—

ARCHIGRAM

53. Endell Street, WC2. 01·240·0141

Archigram Architects (Peter Cook, Dennis Crompton, Ron Herron, partners), postcard, c. 1971, advertising Archigram Architects' relocated office and Adhocs (Addhox) gallery in Covent Garden, London. Archigram Architects first opened in 1970 near the Architectural Association, confirming the ambition of some contributors to Archigram *magazine to proceed from provocation to practice. Archigram Architects closed circa 1975.*

ARCHIGRAM

ARCHITECTURE WITHOUT ARCHITECTURE

—

SIMON SADLER

THE MIT PRESS   CAMBRIDGE, MASSACHUSETTS   LONDON, ENGLAND

Press books may be purchased at special quantity discounts for business or sales promotional use. For information, please email special_sales@mitpress.mit.edu or write to Special Sales Department, The MIT Press, 55 Hayward Street, Cambridge, MA 02142.

This book was set in Chapparal and Magda Clean by Graphic Composition, Inc., and was printed and bound in China.

Library of Congress Cataloging-in-Publication Data

Sadler, Simon.
Archigram : architecture without architecture / Simon Sadler.
p. cm.
Includes bibliographical references and index.
Contents: A new generation: Archigram's formation and its context—The living city: Pop urbanism circa 1963—Beyond architecture: Indeterminacy, systems, and the dissolution of buildings—The zoom wave: Archigram's teaching and reception—Conclusions.
ISBN 978-0-262-69322-6 (alk. paper)
1. Archigram (Group)—Criticism and interpretation. 2. Architecture—England—20th century. 3. Avant-garde (Aesthetics)—England—History—20th century. I. Title.

NA997.a825s23 2005
720′.92′2—dc22

2004065582

10 9 8 7 6 5 4 3

TO MY SON, HENRY

CONTENTS

—

PREFACE

An understanding of neo-avant-garde architecture requires a critical summary of Archigram's achievement, and in 1994 I started research on the problem at the Open University. As good-quality essays and catalogues on Archigram have appeared over the last decade,[1] the absence of a full-length monograph has only become more noticeable. Given the rapid recent evolution of scholarly research into architectural neo-avant-gardes, we can likely look forward to further publications on more discrete aspects of Archigram's work, or which conversely merge this work with other discourses. But for now, a book-length study presents the opportunity, as far as such a thing is possible, for an excursion into the Archigram moment as a whole.

This permits it to be seen as cultural, and not just narrowly architectural. Because Archigram was a partisan intervention into practice and publishing, the group's drawings and texts are just as rewarding when read iconologically—as arguments about style, society, modernity, technology, and the architectural profession in the sixties—as they are when scrutinized for facts of architectural technique or principle, which often melt into the spectral haze of Archigram's distinctive presentational style.

For more than forty years the provocative material recounted in this book has drawn both critique and apologia. Tempting though it is to write in similar veins, pursuant to the requirements of a credible architectural history this book neither scoffs at Archigram's venture nor presents an "authorized biography" of the group. The latter would have been an exercise in futility even had I wanted to write one, since the careful observation of Archigram reveals subtle distinctions between its members' purposes (despite attempts by the group and subsequent commentary to present the group as univocal). In addition, this book has to allow views of Archigram from outside observers—laudatory and antagonistic—to accompany Archigram's self-perceptions.

Given my lack of accountability to the surviving members of the group which created my subject matter—Peter Cook, Dennis Crompton, David Greene, and Michael Webb—

it is surely a tribute to their magnanimity that they listened to me in symposia, discussed their work with me, authorized its reproduction in my articles and chapters,[2] and acceded de facto to the publication of this study when Archigram Archives released picture permissions (including those for Warren Chalk, who died in 1987) following complex negotiations in 2003–2004. Permission for the reprinting of work by Ron Herron, who died in 1994, was granted me by the Herron Estate.

The penalty for independent scholarship is that it cannot be privy to all extant records and artifacts, because the group's various archives are not yet in the public realm. The interests of custodians and researchers should soon be reconciled, however, pending a joint funding bid between the University of Westminster, the Victoria and Albert Museum, the Archigram Archives, and the Herron Archives which will finally see Archigram's physical effects catalogued, digitized, and transferred from their present confinement "under beds or behind walls."[3] It is also likely that additional archival material will be published in the near future.[4] I remain beholden, in the interim, to Dennis Crompton of the Archigram Archives, and Simon Herron of the Herron Archives, for answering my steady stream of inquiries, retrieving archival material, and preparing it for this book.[5]

Meanwhile the quantity of more readily available information pertaining to Archigram remains formidable. Whereas research for my previous MIT Press publication (on situationist urbanism) had to magnify evidence gleaned from libraries, long walks, conversational hints, fringe publications, and museum basements, reading rooms, and newly accessioned archives (which yielded the book's arcane cover image), it is the task of the present publication somehow to survey and sample a prodigious bounty. An enormous number of Archigram's drawings, models, and documents have become accessible through the big retrospective exhibitions that began with the Centre Pompidou show of 1994. Archigram published copiously, including its run of the legendary *Archigram* magazine, and it was discussed in dozens of articles and books around the world. There are any number of opinions and memories of the group to be logged and sifted, and the circumstantial record of the pop, technological, and libertarian cultures to which Archigram related is practically infinite.

Mentors, colleagues, and correspondents inestimably assisted with the assignment, though of course they will not necessarily sanction the book's findings. Special mention must be made of the supervisors of the dissertation from which this book originated, Tim Benton and Barry Curtis, and of the further insight gained from examination by Iain Boyd Whyte and Nicholas Bullock. Other encounters—with Mary Banham, Hazel Cook, the late Catherine Cooke, François Dallegret, Paul Davies, Mark Fisher, Yona Friedman, Simon Herron, Malcolm Higgs, Craig Hodgetts, Diana Jowsey, the late Roy Landau, Arthur Marwick, Peter Murray, Brian Nicholls, Martin Pawley, Roy Payne, Monica Pidgeon, the late Cedric Price, Mary Quant, Tony Rickaby, Gordon Sainsbury, Paul Shepheard, Alan Stanton, and Peter Taylor—added detail and texture to my work. My hosts while visiting Michael Webb were Diane and Bill Menking.

I have been privileged to work again with the MIT Press and its staff, in particular executive editor Roger Conover, whose resolve is imprinted upon this book. Matthew Abbate and Derek George, production editor and designer respectively, saw the book to press.

Work on this study and its subsequent publication were made possible by generous financial aid from the Open University, Milton Keynes, 1995–1998; from the Paul Mellon Centre for Studies in British Art, London, 2002; and from the University of California, Davis, 2004.

Unexpectedly taxing in itself, this project was one strand of a challenging period in my life, into which Jan Wagstaff entered and thankfully stayed. Suffice it to say there are other people, some now distant from me or who played their parts perhaps unwittingly, whom I would acknowledge less notionally if I knew where to start or what to say to them.

—

ARCHIGRAM

—

INTRODUCTION

Archigram can be fairly claimed as the preeminent architectural avant-garde of its day. Its ideas and images were invariably extreme, depicting scenes of quite rampant modernity. Little more than a compilation of offbeat student projects at first, the gloriously shoestring *Archigram* newsletter became the focal point of radical architecture locally and globally, published from London in nine main issues between 1961 and 1970. *Archigram*'s coterie began as an informal consortium, with its core membership of six men (Warren Chalk, Peter Cook, Dennis Crompton, David Greene, Ron Herron, and Michael Webb) emerging by the third edition of the magazine in 1963 and assuming the Archigram name as a group label. Three of the members were recent graduates with impressive student careers, and three of them were veterans of the mighty London County Council Architects Department. Their relationship solidified while employed at Taylor Woodrow Construction between 1962 and 1965, leading to extensive teaching and exhibition collaborations. In 1970 some members started an office, Archigram Architects, which closed around 1975 after its major project, an Entertainments Centre for Monte Carlo, was shelved.

Archigram passed into legend: "Archigram is a marvellously fitting choice for a Royal Gold Medal for the beginning of the 21st century," read the citation for the highest architectural honor in Great Britain, bestowed upon the group in 2002. "Archigram belonged to a new sensibility which sought to re-evaluate architectural practice and to redefine the nature of architecture itself."[1] This book returns to the period when Archigram was the irritant, not the toast, of the Royal Institute of British Architects.

Archigram's production took place mainly on paper, not on the ground. Archigram's architectural images rank as the most memorable of the 1960s and among the most remarkable ever made. Yet this unfettered creativity, more usually enjoyed by artists, practically precludes Archigram as a topic for the conventional history of architecture, as if the "blue sky" of pure architectural imagination were less fascinating (and influential) than the leaden, built "facts" of completed buildings—including the buildings that followed Archigram's wake. Archigram became marginal to the history and theory of architecture much as it was sidelined by most architects in its own day.

Archigram and its major interlocutor, the critic-historian Peter Reyner Banham, alternately dissuaded people from critical engagement and begged for a fight. "Hard as it may be for the average Cand. Phil. from Gothenberg or Lisbon to comprehend, it's all done for the giggle," Banham wrote in 1972.[2] "People draw a big distinction between projects and buildings but I don't," commented Peter Cook in an interview in 1970. "A lot of our projects are highly serious and a lot of built buildings are a sort of bad joke."[3] Flush with the Monte Carlo job and settling into its own premises in 1970, Archigram still could not play it quite straight, reproducing madcap and commissioned projects side by side on the invitations to their office: "seriously (ha!) . . . now you know where we are and what we've been up to."[4] Was Archigram a serious intervention in architecture, and should it receive the thoughtful attention of those interested in the history, practice, and theory of architecture?

When Archigram is admitted to the historical narrative, it is as a hyperfunctionalist stunt, modernism's last fling, and terribly "sixties." And there may be a grain of truth in this perception, but the present book further contends that Archigram's historical significance was as an origin of combative neo-avant-garde attitudes and techniques that became stock-in-trade to practitioners keen to rethink architectural space and architectural technology. That rethinking naturally endowed the Archigram phenomenon with a theoretical as well as historical dimension, liquidating the philosophical foundations of architecture as it anticipated wider, "postmodern" anxieties.

Overall the book argues that, if anything, the more cartoon-like Archigram became and the more preposterous its proposals, the more it merits sustained attention. In the early twentieth century, modernism licensed radical approaches to the way human experience is shaped. Archigram continued this pursuit into the second half of the century. If Archigram seemed a little too boisterous, it may be because in the architectural pro-

fession at large, those who regarded themselves as "modernist" had emerged as the new establishment. To some extent then, the history of Archigram is part of the history of the architectural profession. This is particularly apparent in the first and last chapters of this book.

If the machinations of the architectural profession seem at first an unexciting temptation to reading, consider why architects love(d) as well as hate(d) Archigram. The respect traditionally accorded to paper projects, from Boullée or Ledoux or Piranesi in the eighteenth century to the unbuilt work to be found in De Stijl, the Glass Chain, and Le Corbusier's *Oeuvre complète* in the twentieth, was generally withheld from Archigram. Archigram was easily dismissed as fantastical, despite the detailing of its renderings and (as this book maintains in its third chapter) the investigative and predictive value of its projects.

Two suggestions can be offered here for why Archigram spent a long time in the architectural asylum. First, the heat and humor of its images and texts threatened to shift architecture from reason to seduction, inciting a return to the avant-garde riots that were meant to have been quelled in the 1920s. Second—and looking beyond the front rows of the profession to the galleries of "the public"—Archigram asked again what it was that "we," the "consumers," really wanted from architecture. So shocking were the questions that Archigram asked of "us" that, beneath the pop art styling, it had started to ask all over again just what exactly architecture is.

THE VISIONARY AND THE REAL

The return of a "visionary" architecture must have seemed regressive to many modernist architects in the 1960s. The codification of an International Style in the 1920s had broadly settled the debates about what modern architecture should be; why undo this only forty years later, just as cities were triumphantly being built in the image of the Bauhaus and the International Style? A mainstream modernism of International Style vocabulary and functionalist rationale provided a norm that made even departures from it—like Le Corbusier's Ronchamp (1950–1955), Frank Lloyd Wright's New York Guggenheim (1943–1959), or Louis Kahn's Salk Institute in La Jolla (1959–1965)—all the more enchanting. Archigram's transcendence of this arrangement, its demand that *every* design be born of inspiration, implied rebellion against an architectural profession intent upon training, in the main, competent technicians.

And in what technique, *Archigram* asked, were these functionaries being trained? The myth of modernist "technique" had exploded in the 1950s with the "brutalist" fashion for showcasing the base, nineteenth-century building matter that lay behind the International Style—reinforced concrete, plate glass, ducts, and brickwork. Archigram architects were initially fascinated by the brutalist exposé, and several of them were responsible for the design of one of the most extreme examples of brutalism: the South Bank Centre in London (1960–1964). This done, they proposed that modernism try again at being technologically determined—*really* fabricating the "machine for living in" promised by early modernism, assembled from postwar technologies transferred from the chemicals, electronics, and aeronautics industries. Archigram was a reminder that modernism had lost its technological nerve. Only its preoccupation with the inhabitation of space demarcated Archigram's practice of architecture from the (supposedly lowlier) discipline of industrial design.

In the 1950s, brutalist architects Alison and Peter Smithson had reread the history of the modern movement to assert the birthright of young architects to be creative, assembling an inventory of pioneer form which they wished to rework. The American neo-avant-garde of the 1970s would return to the same sources—early Le Corbusier, early Mies van der Rohe, De Stijl, Italian futurism, and Russian constructivism. Archigram's use of modernist history was less academic. Its designs began by paying homage to pioneer form (futurism, constructivism, Le Corbusier), as at the South Bank Centre, but quickly took off into modernist fantasy, legitimated not by the architecture of the pioneers but by what was considered to be the pioneers' spirit—their inspiration by the experience of *modernity*. Archigram thereby embodied a felicitous notion of what it was to be avant-garde, unburdened even by the weight of history and destiny that the brutalists carried. Archigram was discomforting not only to the mainstream of modernism but to the group's brutalist forebears too.

Any architectural rendering is otherworldly, presenting a design more romantically or structurally perceptible than it will ever be if actually built, but something especially oneiric was happening in Archigram's blueprints. The artful proximity in Archigram's work between the buildable and caprice can be seen in the collages bordering the opening pages of their anthology of 1972, in which a wholly workable competition entry for halls of residence at Liverpool University (1962) was printed alongside the extraordinary spectacle of two people bonding in a Suitaloon (1968, figure 3.29). The parallel reality of a Suitaloon was comparable to the interior of a science fiction novel. Yet Archigram's embrace of modernity—that is, of the *actual* phenomena of the contemporary world, from advertising to the space race—made it impossible to write it off as divorced from reality. Archigram's proposals may sometimes have been misguided, but they were always skillful extemporizations upon live technologies, or problems, or discourses. At a time of rapid university expansion, Archigram's proposals for the Liverpool halls of residence met a need. Unlike other architects, however, Archigram chose to do more, by addressing an "expanded field" of social, cultural, and technological facts. Nineteen sixty-one, the year of *Archigram* no. 1, saw Yuri Gagarin, John F. Kennedy, and the "Pill" open the "new frontiers" of space, social policy, and the body. Would architects stake their own claim?

It was within such global contexts that the Suitaloon, the architectural equivalent of the space suit, was drawn. It was simultaneously realistic and crazy, and by accepting a ride with Archigram, as this book does for some of the distance, the solemnity and inertia that beset architecture can be more clearly perceived. The book also takes advantage of a certain remove, stepping off the cavalcade to inspect the imaginative and optimistic assumptions under which Archigram worked.

A KIND OF RADICALISM

Archigram's scatty presentation disguised the radicalism of its argument about architecture. Broadly, it contended that architecture should not create fixed volumes of space to be mutely inhabited, less still shaped masses of masonry, but must provide the equipment for "living," for "being." The extent to which the architectural profession was failing to design this equipment revealed to Archigram that technological modernism was an incomplete revolution, reduced to a dowdy, killjoy version of itself, colorless, hard-edged, frugal, planned rather than chosen. Architectures of serious fun provided Archigram with a way out of the modernist impasse without having to backtrack to premodernist "tradition."

However problematic Archigram's reopening of architectural possibility may have been (and it was very problematic), mainstream modernism's foreclosure of architecture was no better conceived, choosing to sit tight in a position once occupied by classicism. "Architecture is, and always will be concerned, roughly speaking, with 'carefully balancing horizontal things on top of vertical things,'"[5] declared James Cubitt, the established London architect who provided respectable employment to David Greene and Peter Cook as they were plotting the launch of *Archigram*. Cubitt was only articulating the "common sense" that permeated not just the modernist mainstream but alternatives like brutalism too. To a changing world, modernism was content to provide an idealizing architecture of static trabeation. Pitched against this, Archigram's designs destabilized the fundamental assumption that architecture is a static art: Archigram was unconvinced that a building's *firmitas* (solidity) was the necessary precondition of its *utilitas* and *venustas* (utility and beauty), as Vitruvius's foundational equation of the Western architectural tradition had ordained. With Archigram, architecture's mobile "outsiders"—awnings, tents, caravans—had modernist company. Ordinarily, architects removed architecture from the vicissitudes of everyday life. Subjecting architecture to whimsy, adopting indeterminacy as a design paradigm, Archigram made sure that architecture could be seen as the essentially conservative practice that it is. Archigram was not antiarchitecture; rather, Archigram loved architecture enough to want to save it from ignominy, dodged by the traffic and cut through by the telecommunications that were rapidly weaving new social configurations.

If Archigram seemed like a prank, then, it was no less serious than contemporaneous cultural agitants, such as those of Britain's "satire boom" gathered around London's jokingly named Establishment Club (coincidentally opened in 1961 by another Peter Cook). The "establishment" was the vaguely

defined but all-pervasive enemy for the arts in Britain in the 1960s, and Archigram's drawings graffitied over all of its sacred truths—that architecture was big and heavy, that civic life was different from shopping, that the sea was not a suitable place for buildings. Archigram's mischievous approach to everyday life marked the group apart even from many of its fellow travelers in alternative architecture (the metabolists, GEAM, the editors of *Ekistics*) in the early 1960s. True, Archigram does not feel very *dangerous* in the way that we might expect an "avant-garde" to feel; there is not about it the combativeness of, say, the Situationist International, notorious for being absolutely confrontational with dominant (bourgeois) culture. Compared to the transgressive cachet of contemporary "countercultural" bodies (such as Ken Kesey's Merry Pranksters in the United States), Archigram's eccentricity was truly studied, that is to say the product, more often than not, of a logic pursued to a point of absurdity.

In fact, Archigram could be placed within a conservative English tradition, founded by the arts and crafts and garden city movements, in which architecture cushions the impact of industrialization.[6] Yet Archigram can feel more *subversive* than every other harbinger of a new world. As we chew upon the bubblegum of Archigram's drawings and writings, we barely notice that we are being systematically deprived of certainty. The shock of pure indeterminacy is the subject in particular of the third chapter of this book. At least the situationists steadied themselves against the handrail of Marxism, in the tradition of the pioneering "historical" avant-gardes of the 1920s and 1930s. Tradition, cultural continuity, and clearly assigned meanings and functions fell by the wayside in the world of Archigram. Political commitment to a firmly defined left was one of the things Archigram felt it could do without in pursuit of its main goal, to make living new. Simultaneously, its passion for the future made it overwhelmingly avant-garde, while its abandonment of Marxism made it suspiciously reactionary—and a prime example of what would soon be described as a "neo-avant-garde," the "neo-" prefix designating ideological as well as temporal distance from the "historical" avant-gardes.

One of the questions that this book ponders is what sort of economy was to support Archigram's architecture of flux and fun. In the 1950s and early 1960s, sections of the European avant-garde were slowly seduced by the market-driven confidence of the United States, its wealth, and above all the brilliance of its popular culture—ever more difficult to resist with the increased prosperity of masses of ordinary western European people. The entente between the avant-garde and "popularity" has perhaps been the most important development in avant-garde culture since the Second World War, and one of the severest tests of its nerve. If avant-garde activity was once defined by its very inaccessibility to the general public and its onslaught upon bourgeois culture, how could it survive the breakdown in distinction between the "high" and the "low," the "valuable" and the "kitsch," the "authentic" and the "inauthentic"? If the avant-garde was once considered to be, by its very nature, oppositional to the status quo, how could it even think about assimilating late capitalism, let alone imitate its operations?

The process signaled a shifting feeling among intellectuals about the nature of social change: that it might occur not through a sudden revolution of subjects linking arms, but by an irreversible escalation in the day-to-day demands of "ordinary people" for greater access to goods, services, and culture. In the 1950s, many Europeans acquired fully plumbed, indoor lavatories for the first time. Such a simple, plain fact; and yet for many people (the grandmother of Archigram member Dennis Crompton was one),[7] the impact upon the quality of life was profound. This prosaic revolution became dizzying as private telephones, refrigerators, washing machines, and even scooters and automobiles became "plugged in" (to employ Archigram terminology) to the household as well. As it invented more and more ways in which individual lives could be "revolutionized," Archigram was frankly unconcerned with how such goods were acquired. Its work was part of a larger shift in avant-garde concern in the 1950s and 1960s, from the creation of singular "works of art" such as paintings and buildings to the exploration of art as a *lived* medium, as a way of structuring everyday life for all. In order to do this, Archigram (this book suggests) was willing to see the transformation of the working class as the work of that class became automated, making us all bourgeois if need be. Archigram's revision of the political relationship between social class and architecture was heresy to avant-garde and mainstream modernist assumptions alike.

Archigram's program, which emerges in retrospect as a juncture between "modernism" and "postmodernism" in architecture, was all the more shocking for the way in which it was left so vaguely stated. Like its designs, it was indeterminate, almost a chameleon, so that as another form of popular address—that of direct action—acquired currency in progressive artistic and cultural circles in the later sixties, Archigram remained superficially relevant. It also gained an avant-garde, "revolutionary" kudos by consistently targeting youth (in the schools of architecture) as potential agents for change, portraying architecture as being in the throes of a generational struggle. By finding an "establishment" enemy—the "drearies"[8] of architecture, salaried and replaying the repertoire of mainstream modernism without thought to technological and social change, let alone individual expression—Archigram had an almost classically avant-garde modus operandi, executed through little magazines, demonstrative exhibitions, and polemic; Archigram knew all about Dada, the expressionists, and the futurists.

Though only a handful of minor buildings can be ascribed directly to the Archigram group, its catchy style, the dissemination of its ideas through *Archigram* and other media, and its members' teaching (particularly in the United States and Britain, where the award of the RIBA Gold Medal coincided in 2002 with the award of the RIBA's Spink Prize for Teaching to Archigram's David Greene and Peter Cook) left a disproportionate bounty. An account of its outreach has also to take special account of the influential proselytizers of Archigram's vision, most notably Reyner Banham. Potlatching its ideas let Archigram have its cake and eat it, playing to an international audience (particularly in Germany, Austria, France, the United States, and Japan) while celebrating its "Englishness."

THE BOOK IN BRIEF

The first chapter of this book, "A New Generation," introduces Archigram as an attempt to recover the thrill of modernism's pioneering phase, in protest against its later marshaling into a discipline. Occupying the ground already cleared by the London vanguards of the 1950s, the new brutalists and Independent

Group, Archigram attempted to bring architecture up to speed with leading artistic, technological, and cultural tendencies—"pop" influences in particular.

This could be seen at Archigram's 1963 show at the Institute of Contemporary Arts in London, "Living City," the subject of the second chapter. "Living City" heralded a way of thinking about cities that later became commonplace: that cities, being more than mere functional organizations of space, are the life-support machinery of a culture in perpetual change. The exhibition's fascination with the ephemeral made it significant to the longer trajectory that Archigram was taking: one that would affect the "disappearance" of architecture.

This was the most remarkable aspect of Archigram's work at its peak, and is described in the third chapter, "Beyond Architecture." Architectural disappearance was the logical outcome of the thus-far "repressed" strain of modernism: the one that wanted to defeat monumentality by composing buildings out of industrially produced, interchangeable and ultimately disposable "kits-of-parts." Thereby the task of architecture would be passed from the architect to the user-client. The context of this project was a dispersed range of ideas from the 1960s about the nature of freedom—spatial, creative, consumerist, political, echoed in the fine arts at that time by the drive "beyond the object" and amongst other architectural provocateurs such as Bernard Rudofsky (whose famous 1964 exhibition and catalogue *Architecture without Architects* is a reference for this book's title).

A very peculiar politics thus emerges around Archigram, often rendered insensitive to emergent political movements (especially feminism and ecology) by its sheer macho enthusiasm for modernity. And this, the book suggests, is one of the things that makes Archigram a case study of the ideological disorder encountered in a bid for complete freedom. Archigram indicates a version of the sixties that does not readily emerge in histories of the period—avowedly "apolitical" rather than "engaged," technocratic rather than anarchic, individualist rather than "hippie," grounded as much in 1950s assumptions of affluence as 1960s commitments to redistribution.

These politics are discussed as well in the fourth and final chapter, "The Zoom Wave," where Archigram's influences, on segments of the student populace in particular, are outlined. The limits of its reach are also plotted. To a great extent Archigram came out of, and was sustained by, the schools of architecture, and it was nourished by a high ideal of what education, and architectural education in particular, should be about: the cultivation of individuals working in concert, uninstitutionalized.

More visibly, Archigram created a style—assembled from nineteenth-century industrial architecture, twentieth-century manufacturing, military apparatus, science fiction, biology, technology, electronics, constructivism, pop art, cutaway technical illustration, psychedelia, and the English seaside—which would serve as an inspiration for an architectural movement, high-tech, and feed into the stream of postmodern/deconstructivist trends of the 1970s, 1980s, and 1990s. In the process of demonstrating the potential of technology to create deformations and nonmonumental networks, Archigram became radical stylists of technology. More yet than Archigram's hero Richard Buckminster Fuller (widely remembered for the geodesic dome), the new prophets of architectural antiform turned out to have an antithetical legacy as form-givers, tethering domes, inflatables, pods, and billboards with wires, gantries, tubes, tracks, trucks, and logs. The group imagined releasing building's latent energy not through sculpting but through electrical and mechanical impulses, dictated by social activity and projected by images and writhing vinyl. With its instantly recognizable style, Archigram had paradoxically found form in the equipment of events.

If Archigram's contribution to the arts of the sixties and its stylistic bequest to high-tech architecture are now historically acknowledged, its counsel on designing in a "postindustrial," "informational," "globalized" age might be less apparent—and could account for the resurgence of curiosity about Archigram three decades after it closed its office. Because while many of the marvels *Archigram* predicted eventually became accessible through the flat screen of the computer monitor, few manifested themselves three-dimensionally or with such flair.

1

A NEW GENERATION

ARCHIGRAM'S FORMATION AND ITS CONTEXT

frustration, giving way to moral indignation and ambition, prompted the appear ance of *Archigram* magazine in London in May 1961 (figure 1.1). Over the following decade, Archigram's initially insular disquiet with architecture expanded into an agenda for social renovation. "The first *Archigram* was an outburst against the crap going up in London, against the attitude of a continuing European tradition of well-mannered but gutless architecture that had absorbed the label 'Modern,' but had betrayed most of the philosophies of the earliest 'Modern,'" Peter Cook told American readers, in no uncertain terms, in 1967.[1] *Archigram*'s insistence that modernism should celebrate all that is new reacted against the routines of day-to-day architectural education and practice.

Glass curtain walls, a vision that had roused architects to states of high excitement two generations earlier, had begun to seal city streets. Lustrous office block surfaces emulated the major buildings to be completed in New York and London in 1961, the Union Carbide Building and Castrol House: the future employer of the Archigram group members, Taylor Woodrow, advertised its expertise in this corporate modern mode in the catalogue for Archigram's first exhibition (figure 1.2).[2] As Archigram architects turned the pages of *Architectural Design,* or of its foreign counterparts like *Bauen + Wohnen* or *Architecture d'Aujourd'hui,* the grip of curtain walls, rectilinearity, reinforced concrete, and fastidious planning was overwhelming, and these were examples of the more progressive journals of Britain, Germany, and France. Modernists experimented with any number of techniques of construction, of materials, of surface treatment, of site, and of plan, but the nuances could be properly appreciated only by a member of the specialist technical corps of modernism. The gloom was summarized in an editorial in *Architectural Design* in November 1961 which claimed that "ninety-nine percent of [London's architects] continue in mediocrity until senility intervenes."[3]

1.1 *Main spread of* Archigram no. 1, 1961: *architecture "lifts off" in the same month that President Kennedy announces the Apollo missions. Student work from London, principally inspired by futurism and expressionism, is here knitted together into a protest at contemporary British architecture.*

The triumph of mainstream modernism had been to interpret and institutionalize the work of the modernist pioneers, redeploying the pre–Second World War "heroic phase"[4] as the house style of corporate-democratic postwar reconstruction. By the 1950s, modernism was foregrounding an image of tidy and fair cultural order that drew upon De Stijl and Bauhaus work of the 1920s. Official sanction of modernism deprived it of its inherent avant-garde quality. Nowhere was this more true than in Great Britain. In the process, the "second generation"[5] of modern architects, the generation after the pioneers, had installed itself as a new "establishment." In his review of the 1955 exhibition "Ten Years of British Architecture 1945–1955," the eminent architectural historian John Summerson reckoned that it would be a little misleading for him to describe the buildings illustrated as being part of the modern movement, because "the 'modern movement' implied movement within a state of affairs alien to the ideas by which the movement was inspired and that state of affairs no longer exists. Which is simply to say that a generation has passed . . . and the movement

1.2 "Changing London's Skyline," advertisement for Taylor Woodrow, Living Arts no. 2, 1963. The Archigram group was a reaction against the generic, glass-and-concrete grids of early sixties "modern architecture"; yet one of the thriving exponents of such architecture, Taylor Woodrow Construction, employed all the members of the nascent Archigram group and encouraged their experimental work.

itself is very respectably old, its still acknowledged leaders bemedalled veterans."[6]

Just a decade prior to the publication of *Archigram*, a British modernist idiom had triumphed on London's South Bank at the 1951 Festival of Britain, technically sophisticated though stylistically loyal to the 1930s. "Festival Style" offered the British public a bouncy, decorative modernism, its newfangled scientistic iconography of atoms and saucers tempered by a feeling for the English picturesque.[7] Summerson, who had sympathies with the picturesque planning of the Festival,[8] admitted that "the South Bank was a nostalgic echo from the 'thirties rather than a confession of faith in present time and circumstance."[9] Postwar town planning under the auspices of the "second generation" similarly tended toward compromise. English architect-planners had been empowered by the 1947 Town and Country Planning Act and the 1939 Barlow Report's proposals for New Towns to consider the wholesale remaking of the environment. The results were often bold as social experiments but architecturally received with lukewarm appreciation even by the most sympathetic observers.[10] Cedric Price, a well-known radical architect who published one of his first articles in *Archigram*,[11] satirized the typical Festival-style New Town plan with its "town hall in the middle, shouting its importance to a lot of people who don't want to know," centralized and unamenable to the car, leaving its citizens "hobbling over the cobbles."[12]

New buildings in Britain were generally modern enough, and their settings landscaped enough, to signify a break with the past, but radicalism was eschewed.[13] The unprecedented powers bestowed upon architects were (in practice) perceived as reactive rather than active—the demarcation of green belt and suppression of ribbon developments,[14] barely relevant to the uncompromisingly modern aspirations of the people who would make *Archigram*. As the leading British planner Thomas Sharp asserted in 1957, "what is most disliked about us . . . is the control which we exercise over other people's activities with so little obvious and acceptable result. . . . It seems to me that our plans today are so small and dreary and are made known so dimly and grudgingly that in the main they deserve the indifference and even, perhaps, the contempt they get."[15] Sharp would repeat his sentiments to readers of the *Sunday Times* in August 1964.[16] The following month, the same readers were confronted by a counterproposal, for a "Plug-In City," by a young architect called Peter Cook: nothing small and dreary this time (figure 1.3).[17]

PLUG-IN

Ron Herron's outlandish Walking City of 1964 might be the best-known image to come out of Archigram in the long term (figure 1.32), but Peter Cook's iconic Plug-In City scheme most thoroughly encapsulates the preoccupations of Archigram in its early years. An examination of Plug-In City makes it possible to appreciate the scale of Archigram's ambition. Plug-In reinstated the avant-garde impulse that had inspired the first generation of modernists and had been put out to seed by the second generation. A megastructure devoted to continual circulation, its functions scrambled, its boundaries blurred, it reprieved the promise of collective living from a creeping pessimism about "urbanism."

Forging ahead with the building of the future, Plug-In City reworked two slightly repressed motifs to be found in modernism: those of the megastructure[18] and the "building-in-becoming." They had been tried in theory in Le Corbusier's Algiers project (1931) and in the Soviet linear city projects of the 1920s;[19] megastructures existed in built form in Karl Ehn's Karl-Marx-Hof in Vienna (1927) and Le Corbusier's Unité d'Habitation in Marseilles (1947–1953). Plug-In City combined elements of all of these precedents—the principle of collectivity, of interchangeable apartment units, and the incorporation of rapid transport links. In this there was a disarming reasonableness about the Plug-In proposal, with its attempt to keep cities viable in an era of rapid change. It was an expression of solidarity with other megastructures being projected as the urban future in the 1950s–1960s, particularly the Philadelphia City Tower project created circa 1954 by Louis Kahn and Anne Tyng, and Kisho Kurokawa's helicoidal towers project of 1961. The aesthetic of incompleteness, apparent throughout the Plug-In scheme and more marked than in megastructural precedents, may have derived from the construction sites of the building boom that followed the economic reconstruction of Europe. This modernization was accelerating in Archigram's property-boom-fueled London of the 1960s, as the service cores of office blocks rose above the city prior to the addition of floor slabs and curtain walls. The aesthetic had good modernist ancestry; Erich Mendelsohn had photographed buildings under construction in the 1920s, coining the phrase "X-ray view" in his picture books *Amerika* (1926) and *Russland, Europa, Amerika* (1929).[20]

Yet Plug-In City, heaped up in cliffs of architecture, could not be mistaken for any one antecedent. There was an intoxicated sense of chaos in it unshared by models so sensibly bracketed by frames, good taste, economy, and spatial evenness. With Plug-In, we are at the outer edge of the early sixties avant-garde, primarily motivated not to make architecture better behaved but to make architecture change life, much like the early avant-gardes. Cook's unrepentant modernism was fired by a conviction that the qualities of the everyday could be enhanced by design.

The plug-in principle had taken a hold in Cook's work by the time of the Shopping Centre project of 1962 for the English Midlands city of Nottingham, hatched with David Greene who had known the city as a student (figure 1.4). The center of Nottingham, created by the lace industry, was hurtled in Cook and Greene's vision from grimy Victoriana into a future of stacked geodesic and inverted-U-shaped units. The units were inched into place by all-surveying cranes on a circular rail above, which also fed supplies down chutes to the shops. By the time of the Europa/Kent Businesstown scheme of 1963–1964, Cook was verging on a full plug-in urbanism. It still deployed the cranes and standardized units, but now emphasized the twin design features of vertical silos of units bridged by lateral chutes. It was a manner found in the City Interchange scheme of 1963 by Archigram colleagues Ron Herron and Warren Chalk, and was traceable in turn to science fiction comics and the conveyance bridges of Brinkman and Van der Vlugt's iconic Van Nelle Factory, Rotterdam, of 1925–1931. To complete the total Plug-In City effect in 1964, Cook repeated the tubular "plumbing" as a diamond-shaped lattice that acted as a structural support for units and more random elements such as inflatables,[21] then deposited the whole package along lines of transportation.

1.3 *Peter Cook, Plug-In City, axonometric overhead view of local district in medium-pressure area, 1964. A mass-circulating image, Cook's Plug-In City provided Archigram's early interest in rapidly adapting urbanism with engrossing aesthetic interest.*

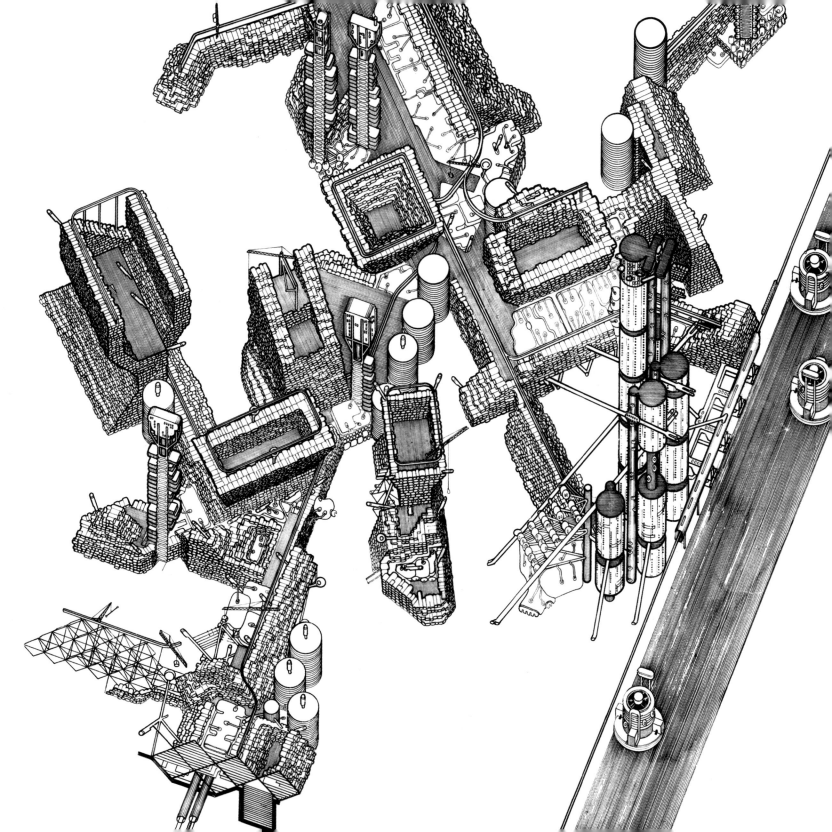

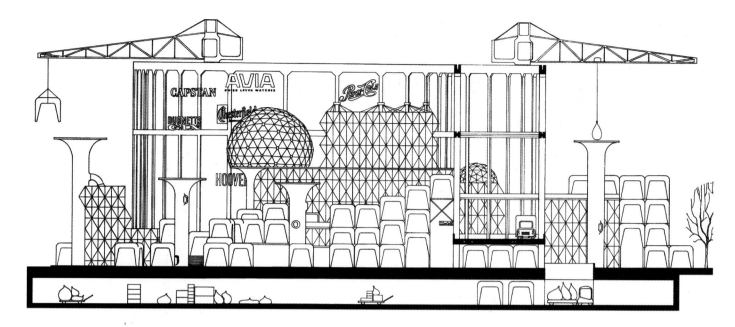

Plug-In City was devised to prompt circulation and accelerate the city-in-flux. The clean, zoned, hierarchical separation that characterized orthodox urban planning gave way to what Cook would call the "come-go" of Plug-In City. Urban experience would consequently be less determinate, physically and mentally. If city planning had traditionally encouraged contemplation of the fixed and ideal architectural object, Plug-In planning promoted architecture as an *event* that could only be realized by the active involvement of its inhabitants. It was a supposition that would be generally accepted by avant-gardes working in the wake of Archigram in the 1960s, such as Coop Himmelblau, Haus-Rucker-Co, and Utopie.

Plug-In superseded not only mainstream British modernism but also the current bearer of the vanguard crown, the so-called new brutalism. In the 1950s, new brutalists, led by architects Alison and Peter Smithson, demanded a return to the unprettified but poetic "truth" that they believed had guided the pioneers of modern architecture, Le Corbusier above all: truth to materials, site, method, and program. Brutalists and their associates in their international discussion group, Team 10,

challenged designers to create textured surfaces and plans as intricate as the societies they would contain. The giant machinery of Plug-In City arguably generated those textures, but was hardly what the brutalists—seeking the essential, frozen, built image of the contemporary world—had in mind. For a kinetic vision of modernity in motion, Archigram turned to the Japanese avant-garde, which had found itself, in Peter Cook's summation, "sometimes . . . treated with very harsh criticism by the European élite" of Team 10.[22]

One visitor to the Team 10 meetings, the architect Kenzo Tange, had embarked upon megastructural schemes of such ambition that Plug-In City (at least in the small portions published) seemed modest. Tange's Tokyo Bay project of 1960 (as featured in *Archigram* in 1964) extended its causeway network across the sea (figure 1.5). Architects in Tange's office at the time were meanwhile publicizing the message of what they called "metabolism": the design of long-term structures to support short-term components.[23] This was the principle transferred to the heart of Plug-In City. Cook annotated the diagrams of Plug-In City with indications of the lifetime of the various compo-

1.4 *Peter Cook and David Greene, Nottingham Craneway (Shopping Viaduct) project, section, 1962. The kinesis of the proposed Craneway would have radically differed not just from its red-brick Victorian context but from the bunker shopping centers that encased Nottingham's city center in the later sixties.*

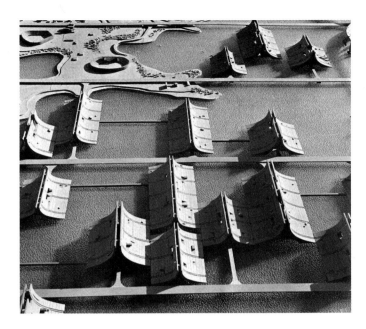

nents—forty years for the tubular structure of the city, twenty-five years for, say, a hotel "core," three years for the hotel rooms plugged into it.

Plug-In City had to be judged on whether it showed the world a better way of building. The metabolists claimed that theirs was the only solution to building a Japanese economy in rapid development. Plug-In was justified in similar terms, but it was not merely economically judicious. Inspired by futurism, Plug-In wanted to make the kinesis and transformation of the modern city more legible, and the metabolist separation of support from additive units alone might not achieve this. Tange and the metabolists generated (and built) some striking elevations, such as Tange's Broadcasting Centers in Kofu and Tokyo, 1966–1967, and Kiyonori Kikutake's Miyakonojo City Hall, 1966; but Plug-In packed the biggest punch yet as an "image," even if it did not surpass the Japanese conceptually and remained a long way from actual construction. It was the same story with Cook's unbuilt Expo Tower for Montreal's 1967 world's fair (designed 1963–1964, figure 1.6), which borrowed a length of Kikutake's Marine Civilization project of 1960 but amalgamated it into a

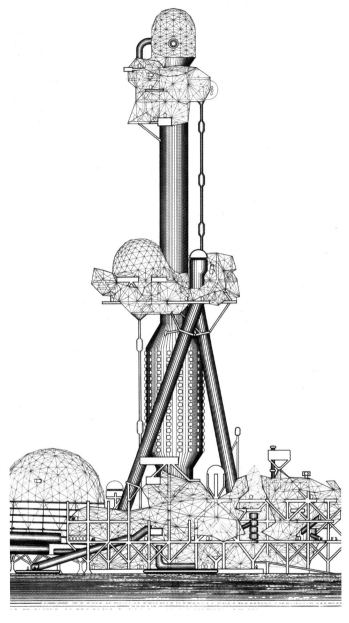

1.5 *Kenzo Tange and team, Tokyo Bay project, model, 1960. The authoritative megastructures, projected and built, came not from Britain but from Japan. Archigram's contribution to the genre was to extemporize on the visual and consumer delights possible within an approach to design that might otherwise appear utilitarian on a massive scale.*   **1.6** *Peter Cook for Taylor Woodrow Design Group, Montreal Expo '67 Tower project, elevation, 1963–1964. A relatively prosaic tower and substructure are engulfed by geodesic domes, expressionist crystals, and futurist elevators: the forms expressed the energy of the Expo.*

thrusting, complex, pictorial assemblage rather than presenting it in the straight-up-and-down fashion of its source; Kikutake duly built aspects of Cook's Montreal silhouette back into the Expo Tower for the 1970 world's fair in Osaka.

So began the precarious relationship between the "ethics" and "aesthetics" of Archigram's work (a conundrum previously lodged in new brutalism).[24] The dynamic processes of Plug-In— its ethic—had to be made visible, and so become an aesthetic. Plug-In City turned architecture inside-out to make its interior life anterior; expendable apartments were slung happily down the outside of the huge A-frame substructures, rearranged by the cranes sliding back and forth above. The effect can be pictured in the mind's eye. Plug-In City would be like an inland port, goods arriving by monorail and transferred by gantry, weather barrage balloons bobbing above, sounds of delight drifting through the open framework from the colorful leisure sectors

within. Plug-In had to show that the frame-and-unit method would eventually aggregate into urbanism of equivalent quality to what it would supplant, functionally *and* artistically. Plug-In's units stacked into profiles that, far from being repetitive, bordered on the picturesque, clustered like coral and tumbling down the megastructural precipices like troglodytes. It was systematic gaiety. This was the most striking aspect of the big drawings of the Plug-In skyline that became so widely known.

A typical British boy of Archigram's generation, growing up in the 1940s, was apt to play with Meccano sets;[25] and ranking among Britain's best contributions to postwar modern architecture were the Meccano-like Hertfordshire and CLASP prefabricated school buildings. We might credit to the rivet-and-connector set the same influence upon the formative Archigram architect as has been ascribed to the Froebel blocks at the disposal of Frank Lloyd Wright in kindergarten. *Archigram* no. 7 in

1.7 *Plug-In City, Paddington East version, 1966. Archigram's models were usually realistically detailed, but this is more abstract, portraying the relationship between rigidly bonded subframe and transitory architectural units. By a further nuance, the studs on the pieces of Lego are visually suggestive of porthole windows, and are functionally analogous to the dream of plug-in architecture.*

1966 included a cutout constructor set by which an architect could play with pseudo-industrial building elements (figure 3.10), and Plug-In City deployed a very Meccano-like iconography. Yet it had a Lego-like quality too, which is intriguing because Lego (which partly supplanted Meccano as a toy) has stood accused of producing less didactic structures and even of bearing a responsibility for the decline in British engineering.[26] In one of the most "conjectural" and "abstract" models that Archigram produced—that of Plug-In City, Paddington East version, 1966[27] (figure 1.7)—pieces of Lego were inserted into the metal frame: whatever the diligent joys of its Meccano-like armature, Plug-In City implied a Lego-like convenience and instantaneous gratification. Archigram rarely troubled itself with the smallest structural details—the task of joining a capsule to a frame would be relished by high-tech progenies of the 1970s—but Archigram nevertheless dreamed of the straight,

clean, plug-in/plug-out joint that had been perfected by the ABS plastic stud-and-tube technology of Lego.

Plug-In City was projected to extend across Britain and across the Channel to continental Europe, but pure lateral extension was not Cook's prime interest with Plug-In; stacking was just as important, hence the desire for the clean joint. In the early sixties, Archigram knew that much good investigative work had already been carried out on lateral extension, not least by Tange and by Team 10. Plug-In sections now concentrated upon *conjoining* events, not only along the horizontal axis, nor even just around the vertical axis but through the *oblique,* and the Plug-In section was able to show this diagrammatically (figure 1.8). Connections could be made and disconnected at will, like an endless syntax.

Awaking in the morning in her or his little apartment-capsule—of the sort shown in close-up in Warren Chalk's Capsule

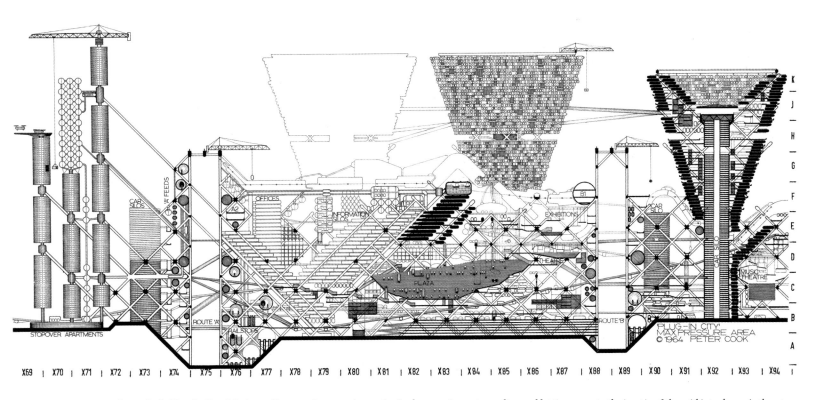

1.8 *Peter Cook, Plug-In City: Maximum Pressure Area, section, 1964. In the new city center, a diamond lattice converts the inertia of the grid into dynamic thrust, literally a framework for crossover events.*

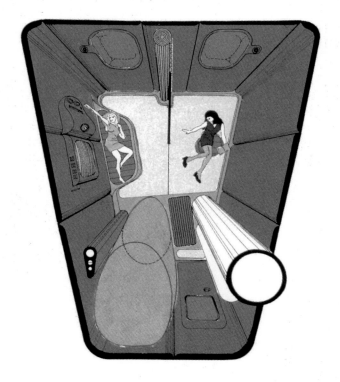

region, and propelled by newly invented hovercraft levitation, called at local clusters.

Cook's vision brought the feverish bustle of the metropolis to all places willing to plug in to the network, but it also tackled the problems of population growth, land use, and traffic that were thought at the time to render great cities unsustainable. Outright chaos was checked by the "systems approach," a universal technology directing "a hundred or a thousand different things, all happening at once."[28] A Computer City diagram (1964), drawn by Cook's Archigram colleague Dennis Crompton, abstracted the sorts of monitoring systems—borrowed from radio-controlled taxis, ambulance services, and airports—that permitted Plug-In City to operate smoothly (figure 1.10).[29]

RESISTANCE

Plug-In went against the grain of architectural training. For the ambitious architect in the late 1950s and early 1960s, whether student or professional, there were few alternatives to orthodox modernism. The Royal Institute of British Architects' 1958 Oxford Conference established what historians Mark Crinson and Jules Lubbock have called the "Official System"[30] in British architectural schools: a technocratic modernist hegemony policed by the Visiting Boards of the Royal Institute of British Architects (RIBA). William Allen, author of the agenda at the Oxford Conference, and new head of London's Architectural Association from 1961 (from whence *Archigram* no. 1 appeared), was among those imposing a positivist, scientistic approach upon the country's leading schools. The Oxford Conference also confirmed the British architectural syllabus as full-time and university-based, eroding the more artisan route into architecture taken by several Archigram members through pupilages and part-time courses at art and technical colleges.[31]

The time traditionally spent on drawing and design was being reallocated by architecture schools in favor of pure and social sciences; it was expected that the architect would concentrate on a policy-making role. So Archigram's resplendent Pantone and felt-tip color drawings, with their richness of incident, reasserted the impatient visionary genius of the architect, resisting the pincer movement that was closing in on creative

Homes study of 1964 (figure 1.9)—the Plug-In citizen would have encountered views from the window much like those greeting occupants of the new *Terrassenhäuser* schemes (such as Patrick Hodgkinson's Brunswick Centre, London, 1962–1973). The Plug-In citizen was almost certainly employed in a white-collar occupation: factories were not apparent in Plug-In City, no matter that its form drew on oil refineries and assembly plants. Plug-In adopted the common 1960s ambition that repetitive physical labor should be ended by automation. The journey to work could be very short, along weatherproof tubes, and the workplace was probably piled against shops or an entertainments center, generating multiactivity leisure. Longer journeys to other centers could be taken by cars that were stored within local silos—though as Plug-In City was strung out in clusters across linear communications routes, it would make equal sense to hop on the fast monorail. Or the journey might be unnecessary, since mobile buildings serving the entire

1.9 *Warren Chalk, Capsule Homes project, view of a typical interior, 1964. Plug-in living close up: lifting the lid on an Archigram "pad" reveals miniskirted roommates (or a bachelor fantasy) where day-to-day survival hinges around choices between going out, staying in, reading, or watching television. The drawing emphasizes the packaging of space through lightweight, prefabricated interlocking components of a type that might be lifted and suspended from a plug-in superstructure.*

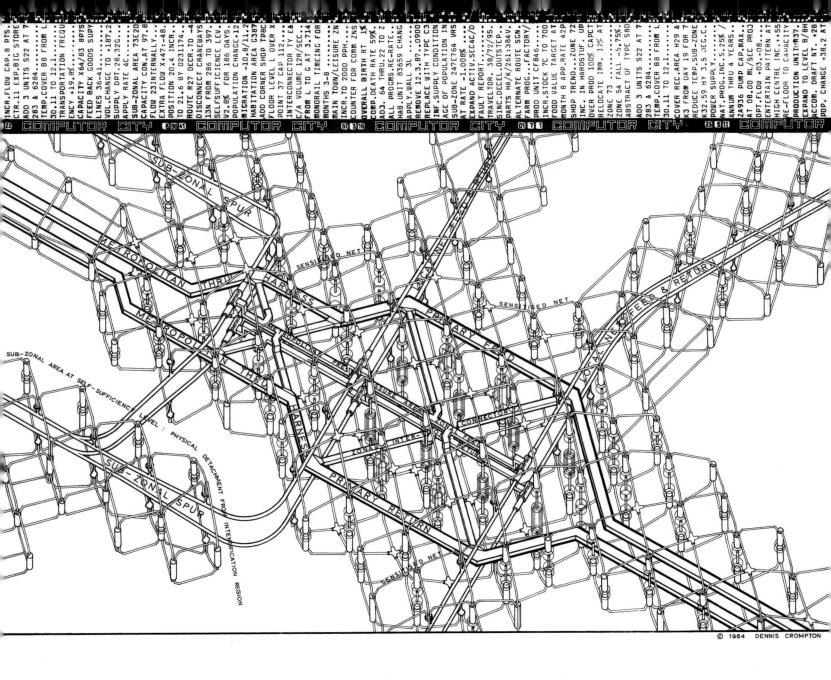

1.10 *Dennis Crompton, Computer City, 1964. Computer City described the city as a network of flows—flows of traffic, goods, people, and above all information. Strongly reminiscent of diodes and electrical substations, it was probably posited not so much as an alternative to the spawning urban forms of Plug-In City but, floating in abstract space, as a diagram of the systems that would let Plug-In City work, their chatter of data spooling across the top.*

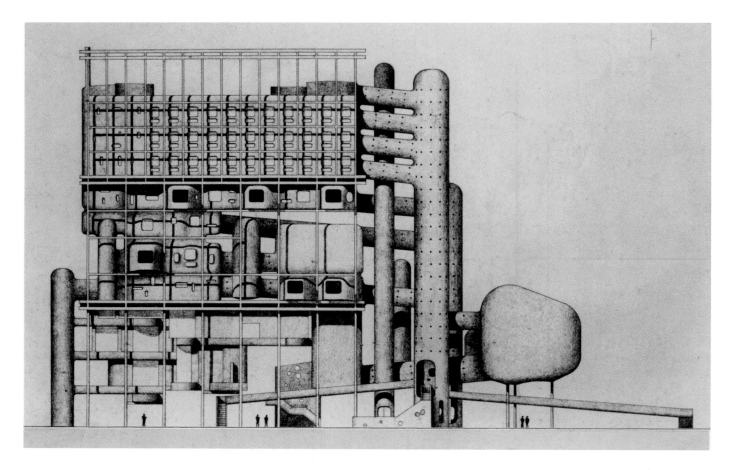

design from the housing targets of the state and the profit motives of developers. By revealing the beauty of technological process, Archigram could bridge the dispute that emerged in 1960s British architecture between the "System Boys" and the "Art Boys."[32] The group's rapture in drawing became a central (though not entirely accurate) organizing myth. According to Archigram's official biographical details of 1972, Peter Cook "enjoys drawing" his ideas "rather than writing about them"; Ron Herron "draws like a dream . . . apparently effortlessly."[33] Behind Archigram's published drawings were more working drawings, as many as fifteen hundred it is thought, most of them lost.[34] Historian and critic Reyner Banham attributed more "draughtsmanly talent" to Archigram than to any architectural body since Christopher Wren's Royal Works.[35]

If, in fact, David Greene and Warren Chalk kept their distance from the group's arduous production of drawings, it was to enable them to concentrate on a distinctive mode of architectural reverie that no less resisted the profession's default to established procedure. Connecting with a new culture of beat literature,[36] angry young men, abstract expressionism, and existentialism, this reverie counterbalanced the policy-making positivism that confined inquiry in schools and offices in the early sixties to narrowly defined research programs—construction systems, lighting, building density, and the like. Architec-

ature (received wisdom held) was basically a rational business best left to big offices, preferably in the public sector. "The obverse of public patronage," Anthony Jackson noted in his 1970 examination of the architectural profession in Britain, "was a disinclination for unconforming genius."[37]

The postwar period had mass-employed a crush of architects in which there were ever fewer opportunities for the architect to put her or his personal mark on a project. The *Architectural Review* blamed the loss of senior talent from public to private practice on the lure of individual vision.[38] The samizdat system established by the *Archigram* magazine, and enabled by cheap offset lithography[39] and Roneo machines, was a liberation from the open prison of public and construction company teamwork.

Archigram's first two editions, which represented a broad church of young, dissenting London architects, exploited an ill-tempered generation gap in British architecture. Even as RIBA policy insisted on the systematization of design skills, students could find themselves panned for lacking the personal expressiveness of "the masters"; equally, students had to moderate their homage to the masters and remain strictly "rational" in their designs. At the 1961 RIBA student award ceremony, architect Richard Sheppard chided his audience by showing "a few slides of buildings by [Louis] Kahn and Le Corbusier and others whom I would have thought would act as catalysts in your minds."[40] And yet, when future *Archigram* contributor Michael Webb paid an exaggerated homage to Kahn's "servant-and-served" concept[41] in a 1957–1958 fourth-year project at London's Regent Street Polytechnic, he was accused of defying the rationality that was meant to underwrite modernism (figures 1.11, 1.12). Historian and critic Nikolaus Pevsner took the matter up with the RIBA, dismissing Webb's scheme as an attempt to "out-Gaudí Gaudí"[42] and contrasting the generally "promising" state of mainstream British modernism with student work.[43]

"What will happen with students," asked Reyner Banham in his rejoinder to Pevsner, "when what they see in their history lectures is stronger and tougher stuff than they get taught in their studio instruction? What happens when the practising masters of the day produce only near-beer, and the slides that are shown in the history lectures are 80° proof?"[44] With this, Banham fanned the flames of a generational struggle (Pevsner was Banham's doctoral supervisor). Banham's friends, architects James Stirling and James Gowan, had also been looking at their history slides. They were completing their much-discussed Leicester University Engineering Building (1959–1964) in an avant-garde manner of recovered Corbusian, futurist, and constructivist sources (figure 1.13), and Gowan generously featured Webb's Furniture Manufacturers Building and other "futurist-flavored" projects in his model curriculum published in *Architectural Review* in December of 1959.[45]

1.11, 1.12 *Michael Webb, Furniture Manufacturers Association Building in High Wycombe project, front and side elevations (Regent Street Polytechnic fourth year, 1957–1958). Flagship of a micromovement in architecture, bowellism, this was probably the most notorious student project of the late fifties, and was selected by the New York Museum of Modern Art in 1961 as an example of "visionary" architecture.*

Another futurist-flavored scheme chosen by Gowan was one for a Concert Hall by student John Outram, which would be included in the first edition of *Archigram* (figure 1.1). Outram had transferred in 1958 from Regent Street Polytechnic to the rival Architectural Association school, finding there tutors such as James Gowan, students such as Peter Cook, and sympathy for Webb's scandalous Furniture Manufacturers scheme. Restlessness had been apparent at Regent Street since 1956 in the pages of its student magazine *Polygon,* edited by Outram and Wilfred Marden (who also sought asylum at the Architectural Association).[46] *Polygon* fed into the wider student discontent that became apparent with the formation of the British Architectural Students Association (BASA) in 1958,[47] representing twenty-five schools and destined to be a sparring partner of Archigram. In a generous attempt to help a student body that was traditionally "transient . . . deficient in funds, organization, and a means of mass communication,"[48] in 1959 the *Architects' Journal* offered BASA a few pages on a regular basis—"and if lank editorial hair goes white with shock," the *Architects' Journal* cautioned, "so, presumably, will the locks of some of its readers."[49] The first BASA "Student Section" in the *Architects' Journal* borrowed material from *Polygon,* with articles by Outram and Marden mapping out the preoccupations that were revisited by *Archigram* in the sixties. As if forewarning of beasts like Plug-In City, Outram and

Marden talked of new building technologies such as glue, plastics, and mechanical systems, and of how "the environment would adapt in a manner more flexible than any living organism." They foresaw the sort of designer who would devise Plug-In, too, conversant with systems, unafraid of the multilevel city (traffic below, "air-conditioned arcades" above, filled with "experimental, impermanent, structures").[50]

The jewel in the student crown remained, in the meantime, Webb's Furniture Manufacturers Building, published in detail in the *Architects' Journal*'s BASA section under the appellation "Michael de Webb" (reverence for Webb had now jokingly elevated him to the architectural nobility).[51] So much interest had Webb's scheme accrued, even prior to its reappearance in *Archigram* no. 1, that it "was able to draw much comment from the pundits as to its antecedents in the twenties, nineties, etc.," as *Architectural Design* later observed.[52] The 1920s, 1890s, etc.? Was Webb working in the image of the "pioneer generations" of modern architects? It was an accolade that was lent further credibility by the New York Museum of Modern Art's decision to hang the Furniture Manufacturers project alongside works by El Lissitzky, Frederick Kiesler, and Hans Poelzig in a 1961 show. The pioneer influences of Lissitzky, Kiesler, and Poelzig would later be discernible among other Archigram architects, though Webb and his new *Archigram* collaborators also made it clear that their working principles had been brought thoroughly up to date by the mediation of a more recent vanguard.[53] Archigram designers openly conceded their debt to Team 10 and the new brutalists.

BEYOND BRUTALISM

New brutalism had been nothing short of a revelation to the future members of Archigram. The first truly modern building David Greene could recall seeing was the iconic Hunstanton school (1949–1954) by brutalist ringleaders Alison and Peter Smithson.[54] Cook received brutalism directly from Peter Smithson, through tuition at the Architectural Association; and Crompton, Chalk, and Herron, working in an architectural office at the London County Council (LCC) that had once employed the Smithsons and their brutalist compadres William Howell and John Killick,[55] set about applying brutalism's lessons to LCC work.

1.13 *James Stirling and James Gowan, Engineering Building, Leicester University, 1959–1964: perhaps the most avant-garde building actually constructed in Britain at the time* Archigram *was launched, it demonstrated the unabashed pleasures in form to be found in Corbusian, futurist, expressionist, and constructivist sources, ranging from the red-brick tower to the dramatically freestanding stack and the ridge-and-furrow glazing. The work of Stirling and Gowan was numbered among the inspirations for* Archigram.

Yet Archigram's exuberance was antagonistic not only to the architectural establishment but to brutalism too. By the beginning of the 1960s, brutalism, once touted as an ethic, was settling into an aesthetic of molded concrete aggregate,[56] much as the whirlwind of early modernism had settled into the white villa style of the 1930s. "This'll upset them," Archigram members would joke as they dispatched new sets of drawings, the "them" being *every* establishment body in architecture, including the now-established brutalists.[57] Believing that modernism was destined to recreate itself with each generation of architects, *Archigram* audaciously hinted that the avant-garde mantle might soon be theirs. As *Archigram* no. 1 declared in 1961, "A new generation of architecture must arise." Archigram dared to turn the purported ethos of the new brutalism in upon itself: if the brutalists wanted a frank exposure of form, circulation, site, and technology, Archigram would carry on meting it out, in spades. "At that time," Cook recalled, "the more intelligent of London's architectural thinkers . . . were turning their backs on fifties expressionism. To them, the crystalline, lumpy, bowellist world of *Polygon* was a nasty little turn. The Smithsons had . . . returned to a classicist interpretation of architecture reminiscent of their early work."[58] As Alison and Peter Smithson's Economist Building, London (1960–1964), showed, not even brutalism had achieved the escape velocity needed to pull out of the orbit of solemn, trabeated structure.

Webb's Furniture Manufacturers Building showed how far brutalist principles of uncompromised truth and modernity could be pushed, and the results were, if anything, too avant-garde—a "cartoon architecture" too flashy to qualify as brutalism.[59] One could legitimately expose the services, such as the water tower at Hunstanton School. But a building like the Furniture Manufacturers that was apparently nothing *but* services, stacked crazily in a frame, lacked gravitas. As in the later buildings by the brutalists, Webb left its concrete surfaces rude and undisguised. But molded, form-worked mass, the hallmark of brutalist *béton brut* (raw concrete), was here flayed down to its bones, concrete troweled and sprayed onto the steel mesh using the daring methods of the latest master of concrete construction, the engineer Pier Luigi Nervi.

It resembled "a stomach on a plate, or 'bowels.'"[60] An abnormal meeting between the Cartesian and the biomorphic, the building's frame gingerly held its entrails in place, swallowing up a showroom and company offices on the lower floors, rentable office space in attic stories, and a bulbous auditorium clinging to the side through umbilical cords. Greene took up the cue in his still more bizarre 1961 Seaside Entertainments Building, its main chambers hovering like the muscles of a heart from an aorta service tower (figure 1.14). The implication was that the Seaside Building could comfortably become part of a larger architectural-biological machine, possibly plugged in to a Cook megastructure. Webb took the crossover between architecture,

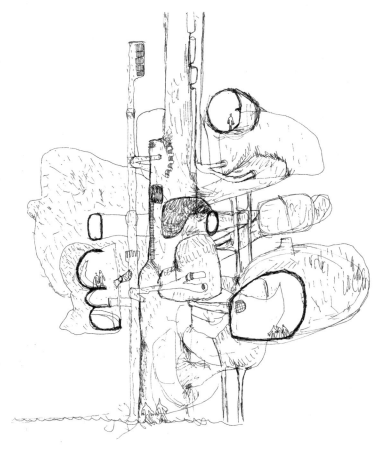

1.14 *David Greene, Seaside Entertainments Building project (Cliffside Entertainments Building), drawing, 1961. Whatever antecedence Greene's work may have had in Frederick Kiesler's Endless House schemes, design did not get much more radical in 1961 than this bowellist sketch of stacked chambers. From the textures of concrete to womblike spaces and electronic stimulation, intimacy with the body and its senses became a prime concern of Archigram's architecture.*

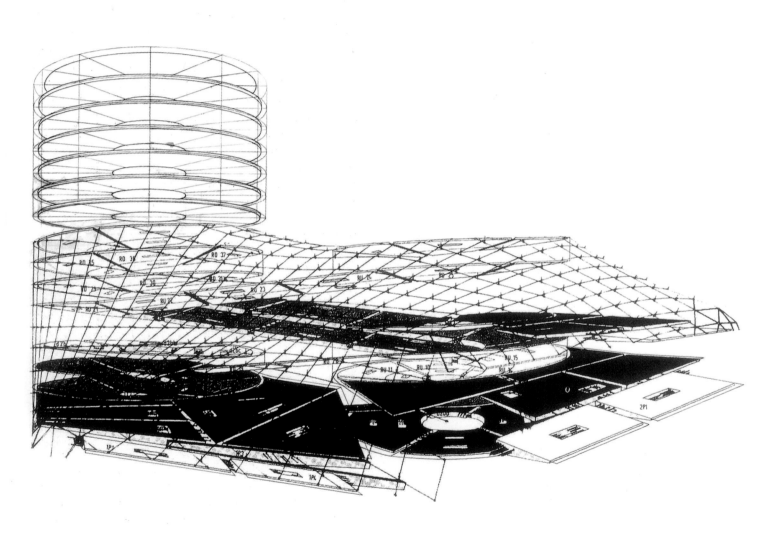

1.15 *Michael Webb, Entertainments Centre (The Sin Centre) for Leicester Square project, diagrammatic perspective of the interior illustrating the suspended covering of plastic sheet and steel cable, 1959–1962, redrawn 2004. Almost as infamous as his earlier Furniture Manufacturers Association Building project, Webb's Sin Centre projected a high-tech style and such potent organic metaphors as transparent skin. Its tower was reminiscent of Frank Lloyd Wright's New York Guggenheim Museum, which opened the year Webb began work on the Sin Centre.*

biology, and the machine a stage further with his seminal 1959–1963 Sin Centre Project for Leicester Square, a fifth-year thesis project (published in *Archigram* no. 2) that Regent Street Polytechnic's examiners persistently failed (figure 1.15).[61] The skeletal services of the building, and its bloodstream of moving cars and crowds, were to be visible through the building's geodesic skin, which cascaded down from the parking tower to the main foyers.

Reyner Banham labeled this new fascination with visible circulation "bowellism" (a biological metaphor), just as he had earlier described an aspect of brutalism as "topological" (a term derived from mathematics and geography). The term "topological" pinpointed the compositional formlessness, derived from circulation between nodes and a complex, "organic" relationship to site, as found in schemes such as the Smithsons' much-reprinted 1953 Sheffield University competition entry, its walkways tying together irregularly massed superblocks (figure 1.16). The departure point of Archigram was a topology gone berserk, multilevel decks surmounting mounds, ducts feeding air into brutalist clusters, plans as smeared as abstract expressionism, *béton brut* as rough as *art brut*. These were the qualities that Webb, Greene, and Cook also noticed in various competition entries by LCC employees Chalk, Crompton, and Herron.

The LCC group was subsequently invited to contribute to the second edition of *Archigram* in 1962, bringing practitioner kudos to a magazine otherwise dominated by student projects. Able to take advantage of their relative freedom as recent graduates, Cook, Greene, and Webb had been cultivating work that was more romantic than that of their colleagues working in the real-world grind of the LCC: respective entries to the 1961 Lincoln Civic Centre Competition made this much clear. The Chalk, Herron, and Crompton entry (figures 1.17, 1.18), which gained a commendation, was in the late brutalist style: a "topological" plan, incorporating any number of irregular polygonal shapes, stacked in elevation over several levels, pulled together by a few deftly placed walkways. Contrasting with the hardedge approach of the LCC team were Cook and Greene's more bowellist, soft, poetic, low-rise elevations, hugging a landscaped site (figures 1.19, 1.20).[62] Notably common to both entries,

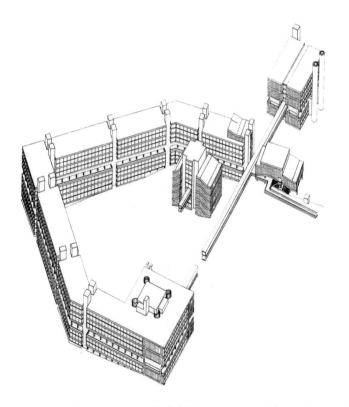

1.16 *Alison and Peter Smithson, Sheffield University competition project, 1953. This scheme showed Archigram members that satisfying architectural composition could be achieved, paradoxically, by surrendering to local topography, patterns of circulation, mechanical servicing, repetitive functions, and standardization.*

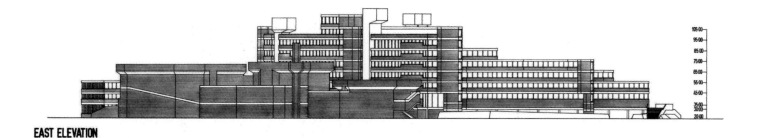

EAST ELEVATION

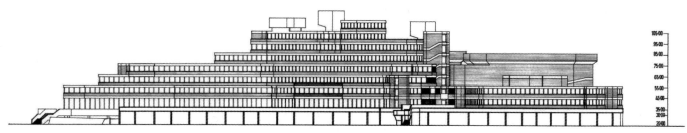

WEST ELEVATION

LCC 10

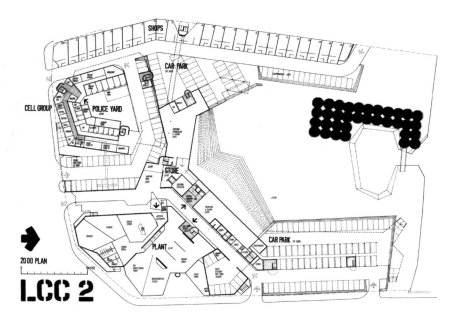

LCC 2

2000 PLAN

1.17, 1.18 *Warren Chalk, Ron Herron, and Dennis Crompton with John Attenborough, Terry Kennedy, John Roberts, and Alan Waterhouse, Lincoln Civic Centre Competition, elevations and plan, 1961. Here, one-half of the future Archigram group showcases advanced brutalist techniques: a highly irregular plan generated by patterns of circulation, echoed through stacked concrete, glazing, and service towers in its elevation. Something of the scheme would be felt in the South Bank Centre (figures 1.22–1.26).*

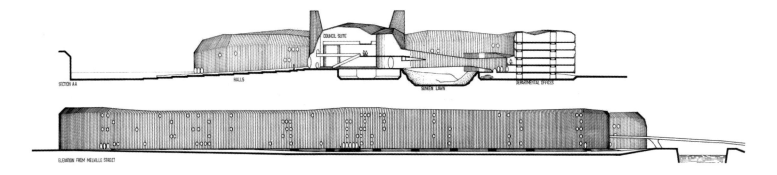

SECTION AA — HALLS — COUNCIL SUITE — SUNKEN LAWN — DEPARTMENTAL OFFICES

ELEVATION FROM MELVILLE STREET

Lincoln Civic Centre Comp. 1961 Elevations reconstructed from plans (originals lost). Project by Peter Cook & David Greene + Mike Webb and Crispin Osborne.

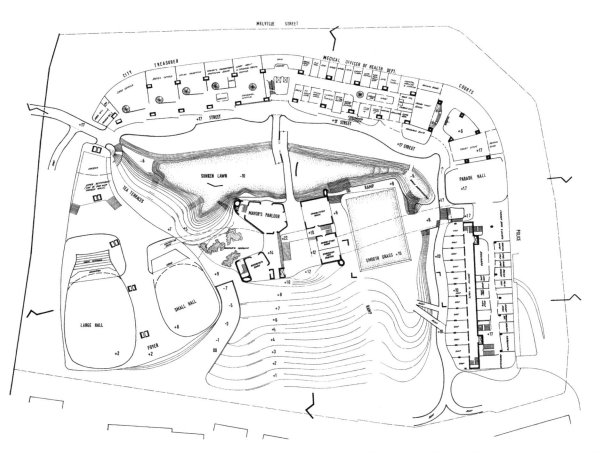

1.19, 1.20 *Peter Cook and David Greene with Michael Webb and Crispin Osborne, Lincoln Civic Centre Competition, elevation and plan, 1961 (elevation reconstructed, original lost). Compare with figures 1.17 and 1.18: more members of the nascent Archigram group push beyond brutalism, almost abandoning machine form to find inspiration in the natural topography of the land and in late expressionism (such as Hans Scharoun's Berlin Philharmonic Hall, then under construction). Mound and architecture would regularly meet in Archigram's work.*

though, was a love of moundlike buildings which would emerge as a key theme in Archigram designs.

Ron Herron had joined the LCC's Schools Division in 1954. It was at the LCC that Herron met Warren Chalk, who joined the same year, and they became inseparable.[63] Between 1956 and 1958 Chalk and Herron's designs combined 1920s Corbusian styling with a certain brutalist ruggedness.[64] Herron's 1957 St. Pancras Starcross (Prospect) Secondary School (with Peter Nicholl) was regarded as an exemplar of young LCC architecture[65] (figure 1.21) and featured in G. E. Kidder-Smith's 1962 anthology *The New Architecture of Europe*.[66] The building hinted that it could be enlarged and changed, anticipating the architecture of endless "becoming" that would preoccupy Archigram. The striking multilevel elevation at Starcross achieved by its concourse bridge was exaggerated by excavating the basements of the houses previously on the site, permitting a sunken playground to flow beneath the teaching block—an appetizer for the infamous undercroft of the South Bank Centre (figure 1.22).

The LCC's controversial addition to the South Bank arts complex (first designed in 1960, completed in 1964, and officially opened in 1967), on the site once occupied by the Festival of Britain, was a snapshot of advanced architectural interests at

1.21 *Ron Herron and Peter Nicholl for London County Council, Starcross (Prospect) Secondary School, St. Pancras, London, 1957. Regarded as an exemplar of work by younger architects at the London County Council, Starcross anticipated Herron's preoccupation with structures receptive to multilevel movement and alteration, though it remained stylistically indebted to early Le Corbusier.* **1.22** *Warren Chalk, Ron Herron, Dennis Crompton, and John Attenborough, for group leader Norman Engleback at the Special Works Division of the LCC, South Bank Arts Centre, London, 1960–1967, undercroft. It had been a Corbusian dictum that buildings should be raised from the ground, but the unusual size of the South Bank Centre's undercroft made the building "get up" and "walk away." The optimism of the scheme (typical of the architecture of the period) is apparent in its assumption that the spaces would be immune from crime.* **1.23** *Warren Chalk, Ron Herron, Dennis Crompton, and John Attenborough, for group leader Norman Engleback at the Special Works Division of the LCC, South Bank Arts Centre, London, 1960–1967. An aerial view illustrates the contrast between the South Bank Arts Centre's rough concrete brutalism, the bright, crisp envelope of the Royal Festival Hall (1948–1951) in the foreground, and the well-mannered terraces of the National Theatre by Denys Lasdun (1967–1977) at the rear; sandwiched between, the South Bank Centre seems to savor its "accidental" quality.*

the turn of the new decade, and its challenge to public taste proved enduring (figure 1.23). It became a battle line for intergenerational struggle: when LCC chief architect Hubert Bennett attempted to redesign the scheme, its young architects resigned. They were reinstated following the intervention of the architecture critic of the *Guardian* newspaper and questions in Parliament.[67] For its design, Warren Chalk and Ron Herron were joined in the LCC Special Works Division by Dennis Crompton. They had lured him from Frederick Gibberd's office, upon recommendation from a friend, in 1960.[68] Designed by Chalk, Herron, Crompton, and John Attenborough for group leader Norman Engleback,[69] the South Bank Arts Centre finally juxtaposed the new brutalism with the great achievement of the earlier generation of British modernists, the Royal Festival Hall (1948–1951), which was being remodeled at the same time. Contrary to the Festival Hall's bright, civic, slightly nautical and unerringly rational confidence, the South Bank Centre truculently crumbled its two shuttered-concrete concert halls (the Queen Elizabeth Hall and Purcell Room) and gallery (the Hayward) into the riverside.

With blind bends and furtive staircases, the Centre deflected any hint of a processional route, reluctant to reveal so much as a front door (figure 1.24). Though powerfully sculptural, the Centre's resistance to being a resolved composition was underlined when its superficially similar cubist neighbor, Denys Lasdun's National Theatre (1967–1977), was erected on the other side. Lasdun held his elevations in check with regulating horizontal layers and crisp corners. By contrast, critics and admirers alike soon noted the willful expressionism of the South Bank Centre.[70] Debts to the 1920s, to Le Corbusier and Konstantin Melnikov, even to Rudolf Steiner could be detected, but in a state too dreamlike to be nailed down as straight historical antecedents (with occasional exceptions like the Unité d'Habitation-derived staircase on the Queen Elizabeth Hall). Imagery was potent but abstract, the pyramid skylights making the silhouette bristle

(a little like the ridges and furrows of Stirling and Gowan's contemporaneous Leicester University Engineering Workshops [figure 1.13]), the Hayward's west window like a pillbox gun installation or a visor (figure 1.25); yet the aggression of the whole ensemble was tempered by a comic-book eclecticism of the sort put on display in *Archigram* no. 4, 1964 (figure 1.31).

The South Bank was an essay on brutalism's procedures. The building seemed to have a disproportionate amount of "exterior," solving at the same time the classic design problem of articulating

1.24 *Warren Chalk, Ron Herron, Dennis Crompton, and John Attenborough, for group leader Norman Engleback at the Special Works Division of the LCC, South Bank Arts Centre, London, 1960–1967, seen from the pedestrian deck to the southwest. The South Bank Centre cast off any rules of architectural composition that would require the building to distinguish front from back, top from bottom, inside from outside. Simultaneously challenging and self-effacing, it expressed its internal volumes monolithically but apparently randomly, greeting the immaterial interactions with its environment—the movements of pedestrians, traffic, ventilation—with gallant walkways, underpasses, overpasses, ducts. The pedestrian deck in the foreground is now demolished, a fretful severance of one of the most daring public buildings in Britain.* **1.25** *Warren Chalk, Ron Herron, Dennis Crompton, and John Attenborough, for group leader Norman Engleback at the Special Works Division of the LCC, South Bank Arts Centre, London, 1960–1967, west window: the aggressive imagery of a gun installation with spines is tempered by reminiscences of comic books and dinosaur movies.*

the blank elevation of an auditorium. Surface textures were selected from surrounding buildings—John Miller and Christopher Dean's much-discussed brutalist Old Vic Theatre workshops (1957–1958, for Lyons Israel and Ellis), and the Sainsbury warehouse in Stamford Street by Owen Williams.[71] The South Bank Centre's ducts were heroically scaled, standing proud of the volumes they served.[72] More profound was the Centre's tribute to the walkways of Sheffield's famous, brutalist Park Hill estate (J. L. Womersley, Jack Lynn, and Ivor Smith, 1953–1959), and its adaptation of the "topological" pedestrian web devised by the Smithsons in their 1953 Sheffield University and 1956 Berlin Hauptstadt projects (figure 1.16). So it was that brutalism reached its apogee not so much under the brutalist avant-garde itself, but under a "retardataire" group of architects at the LCC. Warren Chalk, the eldest member of the Archigram group, conceded that he could have fallen in with the earlier camp of brutalists: "I joined your lot. I could have joined the other lot."[73]

Its ravines of imaginary vehicular traffic separated from pedestrian circulation above, the South Bank Centre was the first chunk in a fantasy-brutalist multilevel city. Chalk was assigned to design the walkways and approaches to the Centre,[74] originally planned to reach out to Waterloo station[75] and extend to jetties on the Thames, and extruding a new pedestrian deck from the Festival Hall's terrace level. But the circulation plan of the South Bank Centre was primarily experiential, not functional (figure 1.26). As critics Edward Jones and Christopher Woodward later noted in a tone that was typical of the hostility engendered by the complex, in the event "the raised pedestrian decks and bridges seem both inconvenient and irrelevant on this quiet site, with no through traffic from which pedestrians might need protection. The decks are windy, offering no protection from the weather, and are difficult for the frail or disabled to negotiate."[76] It is a criticism that benefits from hindsight, and the adventure of visiting the complex has since been curtailed by blocked staircases and closed terraces, sacrificed to cheap architectural crime prevention (the Metropolitan Police wanted nothing to do with the new labyrinth)[77] and the passage of architectural fashion. Yet the South Bank Centre's insensitivity to the infirm did perhaps betray its futurist origins, prioritizing the flow of the young and able-bodied, motorized vehicles, and air. It was somehow appropriate that the Centre later became a mecca for skateboarders (figure 1.22).

"The original basic concept," Chalk recalled in 1966, "was to produce an anonymous pile, subservient to a series of pedestrian walkways, a sort of Mappin Terrace [the artificial mountain at London Zoo] for people instead of goats."[78] The exposure of pedestrians to the weather as they hiked along the bridges, ridges, and plateaus of the South Bank emphasized the designers' preoccupation with styling the building as some sort of natural or organic feature. Alluding to geology and weathering, sheer cliffs of shuttered wood-grained concrete were offset by overscaled rounded deck walls, and in Archigram's self-penned 1971 anthology the South Bank Centre was covered in a discussion of the group's fascination with "mounds" and "crusts" (themes examined in *Archigram* no. 5, 1964). One drawing by Herron even proposed grassing over the entire structure.[79] The "geological" effect was upset only by the grid of precast concrete panels, a hangover of Hubert Bennett's intervention.[80] And so the nearest Archigram came to major built statements began and ended with the metaphor of the mound: the stillborn Monte Carlo Entertainments Centre (1969–1973) was to have been built literally beneath the topsoil (see figure 4.25).

UNFINISHED BUSINESS: POP

The original brutalists had been closely associated with the Independent Group, an architecture-dominated discussion group for junior members of the Institute of Contemporary Arts (ICA), a London-headquartered arts club that from 1948 provided refuge to young avant-garde coalitions amidst a pervasively conservative postwar British arts scene.[81] The Independent Group's meetings lasted from about 1952 to 1955, a pool of interdisciplinary dissent against the modernist establishment that spilled over into a new stream of cultural thinking of its own. What it became best known for, and the reason why it was a key antecedent for Archigram, was its interests in pop: in the culture of mass media, consumption, and leisure.

By the turn of the sixties, Independent Group theory was unavoidable for an informed progressive artist or architect in

Though hard to spot in brutalist buildings, there was an essential overlap between the brutalist ethos and pop. In 1956, the Smithsons brazenly announced that "Today We Collect Ads."[85] "Brutalism," the Smithsons claimed the following year, "tries to face up to a mass-production society, and drag a rough poetry out of the confused and powerful forces which are at work."[86] This urge to appreciate the "long front of culture" (to use an Independent Group expression)—popular culture as well as elite culture—probably explains why the brutalists found the free-ranging discussions at the ICA valuable. The Smithsons soon distanced themselves from the more complete seduction of the Independent Group by popular culture per se. The quest for a poetry of mass production, initiated by Le Corbusier two generations before and rediscovered by the Smithsons, was then adopted by Archigram. Archigram architects were unashamed of the reality of popular taste: they did not try to drain their designs of color; they did not shy from plastic; they did not fear fashion and the possibility that their buildings would one day be carted away by the cleansing department.

Cook's Car Body/Pressed Metal Cabin student housing project of 1961–1962, for example, seemed almost literal in its transcription of automobile design (figure 1.27). Archigram tried to show that Detroit-styled houses were not a proposition for twenty-five years hence, as the Smithsons were at pains to claim in regard to their celebrated, but one-off, House of the Future for the 1956 Ideal Home Exhibition (figure 1.28). As far as Cook was concerned, the pop house, mass-produced from plastic and metal and filled with gadgets, was for the here-and-now of the 1960s. Thus, Cook and Archigram were perplexed by the Smithsons' increasing austerity and concrete fixity. "When, eventually, our own Archigram group began to articulate our homage to their work—and take up their Experiment where their own 'House of Tomorrow' had left off—they were frankly embarrassed," Cook would admit.[87]

When Reyner Banham caught up with Archigram work around 1963 (by odd coincidence his house was on Aberdare Gardens, the same prosaic north London street as Cook's flat that doubled as Archigram's editorial office),[88] he was *not* embarrassed by its embrace of the Independent Group's pop legacy.

Britain.[82] Though members of Archigram had no direct involvement with the Independent Group, that hardly impaired their retrospective reception of the Independent Group's ideas. When the Archigram members were employed at Taylor Woodrow Construction in the early sixties, their manager was the designer Theo Crosby, who had curated the nearest thing to a group manifestation that the Independent Group made: the spectacularly successful 1956 Whitechapel Gallery exhibition "This Is Tomorrow."[83] As well as Crosby, Archigram would come to number among its supporters former Independent Group convener Reyner Banham. And as a student at the Architectural Association, Peter Cook was worked upon directly by Independent Group/brutalist thinkers Peter Smithson, John Voelcker, James Stirling (who also tutored Webb at Regent Street), and Eduardo Paolozzi. Paolozzi delivered the first lecture that Cook attended as a student at the Architectural Association in 1958, packed with "lots of slides of funny things"—packages, advertisements, gadgets.[84]

1.26 *Warren Chalk, Ron Herron, Dennis Crompton, and John Attenborough, for group leader Norman Engleback at the Special Works Division of the LCC, South Bank Arts Centre, London, 1960–1967, staircase and walkways: the building as an anonymous pile, with visitors free to walk over it, through it, under it.*

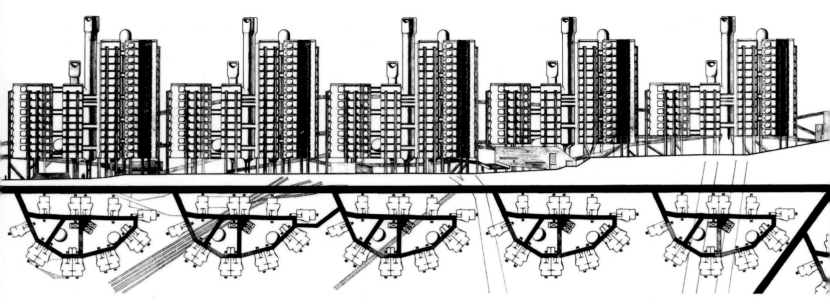

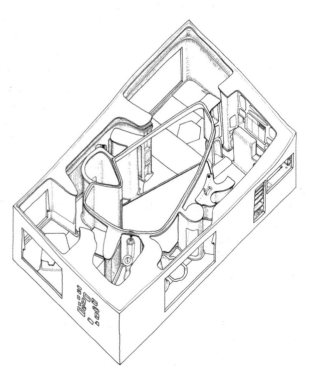

By this date Banham was at the forefront of British architectural history and criticism. Embarking on a series of Independent Group lectures on car styling and product design, Banham had been the first British critic to openly admit liking the populist industrial design of the United States, defying its official condemnation by the modernist establishment. Reading the third edition of *Archigram* in 1963, it was clear to Banham that the way was open for this new consortium to retrieve the incomplete pop project in architecture, deserted by his Independent Group colleagues in the previous decade. In a key address at London's Institute of Contemporary Arts in November 1963, Banham told his audience:

> It's interesting to see how many architects who at one time were with the Pop scene, have in their various ways resigned or withdrawn from it. Peter Smithson in his House of the Future was designing a fully styled-up house intended to be styled-up, in order to make it desirable. The House of the Future had token chrome strips painted round it, and so on. It was to be a fully Pop product so that it would move realistically on the Pop market—it had the sort of gimmicks that were thought necessary then in order to make it viable on the Pop scene.[89]

1.27 *Peter Cook, Car Body/Pressed Metal Cabin Student Housing project, plan and elevation, 1961–1962. Pop is transferred from art to architecture, via brutalism: housing units, mass-produced like Detroit autos, are stacked around common service towers. The image would find echoes in high-tech buildings of the 1980s.*
1.28 *Alison and Peter Smithson, House of the Future, for the Ideal Home Exhibition, London, axonometric, 1956. In this forerunner of Peter Cook's pressed-metal housing and many other schemes for "monocoque" housing units, the Smithsons unwittingly produced an icon. The House of the Future was itself a fanciful development of Buckminster Fuller's 1938 Dymaxion Bathroom (figure 3.11).*

Things had also moved on very rapidly since the 1950s, when the products of the American way were still being experienced as exotic, as a desired "other," even by the Independent Group. Consumer objects were depicted by Independent Group painters such as Richard Hamilton as though they were sacred. But for the generation of the 1960s, pop consumerism was more quotidian and experienced firsthand. Painters of about the same age as the members of Archigram emerged from the Royal College of Art painting pop in intimate detail, publishing the findings in the Royal College's magazine ARK [90] (once a vehicle for the Independent Group and briefly edited by Warren Chalk's brother, Michael);[91] and British pop art was placed on show at the "Young Contemporaries" show of 1961, three months before the launch of *Archigram*.[92]

Archigram members had an arty predisposition that made them receptive to such trends.[93] Greene, Cook, and Chalk had all studied architecture at art schools; in 1965, Cook and Crompton took teaching positions at Hornsey College of Art, a crucible of the British arts scene. Webb early on admitted silver to the already free-ranging palette of his architectural drawings,[94] Chalk surreptitiously practiced painting, and the bright colors typical of pop painting came to characterize Archigram's "poster" mode of presentation. Archigram's cheap, high-impact graphics prepared the public for the cost and commitment of actual pop building through two-dimensional visual seduction. Already sandwiched into pop art, pop eventually had to be *lived* directly through architecture.[95] Archigram broadcasted this message beyond narrow professional architectural audiences by adapting the visual deluge of mass media.

Reyner Banham quickly recognized Archigram's breakthrough in promising an *expendable* environment, apparent in the various plug-in and capsule projects that *Archigram* was amassing and publishing in its third issue, dedicated to "Expendability" (figure 1.29). "I think it does great credit to Peter Cook and the boys . . . that they are trying to grapple with the problem,"[96] Banham noted in the same 1963 lecture in which he lamented the Smithsons' loss of pop nerve. From now on, the ideal building would be as desirable as a new car, and as disposable as an old one. King and queen consumer were in the driving

1.29 *Peter Taylor,* Expendability, *cover of* Archigram *no. 3, August 1963. The acceptance that architecture was expendable was a foundation of the Archigram group's work: issue no. 3 of* Archigram *showed readers the array of disposable buildings already available, including a plastic telephone exchange building (top), Cook and Greene's 1963 City Within Existing Technology (bottom), and the famous photograph of a Buckminster Fuller geodesic dome suspended beneath a US Marine helicopter (center).*

seat. Expendability struck at the very soul of the British design establishment circulating around the Royal Institute of British Architects and the Design Council, with their high regard for the *durability* of "good design"—a hangover of both connoisseurship and war-induced frugality. In fact, disposability had been another outcome of the war, prompted by overproduction after 1945 of new materials like polythene, which now found itself used for packaging food rather than electrical cables.[97]

Cultural critic Christopher Booker described the context for the changeover from austerity to "plenty" at the end of the fifties and dawn of the sixties, as the British public encountered a new prosperity, an expansion in advertising with the arrival of commercial television, even a shift in diet thanks to deep freezes, TV dinners, and fish fingers:

> with so many bright new packages on the shelves, so many new gadgets to be bought, so much new magic in the dreary air of industrial Britain, there was a feeling of modernity and adventure that would never be won so easily again. For never again would so many English families be buying their first car, installing their first refrigerator, taking their first continental holiday. Never again would such ubiquitous novelty be found as in that dawn of the age of affluence.[98]

The same observations had been made at governmental level, in the Ministry of Housing and Local Government's widely read *Parker Morris Report* of 1961 on "Homes for Today and Tomorrow."[99] Though later dismissed by David Greene as "an environmental Mickey Mouse,"[100] the *Report* was clear that British aspirations were being irreversibly transformed by increased consumption and travel.

What this augured was a shift in the social reproduction of architecture.[101] The built environment was being redirected to service a liberal, not centrally planned economy; to house consumers, not workers; to delight the body, not discipline it. In the late fifties Team 10 nurtured what they identified as traditional, seemingly immutable, close-knit social structures. Sporting their "mod" short haircuts and treated warily by Team 10 acolytes "with fringes,"[102] Archigrammers had other ideas of social

improvement. The social body would be liberated through affluence and leisure: through pop, in short. Analysts in the early sixties forecast that huge chunks of the working week were on the verge of disappearance, prompting the avant-garde to invent an architecture of leisure as a matter of urgency— perhaps to accelerate social change, perhaps to stabilize it. One outcome was the infamous Fun Palace project devised in 1961 by Archigram's friend Cedric Price and radical theater impresario Joan Littlewood (figure 1.30).[103] Archigram architects similarly promoted an architecture of fun, "up West" at Webb's Sin Centre for the London entertainments district of Leicester Square (figure 1.15), over at Greene's Seaside Entertainments Building (figure 1.14), and indeed at the LCC's South Bank Centre (figure 1.23). When developing Archigram's festive iconography, Cook and Crompton fondly looked back to their own seaside origins (genteel Bournemouth and working-class Blackpool/Southend-on-Sea respectively), and Michael Webb recalled the boating regatta of his native Henley-on-Thames.[104]

Early issues of *Archigram* replayed, to some extent, the programs of the 1930s, when an architecture of pleasure (cinemas, seaside pavilions) sprang up alongside the architecture of conscience (social housing, health centers). Something of the tension had been seen in the Smithsons' own collages, incongruously bringing honeymooning pop icons Joe DiMaggio and Marilyn Monroe to the spartan access decks of east London mass housing. A cultural shift from northern social realism to swinging London, seen in drama and literature, was pronounced in the first few issues of *Archigram*. Timothy Tinker's fourth-year project for a cinema in west London was central to *Archigram* no. 1, but his fifth-year thesis for Housing at Moldgreen

1.30 *Cedric Price with Joan Littlewood,* Movement, *Fun Palace project, photo diagram, 1961. In the year that* Archigram *was launched, Price and Littlewood's sensational Fun Palace proposal established an agenda for architecture as a "neutral" support servicing leisure. The scheme stubbornly permeated sixties architecture until it was adapted to Piano and Rogers's project for the Pompidou Center (figure 4.19).*

(1960), which clung to the "grim North" and the "kitchen sink," was relegated to marginalia for *Archigram* no. 2.[105] In the thirties the architectures of conscience and delight were regarded as complementary: one providing Monday to Friday decency and the other a weekend release. This distinction was no longer valid to the architectural pace-setters of the sixties. Conscience dictated that the common man and woman be delighted seven days a week. Pop promised that.

Instead of confining the working class to mass-housing quarters, Archigram was unashamedly transferring tenants to hip, dispersed living pods with direct access to goods and leisure. "It was a commonplace of American sociology at the time," notes historian Arthur Marwick of thinking that was being imported into Britain, "that urbanization was converting the extended family of earlier times into isolated nuclear units."[106] The career of the prominent sociologist Michael Young, whose observations of the organic patterns of working-class life had informed the Smithsons' assumptions, encapsulated the transition from a pre- to postconsumerist mindset: in the same year that he published *Family and Kinship in East London* (with Peter Willmott, 1957),[107] which was standard reading for architects, he founded a new political body called the Consumer Party and launched the product rating magazine *Which?*

Little more than a decade later the British social housing program, the architectural backbone of the centrally planned welfare state economy, collapsed and was partly blamed for stifling an enterprise economy that demanded (to borrow an Archigram phrase) "housing as a consumer product."[108] Archigram, it is fair to speculate, wanted to wave a pop wand over mass housing and so rescue the promise of a better tomorrow before it was too late. Archigram's members had been shocked at the backwardness of a great deal of the British housing stock extant in the postwar decades. In 1950, Dennis Crompton's grandmother's Leverhulme house in Manchester had no toilet, no electricity, and was lit by gas,[109] and a decade later a third of British homes still had no bathroom.[110] The problem of outright homelessness was perceived to be so great that the British Minister of Housing spent 1962 investigating the potential of temporary shelters and mobile homes.[111]

Thus it was that the bolt-on, car-body, disposable pop home could be regarded by Archigram not as a fanciful diversion but as the solution to housing an economically transformed society. Four hundred thousand new homes a year were projected by the British government in the mid-sixties, and Archigram members decided that the factory-made shelter was the only way the target could be realized.[112] Plug-In City was, perhaps, a "third way" between public- and private-sector housing, privately selected capsules clinging like limpets to the public infrastructure. "It is arguable that the rigid departmentalization of the Welfare State bureaucracy, with its emphasis on the *relief* of poverty, is due to make some form of attempt at social coordination and programming," one skeptical commentary on the technostructure of British planning trends later noted. "This would have as its main objective the minimization of the need for relief mechanisms, and the creation of a consumer society in which all members participate through their own unaided efforts."[113]

At Taylor Woodrow Construction, the Archigram architects were encouraged to assess and develop prefabricated building systems,[114] inspiring as a spin-off Chalk's interest in a new sort of capsule housing allied to Cook's Plug-In City concrete infrastructure (figure 1.3).[115] Archigram embarked upon a rapprochement with new technology more intrepid even than that attempted by the Smithsons' House of the Future. Archigram learned about the cutting-edge architectural engineering of Konrad Wachsmann, Eckhard Schulze-Fielitz, Frei Otto, and Jean Prouvé;[116] Crosby's *Architectural Design* magazine, meanwhile, propagated radical technologies,[117] working particularly hard to interpolate the ideas of the renegade American architectural inventor Buckminster Fuller, whose stratospheric theories were translated by Independent Group member John McHale into a language accessible to *Architectural Design*'s readers.[118]

That Fuller's work often had a science fiction aura about it only added to its pop cachet. Banham asserted to architects in 1958 that science fiction was "one of the great mind-stretchers, specialization-smashers of our day. . . . It is part of the essential education of the imagination of every technologist."[119] This education mattered because recent advances in technology, especially in rocket science and computing, were blurring the distinctions between the extant and the possible. Mainstream modernism had boasted of being technologically determined, yet declined to respond to the catalogue of technological achievements of the decade or so leading up to the launch of *Archigram*—including the bomb (acquired by Britain 1952), electronic computers, television, and manned space flight (1961). *Archigram* no. 4, 1964, returned to science fiction and comic book sources similar to those used by the Independent Group (figure 1.31). A strong factual thread ran through British boys' comics of the 1950s (girls' comics tended to revolve around photo stories), sincerely attempting to predict and inform youthful readers about short-hop air transportation and space travel. An almost postmodern quality pervaded the scenography of the comic strips, and the optimism of the new Elizabethan age pulled the future toward the near horizon.[120]

In 1955 Richard Hamilton opened his ICA show "Man, Machine and Motion," containing more than two hundred photographs and copies of drawings illustrating devices that had allowed humans to conquer land, sea, air, and space.[121] A decade later and Archigram would be drawing *architecture* that did the same jobs: a Walking City (figure 1.32), an Underwater City (figure 1.33), an Instant City borne by airships (figures 4.1, 4.39), and a Living Pod (figure 3.5) that brought the hermetic environmental conditioning of the Apollo missions back to Earth.[122] It was wayward, it was "boys' stuff," excited by implements, noises, and frontiers, but it had a rationale. Archigram projects demonstrated that architecture was an escape hatch from environmental conditions, not an internment within them. Here was the architecture of rescue, partly inspired by the tents and field hospitals of humanitarian relief efforts; Walking City, or a less fanciful version of it, might one day deliver a community of United Nations administrators to a crisis area within days.[123] Humanity stood shoulder to shoulder, as in 1950s comics,[124] or like the Allies in the 1940s. The vision was touched with mythic heroism. Indeed, one commentator has concluded that the architect *is* the comic strip hero of *Archigram* no. 4.[125]

1.31 *Warren Chalk, typical page from* Archigram *no. 4, 1964: architectural form is culled from sci-fi comics and Archigram's own doodles, disrupting "the 'straight-up-and-down' formal vacuum" of contemporary British architecture. Appropriate to its message, it was with issue no. 4 that* Archigram *really took off, selling about one thousand copies and igniting architectural "zoom."*

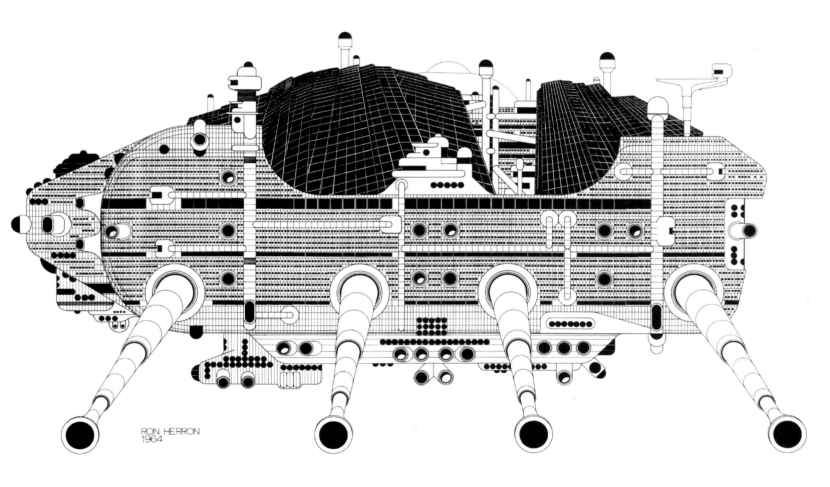

1.32 *Ron Herron, Walking City, 1964. Possibly because it was so implausible, Walking City became one of Archigram's best-known images. Despite its fastidious surface detailing, it is hard to interpret literally: Could a big aircraft undercarriage support a building? Could a landscape bear the load? Could Walking City paddle in the sea, as other versions of the picture suggested? Even read metaphorically, questions proliferated: Did Walking City come in peace? Nonetheless, it was a bold memorandum of forgotten modernist ambitions: to make collective dwellings, transcend national boundaries, build machines for living in, extend human dominion, alter everyday perception, bring people into contact with the elements, and simply to excite the public about the future.*

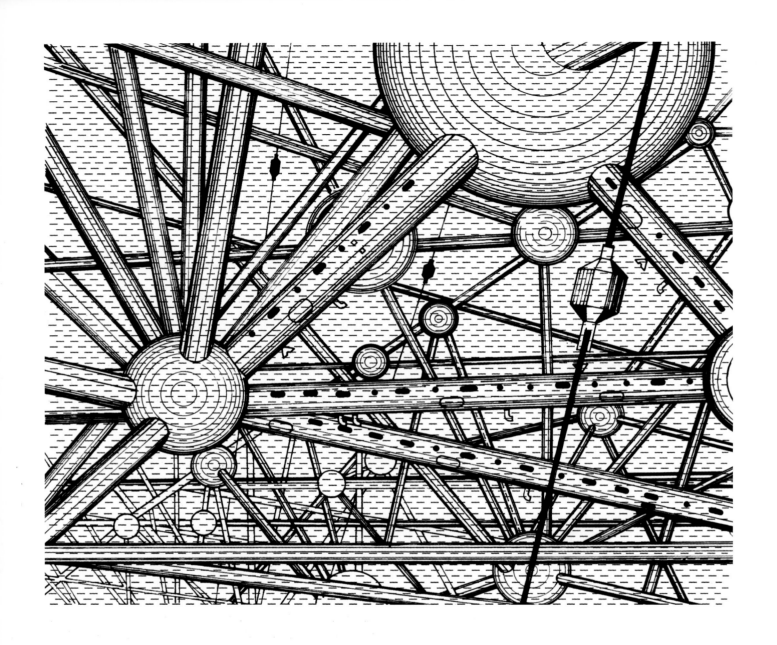

1.33 *Warren Chalk, Underwater City, drawing, 1964. Underwater City was of the suite of Archigram drawings that saw architecture as a way of breaching the Earth's frontiers and extending the "kit" language of architecture: here Chalk explores the formal possibilities of repeated nodes and connectors.*

Modernism had repeatedly fostered in its young followers a taste for avant-garde adventure. Ron Herron's mentor at Brixton School of Building, Julius Posener, a veteran of German modern architecture, recorded as early as the 1930s how, in the eyes of young architects, pioneer figures like Gropius, Mies, and Ernst May lost their shine when they hit their forties: "They tried to close the profession within clearly visible limits . . . to begin to value habit as an important factor in the designing of dwellings, rather than re-casting them according to the image of a new way of life."[126] Indeed, the generation that represented the establishment to Archigram had in turn, as students, exhibited contempt for authority (in 1930s England, still founded upon Beaux-Arts principles). The publication in 1938 of *Focus* magazine by Architectural Association students (which contributed to the tradition of the little magazine in Britain from *Blast* to *Archigram* and beyond) announced, "We were born into a civilisation whose leaders, whose ideals, whose culture had failed. They are still in power today. But we, the generation who follow, cannot accept their domination. They lead us always deeper into reaction that we are convinced can only end in disaster."[127]

Young English modernists of the 1930s asserted the same impetuousness of youth that gave the Smithsons in the 1950s and Archigram in the 1960s the notion that the profession should pay attention to architects still in their twenties.[128] It was not Archigram but their new brutalist forerunners who first challenged the gestating Official System in architectural education and dogma in architectural practice. As students themselves at the Architectural Association, brutalists John Killick and William Howell had challenged the theoretical roots of English modernism in the student journal *PLAN* (1943–1950),[129] emboldening them to take on the international body of modern architects itself, the Congrès Internationaux d'Architecture Moderne (CIAM). A deep-seated memory of avant-garde resistance and little magazines persisted in the English modern movement: "after we had finally all met," Cook has recalled of Archigram's formation, "we started to share some secrets with each other and started to grumble. This attitude hardened and

focused upon an assumed 'enemy.' Had not Gropius, Le Corbusier and the Smithsons had conspicuous enemies?"[130] Archigram subscribed to a myth that modernism was renewed by acts of heroism. Archigram would perpetuate the revolution by taking a collective stand against those who wanted to make modernism into a methodology.

Launched at just the moment when new brutalism was itself slipping down a gear into the municipal, *Archigram* was perfectly in the logic of the avant-garde (figure 1.1). Protagonists knew it at the time: the same sort of friction felt between Archigram and the brutalists had occurred between the Independent Group and the ICA's founder, Herbert Read,[131] and Peter Cook draws a comparison with the tension between Bruno Taut and Hermann Muthesius.[132] "THIS IS ARCHIGRAM—PAPER ONE—A STATEMENT," the cover of the first *Archigram* loudly announced, though it took more than a little effort on the part of the reader to piece the "statement" together. In emulation of the Smithsons' pages in the catalogue to "This Is Tomorrow,"[133] words fell about so that they would be read synchronously, snaking around the page as if their sum meanings were so outrageous to the early sixties design establishment that they should be subject to a controlled release, intelligible only to those who were appropriately youthful:

A new generation of architecture must arise—with forms and spaces that seem to reject the precepts of "Modern" REJECT—curtains—design—history—graphpaper DIG ACCEPT endorse—homogeneity—travelators—Monk—expendability

It was a curious manifesto, accompanied by a medley of rebel designs from the Architectural Association and Regent Street. *Archigram* no. 1's startling rejection of "design" was a traumatic request for architects, and surprising given Archigram's subsequently massive production of drawings. But there it was: design (as in the cut-and-dried presentation of a solution) was too static, premeditated and removed from environmental context to be literally transcribed into built form; there could therefore be no more design in the traditional sense of the word.

Edward Reynolds's project for a Concert Hall at Trafalgar Square was regarded as an exemplar of the "virtuoso free-forming at the AA";[134] its cubist handling of form faceting every surface of the project, first shown at the 1957 AA student exhibition, was heralded as a "breakaway from graphpaper."[135] It seemed to William Howell that the work had marked "both an intellectual and a poetic reaction against the straight-up-and-down, strictly rectangular, tee-square and set-square, exposed frame structure."[136] For all the supposed neutrality of mainstream modernist culture, there was an official style to which the architect was expected to adhere. The grid was the paramount device, with its affectations of "objectivity" and "functionality," reproduced through three dimensions by "modular design."[137] So *Archigram* no. 1 outlawed graph paper; the logic of the studio-produced statistical graph had to go the same way. The jibe was probably aimed at the sort of rationalist/modernist teaching at the key schools. (Part of the first year at London's Bartlett school, for instance, was spent studying science and a choice of "allometry, semiotics, Markovian analysis, sensory thresholds, self-regulating systems, Boolean algebra, theory of measurement or the theory of limits.")[138] In place of such high-sounding approaches, *Archigram* no. 1 was proposing pragmatic "expendability," a permit to do away with designs as soon as their peak of desirability has passed.

The new architecture should "seem to reject precepts of the modern"—the precepts taught in the architectural schools, perhaps, though not necessarily the precepts of the modernist pioneers. As *Archigram* no. 1 further announced, "WE HAVE CHOSEN TO BYPASS THE DECAYING BAUHAUS IMAGE WHICH IS AN INSULT TO FUNCTIONALISM," including the ubiquitous motif of the curtain wall. Instead of the *image* of standardization presented by "curtains" (the curtain wall), true "homogeneity" would return architecture to its dream of interchangeable parts that could be deployed ad hoc. The *spirit* of the machine age would live again, its citizens transported by "travelators." Young architects would recover an uncorrupted architecture of technique. With curtain-walling set aside, the suspended cradle used for cleaning it would be reprieved as a plug-in shuttle servicing kinetic structures,[139] and the tedious problem of water-proofing the curtain wall would advance in 1965 to the hermetically sealed Gasket-Homes by Chalk and Herron.

The modern movement had largely rejected history, or at least the more obvious deference to the classical orders, decoration, symmetry, and hierarchical typologies. Yet it had retained other things, notably proportion, trabeation, and axial planning—one only had to look at the temples in Le Corbusier's *Vers une architecture,* or to John Summerson's final chapter of *The Classical Language of Architecture* (1963), or to Banham's exposé of the Beaux-Arts origins of certain modernist axioms in the first chapter of *Theory and Design in the First Machine Age.* The *Archigram* generation of architects would not submit to these classical hangovers: this time, history really wasn't going to be tolerated. New buildings would be placed on top of and around those existing designs whose fixed plans had outserved their usefulness.

The result would be architectural disjunction, a visual break with yesterday, an anti-idealism. Architecture would embrace discord, like jazz pianist renegade Thelonious Monk, and would adopt the same choppy, streetwise tone in which *Archigram*'s statement was scripted; "DIG," in case the reader of *Archigram* didn't realize, meant "endorse." (Eight years later in *The Neophiliacs,* the conservative 1960s commentator Christopher Booker wearily explained that the embrace both of jazz and sensational language signified the "almost indefinable state of being 'hep' [sic] or 'in the groove.'")[140]

Nature, adopted by *Archigram* no. 1 as another model, was in a condition of constant regeneration and thus unencumbered by history. Nature was the analogue of youth, a visible energy erupting underneath the establishment. Drawing upon one of the old dualities of Western thought, David Greene wrote a poem for *Archigram* no. 1 about nature as the life-giving counterpoint to the idealism of methodical modernism:

synthetic design and instant
plans and niceness and reasonableness
and flat buildings lie heavy in the bowels
As clouds whisper across the sky
and earth smells explode the heart [141]

Nature offered the organic solutions of growth, form, reproduction, and evolution; visions like Plug-In would be the built counterpart. For young architects craving the mantle of the modernist pioneers, the concept of flow and organicism as generators of form was irresistible after Frank Lloyd Wright's sensational New York Guggenheim finally opened in 1959. "This building," *Archigram* no. 1 said, pointing at Timothy Tinker's 1959 project for a cinema, its streamlined curves interrupted only by a little geometric control tower, "illustrates flow as generator of form," an idea enlarged in a stream of consciousness in the corner of the page: "Bulge contain modulating *skin* nut bolted vertebrae *flow* growth plant *cool* movement." The idea pulsed through the page: "MOVEMENT . . . MOVE MOVE."

Heroes lesser known than Wright were spirited up, too; Greene's 1960 Mosque at Baghdad project developed ideas from one of modernism's great outsiders, Frederick Kiesler, whose Endless House schemes of the 1950s, with their cell-like reproduction, womblike hollows, and sensitivity to the spaces of the body, defied Cartesian rationality.[142] "THE *bud* OF SPACE/THE INNER SPACE *PUSHES* THROUGH THE *SKIN*," ran the caption to Greene's Mosque at Baghdad. *Archigram* celebrated skin, then— even though it instructed its readers to reject the ubiquitous modernist membrane of the curtain wall. The problem with the curtain wall, it seemed, was that it superficially functioned as "skin" but was more akin to the encumbrance of clothing, hanging from a grid skeleton. The intent now was to design an interface like biological skin, an active organ.

Archigram aspired to design at the level of nature so that it could reorganize the planet, leading as far as interests in underwater sea-farming. As Dennis Sharp puts it,

> No better word could have been found than the in-word of the late 1960s, "environment," a term which, so far as I can infer, means that when architects use it for "physical" design they include among their problems everything everywhere. From desert landscape to moon landscape through the ocean systems, all is defined as environment. The architect, it seems, can come up with solutions to all of these problems.[143]

Such heroic superstructural and social ambitions were bequeathed to *Archigram* by earlier modernists, such as Cook's teacher at the Architectural Association Arthur Korn, who chaired the Modern Architecture Research Group (MARS) committee that published the outrageously abstract 1944 linear plan for the reconstruction of London.[144] In its syllabus of the 1950s, the RIBA itself emphasized the role of the architect as a "total planner." *Archigram* now extended this calling to its logical ends.

BEING AVANT-GARDE

Often speaking through collage (a medium closely associated with the avant-garde), *Archigram* entered the heroic history of avant-garde renewal. Peter Cook had been startled by a Dada show in Düsseldorf in 1958[145] and was swept up by the rediscovery of constructivism at the Architectural Association at the beginning of the sixties.[146] Constructivism would be influential on Michael Webb, too,[147] and was manifest in Chalk, Crompton, and Herron's South Bank Centre. *Archigram* no. 1 name-checked the futurists, recently recovered from relative obscurity for English-speaking audiences by Reyner Banham in "Futurism and Modern Architecture," 1957,[148] and more prominently in his landmark *Theory and Design in the First Machine Age*, 1960. *Theory and Design* performed a similar service for the old expressionists, and Ron Herron's teacher Julius Posener had earlier introduced German expressionism to an English audience. The extraordinary visions of the early twentieth-century avant-garde were further propagated in Ulrich Conrads and Hans Günther Sperlich's *Phantastische Architektur*, 1960, soon afterward translated into English.[149]

Otto Wagner's organization of the Viennese avant-garde[150] and Bruno Taut's administration of the utopian Crystal Chain correspondence[151] were of particular appeal to Peter Cook. Cook was probably the most interested in endowing Archigram with a cohesive group identity. He quizzed Mary Banham about the social dynamics of the Independent Group when sharing rides in the car to and from Aberdare Gardens.[152] Much as Team 10 had observed the dynamics of the organization they helped to destroy, CIAM, Cook was curious about the self-styled Team 10 family by which CIAM was superseded.[153] He keenly noted the development of the new avant-garde formations in Austria and elsewhere. By his own admission, intrigue with group dynamics and teamwork during his first year at the Architectural Association had made him an "amateur psychologist." Group dynamics, Cook found, were a question of understanding the mix of participants, poor teams resulting from excessive concurrence.[154] This again suggested a pop outlook, a transition from an avant-garde organizational model based on the military to one based on bands and gangs: the arrangement permitted the development of cult figures within the fold.[155]

Archigram's adeptly wrought self-image was one of bright but unpretentious guys doing their thing—inclusive enough to look relaxed, exclusive enough to whittle out an agenda and a contributing caucus of half a dozen after the first two issues of the magazine, when social realists and "Christian Weirdies" were bid farewell.[156] The precipitate that became the "Archigram group" almost reenacted Taut's plan for the Crystal Chain: "Let us consciously be 'imaginary architects'! . . . Quite informally and according to inclination, each of us will draw or write down at regular intervals those of his ideas that he wants to share with our circle, and will then send a copy to each member. In this way an exchange of ideas, questions, answers, and criticism will be established. . . . The mutual sympathy within the circle and the use of terse language will make it difficult for outsiders to understand us."[157] Archigram developed too feisty an identity to suit Cedric Price, who retained an autonomous career and an "avuncular" relationship with the group despite being a similar age and enjoying close connections (Cook met Price when they were at the Architectural Association, Cook in the third year, Price in the fifth).[158] Replacing the earlier modernist principle of anonymous group effort, Archigram acknowledged individual contribution, its drawings almost always attributed and sometimes signed, even copyrighted to an author. Archigram group identity, more than a sum of its considerable parts, was in turn an extension (to pick up on the thinking at the time) of each man. The Archigram arrangement became more corporate by degree, with the production of shows from 1963 onward, the printing of a letterhead in 1965, and eventually the opening of an office in 1970.

Within these parameters, two consistent posts can be identified within the group. Dennis Crompton (known as the Euston team's "Mr. Screwdriver") acted as group technician and archivist; Peter Cook was the group's internal commentator, its most energetic editor (likely the author of many unsigned editorials in *Archigram*), and the member who had the most ambition for the organization. Cook's outlook cherished a belief in "English Empiricism,"[159] in Archigram existing by dint of its production rather than its party line. And production tended to be constituted more through the empirical activity of drawing than the contemplative abstraction of theory. This allowed Archigram to make a big splash very quickly, though it might have had the effect of demoting the more reflective, poetic side of the group. A cavalcade of brash images and can-do rhetoric promoted the group, yet Warren Chalk found drawing a fatigue and David Greene was quietly against it altogether. Greene had been reproached by his teachers at college that he was interested only in "ideas about ideas," and he found the detailing of architectural drawings "boring."[160]

Enthused designs gave Archigram a relentlessly upbeat group persona that belied the romantic melancholia dwelling within. For each optimist in the group poring over a drawing board late at night, one might have found another member brooding uncertainly over the purpose of architecture, though such vocational misgivings were barely apparent to Archigram's public. Even the group's shared technophilia blurred a varied set of personal responses to technology. Peter Cook, for instance, disliked driving, flying, and tall buildings, whereas David Greene yearned to disappear into a machine once and for all;[161] from about 1968, Michael Webb was too preoccupied with matters of vision, speed, and perspective to dedicate more effort to the *machine à habiter*.

In its group manifestation, Archigram certainly appeared to be a successfully updated version of an avant-garde. It was literally a neo-avant-garde, a *revival* of the avant-garde activities that made modernism exciting at its early twentieth-century launch.

John Summerson observed in 1955 that "the reappearance of a radical spirit is especially vital in Britain today because architects here never shared in the radical phase of the modern movement as a whole. It all happened abroad. Modern architecture arrived here in the late 'twenties, already a 'manner,' an 'idiom.'"[162] Early modernism was rediscovered by brutalism and Archigram much as the Renaissance befriended antiquity. (In 1965, *Architectural Design* published the Smithsons' much-thumbed anthology of "The Heroic Period of Architecture," a primer in avant-garde forms.)[163]

The desire to refresh modern architecture did not, however, constitute a fully fledged avant-garde program of itself. Moreover, observers were unconvinced of the importance of Archigram's larger ideological and theoretical contribution. Misgivings that *Archigram* was principally a vehicle for showing off characterized a critique by Denise Scott Brown in 1968. Scott Brown emphasized that the new pack of little magazines, over which *Archigram* reigned supreme, was indeed a "heroic" venture—with all the pathetic gender assumptions that that entailed:

> *Little magazines are usually one-track . . . representing that school at its most iconoclastic. . . . They are written by young men and often emanate from the schools; a school may have its own vehicle, glossy and well-turned, and its back rooms be supporting, unofficially, this other venture. Little magazines are hand-made and usually ill-kempt in appearance, but with a certain flair.*[164]

As well as a gender bias, Scott Brown surmised two other key features of the new avant-garde magazines: that they emulated the self-published efforts of the pioneers—*L'Esprit Nouveau, De Stijl,* the futurist manifestos, and *G*—but were more likely to emanate from the college refectory than from café society.

Scott Brown's somewhat partisan tone was probably provoked by her own sensitivity to the debates motivating Archigram. Studying at the AA in the early 1950s, she was first alerted to the vivaciousness of pop culture by Independent Group ideas, received from the Smithsons and other brutalists who exercised a sustained influence on her.[165] For Scott Brown, and her collaborator from 1960, Robert Venturi, a truly "popular" architecture required not Archigram's perpetual change of super-technological consumerism, but a "homecoming,"[166] a new interest in meaning and legibility, a new vernacular. The belief that architecture can or should change the world through ruthless modernization—one of the prevalent assumptions of the avant-garde—was rejected by Scott Brown and Venturi as modernism's worst habit.

Scott Brown presented the youthfulness of Archigram's new avant-garde as juvenile. However, the young, "studenty," increasingly "zany" image conveyed by *Archigram* belied the fact that it was put together in the spare time of some experienced architects, professionals who had one major project already in construction (the South Bank Centre for the LCC) and another, the massive Euston development, in progress for Taylor Woodrow Construction—though never to see the light of day (figures 1.34, 1.35)[167] Archigram members were tantalizingly close to seeing their projects built, yet they persisted in an avant-garde guise, courting student readers and controversy. Archigram was likely a career gambit, but it was, nonetheless, evidence of a fervent wish to see modernism "kept new"— a flame lit when Archigram members were still training, and which they wanted to keep alight among the "new generations" succeeding their own. Therefore *Archigram*'s language did not preach to students but conspired with them. The drive to innovate took on a combative, avant-garde mode because the "modernist establishment" and the RIBA represented a tangible enemy for Archigram (a polarity which Archigram members admit has since become indistinct).[168] The appeal to youth was tactical, since architectural schools provided space in which architects, both teachers and students, could creatively reflect upon their practice, undistracted by the immediate pressures of clients and work on site. *Archigram* hoped to link up and radicalize architectural students in Britain and abroad, spawning further student-oriented architectural little magazines and posses in the mid-sixties, and prompting Reyner Banham to talk of "the Movement"[169] as though it were a shadow of the 1960s counterculture at large, the student an agent of long-lasting change.

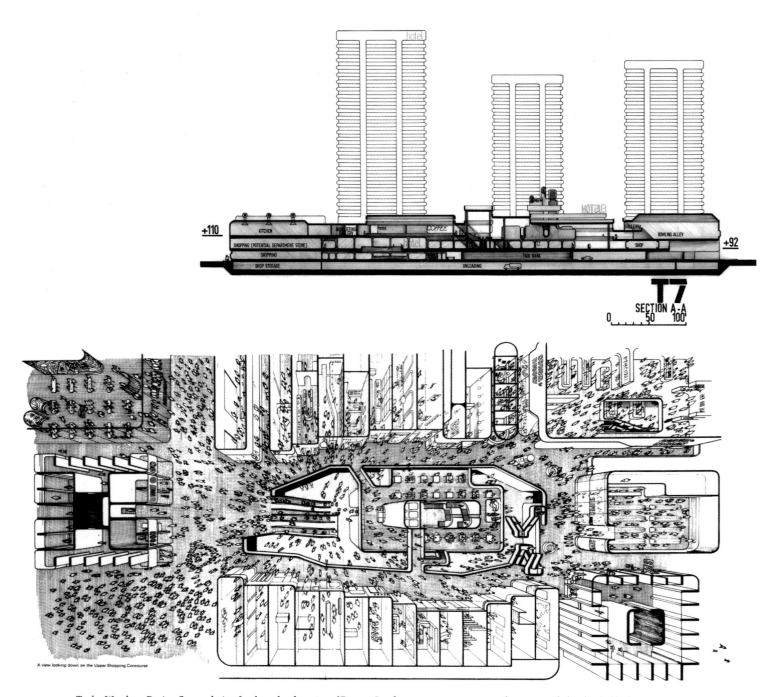

A view looking down on the Upper Shopping Concourse

1.34, 1.35 *Taylor Woodrow Design Group, design for the redevelopment of Euston, London, 1962–1965, section and perspectival plan (probably drawn by Ron Herron). The redevelopment of the Euston area was one of the most contentious in sixties London, and Taylor Woodrow Construction's scheme, illustrated here, was never realized. Under the supervision of Theo Crosby (a leading light of the London arts scene), Taylor Woodrow's Design Group employed all the core members of Archigram as well as Robin Middleton, Brian Richards, Frank Linden, and Alex Pike. Combining offices, retail, and leisure facilities, the Euston scheme's program was typical of the sixties property boom, though its formal qualities suggested new directions for Taylor Woodrow's design language (compare with figure 1.2): geodesic canopies (later deleted), towers like silos, pop signage, rounded corners, ducts, and complex, staggered sections. The populous, single-point perspective of the plan emphasizes the designers' interest in social space.*

The "neo-avant-garde" label, nowadays commonly used for post–Second World War artistic tendencies, acknowledges the antecedence of the "historical" avant-gardes, but it also somehow corroborates the weariness already apparent in Scott Brown's tone in 1968. "Neo-" suggests "pseudo-," a loss of bohemian radical authenticity.[170] This is probably due to the way that neo-avant-gardes were frequently produced by the modernist artistic system itself, quite as much as by a cultural urgency at large: "I always think of it as an architectural thing," Cook has recalled of the Archigram phenomenon. "We knew more about [Erich] Mendelsohn than we knew about Mary Quant."[171] Mary Quant—the designer of the sartorial emblem of the sixties, the miniskirt—meanwhile knew nothing of Archigram.[172] Archigram was a product of architectural discourse before it addressed wider cultural turbulence. Viewed as only one more episode in the architectural profession's intergenerational struggle, Archigram principally remained subject to the logic of modernism as well as a challenge to it. As Crinson and Lubbock have convincingly argued, the British architectural avant-garde was institutionalized, enjoying inclusion *inside* the modernist curriculum:

> an internal modernist "avant-garde," quite unlike the anti-
> establishment avant-gardes of early modernism, has developed
> since the 1950s that asks questions that are only comprehen-
> sible, indeed perhaps only conceivable, within the paradigm. . . .
> Furthermore, it is often germinated and spread within the cul-
> ture of the architecture schools—through teaching, peer contact
> and the student magazines that multiplied after 1955—and it
> provides the system with profuse design theories for its voracious
> studio system.[173]

Given Archigram's involvement with architectural education, it was appropriate that reaction against Archigram eventually came, in the late sixties, from students. By that time, many students were skeptical about pop: in fact, rapprochement with bourgeois capitalism was precisely a factor that identified the pop art movement as a "neo-avant-garde" in the denigrating sense of the term. Was Archigram so toothless politically and culturally? Describing it as an avant-garde makes the term very inclusive and upsets the neat orthodoxy that grounds the avant-garde in the hard left. But balking at describing Archigram as "avant-garde" may not be helpful in analyzing a small, youthful, antiestablishment, iconoclastic body in the arts that acquired beliefs in some sort of social redemption through modernization and creativity, and which most likely looked, to the vast majority of observers at the time, like a regular avant-garde. Archigram, this book is arguing, gradually correlated its parochial concerns with modernism and the architectural profession to broad issues of social (and economic) organization in space. Archigram, this book further argues, thought that a pop sensibility could divert market mechanisms and the military-industrial complex to the benefit of social progress, much as the avant-gardes of the 1910s, 1920s, and 1930s hoped they could recoup industrialization for socialism. This reined in "avant-garde" ambition to something close to liberalism precisely in order to salvage avant-garde beliefs in emancipation. More Marxist-oriented commentators found the position naive; Archigram found more Marxist-oriented positions naive. Archigram inclined toward a belief that the architect with the least party-political commitment was best able to respond to a world undergoing the rapid transformations wrought by capitalism, scientific change, and accelerated communications.

PERPETUAL BECOMING

Archigram defied all closures, preferring a dialectical relationship between its mutable designs and its elastic ideology. *Archigram* magazine clipped together news items, advertisements, technical releases, and architectural history into new architectural assemblies. This was Archigram's supermodernist aesthetic *and* its avant-garde ethic: to promote a world of perpetual becoming. Endless permutations of existing forms or extreme outcomes for established methods were to be discovered. The viewer was reminded of Le Corbusier's scorn for those who have "eyes which do not see."[174] As anyone reading *Archigram* could see, the sources for the new were already "out there": not now the sources for purism, but for a technological eclecticism.

Archigram portrayed the experience of modernity as fractured, simultaneous, transitory, magnificently inarticulate, a reversal of the "call to order" in the 1920s that turned avant-gardism into the modern movement. Readings had to be kept open if they were to represent the unclassifiable nature of reality in the mid-twentieth century after the certainties of the twenties.[175] If Archigram eschewed the polemical force of those manifestations issued by the first avant-gardes, it was partly because they refused to be encumbered with hard-and-fast rules—actually a highly strategic way of tackling orthodox modernism.[176] Archigram's laissez-faire outflanked even those modernist maxims to which Team 10 and the brutalists had remained loyal. Team 10 had stormed the palace of modernism, taking control of CIAM, dissolving it and reframing the debates about housing estates and the like, whereas Archigram largely *ignored* the institutions and debates that preoccupied the establishment. Archigram simply walked away from mass housing estates, the Roehamptons and Park Hills, the brutalist battlegrounds of the 1950s, so as to indulge an interest in hip city centers and pleasure parks.

Archigram shifted the rules of engagement in a move analogous to the new modes of guerrilla engagement in postcolonial war. The architectural profession in Britain, which had tried so hard to establish itself as a level-headed and distinct profession, jealously patrolling its borders against incursion from neighboring professions and even from public opinion, now found a cell operating within it that apparently wished to promote popular, frivolous, and unorthodox approaches: "it upset a lot of people who still felt that architecture was somehow a sacred discipline that should not be played with and certainly not placed at the same level as comics or things like that."[177] From the outset Archigram prided itself on its indeterminacy, right down to the way in which its membership, like its images, "fell together" by circumstance.[178] Like Team 10 and the Independent Group before it, Archigram was keen to stress that its members were ultimately autonomous, only briefly and partially formalizing their partnership as the Archigram Architects from 1970 to circa 1975. In the interim it was like a study group, an ongoing "conversation,"[179] so speculative that its output was largely confined to paper and teaching rather than actual construction.

Archigram may tell us as much about modernism and the architectural profession as about the wider world, but Archigram's breathless rush was inevitably related to its era. Sixties Britain was a time and place willing to appraise visions and gestures that might otherwise have been dismissed as delirious. As Christopher Booker described it, there was in the air "a new wind of essentially youthful hostility to every kind of established convention and traditional authority . . . a sense that society was being carried rapidly forward into some nebulously 'modernistic' future."[180] Booker disparagingly compared the 1960s to earlier periods of social and economic upheaval, like the age of the romantics and the roaring twenties, moments, he said, that

fire men's imaginations, arousing them to the intense mental activity that has represented their attempt to reestablish a relationship with the world and with reality. But it is also at such times that for many people, even for whole classes and nations, a hold on reality becomes hardest to achieve. Unbalanced by change, they display, like an uncertain adolescent, all the symptoms of insecurity. . . . They are, in short, the results of trying to resolve an insecurity through what we may call the dream or fantasy level of the mind.[181]

The apparent madness of *Archigram* was an antiestablishment tactic[182] comparable to two other experiments launched in 1961, *Private Eye*[183] (the first editor of which was none other than Booker, prior to his deliverance), and the Establishment Club, its interiors partly designed by Cedric Price, Archigram's friend with extensive connections in the new "antiestablishment."[184] Zaniness was being funneled through art colleges into pop groups like the Bonzo Dog Do Da Band and the Beatles. Even madness as a mental condition was reappraised in the radical psychology of R. D. Laing and in the drama *Morgan: A Suitable Case for Treatment* (adapted by BBC television in 1962).[185] Romanticism had long associated "madness" with the genius of the visionary, and it was in this direction that Archigram wanted to steer interpretation of its work. In 1965 Warren Chalk defended the work "optimistically lumped together and . . . classified under the label of 'Fantastic Architecture'":

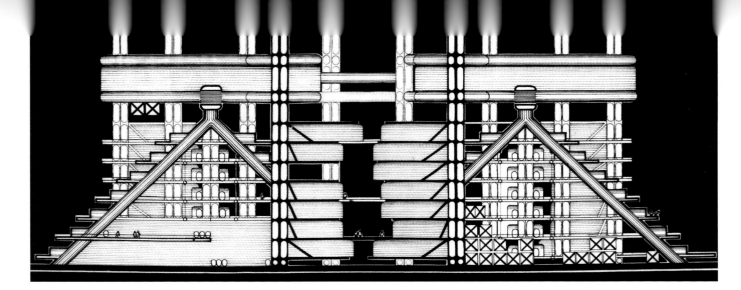

Contrary to the belief that pioneer architecture is over and that "the revolution finished twenty years ago," there is evidence of an increasing interest in that diverse congregation of revolutionaries whose drive springs from a desire to transcend the cultivated academic doctrines and disciplines of the Modern Movement and operate in an area at once chaotic and ingenious, irrational and inspired.[186]

It therefore mattered whether Archigram's work was catalogued as "fantastic" or "visionary." In 1961, Webb's Furniture Factory was classified by the Museum of Modern Art (MoMA) as "Visionary Architecture," a category that did not sideline the work in quite the same way as the then more popular tag of "Fantastic Architecture," which was used by *Architecture d'Aujourd'hui*[187] and by the Bannister Fletcher Library at the RIBA. For *Architectural Design,* there were some critical distinctions to be made between the works on show at MoMA. Frederick Kiesler, enjoying a resurgence of patronage, was actually not to be taken too seriously: "it reminds one of that car-of-the-future that Detroit is always bandying about and with very much the same result, that really underneath all the stuff is the same old transmission, engine, and suspension."[188] *Architectural Design* preferred that architecture address an argument, a structural or

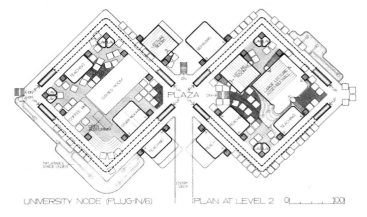

functional logic. This more accurately represented the motive for the bulk of Archigram's projects, whatever their admiration for Kiesler. Archigram's projects tended to have their roots in the surprisingly conventional problems of postwar architecture. Like Cedric Price's Potteries Thinkbelt (1964), for instance, Peter Cook's University Node project (1965, figures 1.36, 1.37) answered the rapid expansion of universities and the need to democratize education following the Crowther Report of 1959;[189] and as Ron Herron admitted in 1972, the foundation in Britain of the Open University almost matched Archigram's

1.36, 1.37 *Peter Cook, Plug-In University Node project (detail), elevation and plan, 1965. If oneiric, sensory concerns guided designs by Archigram members like David Greene and Michael Webb, other members, particularly Peter Cook, offered radical solutions to socioeconomic problems—as here, where plug-in technology manages the rapid expansion of British higher education.*

vision of a radically decentered and nonelitist higher educa-tion.[190] Cook's Plug-In City, meanwhile, could be read as an extension of new-town linear city theories being expounded in the United States and Great Britain, by both progressive and mainstream planners, as a way of relieving the population crush in the old cities,[191] taking advantage of occupation densities made safe again by the Clean Air Act (1955) and the increasingly adept control of disease.[192]

Archigram responded to a Britain undergoing a huge build-ing boom controlled in the public sector by architects with unprecedented budgets and powers, and in the private sector by the speculators of the property boom, which peaked in the mid-fifties and early sixties.[193] In place of the static, unimaginative, anonymous mass of late International Style office development that was so far meeting demand, Archigram posited a dynamic architectural language of growth, rethinking architectural aesthetics much as Louis Sullivan felt compelled to devise an appropriate dressing for the tall office building in the 1890s. Archigram's ad hoc alterations to the built environment would have no greater impact than the schemes for comprehensive redevelopment undertaken by dozens of British towns and cities. For a world undergoing such rapid transformation, Archi-gram proposed organic change rather than total, sudden, cen-tralized projects.

Ultimately Archigram's vision redeemed the technological apocalypse. "Now, after the Second World War," wrote CIAM's secretary, historian Sigfried Giedion, in 1948, "it may well be that there are no people left, however remote, who have not lost their faith in progress. . . . And it began so marvelously."[194] In the Cold War age of the atomic bomb and the conquest of space, technology was perceived as both savior and destroyer of civi-lization. Perhaps Archigram's sheer optimism would win over some waverers. "We want to drag into building / som[e] of the poetry of countdown, / orbital helmets . . ." Greene mused in *Archigram* no. 1, the same month that Kennedy committed America to a space program that would land a man on the Moon by 1969.

Affluence, comfort, and progress attended the technological revolution, it was assumed. Ronald Bryden, in a witty article for a special issue of *Town* devoted to youth in 1962, portrayed "these future rulers of ours." "They will see no reason why we shouldn't follow European experiments with monorails, hydro-foils and district heating," Bryden wrote, as if he had already seen Cook's drawings for Plug-In City. "They'll probably feel the cold less," Bryden thought, as Archigram examined the possibil-ity of architecture as a second skin. "They will be cleverer than us"—or, if not cleverer, perhaps wired into Archigram's net-works of information technology. One paragraph by Bryden summarized Archigram's preferred social vision:

> they're going to be classless. Their clothes already are. So are the things and places they like most—Wimpey [sic] [hamburger] Bars, bowling alleys, the M1 [Britain's first high-speed road]: all too new to have any connotation of upper or lower, in-group or out-group. When they come to furnish homes they'll pick "con-temporary" design with none of the connotations antiques carry of a bygone, aristocratic taste.[195]

Classless, popular, high-tech, go-with-the-flow—Archigram had devised an exhilarating alternative to doctrine.

2
—

THE LIVING CITY
POP URBANISM CIRCA 1963

The six core members of Archigram began to work as a collective in the summer of 1963,[1] trading not eponymously as the publishers of the *Archigram* newsletter (the third issue of which was about to appear),[2] nor as employees of Taylor Woodrow Construction (which they all were), but as the creators of a major installation at the Institute of Contemporary Arts (ICA) in London (figures 2.1, 2.2).[3]

Aslant as it was from the governing institutions of British architecture, such as the Royal Institute of British Architects, the ICA offered Archigram space in which to reflect upon the conditions of modernity and the role of the modern architect. If 1964 would see Archigram emerge as hugely confident—with Plug-In City, Walking City, Computer City, Underwater City, and so on—a year earlier their ideas appeared more hesitant, formative, and poetic. Avant-garde nonetheless, this collaboration with furniture designer Ben Fether and graphic designer Peter Taylor[4] was "a vision of the city as an environment conditioning our emotions,"[5] and it was called "Living City." A sense of living: This was the quintessential quality sought by the "new generation." Through image, text, sound, and light, this "assault on the senses"[6] that physically enveloped visitors attempted to convey the essential property of the city as being in a state of continual becoming, and to enshrine physical and cultural pluralism as an indispensable quality of urbanism. "Living City" proposed an "existentialist" approach to design: the problem of being had to take precedence over that of knowledge, with the architect no longer able to "stand outside" his (or more problematically her) subject.

"Living City" straightaway made Archigram the subject of partisanship: "half the world gasped in horror," critic-historian Charles Jencks later joked.[7] Constantin Doxiadis, an architect himself engaged in radicalizing the public's concept of settlement, found "Living City" beyond the pale, recalling "a London 1963 exhibition" that sowed the seeds of "an inhuman conception of the city of the future by a small group of

people," all the more "appalling . . . because it received wide publicity without, as far as I know, any corresponding protest."[8] "Living City" was certain about its importance as an avant-garde intervention. Like Alison and Peter Smithson pitching their "Parallel of Life and Art" show to the ICA a decade earlier (figure 2.3),[9] "Living City" introduced itself as the latest installment in the history of modernist exhibitions, from the "demonstrations" of "the 1910's in Germany, 1920's in France and Italy, 1930's in Sweden and so on" to the "reviews" more typical of England — the 1938 MARS group exhibition and the Festival of Britain.[10]

Yet "Parallel of Life and Art" and "Living City" were not programmatic in the manner of these forebears. They stood in place of manifestos as improvised, visual antimanifestos. "Parallel of Life and Art" had displayed iconic images culled from anthropology, biology, and technology as prearchitectural raw material.[11] "Living City" curator Ron Herron described his appreciation of "Parallel of Art and Life":

> It was most extraordinary because it was primarily photographic and with apparently no sequence; it jumped around like anything. But it had just amazing images; things that one had never thought of looking at in that sort of way, in exhibition terms. And the juxtaposition of all those images! I was just knocked out by it.[12]

As the Smithsons' Independent Group colleague John Voelcker explained the shift in the mood of the avant-garde after the 1939–1945 war: "1930. The frame building and the multilevel high-rise city, images which contained a complete urban system. 1950. Random images drawn from many sources containing single ideas which, one by one, contribute to, change, and extend the experience of space."[13] And so it would be at "Living City."

Visitors hoping to see in "Living City" the buildings of tomorrow had to look hard, studying the catalogue, peering into the dazzling collages, or standing back to ponder the crumpled walk-in environment display structure improvised by the group (figure 2.4). The very clutter of the presentation seemed unarchitectural. The geodesic triangulation of the display structure was chosen for its amenability to free form and ease of fabrication and "nothing more was intended"[14] (the structure was

2.1 *Peter Taylor, "Living City" logo, 1963. The logo of Archigram's first group exhibition signified the core, periphery, and communication route of the city.* **2.2** *Team preparing the "Living City" exhibition, Institute of Contemporary Arts, London, 1963. From left: Harry Powley (a friend of Peter and Hazel Cook, and resident of Aberdare Gardens); Peter Cook; Warren Chalk; Ron Herron; Dennis Crompton; Brian Harvey.* **2.3** *Installation view of "Parallel of Life and Art," Institute of Contemporary Arts, September-October 1953. Juxtaposing fragments of the modern condition a decade earlier, Alison and Peter Smithson's "Parallel of Life and Art" was an inspiration to the organizers of "Living City."*

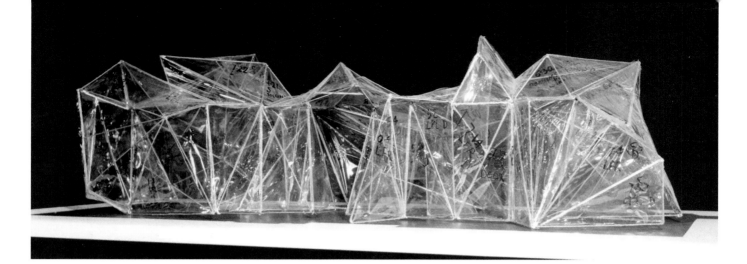

originally intended to be made from still more amorphous spray plastic). "Living City" and its catalogue were not about traditional architectural form, but its opposite: the formlessness of space, behavior, life.[15]

In the 1950s and 1960s, avant-gardes widely abandoned the intellectual and artistic certainties of historical materialism so as to acknowledge the diversity and untidiness of the material world, and of social and psychological experience. In painting, the avant-garde had preferred the *informe* to the modernist grid. And now in architecture, "Living City" was a statement of faith that built form was only one half, possibly the lesser half, of the architectural experience. "When it is raining in Oxford Street the architecture is no more important than the rain, in fact the weather has probably more to do with the pulsation of the Living City at that given moment."[16] The "Living City" exhibition tried to account for an urban experience unregistered in the purviews of maps, plans, elevations, and statistical analyses. Hurriedly raiding shop displays and ripping up magazines, Archigram's own drawings, modernist texts, comics, catalogues, and film posters,[17] the organizers of "Living City" zoomed in on space and experience at a micro scale, and delved into the secret daydreams and desires of the city dweller. "Living City" abandoned architecture's pretense to account for the urban condition, preferring to condense a sense of *being,* of joyful survival in an urban landscape without clear meaning and undergoing rapid change.

London, the emergent swinging city,[18] was the venue and effectively the subject of "Living City," exemplifying the architectural and cultural modernization of British cities from the mid-fifties to the mid-sixties. There was, the commentator Christopher Booker remarked, "the same visual violence everywhere; in the ubiquitous neon-lighting, on shop-fronts, on advertisements, in the more garishly decorated restaurants."[19] Booker found the scene barbarous, and at the time of "Living City," few urban planners would have admitted a fondness for London's newly found raciness. The ICA circuit—first the Independent Group, then Archigram—set about affecting a perceptual shift, inspired by the bright lights of Piccadilly Circus, Times Square, and photographs of Weimar Berlin.[20]

Archigram welcomed the vastly expanded range of visual effects and cultural references available to architects willing to embrace the illuminated pop city. "Living City" was lit by a Flicker Machine,[21] a rotating slotted lampshade that, when looked at with closed eyes, was "a crazy but effective way of stimulating interest in the possibilities of moving light" (figures 2.5, 2.6).[22] Sensorially, it summoned not immobile structure but what Bauhaus veteran László Moholy-Nagy called *Vision in Motion* (the title of a 1947 book that had a sizeable impact upon the postwar British avant-garde).[23] Architects were fussing over the detailing of their buildings when the reception of the city by those down on the street was generally fractured, immaterial,

2.4 *Model of the Total Exhibition Structure, "Living City," 1963. Unable to realize the ideal solution of a plastic bubble, the designers of "Living City" opted for a lightweight, transportable triangulated metal frame with panels, familiar in geodesics. A paradox became well known to Archigram architects: the disavowal of form (the subject of the exhibition was urban mood) created dynamic forms.*

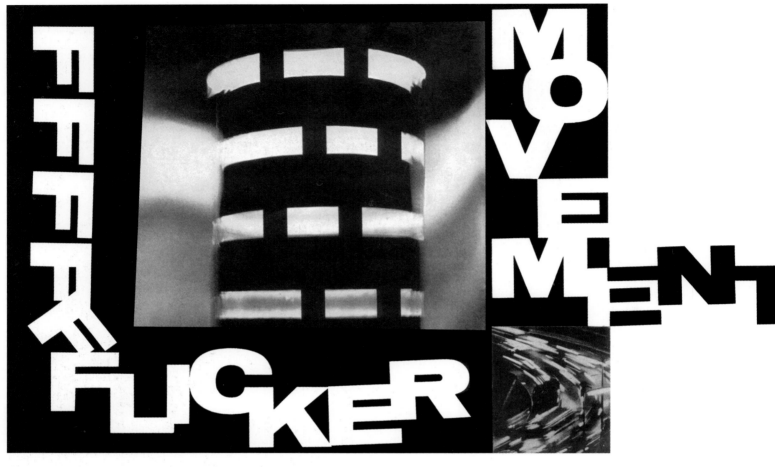

and kinetic: the Flicker Machine was juxtaposed at "Living City" with a long-exposure photograph of traffic moving at night.[24]

Urban managers continued to withstand the slurring of spatial and verbal grammar; the motorists of 1963, for instance, saw the introduction to the highways of the unitary system of traffic signs by Jock Kinneir and Margaret Calvert.[25] But "Living City" wanted to make jumbled-movement communication into a medium workable by the architect, without robbing it of its natural, unkempt charm. Such was the kinetic city's vibrancy that the most civilized act of the architect was a "tuning," perhaps even an "amplification," of the city's (non)communications.

"Living City" attempted to identify and classify "movement-cycles," "the point of origin or destination, direction, route and speed of individuals or crowds."[26] Archigram borrowed the new theory of communicative "feedback" intending to make the communicative cycle more symphonic, even while originators of communications theory were trying to remove "noise" from the communicative system. (Colin Cherry, a professor at London's Imperial College and the most immediate authority on communication theory for ICA circles, eliminated the communicative pollution of cereal packets from his breakfast table.)[27] "Watch it happen + listen to the sound + see it flow," "Living City's"

2.5, 2.6 Anon., Flicker, *montage and view of the "Living City" installation at the Institute of Contemporary Arts, London, 1963. Coincident with broader op-art trends, the flickering light in "Living City" alluded to the escalating energy of sixties London, a notoriously drab city in the previous decade.*

telegram script on "Communications" rattled out through clouds of trains, telephones, remote controls, freeway intersections, film spools, records, and televisions (figure 2.7).[28] For the designer of film, television, and the urban environment—where typography was liberated from the mechanical letterpress and hurled into freeform motion—the best lessons came from futurist and dadaist recklessness, not Bauhaus and Festival of Britain prudence, "Living City's" graphic designer Peter Taylor believed.[29]

Interest in the relationship between language and urbanism, and the most exotic celebration of formless ephemerality, hailed as well from situationism. The situationists were engaged at the time in raising the art of city living to the level of politics. Their influence had been imported into the ICA by Ralph Rumney, a founding member of the Situationist International in 1957,[30] and the group made an infamous appearance at the ICA in 1960, a few months after the ICA's screening of the early situationist film *Hurlements en faveur de Sade* had created scenes of unprecedented ill-temper.[31] When the situationist Constant spoke at the ICA in November 1963, Archigram personnel Peter Cook,

Michael Webb, and their friend Cedric Price joined the audience,[32] and Archigram made some effort to stay in touch with him.[33] Ron Herron purported to find Constant's theories baffling, and Dennis Crompton was disappointed by the lack of structural detail in Constant's architectural designs, but in retrospect the failure to cultivate closer contacts with the situationists was one of David Greene's great regrets for Archigram's development.[34] That the affair between Archigram and the situationists remained unconsummated says something about the Archigram project: opportunist, empiricist, and "English," while the Paris-centered group pursued the theoretically elaborate, politicized "grand plan." If these differences between British and Continental approaches were not explicit in the early sixties, by the end of the decade Archigram had been made acutely aware of them (as will be discussed in chapter 4), defiantly celebrating their supposed freedom from dogma as they were questioned by the left.

At "Living City," the attraction to situationism, while never cited explicitly, was made clear by the little show's culmination in a section on "Situation" (figure 2.8): "all of us in varying

2.7 *Anon.,* Communications in Living City, *montage for "Living City," 1963. By celebrating environmental noise, the new associates of* Archigram *were doing the exact opposite of what urban designers were meant to do.*

degrees, according to our perceptiveness, find Living City in *Situation*."[35] Originally a term borrowed from the existentialism of Jean-Paul Sartre, it referred to the complex of living conditions which, moment to moment, the individual must negotiate. The notion of *situation* had been appropriated by situationists in the mid-1950s to denote moments and places where potentially revolutionary environmental conditions prevail. A situation had clearly existed in the declaration of the Paris Commune, situationists argued, and situations still existed beneath the surface organization of latter-day Paris. Outright social revolution was not Archigram's bag, but the group did revel in London's social frisson, seeing in the notion of situation a forceful informality. "In this second half of the twentieth century, the old idols are crumbling, the old precepts strangely irrelevant, the old dogmas no longer valid," Archigram's assessment of "Situation" claimed. Much beyond this, Archigram was reluctant to comment too much about situation's antiestablishment qualities. Situation was simply a source of street-level pleasure for architects to study firsthand, the raw material of a new architecture of events. Archigram conceived of situation in a more architectural, more plastic way than the situationists. Situation was

an ideas generator in creating Living City. Cities should generate, reflect, and activate life, their environment organized to precipitate life and movement. Situation, the happenings within spaces in the city, the transient throw-away objects, the passing presence of cars and people are as important, possibly more important, than the built demarcation of space. Situation can be caused by a single individual, by groups or a crowd, their particular purpose, occupation, movement, or direction. Situation can be traffic, its speed, direction, classification. Situation may occur with change of weather, time of day or night.[36]

A likely source of "Living City's" adaptation of situation was Reyner Banham's article of 1959, "The City as Scrambled Egg."[37] It was published in the Independent Group-influenced journal *Cambridge Opinion*, which read almost as a primer for the themes of "Living City," with issues dedicated to "Race," "Predictions,"

2.8 Anon., Situation, *montage for "Living City," 1963. The word "Situation" referenced the existentialism and cultural radicalism of continental Europe, but the diorama was more urban jumble than urban jungle: this was Swinging London Picturesque.*

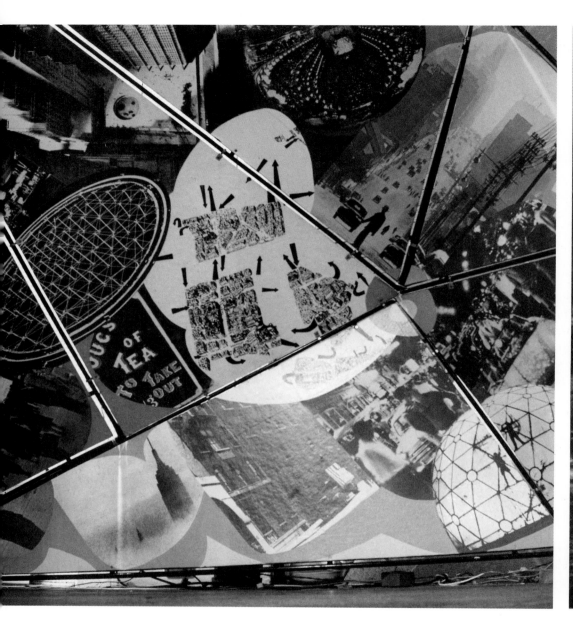

THE PASSING PRESENCE

2.9 *View inside the "Living City" installation, showing Guy Debord and Asger Jorn's situationist* Psychogeographic Guide to Paris *(1956). In drawing the visitor's attention to the psychic qualities of metropolitan social space, London's avant-garde references the work of Parisian revolutionaries.* **2.10** *Anon.,* The Passing Presence, *montage for "Living City," 1963. In common with nineteenth-century observers of "modernity," "Living City" identified momentary encounters in the street as life-enhancing, though no acknowledgment was made of the sexual frisson between model and presumed male observer (compare with the mannequin legs and high heels of figure 2.12).*

and latterly "Living with the 60s"—"in this issue we look at certain aspects of our cultural SITUATION in terms of COMMUNICATION."[38] Writing in *Cambridge Opinion*, Banham felt that the situationists had cracked the problem of reading the "scrambled," living city with their technique of "psychogeographical drift" ("the study of the specific effects of the geographical environment, consciously organized or not, on the emotions and behavior of individuals").[39] The creators of "Living City" agreed: "The overall configuration of mass movement is also significant in predicting the behavior patterns of man in motion. These patterns have the effect of splitting and isolating known city environments in loosely defined but distinct areas or locations of psycho-geographical drift."[40] To demonstrate the technique, "Living City" included Guy Debord and Asger Jorn's situationist *Psychogeographic Guide to Paris*, 1956,[41] its chunks of markedly atmospheric city floating in a sea of movement (figure 2.9). Significantly, though, the Gallic subtleties of psychogeography and the neo-Marxist politics that underwrote it were lost in translation into Archigram's own British pop tongue.

Psychogeography reinvented the old technique of *flânerie*, of strolling around the city in order to better understand its cultural and geographical dynamics; "Living City" was redolent of the transient, erotic urban experience of such *flâneurs* as Charles Baudelaire and the surrealists. Fundamental Baudelairean preoccupations were at "Living City," right down to the defensive celebration of "Fashion," which, along with the words "Temporary" and "Flashy," Cook felt had been wrongly castigated as "a dirty word."[42] "Living City" appreciated that the commotion of crowds slipping through the streets was one of "come-go," "the key to the vitality of the city."[43] "Living City" was an invitation to the roving male eye of the voyeur and fetishist: "two periscopes arranged in bright metal ducting gave fleeting glimpses of girls in Dover Street or faces at the bar" (figure 2.15).[44] Archigram illustrated the idea of "Situation" with a photograph of a glamorous young woman straightening her stocking in the rain-swept metropolis, throwing a backward glance at the photographer-*flâneur*: "the passing presence," the picture was titled, an embodiment of the *éphémère*, of men fantasizing flirtatious encounters with women (figure 2.10).

Like Baudelaire, the architects of "Living City" regarded the relative permanence of the city's built form as the glorious life support machine for a culture in perpetual flux. As Baudelaire succinctly explained in 1863, "By 'modernity' I mean the ephemeral, the fugitive, the contingent, the half of art whose other half is the eternal and the immutable."[45] "What have cities been doing over the few thousand years in which they have existed?" Peter Cook asked.

> They have provided society with a physical centre—a place where so much is happening that one activity is stimulated by all the rest. It is the collection of everything and everyone into a tight space that has enabled the cross stimulus to continue. Trends originated in cities. The mood of cities is frantic. It is all happening—all the time. However decadent society may be, it is reflected most clearly and demonstratively in the metropolitan way of life.[46]

In its designs, Archigram often allowed for permanence, as in its provision of an underlying urban infrastructure (Plug-In City was a good example), or through its retention of certain historic monuments (as when its linear city threaded its way through old London in the "Living City" catalogue) (figure 2.11). And yet, in his pursuit for the truly "living city," Cook was prepared to loosen even these ties to "the eternal and the immutable." "In old cities," Cook wrote,

> there comes a time when the cycle of interaction and regeneration has become so established as a pattern that the true reason for their existence is clouded over. There is the obvious aggregate of a metropolis: palaces, places of government or control, monuments, symbols of an established centre; but these are not the vital part of cities. . . . The thread connecting the city state of Athens with present-day New York is not that they both possess such monuments, but that they share the coming together of many minds, and they are vital.[47]

This lack of sentimentality for the monument—for the structural and symbolic permanence of architecture—was the radical strand in Archigram's thinking. Even the sponsor of Archigram

---

2.11 (following pages) *Anon. [Peter Cook?], Come-Go, montage for "Living City," 1963. As they rove London, Cook's Car Body Housing, City Within Existing Technology, and Craneway (produced with Greene) doff hats to Westminster, Trafalgar Square, and Piccadilly Circus, and claim ancestry from London's existing "kinetic" architecture—Tower Bridge, the riverfront, and the markets.*

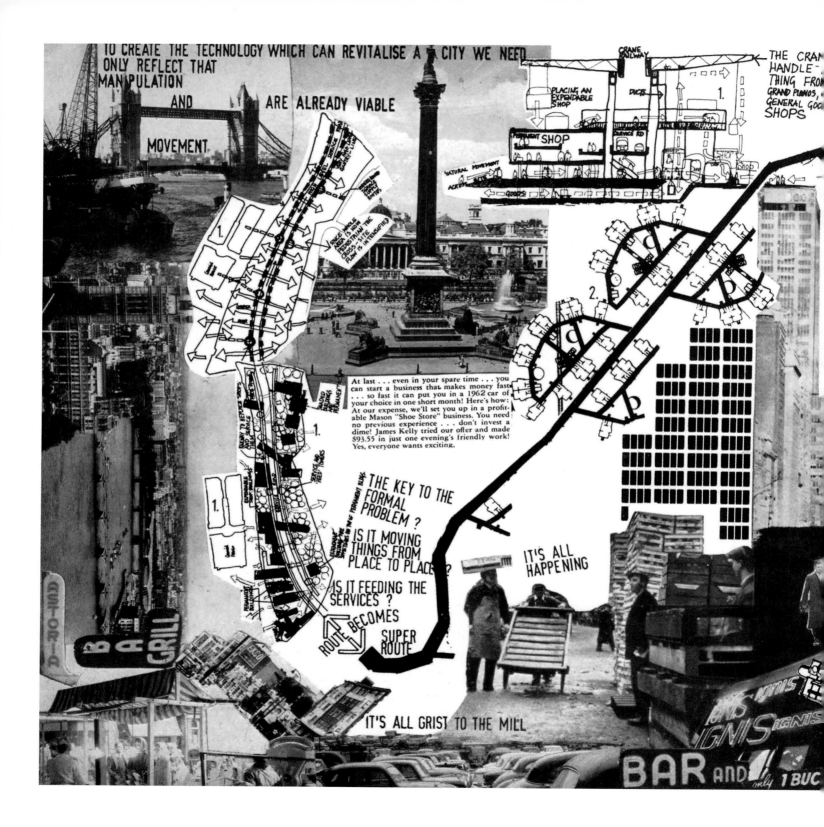

TO CREATE THE TECHNOLOGY WHICH CAN REVITALISE A CITY WE NEED ONLY REFLECT THAT MANIPULATION AND MOVEMENT ARE ALREADY VIABLE

THE CRANE HANDLE-THING FROM GRAND PIANOS, GENERAL GOODS SHOPS

At last . . . even in your spare time . . . you can start a business that makes money fast . . . so fast it can put you in a 1962 car of your choice in one short month! Here's how: At our expense, we'll set you up in a profitable Mason "Shoe Store" business. You need no previous experience . . . don't invest a dime! James Kelly tried our offer and made $93.55 in just one evening's friendly work! Yes, everyone wants exciting.

THE KEY TO THE FORMAL PROBLEM ?

IS IT MOVING THINGS FROM PLACE TO PLACE ?

IS IT FEEDING THE SERVICES ?

ROUTE BECOMES SUPER ROUTE

IT'S ALL HAPPENING

IT'S ALL GRIST TO THE MILL

BAR and only 1 BUC

and the "Living City" show, Theo Crosby, eventually felt compelled to capitulate to the "necessity" of the monument.[48]

Six years before "Living City," Crosby had curated "This Is Tomorrow." Those sections of the show devised by Independent Group members had very publicly demonstrated the shift toward informality and pop in British modernism. "The architects of 'This Is Tomorrow,'" Cook reverently acknowledged, "have had great influence on the generation of organizers of 'Living City.'"[49] A pop formlessness was evident in the "bubble" sculpture of Richard Matthews, Michael Pine, and James Stirling ("Group Eight"),[50] and in the loose assemblage of visual information pinned to a "tackboard" by Group Twelve (Lawrence Alloway, Geoffrey Holroyd, and Toni del Renzio).[51] Two more sections of "This Is Tomorrow," by Group Two and Group Six, were of special significance to the creators of "Living City." Group Two's disarming, hedonistic structure—assembled by Richard Hamilton, John McHale, and John Voelcker as the opening salvo for pop art in Britain—threw out cultural distinctions with abandon, licensing pop culture as a resource for artists, designers, and intellectuals. Without this precedent, "Living City" was almost inconceivable.[52] "Living City" paid homage by including a picture of Group Two's mascot Robbie the Robot (figure 2.12), and a giant bottle of Skol stood in for Group Two's huge bottle of Guinness; Archigram threw in an extra display-scale bottle of Heinz Tomato Ketchup for good measure.

Was it possible, then, to confuse Archigram's work for Group Two's? Group Two's stand was packed full of visual gimmicks, Duchamp rotoreliefs and Bauhaus optical illusions to stimulate the viewer. If it had a deeper purpose, it was to force the viewer to question the boundary between the fine and the popular arts. It remained closer to pop art than pop architecture. There was little point in Archigram retracing Group Two's footsteps; by 1963, the legitimacy of pop art was a fait accompli. Archigram was now interested in how commercial imagery described the urban scene as a whole, and what implications this material had for actual architectural practice. These issues had been raised repeatedly by the Independent Group but never properly resolved, hence the pertinence of the question about the relationship between pop and building, implied by the headline of

Archigram no. 4, "'Zoom' and Real Architecture." If the status of pop art was undisputed in 1963, the status of pop architecture was uncertain.

Meanwhile, "This Is Tomorrow's" Group Six (Nigel Henderson, Eduardo Paolozzi, and Alison and Peter Smithson) had ventured far into formlessness with their "Patio and Pavilion," a scattering of *art brut* and folksy *objets trouvés* across a casually constructed enclosure. This peculiar compositional aspect signaled the quite exceptional informality now possible in the arts, though it was perhaps the *symbolic* allusions of the piece that were more relevant to the making of "Living City." If, as intimated, this was a vision of tomorrow, it was prescient. Rather than being completely remade from modern forms and materials, the future would probably be cobbled together from bits of the old and bits of the new, the crude slats of the pavilion and

2.12 *View inside the "Living City" installation, showing Robbie the Robot, 1963. Six years before "Living City," its patron Theo Crosby had curated the sensational Whitechapel Gallery show "This Is Tomorrow," which was opened by science fiction "star" Robbie the Robot. Robbie reappeared at "Living City" amidst other pop paraphernalia, as though discovered in an attic.*

Play the socio-psycho game
The chips are down
The stakes are low
Man in the city the ultimate goal
Throw the dice and
learn about yourself and how
you fit in the pattern
that is 'Living City'

neither is a Living City. Perhaps in fifty years, or a hundred? But it will be almost despite the architecture rather than because of it."[55] Cook expanded:

When we try to continue a city in physical terms, we tend to start from the assumption that there are certain basics of living, and that there is a single way of providing for these at any one time. Our cities extend and regenerate spaces by way of bricks and mortar and roads and sewers; and people are inside somewhere. . . . If we build into this brief "qualities" or provision for things beyond, it becomes a forced or deliberate environment.[56]

If language and situation were to be the models for the city's built form, architecture would have to be perpetually provisional. Peter Taylor explained that "we should resist the temptation to evolve an 'ideal' form of lettering for the Living City. . . . The form and function of the alphabet changes continually, just as language changes. Yesterday's slang becomes today's common speech, and tomorrow's archaism. . . . Buildings are permanent, and lettering is transient, so goes the thinking; but in the Living City everything will be subject to constant change."[57] Over the next few years, Archigram would design indeterminate architectures, but few of the blueprints were ready in time for "Living City." That exhibition was the occasion for Archigram members to curb any differences and agree upon a general *philosophical* framework. "Living City's" credo of informality would approximate—it transpired—to social, political, and economic liberalism.

INDIVIDUALISM AND LIBERALISM

The true subject of architecture, the avant-garde of the 1950s and 1960s concluded, was the individual, the "bare and naked man,"[58] with his complex of personal beliefs and motives. Excavated by existentialism, "Man" stumbled into the limelight of modernist discourse at CIAM's Hoddesdon meeting in July 1951,[59] blinked out from his shelter at Group Six's Patio and Pavilion, and earned his own display at "Living City" (figure 2.13).[60] The dogmas of collectivism that had once dominated modernism were demonstrably abandoned. The very preparation of "Living

battered cog- and bike wheel remnants of the First Machine Age reflected in the rippling, mirror-finished, aerospace-style sheet aluminum of the Second Machine Age enclosure. And the future would not be the architect's total design, but a *collaboration* between architect and inhabitant (a process simulated when the Smithsons departed for Dubrovnik,[53] leaving behind them at the Whitechapel Gallery an environment for Paolozzi and Henderson to fill with signs of habitation).[54]

Such *tinkering* with the environment would be a key interest of the Archigram group, bolting high-tech additions onto traditional English towns and buildings. Noncommittal, piecemeal architecture was the way to go: "There is no comfort from the dusts of Brasilia or Chandigarh, the two opportunities in recent years for a city to be created *in toto*," Cook claimed at "Living City." "Whether we have a liking for their aesthetics or not,

2.13 *Peter Taylor,* Man, *montage for "Living City," 1963: the catalogue banner for one of the exhibition's themed sections introduced "Man"—not the wall, column, or street—as the central subject of architecture. "Man" was meant in a generic, humanist sense, though males were also depicted, adding to the likelihood that the exhibition described a predominantly masculine perception of the city.*

City" by individuals working in concert represented "personal interests and the angle from which we have individually approached the problem of the Living City."[61] For Archigram, it was high time that the avant-garde permitted individuality of thought, emotion, action, and space—even of property and consumption.

Existentialism had been a select mode of thought in continental Europe between the world wars, and became more widespread among the postwar intelligentsia. It was slower to take root in a Britain dominated by homegrown empiricism (which was visible, not least, through translation into matter-of-fact welfare state architecture). "Living City" showed existentialism's belated, impressionistic assimilation by the British avant-garde, the exhibition's themed sections ("gloops") amorphously and uncertainly combining into a psychic exploration of urban life (figures 2.14, 2.15).[62] "Living City" took the visitor on a sort of existential trip through the city. Our lives in the city are not merely a mass of unconnected chance occurrences, a stroll around the seven gloops of "Living City" implied. They are instead journeys, series of seemingly shapeless and chaotic "situations" that we willfully negotiate and mold to our own requirements in the effort to define ourselves.

Starting at the gloop on "Man," visitors would be reminded of the relationship between themselves as individuals and the apparently alien world of objects and people in the city around them. "Play the socio-psycho game," the "Living City" catalogue implored,

The chips are down
The stakes are low
Man in the city the ultimate goal
Throw the dice and
learn about yourself and how
you fit in the pattern
that is "Living City."[63]

There was a distinctly Nietzschean feel to the invitation, the "socio-psycho game" of our lives envisaged as a contest between a choice of alter egos, Superman, Adam Strange, and Alanna of the Planet Rann (figure 2.16). "Survival," the second gloop, was apparently a matter of negotiating one's "physical defects" and taking advantages of one's "muscles," "intelligence," "physique," and "personality,"[64] and, judging from the magnificent display of consumer items, one's access to goods and services. Even if these personal attributes proved insufficient, there was the promise of prosthetic extension. "The robot figure [Group Two's Robbie the Robot] that opened 'This is Tomorrow' has been superseded by today's spaceman, the nearest man has yet come to realizing the ideal SUPERMAN dream, the ultimate in physical and mental development," explained the exhibition catalogue.[65]

The citizen's individuality was put to its greatest test when it merged with the "Crowd," the third gloop. Contrary to the assurance that "the stakes are low" in the socio-psycho game, just two places short of its "Jackpot" was a square marked "Go Bonkers." This was pretty much the fate predicted for the city dweller by the many critics, from Friedrich Nietzsche to Ebenezer Howard, who believed that the modern metropolis would swallow the individual whole. Reinventing Howard's ideas for mid-twentieth-century America in messianic tones, Frank Lloyd Wright had contrasted his own spacious vision of Broadacre City with Manhattan's gridiron compression of vehicular and human traffic: "Incongruous mantrap of monstrous dimensions! Enormity devouring manhood, confusing personality by frustration of individuality? Is this not Anti-Christ? The Moloch that knows no God but *more*?"[66] This in a book called *The Living City,* and published as recently as 1958.[67]

In their "Living City," however, Archigram perceived the crowd as supremely positive evidence of the resilience of individuality. Georg Simmel expressed the sentiment best in his turn-of-the-century essay on "The Metropolis and Mental Life," where he reassessed the findings of urban critics. Threatened by the onslaught of the crowd and mass urban culture, Simmel argued, the individual in fact summons

the utmost in uniqueness and particularization, in order to preserve his most personal core. He has to exaggerate this personal element in order to remain audible even to himself. The atrophy of individual culture through the hypertrophy of objective culture

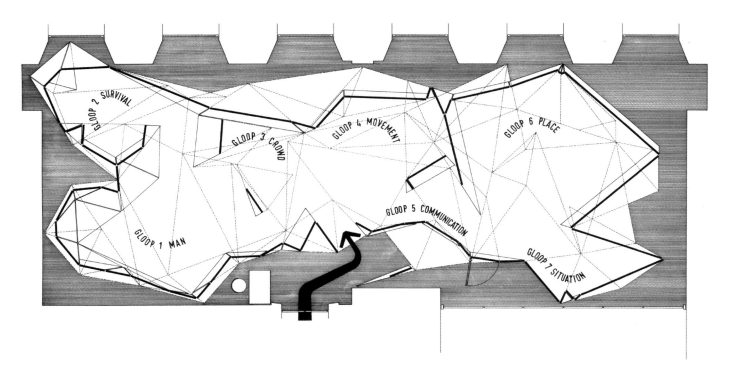

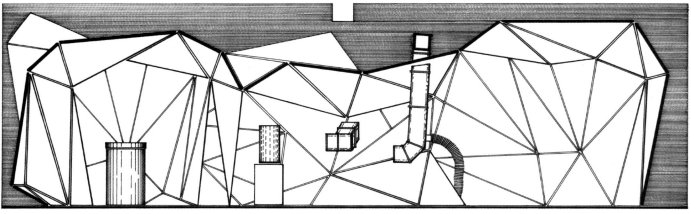

LIVING CITY exhibition
SECTION.

2.14, 2.15 *Archigram group, plan and section of the "Living City" installation, 1963, showing its arrangement into "gloops." The themes elide, like the moods of the city dweller wandering the street. The installation was linked to Dover Street and the ICA bar by the two periscopes shown in the sectional drawing.*

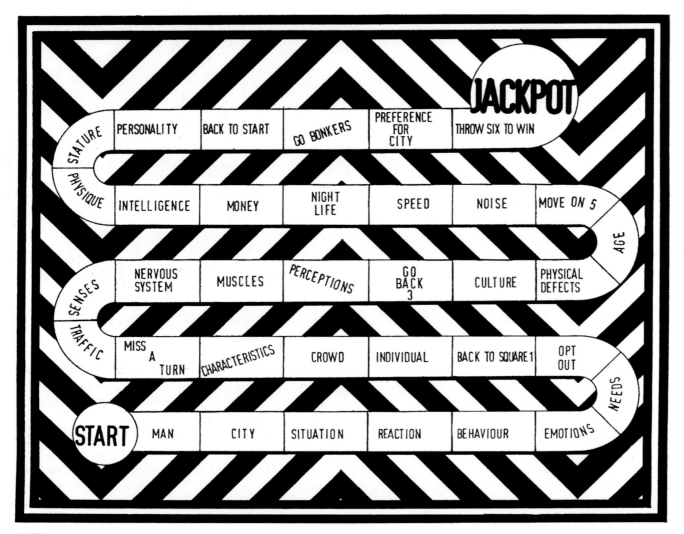

The board game contains the following labels:

JACKPOT

STATURE	PERSONALITY	BACK TO START	GO BONKERS	PREFERENCE FOR CITY	THROW SIX TO WIN
PHYSIQUE	INTELLIGENCE	MONEY	NIGHT LIFE	SPEED	NOISE	MOVE ON 5
						AGE
SENSES	NERVOUS SYSTEM	MUSCLES	PERCEPTIONS	GO BACK 3	CULTURE	PHYSICAL DEFECTS
TRAFFIC	MISS A TURN	CHARACTERISTICS	CROWD	INDIVIDUAL	BACK TO SQUARE 1	OPT OUT
						NEEDS
START	MAN	CITY	SITUATION	REACTION	BEHAVIOUR	EMOTIONS

Trace on a postcard Adam Strange, Superman and Alanna of the planet Rann. (If you do this you will not spoil the magazine.) Colour with your paints or crayons and insert the base of each figure in a slit made in the top of three small corks. Push a pin through the centre of the 'dice' for spinning. The one to spin a six first starts the game.

2.16 *Ben Fether, game from "Man" gloop, "Living City," 1963. A natural existentialist, the Living Citizen progresses through the city move by move, matching her or his inner powers to the game of life.*

is one reason for the bitter hatred which the preachers of the most extreme individualism, above all Nietzsche, harbor against the metropolis. But it is, indeed, also a reason why these preachers are so passionately loved in the metropolis and why they appear to the metropolitan man as the prophets and saviors of his most unsatisfied yearnings.[68]

In Archigram's "Living City," a giant kaleidoscope symbolized "the coming together of all manner and types of man and the way in which they interact upon one another in the shared experience of living city" (figure 2.17).[69] "The masses" were in fact aggregates of *individuals,* freed from the yoke of collectivism by their own, personal agendas for the city. There could be as many Living Cities as there were subjectivities. This was how Archigram attempted to explain its rather woolly sense of "Situation":

This thing we call Living City contains many associative ideas and emotions and can mean many things to many people: liking it or not liking it, understanding it or not understanding it, depends on these personal associations. There is no desire to communicate with everybody, only with those whose thoughts and feelings are related to our own.[70]

Archigram made a stuttering acknowledgment of the fluidity of individual perception: "*Situation Change,* as spectator changes—the moving eye—sees, an environment and situation related to individual perception, mood, purpose, direction, and the place of the individual in the environment."[71]

"Living City's" reverie upon "Situation" aspired toward an architectural methodology. Just as the situationists in Paris had come to believe that their insights into the character of the city were pointers toward a revolutionary program, Archigram drew practical conclusions from their meditations. "What we think and feel about city is not new in the sense that it was unthought of before," the group admitted, "but only in that the idea of Living City has not been acted upon before by our generation. . . . This time/movement/situation thing is important in determining our whole future attitude to the visualization and realization of city; it can give a clue, a key, in our effort to escape

the brittle ingratiating world of the architect/aesthete, to break away into the real world and take in the scene."[72] The flux of the "Living City" would not be arrested by fixed buildings dropped from the drawing board into the human pool.

In this, "Living City" reacted against the pretense to rational objectivity assumed by architectural planners. In 1961, *The Death and Life of Great American Cities,* the book by New York journalist and urban activist Jane Jacobs, began to rock the assumptions of city planning.[73] Jacobs accused the planning profession of undermining the acculturation of city streets in favor of vacuous, zoned spaces. Jacobs's angry attack on this decline in the sense of place within cities fell into Archigram's hands, joining another closely argued account that had just arrived from America, William H. Whyte's *Exploding Metropolis* (1958). Whyte was already famous as a critic of bureaucratic modernity's subsumption of the individual into *The Organization Man,* the title of his book of 1956, and now he turned his attention to the homogenizing effects of the modern city.[74]

2.17 *Peter Taylor, kaleidoscope collage, "Living City," 1963. Pop liberalism: male and female, black and white, Eastern and Western, the everyman and the celebrity, the uniformed and the fetishized, eternally converge and diverge in the cosmopolitan Living City.*

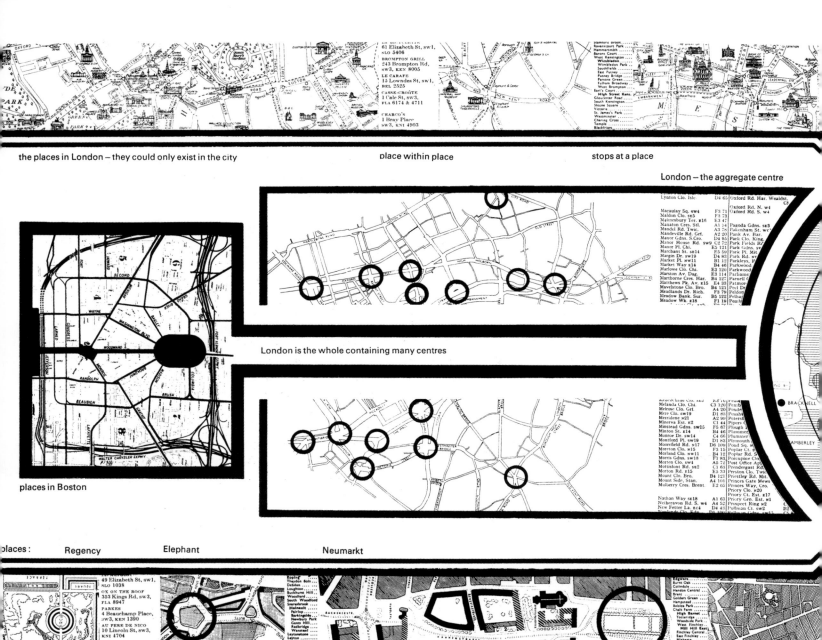

the places in London – they could only exist in the city

place within place

stops at a place

London – the aggregate centre

London is the whole containing many centres

places in Boston

places: Regency   Elephant   Neumarkt

2.18 *Warren Chalk and Ron Herron, Place, "Living City," 1963. The bull's-eyes guided visitors into the epicenters of "place": the USA's northeastern and western seaboards; Rome's Piazza del Popolo and Pantheon; Glasgow and Edinburgh, Liverpool, Birmingham, and above all London. This homage was remarkable coming from architects who would presently propose the dissolution of permanent place.*

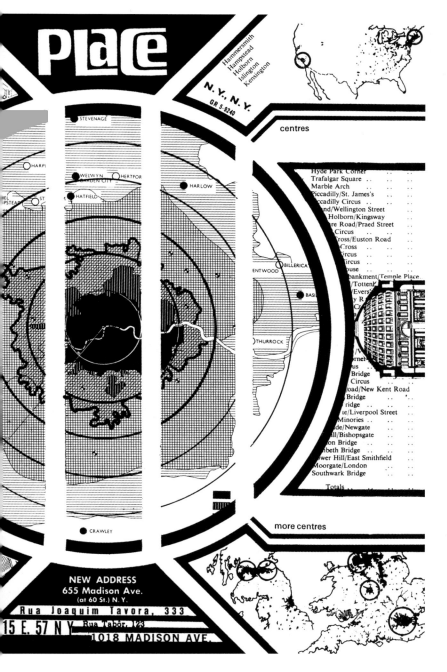

In his foreword to "Living City," Peter Cook described how these books by Jacobs and Whyte

> *treat the threat of the dénouement of city centres with a concern that is at the same time intelligent and frightening. They search hard for any signs of a reverse of the general trend, or a way out, or some path back to the situation when "City" meant something vibrating with life. The Atlantic time-lag is about to catch up with us. The problem facing our cities is not just that of their regeneration, but of their right to an existence.*[75]

Championing the existential liberation facilitated by cities, "Living City" was attempting nothing less than the reversal of an antiurbanism that had characterized British planning since at least the Barlow Report of 1940.[76] This architectural exhibition without architecture, this celebration of nonarchitecture—of the serendipitous orders that come about without planning, and the personal experiences that lay beyond the nib of the architect's pen—remained, after all, an architectural excursion. "Living City" was trying to find an overall vision of the plural, of designs within chaos. In so doing, it contributed to an ongoing paradigm shift in modern architecture from idealism to realism. Brutalism's rugged back-to-basics treatment of the city and its built form had espoused feeling over rationality, community before zoning, everyday life rather than the grand plan, texture beyond the planar. Rather than tell scare stories about metropolitan growth, "Living City" celebrated the city's cultivation of habitat.

So it was that the exhibition's curators expounded the virtues of "Place," sounding more like Team 10 than the harbingers of a radical mobility that they actually were (figure 2.18).[77] "Living City's" relatively sophisticated recognition that the particular spaces of a city are *meaningful* to their occupants permitted the exhibition to oppose the procedures of urban homogenization still fashionable among architect-planners. Locating multiple loci within London, Boston, and Amsterdam, "Living City's" survey of "Place" suggested that cities are like Russian dolls, with centers within centers, places within places, from the conurbation to the local café, and it argued that this pluralism was at risk.

"As the city centres tend to become more and more like one another, so their success and identity will be lost,"[78] the catalogue noted, taking up the challenge of "urban reidentification" that the Smithsons had laid at the feet of CIAM ten years earlier.[79]

"Urban reidentification" was one plank of the Smithsons' architectural brutalism, but the creators of "Living City" avoided prescribing a purely architectural course of treatment for the city. "Architecture alone cannot achieve this feeling of 'place.' It alone is not enough to give identity. It is the content and use that are important."[80] "Living City" was people-centered, a point underscored as if anticipating the charges of antihumanism that would be leveled at Archigram during the coming years. "The image of the city may well be the image of people themselves," Peter Cook reflected, "and we have devoted much of the exhibition to the life-cycle, and survival kit of people within cities"—hence that sense of "Living City"as an existential journey. "Man is the ultimate subject around which we are exhibiting, and he conditions any space into which he comes."[81]

Even CIAM in its last years had recognized this, calling for "the humanization of urban life."[82] The modest suggestion made by "Living City" was that an enjoyment of urban crowds should be the first qualification obtained by an urban designer. The kaleidoscope device at "Living City" represented a plea for liberalism, a convergence of race, sex, and occupation, from Frank Sinatra and Anna Karina[83] on the outer orbit to Sartre[84] and Louis Armstrong on the middle and civil servants on the inner—black, yellow, and white people cheek by jowl.[85] "Who likes it straight?," "Living City" asked (figure 2.23).

Who will buy what?
who believes which?
who lives or dies?
thought, action
chain response
life forces balanced
in tension
the urban community
the city
CROWD[86]

"Living City" rejected the planning profession's architectural, social, economic, moral, and racial purge of city center neighborhoods. The ICA's home turf of Soho had a dim glow compared to red light districts in some other European capitals, but as if to celebrate its risqué, bohemian mélange, "Living City's" kaleidoscope was held together by women's legs, shoes, eyes, and lips. While it maintained masculine domination (substituting voyeurs for patriarchs), "Living City" rejected the prudishness customary to urban planning.

By renegotiating the contract between the city, the citizen and the forces of modernization, "Living City" encouraged socioeconomic liberalism. "Living City" was open to accelerated cultural diversity and economic exchange. Jane Jacobs figured the inner city as a locale of familial neighborly bonhomie, but Archigram intended to retain the inner city as a place of *adventure,* importing into "Living City" some of the seedy glamour of beat, of the hard-boiled detective novel, of film noir; London was an escape for most Archigram members (only Ron Herron was metropolitan by upbringing). For the situationists, the deep living of "situation" would realize nothing short of the destruction of capitalism; for the organizers of "Living City," "situation" primarily fed the pedestrian with novel consumer experiences. While the situationists prepared for the return of the Paris Commune, "Living City" heralded swinging London. "What does a positive view of mass culture have to offer us?" Robert Freeman asked in his editorial to *Cambridge Opinion* no. 17. "Primarily the availability of goods and entertainment to more people than ever before . . . even Henry VIII would be faced with an embarrassment of choice after a short walk down [Soho's] Curzon Street. . . . In all," he summarized, making reference to Prime Minister Harold Macmillan's famous phrase of two years before, "we've never had it so good."[87]

PORTRAIT OF THE ARCHITECT AS A YOUNG MAN

The *Living City Survival Kit,* an image published as a page in the "Living City" catalogue (figure 2.19),[88] looked like one of the product anthologies to be found in the Sunday newspaper supplements and glossy magazines of 1963.[89] It was not selling any particular product, however, and while it consciously imitated

2.19 *Warren Chalk,* Living City Survival Kit, *1963. The "survival kit" is pop, but too formless to be pop art, looking instead like the contents of a man's London bedsit turned out and put on police display. Supposing this is an architect's survival kit for day-to-day life, he seems less the Olympian figure with command of the city, and more like a man of the city, fragile save for his expendable supplies and emotional sustenance.*

the magazine page in the manner of pop art, it was not quite pop art either. It was in fact an image of architecture, which said a good deal about the reordered perceptions of the city and of architectural practice in the decades after the Second World War. Irony, never more apparent than in its *Survival Kit,* helped "Living City" to address such architectural taboos as gender and desire. The *Survival Kit* was a wry, confessional image, produced by Warren Chalk,[90] and it promised survival not just to the citizen, but to the city—and to the modern architect.

It was made up of predominantly lowbrow, everyday, pocket-sized, throwaway, illicit, mass-produced consumer goods, carrying the viewer into the microexperience of space. These were the accoutrements (cigarettes, hankies, snacks, drinks, sunglasses) of a latter-day *flânerie,* of strolling around the city, doing very little except observing its cultural and geographical dynamics. The *Survival Kit* was an invitation to the voyeur, eyes concealed behind the kit's dark glasses, the *éphémère* of a backward glance caught on the kit's roll of film. Although the *Survival Kit* was redolent of the spreads in women's magazines, it was predominantly a survival kit for urban man. The main anomaly in this reading was the inclusion of makeup—although that only figured women as an object of male vision, and was closely aligned with a provocatively unfurled stick of lipstick with the word "sex" Letrasetted along its shaft. To be more specific, the *Survival Kit* staked out the city as the domain of a young, reasonably affluent male, apparently free from family responsibility, and still washing his own shirts with Daz.

By invoking the *flâneur,* the *Survival Kit* portrayed a rather traditional, heterosexual masculinity, compromising what at first appeared to be a genderless, open invitation to urban adventure. But if more innovative configurations of gender and identity were to be found as close by as contemporary British pop painting,[91] they were not to be found elsewhere in architecture. The *Survival Kit* was a frank confession to the role of male subjectivity in architecture, startling for its time. Though the architectural profession at the beginning of the sixties remained overwhelmingly patriarchal in its constituency and outlook, it had brought to perfection an image of itself and its practice as disinterested.[92] If the *Survival Kit* contained the real

tools by which knowledge of the city was obtained, then all the statistical surveys routinely employed by urban designers were at best remote, and at worst a decoy from the urban designer's fallible (male) subjectivity; that the *Survival Kit*'s masculinity was so thinly disguised only confirmed that a gentleman's club atmosphere still pervaded architectural practice. Moreover, the ennobled masculinity of the gentleman's club was in turn being degraded in the image by subscription to a men's club with less exclusive membership: the *Survival Kit* included a copy of *Playboy* magazine. Historian-critic Reyner Banham (a visitor to "Living City") had relayed to the *Architects' Journal* in 1960 how the world of *Playboy* was typically open to a man of "28.3 years," living in one of "168 important metropolitan areas," "for whom a dinner date is a regular and important event."[93]

This particular copy of *Playboy,* from January 1963, featured Norman Mailer, whose 1955 novel *The Deer Park* was placed alongside. Mailer's hard-boiled literature portrayed a cosmopolitan, sexual, political, and drugged subculture. The Soho melee in which "Living City" was staged was a place where someone might submerse into such a jazz-listening, marijuana-smoking urban underbelly, purchasing the more marginal and hedonistic of the goods depicted: a bottle of whiskey, a packet of cigarettes, some hard-bop jazz records, a gun, and "drugs." Yet no harder drug than Alka Seltzer (the corrective for indulgence in the Bell's whiskey) was put on display. To this extent the *Survival Kit* parodied the aggressive masculinity of the likes of Mailer[94] and the fantasy of the metropolis promoted by *Playboy.* The gun looked like a replica in its cowboy-style tasseled holster; the food featured in the image was barely more adult (the slogan of Quaker Puffed Wheat in the 1950s was "shot from guns"); the sports car was no more than a toy. Through its absurd selections and juxtapositions, the *Survival Kit* was depicting an imaginary inner-city living, just as readers of *Playboy* magazine lived out promiscuity and hedonism vicariously. One aerosol product featured was called "Top Secret," hailing the influence of cinematic thrillers (the movie *Dr. No,* the first in the James Bond series, had filled cinemas the previous year), while the assemblage as a whole recalled those made famous by the covers of Len Deighton's paperback thrillers.[95] The aura of sexual deviancy that hung about Mailer's work at the time was "straightened" in the *Survival Kit* into the bathroom paraphernalia promoted by teenage magazines to young men and women on the dating game—lipstick, makeup, razors, deodorant, detergent, toothpaste.

Survival, the adventure of city life, was being represented here as a narrative played out by the citizen with a few basic props—a cigarette to light, a match to flick out, makeup to assist in the creation of a new role (Mailer's *The Deer Park* was set in Hollywood). The notion that the self is a collection of performances that take place across different locations was reminiscent of the findings in Erving Goffman's popular study of the time, *The Presentation of Self in Everyday Life,* 1959,[96] and of existentialism. The city was a mere backdrop for the citizen starring in the "movie" of his (or her) life, and the "living city," with its diversity of urban actors and varied urban décors, was the ideal film lot. It updated urban critic Lewis Mumford's old dream of the city as a multistaged "theatre of social action,"[97] refuting the "survival kit" of rationalization that had characterized urban design from the Renaissance to modernism. Mumford declined an invitation to endorse the rationalist planning principles of CIAM when they were written up by CIAM architect José Luis Sert.[98] *Can Our Cities Survive?* asked the title of Sert's 1942 book; two decades later the *Living City Survival Kit* reported that the city could survive, but only provided its rationalization was curtailed.

Chalk's *Survival Kit* obviously toyed with the pop aesthetic, and sharing the copy of *Living Arts* magazine that served as "Living City's" catalogue was work by the pop pioneer artist Richard Hamilton, who created the mise-en-scène for the cover (figure 2.20). Photographed by Robert Freeman at a Taylor Woodrow building site (presumably accessed by Theo Crosby), Hamilton's cover featured an American footballer and *Playboy* Playmate-style model (the former perched and the latter draped upon a 1963 Ford Thunderbird), a Frigidaire stuffed to capacity, a luxurious white telephone, a Wondergram mini record player and mini typewriter, a chromium-plate toaster, a long-hose vacuum cleaner (of the sort enshrined by Hamilton's famous 1956 "This Is Tomorrow" collage, *Just What Is It That Makes Today's Homes So Different, So Appealing?*), and, particularly impressive, a Mercury space pod.[99]

In comparison, there was something "artless" and formless about the *Living City Survival Kit.* The *Survival Kit* was more literal, didactic, an inventory, declining the smooth compositional qualities of Hamilton's hot-pink shop window of Pax Americana. The *Survival Kit*'s American consumer products (such as the bottles of Coca-Cola) were no more sacred than any other, arrayed upon a level plane. No longer exotic, their significance was as the sort of throwaway artifacts praised in *Archigram* no. 3. They represented packaged and popular taste. American-led mass market ("popular") taste had deeply perturbed modernism: in 1948, Sigfried Giedion had shown his readers a packet of wrapped and sliced Wonder Bread from the United States as an appalling reminder of the impact upon taste when mechanization takes command.[100] Fifteen years later, the *Living City Survival Kit* presented the British variant, the Wonderloaf (which had helped revolutionize UK tastes from about 1953), as an environmental convenience to be consumed without fear of righteous anger.

The Wonderloaf was perhaps an object lesson as well, the forerunner of the modernist construction of the future, stacks of buildings as interchangeable as slices of bread, as expendable as paper wrappers. Messy foodstuffs came packaged and capsuled; could messy life be contained by architectural packets of equal neatness and desirability? Packet cereal and instant coffee had reassembled the postwar British breakfast. Could architecture lose its dependence on mortar and hard labor in the same way that the breakfast table had been unburdened from lard and pans? Raw materials of food could be frozen so that

2.20 *Robert Freeman and Richard Hamilton, cover of* Living Arts *no. 2, 1963. The "artlessness" of the* Living City Survival Kit *(figure 2.19) was confirmed simply by checking it against the cover of the journal in which it was reproduced, which was slickly printed with an image "directed" by the British pop art pioneer Richard Hamilton and the Beatles' photographer Robert Freeman. To borrow car enthusiast terminology (fitting for an arts scene absorbed by Detroit), pop was Hamilton's "Sunday driver," while Warren Chalk and his colleagues from "Living City" used pop as their "daily driver."*

they were available on demand, regardless of the seasons: when would construction sites be this efficient? Heaped up in the *Survival Kit* was a selection of commercial, disposable goods, popular, as found, which the viewer was being asked to regard as a solution to the survival of the city. It did indeed suggest a sort of order in disorder, feeding the crowd yet catering to individuals accepting and rejecting various components of the kit, achieving consistent standards and customer satisfaction.

The danger in this ordering and reordering by supply and demand was that it left the architect redundant. In his "City Notes" of 1959, an essay that anticipated several of the central themes of "Living City," former Independent Group convener Lawrence Alloway reckoned that "architects can never get and keep control of all the factors in a city which exist in the dimensions of patched-up, expendable, and developing forms. The city as an environment has room for a multiplicity of roles, among which the architect's may not be that of unifier."[101] And yet the architect was not yet willing to surrender; the very energy of the "Living City" exhibition showed that architects still saw themselves as active agents in the world. Architect-entrepreneurs would be needed precisely to resist the homogenizing tendencies that monopoly capitalism shared with its supposed opposite, positivist planning. Architects would make sure that everyone got a share of the "living city." And in any case "Living City" implied a richness of urban experience that encompassed a great deal more than the market economy alone. "Living City's" statement of faith in high-density living, to take one example, ran counter to the market-driven urban trends evident in America, its cities spread out thin and far, centers eroded to facilitate the flow of goods and people along superhighways.

Perhaps, then, the architect's role was to be that of facilitator, counseling people on the idea of an architecture of impermanence and exchange. In the interim, "Living City" architects would themselves be the exemplars of the new living, pioneers conveying optimism in the face of the "crisis" of the city. The *Living City Survival Kit* was fun at a time when, less than ten months after the Cuban missile crisis had prompted the assembly of real survival kits, "survival" was no joke. The exhibition was inconclusive—"I'm not quite sure where they have got with it so far,"

admitted Banham in 1963[102]—but determinedly optimistic and proactive. The Living Citizen was neither the American consumer, standing impassive amidst the supermarket shelves now arriving in Britain, nor the resident of the British new town or housing estate, docile under the town planner's command. "Living City" taught its visitors to have *confidence* in their choices—consumer choices and existential choices—and to take joy in multiple identities and lifestyles. Angst—prompted, existentialists argued, by the pressure to make life choices out of the manifold possibilities of which the only certainty was an eventual return to nothingness—was reconfigured as a consumer adventure. Existence and participation in a changing and potentially dangerous world was made safe.

Anticipating the breakup of the single, positivist modernism represented by CIAM, Le Corbusier in 1956 acknowledged the arrival of a younger generation of architects who found themselves "in the heart of the present period . . . feeling actual problems, personally, profoundly, the goals to follow, the means to reach them, the pathetic urgency of the present situation. They are in the know. Their predecessors no longer are, they are out, they are no longer subject to the direct impact of the situation."[103] The *Survival Kit* offered very little in the way of protective gear from the situation of 1963 but warned, in its starkly humorous references to sex, drugs, and hard sounds, that modernity in the 1960s was accelerating well beyond that foreseen even by the Independent Group in the 1950s. Programs to impose order upon chaos would have to be preceded by testimonies of lived experience, of situation. The assumption of the new urbanists—Banham talked in 1959 of "the cool jazz connection, action painters, documentary camera crews, advertising copy-writers"[104]—was that the city would henceforth be created from the street up, not from the drawing office down.

In counterpoint to the role of unifier and good designer—in defiance, that is, of the education of postwar British architects—the architects of "Living City" were teaching an appreciation of the noise and improvisation that filled the spaces of the city with life. The relationship between form and noise could be compared to the method of theme and improvisation found in jazz. The *Survival Kit* featured two groundbreaking jazz albums of 1959, Ornette Coleman's *Tomorrow Is the Question* and John Coltrane's *Giant Steps*. Coltrane and Coleman were building repertoires of brilliant discordance, visually echoed by the fracture and kinesis of "Living City's" displays.

Despite its presentation as a standard-issue kit (its gun, detergent, toothpaste, and razor blades not unfamiliar to someone who had done National Service, abolished the previous year),[105] there was something idiosyncratic about the *Survival Kit*. Symbolically, the jazz albums announced the imperative of greeting the future—tomorrow was the question, Ornette Coleman said, and another of Coltrane's albums of 1960 was entitled *The Avant-Garde*[106]—but they also gave a peak into someone's record collection, and thus into their private life. In the year of ubiquitous Beatlemania, were the esoteric, transatlantic Coltrane and Coleman really essential listening,[107] as central to survival as bread? Such that several copies of one album alone were needed? Juxtaposed against general consumer tat, the presence of these records in the *Survival Kit* spoke of the passion of a connoisseur like Warren Chalk. It was the survival kit of a late night jazz fan, defrosting the peas, lighting up, pouring a whiskey. The *Survival Kit* was, at some level, the self-portrait of a young man (and at thirty-six, Chalk was the oldest of the exhibition organizers by between three and ten years). Richard Hamilton would later decide that his cover for *Living Arts* was a self-portrait, too;[108] both it and the *Survival Kit* could be compared to those dadaist and constructivist portraits of the 1920s and 1930s in which the artist is to be found within a collage of attributes and memorabilia. Chalk had found in his antiheroic self-image an illustration of the new architect: the architect of the streets, the hedonist, the Living Citizen.

TRAFFIC AND DEMOCRACY

A close look at "Living City's" maps of "Places"—places commonly acknowledged as historic centers of national and global culture—delivered a surprise: a dozen or so of London's busiest road junctions had been circled and declared worthy of "place" status. Traffic encroachment, one might have speculated, threatened rather than complemented the pedestrian crowd essential to the living city. And some of the intersections discreetly endorsed by the show—Hyde Park Corner (its generous surface traffic space achieved by lopping off a chunk of Regency architecture),[109] Elephant and Castle—were already controversial as redevelopment schemes.

Nevertheless, the "Living City" curators believed for the time being that traffic interchanges of all kinds (pedestrian *and* automotive) acted as valid urban focal points. The urban model suggested by "Living City" was a further revision of the "cluster" ideas circulating through advanced urbanist ideas at the time.[110] The cluster was interpolated by the Smithsons, who explained in 1957 that "in the Cluster concept there is not one 'centre' but many. Population pressure-points are related to industry and to commerce and these would be the natural points for the vitality of the community to find expression—the bright lights and the moving crowds."[111]

The cluster concept received further attention in Banham's "City as Scrambled Egg." Juxtaposing an aerial photograph of a drive-in cinema with a portion of Debord and Jorn's *Psychogeographic Guide to Paris,* Banham's best-of-both-worlds ideal cross-fertilized Los Angeles freeway sprawl and Parisian pedestrian compactness. The Living City could have two sorts of "place." On the one hand there would be the more deeply rooted *quartiers* (like Soho), home to specialist and elite interests, services and cultures—"jazz-men, wig-makers, sports-car enthusiasts or sculptors." On the other hand, there would be "the radically new centres of popular aggregation produced by the diffuse, well-mechanised culture of motorised conurbations," such as the drive-in cinema and the shopping center.[112] Congestion was to be relieved by its multipolar dispersal. A prime example of this sort of "place" was just reaching completion at the controversial Elephant and Castle development, as gazetteered on the "Living City" map of London.

To some extent the organizers of "Living City," three of whom (Herron, Chalk, and Crompton) had only recently departed from the London County Council and had shaped a sister project at the South Bank (figures 1.22–1.26), had little alternative than to offer a gesture of solidarity with the creators of the Elephant and Castle traffic and shopping complex. But sympathies ran deeper than this. The most fundamental of these was

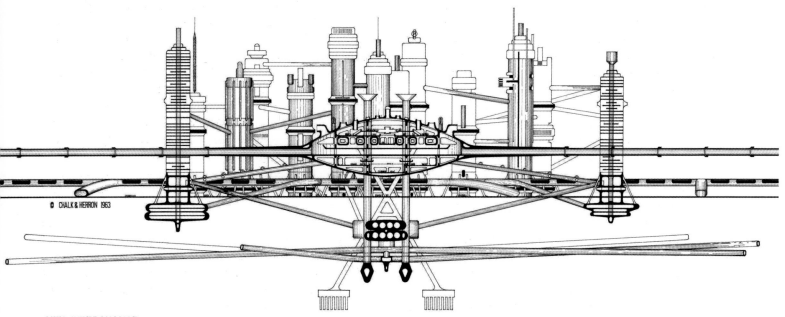

© CHALK & HERRON 1963

CITY INTERCHANGE

Archigram's passion at this time for grand, neofuturist projects; after all, Peter Cook claimed the 1938 MARS show, with its preposterously ambitious scheme for London, as a forerunner of "Living City."[113] With Gordon Sainsbury in 1961, Peter Cook had thrown a traffic interchange project into the fray surrounding the proposed redevelopment of Piccadilly Circus.[114] Even Oxford Circus, as Archigram's 1966 film for the BBC demonstrated, was enjoying a traffic flyover (a third level of circulation, above the road surface and Underground underpasses).[115]

The flow of traffic not only gave the city movement, *Archigram* showed, but it was also a generator of form. Cook filled his new Sant'Elian forum of Piccadilly Circus, published in *Archigram* no. 1 (figure 1.1), with a spaghetti junction, while Warren Chalk and Ron Herron's City Interchange project, a three-dimensional spider's web showcased at "Living City," remodeled the urban core as a multilevel crossover for rail, road, pavement, and air (figure 2.21).[116] "The key to the formal problem?" Cook

asked in his *Come-Go* collage for "Living City." "Is it moving things from place to place? Is it feeding the services?" Here was a tantalizing paradox: the formless as progenitor of form.[117]

It would be easy to misconstrue Archigram's work as comic book caprice. This impression changes the moment it is viewed in the light of contemporary official opinion on the future of cities. The recommendation to enlarge London's traffic intersections had been inherited from the Abercrombie Plan in 1945,[118] and the publication in 1963 of *Traffic in Towns*—the seminal investigation led by Colin Buchanan on behalf of the Ministry of Transport—brought "together two subjects which have usually been treated separately . . . namely the planning and location of buildings and the management of traffic."[119] A comparison of Buchanan and "Living City" is instructive not as evidence of direct correlation but of pervasive trends in architectural and social analysis.[120] Like "Living City," the Buchanan Report set out to deal with "highly complicated issues," but to be

2.21 *Warren Chalk and Ron Herron, City Interchange project, section, ink on tracing paper, 1963. A traffic node clustered into architecture, the City Interchange revised the same designers' ideas for the South Bank Arts Centre in London, giving the drawing vertical thrust and an extrovertly sci-fi profile. But Archigram would later snub the monumentalization of transport interchanges as a throwback to the nineteenth century, as far as possible incorporating transportation into the abode.*

"written in terms that the layman can follow, because public understanding of these problems will be of the greatest importance if successful policies are to be found."[121] Again like Archigram, the Buchanan group strove to present its findings in ways that would be palatable, even attractive, to younger architects and planners. Almost all the fifteen members of the Working Group for the Buchanan Report were registered architects and town planners, and no less than seven of these were graduates of the Architectural Association, bringing with them the Report's Archigramesque marginalia of monorails and jet packs.[122] And at the time of "Living City," Crosby and the Archigram team at Taylor Woodrow were working on a concomitant urban interchange scheme for another government ministry, discussed below.[123]

The cover of the Buchanan Report depicted the consumer and traffic chaos of Oxford Street that interested Archigram (figure 2.22).[124] A large portion of Buchanan's Report was spent weighing up the same freeway projects then being shoehorned into American city centers, which Cook and Sainsbury were mimicking in their Piccadilly Circus project, whose intersection pattern was a slightly less tidy version of a model illustrated

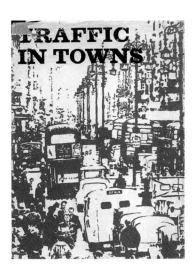

by Buchanan.[125] Viewed in plan on the *Come-Go* collage (figure 2.11), Cook's linear cities of expendable buildings could be seen to be based on the same Radburn model considered in passing by the Buchanan team[126] (with spurs of buildings being fed from a main communications trunk), and on Buchanan's notion that the "rooms" and "corridors" of the ideal city are separated as cleanly as they are in a hospital.[127] Sharing Archigram's impatience with the traditional British city, it was only begrudgingly that Buchanan's team submitted solutions for "partial" and "minimum" redevelopment as appendices to its preferred model of "complete redevelopment."[128] Admittedly, nothing as extraordinary as Archigram's projects would be included in the Buchanan Report. But the Report concluded by inviting "further research" into the same issues preoccupying Archigram, such as "Urban Form," "Movement," "Networks," and "Movement Systems,"[129] and it readily considered the viability of the sorts of radical transportation solutions—monorails, hovercraft, and even personal jet propulsion—that Archigram promoted above and beyond the private car.[130]

Buchanan and Archigram were emphatic: one could not begin to think about the future of the city until one had thought about the future of traffic, in all its forms. The facts seemingly spoke for themselves, and by accepting them Archigram architects could announce themselves as realists, not fantasists. Between 1960 and 1965 the number of cars and vans in Britain, already spiraling, increased from 5.6 million to 9.1 million,[131] and the Buchanan Report concluded that even the threat of the complete saturation of British streets with traffic, such that vehicles ground to a halt, would barely limit exponential growth.[132] Archigram's urbanism was an extreme response to an extreme problem, permitting the city to keep meeting an apparently insatiable demand for mobility. Archigram investigated ways of spreading the traffic load to other forms of transport, incorporating conventional public transport into their interchange schemes and exploring the use of new and theoretical transport technologies, such as air. (In 1966, Archigram forecast a three or four times increase in air travel over the coming twenty years, and domestic air travel in Britain did indeed double between 1961 and 1971.)[133] "Inter-regional rapid

2.22 *Cover of Colin Buchanan et al.,* Traffic in Towns, *1963. The groundbreaking and widely read government report examined traffic and architecture as two sides of the same problem, much as "Living City" did, and featured on its cover the gridlock that was, to the organizers of "Living City," as much a part of London's architecture as the buildings lining Oxford Street.*

transport using linear induction motor propelled trains"[134] would be found in Herron and Chalk's Interchange (figure 2.21) and Cook's Plug-In City (figure 1.3).

Archigram's intrigue with alternative transport was significant, because over the next few years "Living City's" organizers would diverge from the authors of the Buchanan Report on the compatibility of the internal combustion engine and habitation, preferring to integrate mobility *into* architecture as seamlessly and noiselessly as possible (see, for instance, figures 3.7 and 4.3). What remained constant between the traffic architects, Buchanan and Archigram alike, was the assumption that surging mobility was commensurate with good living and with democracy. No attempts were made to slow down the consumption of movement, rather the opposite. This supposition about the value of traffic schemes had been apparent since Baron Haussmann's Paris and Le Corbusier's Radiant City. The spaghetti junction at the heart of Cook and Sainsbury's Piccadilly Circus competition entry (figure 1.1) had words like "movement," "enjoyment," "awareness," and "life" merging like traffic along the model's elevated roadways—a comforting promise for those trapped in the traffic of central London, its average speed down to ten miles per hour by 1960, and predicted to continue dropping.[135] "Before very long, a majority of the electors of this country will be car-owners,"[136] the Steering Group of the Buchanan Report warned the Minister of Transport. "The consumer today is more a participant than a target," Archigram claimed in 1966.[137]

Bowing to the "democratic" imperative of consumerism became regarded in the late fifties and early sixties as the ethical corrective to wartime and immediate postwar rationing, with its admonishment of "unnecessary journeys." Toward the end of *The Long Revolution* (1961), left-leaning cultural critic Raymond Williams noted that "the deep revulsion against general planning . . . is itself in part a consequence of one aspect of the democratic revolution—the determination not to be regimented."[138] The joy of unregulated private motion was intensified with the 1959 debut of the affordable, innovative, and chic Austin Mini, of the one-hundred-and-fifty-miles-per-hour Jaguar E-type in

1961, and with the opening of the Jaguar's natural habitat in the first stretch of the M1 motorway two years before.

In practice, Britain's urban renewal in the sixties did not prove quite the public crusade anticipated, though the Buchanan Report felt confident "that a vigorous programme of modernising our cities, conceived as a whole and carried on in the public eye, would touch a chord of pride in the British people and help to give them that economic and spiritual lift of which they stand in need."[139] It was redolent of the sort of "Britain Can Make It" sentiment that had promoted the Festival of Britain, and something of the same gusto was shared by "Living City." Like the Buchanan Report, Cook threw in an appeal to national identity as a sweetener for traffic architecture, stuffing his *Come-Go* collage with London icons—Tower Bridge, Nelson's Column, Piccadilly, Big Ben (figure 2.11).[140] As backup, however, traffic architects drew upon an idealization of consumer democracy of an entirely different national provenance: that which had been relentlessly exported by the United States since the Second World War.

MODERNIZATION

The shift from contempt for Americanism to its critical reception was characteristic of a generation shift within British modernism. Richard Hamilton's dreamscapes of Detroit car styling and meditations upon traffic, which shared space with coverage of the "Living City" show in *Living Arts* magazine, offered an insight into the Archigram/Buchanan subconscious.

> *In slots between towering glass slabs writhes a sea of jostling metal, fabulously wrought like rocket and space probe, like lipstick sliding out of a lacquered brass sleeve, like waffle, like Jello. Passing UNO, NYC, NY, USA (point a), Sophia floats urbanely on waves of triple-dipped, infra-red-baked pressed steel. To her rear is left the stain of a prolonged breathy fart, the compounded exhaust of 300 brake horses.*[141]

The Buchanan team, reflecting upon much the same scene as Hamilton, quelled its excitement to calmly observe "the silence of the big powerful cars which most Americans favour; and the maturity of the standard of driving. . . . The drivers do not seem to be in a desperate hurry, they seem content to glide along in their big cars in an orderly way."[142] The Buchanan Report equally checked its rapture when reporting that "the American policy of providing motorways for commuters can succeed, even in American conditions, only if there is disregard for all considerations other than the free flow of traffic which seems sometimes to be almost ruthless. Our British cities are not only packed with buildings, they are also packed with history."[143]

Hence the preoccupation of Archigram and Buchanan was to *adapt* the American model to British conditions. "British Made," the "Communication" gloop patriotically flashed (figure 2.7), blurring the distinction between the British and American products on display—Coca-Cola and a shilling coin, a Dictaphone and a Hawker Hunter[144] jet—as if the British economy's assimilation of the American way was a fait accompli. Archigram and the Buchanan team tried to stuff an American standard of living— born, the Buchanan authors assumed, from a fluidity of communication and excess of space (the latter identified by Lawrence Alloway in *Living Arts* as a source of the American sublime)[145]— into the small island on the other side of the Atlantic.

Archigram's New Yorker, mean streets, "Living City" mood later transposed to LA cool: five years after "Living City," in 1968, the lure of the American West Coast proved as irresistible to Archigram members as it had to Reyner Banham (who was researching *Los Angeles: The Architecture of Four Ecologies,* published 1971), and Chalk, Herron, and Cook took up teaching positions at the University of California, Los Angeles, recording the experience of endless sun-drenched LA freeways on cinefilm.[146] In 1963, however, Archigram's ingenuity was still being taxed to devise ways of stacking and miniaturizing Los Angeles into Britain using plug-in cities, hovercraft links, coordinated interchanges, and multilevel precincts. "The city is tight and free and all the city is the centre because the centre is everywhere," Cook claimed of his first sketch for a plug-in city—the City Within Existing Technology, shown at "Living City"— thus importing the phenomenon of decenteredness discovered by the Buchanan team in LA.[147]

"Immediately after the [Second World] war a particular fantasy was exported by the United States, along with the gadgets, techniques, and experts of American capitalism: the fantasy of timeless, even, and limitless development," Kristin Ross has written in her study of postwar France, *Fast Cars, Clean Bodies* (1995).[148] Timeless, even, and limitless development was implied by Peter Cook's urbanism:

> *In many ways the essence of the city is the supreme coming*
> *together of evrything [sic]*
> *of it all*
> *people come and go*
> *it's all moving*
> *the bits and pieces that form the city—they're expendable*
> *it's all come-go.*[149]

In Prime Minister Harold Wilson's Britain, technologically driven economic growth become a vanguard phenomenon thoroughly acceptable to both the right and left of the political mainstream. Political play was generally made of those innovations—the computer, monorail, and hovercraft[150]—that were iconographic to Archigram's plug-in urbanism. Postwar Britain had welcomed the technological dividends of peace. Many domestic applications had been found for the developments of war: atomic power, antibiotics, radar and infrared light; the chemicals industry sought new markets for plastics, artificial fibers, fertilizers, pesticides, and detergents. Two nearly new industries, electronics and optics, had emerged from war, and techniques of engineering, if not all its management and working practices, were in a state of transformation. These were the wonders of untapped architectural potential that would power the pages of *Archigram*. "Scientific knowledge is doubling every nine years," Archigram announced in its 1966 film for the BBC. "90% of all scientists who ever lived are alive today . . . as many scientists were educated in the last fifteen years as in all previous history."[151] But, as historian Arthur Marwick remarks, "many of the great scientific and technological developments could scarcely be attributed to conscious decision-making. Thus, though there was great enthusiasm for, and much talk about, the importance of science and technology to Britain's social regeneration, there was a good deal less understanding of how to set about harnessing science and technology in the most effective manner."[152]

The very vagueness of Harold Wilson's "white heat" rhetoric provided a suitable climate for the open-endedness of Archigram's ideas. In 1960, for example, future Labour MP Anthony Crosland wrote in a major article for the (US-funded) magazine *Encounter* that British institutions were in need of across-the-board modernization; typically, he felt, "our deplorable postwar architecture and city planning demonstrate a failure of nerve in the face of contemporary cultural problems."[153] It is tempting to cast Archigram as budding technocrats, if of a rather avant-garde—and English—kind. While the Archigram image of technocratic solutions was moderated by cheerfulness and boyish enthusiasm, it was quite insistent.

The Archigram men were self-made professionals with few allegiances to traditional social organizations, institutions, or techniques, having ascended the professional ladder by merit alone. Through personal contact and design, Archigram committed itself to networking provincial and outsider creativity and intellect. The meritocracy had risen alongside the anti-establishment Angry Young Men of the 1950s, Christopher Booker claimed, assuming its most potent form in the arts and communications.[154] The publisher of Plug-In City, the *Sunday Times*, was on Booker's list of the magazines fixated with a vaguely defined socialistic "modernization."[155]

Attempts were made by Booker and most famously Richard Hoggart in *The Uses of Literacy* (1957) to ascribe a class origin to the cult of modernization, but the conclusions were unclear.[156] In his insightful and irreverent 1963 speech on the class and ideological roots of ICA culture, "The Atavism of the Short-Distance Mini-Cyclist," Reyner Banham attributed fascination with modern American culture to the postwar British working class, and took 1950s and 1960s British avant-gardism as evidence of class mobility.[157] Yet Cedric Price, held by Banham and Archigram in such esteem for his impatience with tradition, was (like the Independent Group's Colin St. John Wilson, in whose office Ron Herron worked in 1967–1968) very much the Cambridge man.

What counted now, Raymond Williams argued in 1961, was not allegiance to political traditions, but the changing political and social consciousness of voters. "Labour gets a higher percentage of the total vote in the [1960s] period of washing-machines and television than in the [1930s] period of high unemployment," he noted.[158] Though an Archigrammer like Ron Herron seemed to fit Booker's profile of the sort of cultural leader hailing from the "Young Urban Lower Class"[159] (aspirations opened up by National Service, art and technical schools, and prosperity), the social origins of the "modernizer" were (to return to a theme) indeterminate; within the Archigram group as a whole was a mixture of working- and middle-class, southern, Midland, and northern, conservative and socialist. Marwick's observation probably summarizes things best: "Technological change, certainly, brought new obfuscations and subtleties . . . alongside the clearly marked traditional three-tier class structure, there also existed 'non-traditionalists' whose mobility through the technocratic sectors of society was such that they could scarcely be placed in any definite class."[160]

Archigram's external corporate identity doubtless obscured differing motivations and assumptions among the group's members, and even inside the group the assuaging effect of liberalism appears to have ensured that whatever political differences existed between its participants were left at the studio door. During the "Living City" phase, the unofficial line seemed to be that the group operated simply to discover better ways of living through architecture and present them for public consideration. The vision was of the city's resources mobilized, capitalist bounty made accessible to all; it was both socialist and enterprising, a fizzed-up reformulation of the British mixed economy that would get people moving, physically, socially, and technologically. And Archigram was in fact wary of being perceived as a group of faceless technocratic zealots. Archigram's Warren Chalk soon became aware that the image of technology could overrun humanitarian intent:

One of the most flagrant misconceptions held about us is that we are not ultimately concerned with people. This probably arises directly from the type of imagery we use. A section through, say, something like City Interchange [figure 2.21], appears to predict some automated wasteland inhabited only by computers and robots. How much this is justified is difficult to assess, but if our work is studied closely there will be found traces of a very real concern for people and the way in which they might be liberated from the restrictions imposed on them by the existing chaotic situation, in the home, at work and in the total built environment.[161]

The suggestion that the sympathetic observer would pierce the surface of the pop image, and find within it deeper resonances for how humans desire to be, was reminiscent of the Independent Group. The Smithsons wrote in 1956 that advertisements

> are packed with information—data of a way of life they are simultaneously inventing and documenting. . . . As far as architecture is concerned the influence on mass standards and mass aspirations of advertising is now infinitely stronger than the pace-setting of avant-garde architects, and it is taking over the functions of social reformers and politicians.[162]

Archigram now elbowed ahead of advertising executives in the belief that the architectural avant-garde could still stake out the cultural frontier, even if social reformers and politicians had slipped to the back of the pack. "Only people filled with respect and enthusiasm for today's wish-dreams can adequately interpret them into buildings," Archigram insisted in 1966.[163] As the Independent Group's Lawrence Alloway had written in "The Long Front of Culture" in 1959,

> There is no doubt that the humanist acted in the past as taste-giver, opinion-leader, and expected to continue to do so. However, his role is now clearly limited to swaying other humanists and not to steering society. One reason for the failure of the humanists to keep their grip on public values (as they did in the nineteenth century through university and Parliament) is their failure to handle technology, which is both transforming our environment and, through its product the mass media, our ideas about the world and ourselves.[164]

Archigram's role was to liaise between the astonishing forces of modernization and a "public" that might otherwise be overwhelmed, mediating an industrial-consumer democracy in a state of endless flux. This was not quite anonymous technocracy in the sense in which it had been understood in France, then; it was not a means of organization imposed by civil servants and corporations from above. "Pop puts the ultimate command in the hands, if not of the consumer, then at least of the consumer's appointed agents," Banham told his ICA audience in 1963.[165] Unfixed by social status and locale, the citizen of the "living city" would find the city styled in her or his own image, via patterns of consumption and the registry of complex lifestyle choices (symbolized at "Living City" by a computer punch card) (figure 2.23).

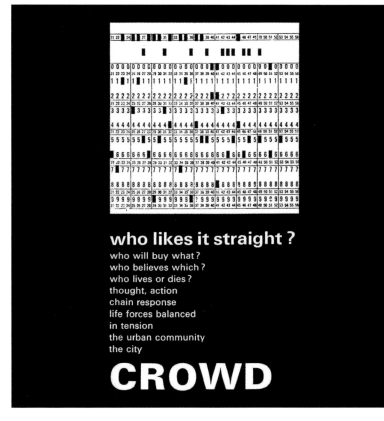

2.23 Anon., illustration from "Crowd" gloop, "Living City," 1963. The computer punch card is a receipt from "the system," an assurance that individual preferences can be tracked just as faithfully as those of the broad masses.

Was the "Living City" more than poetry and image? Was it a trigger for the creation of new architecture? One clue would be found in the publication, again in 1963, of a document by the Taylor Woodrow Group, *Urban Renewal: Fulham Study,* accompanied by an exhibition at the RIBA. The study, which like the Buchanan Report had a semiofficial feel, was for an improbably massive redevelopment of Fulham in west London, and was produced in response to an invitation from the Minister of Housing and Local Government. It was devised by Archigram members working under Theo Crosby.

The *Fulham Study* was a perfect summary of the shifting influences of British modernism. Its housing sections were indebted to the thinking of the Smithsons, designed to a "human scale," derived from precast elements of Georgian proportion (figure 2.24),[166] fed by access decks (in the manner of the Smithsons' Golden Lane project) and by the Corbusian *rue intérieure* (figure 2.25). Some housing bays would project forward in the style of Ernö Goldfinger, a veteran much admired at this time for his defiantly heroic modernist idiom, not least at the Elephant and Castle redevelopment. All this skillfully blended with the stylistic devices of the youngsters: round-cornered glazing (reminiscent of the gasket picture windows of the Comet jet aircraft) and a bristling, futurist elevation of round-cornered towers and silos and bridges (a relative of the City Interchange project by Chalk and Herron publicized by "Living City") (figure 2.21).

A similar mix of influences could be seen in the plan (figure 2.26), the buildings reaching through their site in "topological" chains in homage to the Smithsons' Sheffield University project (1953) (figure 1.16) and networking like the Smithsons' Berlin

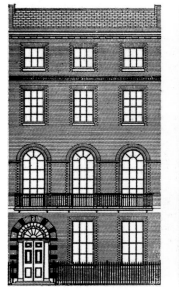   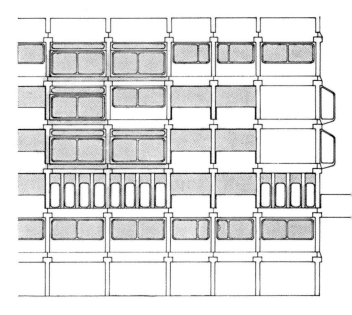

2.24 *Taylor Woodrow Design Group, comparison of Georgian-scale housing and proposed dwellings for Fulham, in Urban Renewal: Fulham Study, 1963. Taylor Woodrow's Fulham scheme, devised by the team behind "Living City," compared the scale and proportions generated by prefabricated modules to the proportional relations governing Georgian townhouses. This appeal to Georgian precedent was a trend in British modern architecture in the 1950s and 1960s. The socioeconomic differentiation between the three Georgian models was absorbed and dissolved by the modular system, however.*

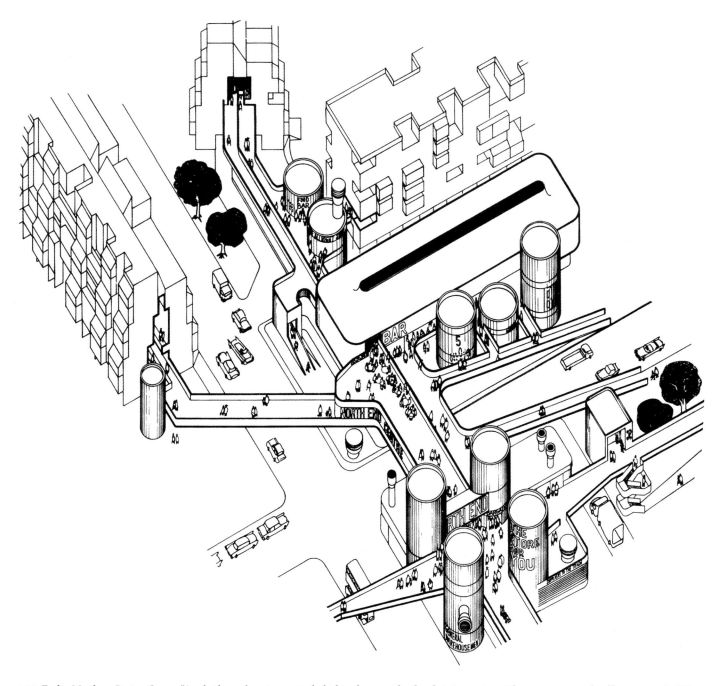

2.25 *Taylor Woodrow Design Group, "A subsidiary shopping centre linked to the upper level pedestrian routes with ramps to street level," axonometric,* Urban Renewal: Fulham Study, 1963. *With the Fulham scheme, the inventory of techniques used by the emergent Archigram group looked assured and convincing. The multilevel separation of vehicular and pedestrian traffic in turn generated a "topological" plan of walkways, fed by elevators styled as silos and acting as cluster points or nodes in a network. Adhering to this substructure are local shopping centers and housing units, which are built from prefabricated parts and articulated by projecting bays.*

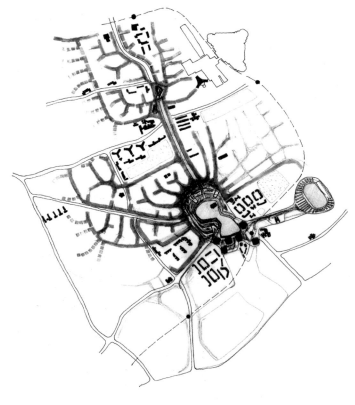

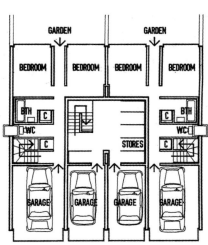

Hauptstadt (1956), but with the expressionist angularity showcased in *Archigram* no. 1 (figure 1.1) and employed at the South Bank Centre (figures 1.22–1.26). The separation of pedestrian and vehicular traffic had also been seen at the South Bank and at the Smithsons' Berlin; but with the *Fulham Study* there was a new Buchananish attention to the practical problem of the car—namely, where it was to be parked. "The 1:1 provision of garages in the study scheme becomes a significant element; in most local authority schemes 1:5 or 6 has been normal."[167] But consumer choice was paramount, since residents of the scheme would have the option to convert the ground level of their flats into bedrooms or garages (figure 2.27). The Fulham homes anticipated the moment when, in 1964, Michael Webb took to heart George Bernard Shaw's observation that "today's homes are little more than a place to sleep next to one's car,"[168] and devised the Drive-In House. And the cars were for escape rather than commuting: Fulham's clustering of functions would help negate long journeys between work, home, shopping, and leisure.

The *Fulham Study* exploited two structural models of urban renewal simultaneously. Urban planner Peter Hall called them the "P"- and "V"-solutions: precinctual and vertical.[169] "Precinct architecture" had dominated postwar British urban renewal and new towns, passing in the 1940s from schemes like those by Patrick Abercrombie for Westminster and Bloomsbury to the shopping precincts of the 1950s onward.[170] At Fulham, the precinct had acquired the altogether more modish label of "piazza" and, raised on a platform, "plaza" (figure 2.28), catering presumably to Theo Crosby's Italianate taste and the Archigram team's predilection for Italian suits.[171] More important, the idea of "piazza" shifted the connotation of the precinct from Oxbridge/Inns of Court collegiate to Mediterranean "come-go."[172]

Meanwhile, Fulham's V-planning was flexed to take traffic pressure head on: "Leonardo understood it," Hall claimed, "in the Adelphi scheme, the brothers Adam used it;[173] it was incorporated in railway building from the start. But very few city rebuilding schemes, anywhere in the world, have yet had the imaginative grasp to accept it wholeheartedly."[174] At Fulham, housing, shopping, leisure, and traffic were stacked and interwoven to create an urban core that was multifunctional and

2.26 *Taylor Woodrow Design Group, preparatory sketch of the pedestrian network for* Urban Renewal: Fulham Study, *1963. Connectivity is all, a social fabric of roving consumers that is the city prior to any buildings.* **2.27** *Taylor Woodrow Design Group, "Ground level plans can be adapted to become extra bedrooms to flats above, or can be given over entirely to garaging," sample residential plans,* Urban Renewal: Fulham Study, *1963. Choice upon choice: for the first time, high-density, inner-city housing permits universal car ownership, yet also allows the legal and rapid conversion of garages to occupancy.*

manageable. Fulham's light manufacturing and blue-collar sectors disappeared, so that the net effect was one of a post-industrial economy geared around white-collar office work, consumption, and leisure. The plan reached over to embrace Stamford Bridge stadium, home to Chelsea Football club, enshrining and sanitizing it in a vast dome.

The formal effect of the dome, as Archigram resorted to free-hand in order to render the myriad of panels on the axonometric,[175] was to lend the entire scheme the geodesic signature of youthful architects. Fulham's industrialized and prefabricated elements marked off the scheme as the work of a new generation (figure 2.29). And it was here that Archigram designers were doing their best to reconcile their own competing preoccupations—messy urban acculturation, choice, and efficient technocratic management: "in a living city there must be a wide possibility of choice to accommodate every family size, and preferably every taste, hobby, or idiosyncrasy. It is for this reason

that much work has been done on the production of an element or panel system, which can be used in a number of different contexts," read paragraph 138 of the Report.[176] Mass-produced, standardized components would cater to individuality (thanks to interchangeability), as in post-Fordist car production. A little earlier in the document, system building was presented as though part of the white heat modernization of British architecture and the British economy simultaneously: "the building site needs to be transformed from guild craft trades operating on

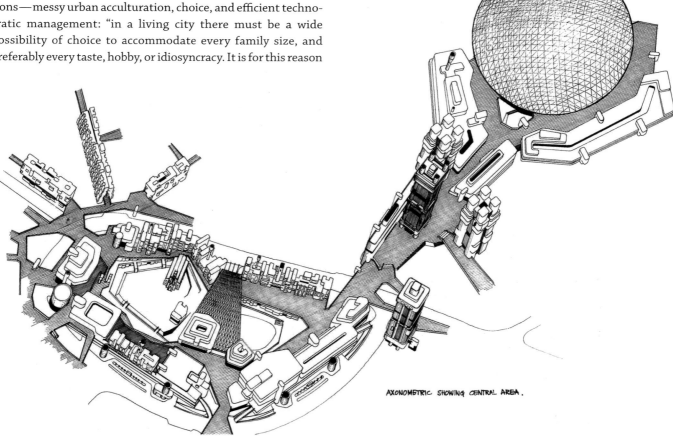

AXONOMETRIC SHOWING CENTRAL AREA.

2.28 *Taylor Woodrow Design Group, axonometric drawing of central area,* Urban Renewal: Fulham Study, *1963. Seen at a distance, the scheme transpires as a flow of elevated plazas supporting building clusters with a formal ruggedness similar to Peter Cook's Plug-In City (compare figure 1.3)—with recollections of Frank Lloyd Wright's Johnson Wax Building, 1947–1950—leading to a geodesic dome of astronomical proportions. The effect is of authentic urban agglomeration, yet Fulham's "pollutants," like manufacturing, have been tidied away.*

a ploughed field to production assembly on a 'factory' floor."[177] Even if the prefabrication of the main structure at Fulham proved impossible, services would still be "rigidly standardised, and the bathrooms/w.c./heater unit/cupboards would be prefabricated, containing all the electrical services and switches."[178] Many things besides—facade elements, panels, balconies, staircases, even tenants' storage—"would be interchangeable within a vigorous dimensional control."[179]

And yet big urban schemes, Archigram began to suspect, were becoming a thing of the past. Nineteen sixty-three was the year in which the City Centre group of top property developers hit crisis and losses. It was also the year, wrote Christopher Booker, of "the first realization of just how ill-fated were to be Britain's two largest shopping precinct schemes, those at the Bull Ring, Birmingham, and at the Elephant and Castle, South London, both of which had been announced in the same month in 1959 and were now nearing completion."[180] The "Living City" catalogue pushed further into the future, beyond traffic intersections and property development, to a moment when the city as we know it has become something else, a "Thing" (figure 2.30):

this thing's come a long way since we started this exhibition wasn't it a great floating city to begin with—a Europe city that spanned the channel [181]
why did we give that idea up?
perhaps because of the purely visionary nature of the idea it'll be years before there's a political set-up sufficient for this thing to come into being and anyway with communications, closed circuit TV we may not want to live in cities any more yeah, I think that's where Keisler [sic] and Schulze Feilitz [sic] with his space frame city fall down
as liberators of ideas they are tremendous but their technology can only answer today's problems [182]

David Greene and Michael Webb were looking forward to a structure more ethereal than the *Fulham Study* or Cook's Plug-In, something like "a vast net encircling the earth," hung from Zeppelins, staffed by cosmonauts. "Living City" reprinted Frederick Kiesler's 1925 description of a "Space City":

A SYSTEM OF TENSION IN FREE SPACE
A CHANGE OF SPACE INTO URBANISM
NO FOUNDATIONS
NO WALLS
DETACHMENT FROM THE EARTH
SUPPRESSION OF THE STATIC AXIS
IN CREATING NEW POSSIBILITIES FOR LIVING IT CREATES A NEW SOCIETY [183]

Archigram's pursuit of this "indeterminist" prophecy would characterize the main thrust of its design work from then on. And citizens too would be refigured, not as "consumers" but—to borrow Raymond Williams's critical distinction of the time—as "users."[184] "Living City," for all its celebration of ordinary citizens—their tastes, habits, and experiences—had tended to portray them as *subjects* to the fixed forms of urban architecture, flowing through the spaces left in between buildings. "Living City" indicated, finally, a more radical possibility, of buildings themselves yielding, bearing no harder on users than any other item of everyday life (clothes, cars, packaging). By the end of its journey, Archigram would pare down even the weight of urban infrastructure, leaving citizens with just the in-between "situations" of encounter, stimulation, and change.

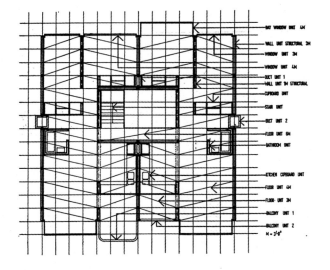

2.29 *Taylor Woodrow Design Group, plan of a housing unit assembled from prefabricated components, on a three-foot module,* Urban Renewal: Fulham Study, *1963. Seamless standardization and interchangeability of windows, walls, stairs, floors, kitchens, bathrooms, cupboards, balconies, and ducts would make housing into a consumer product. Architecture was becoming indeterminate, pointing the way to the Archigram future.*

2.30 *David Greene and Michael Webb,* Story of the Thing *(detail), montage for "Living City," 1963. Archigram here is not designing a building but a placeless triangulated space frame, akin to a Buckminster Fuller tensegrity system: a "thing," a floating plasma with an unstated purpose, hopefully benign, arriving in a bleak (fifties science fiction movie) landscape.*

ALVIN- undersea
research craft

U-Underwat
be for an

3
—

BEYOND ARCHITECTURE

INDETERMINACY, SYSTEMS, AND THE DISSOLUTION OF BUILDINGS

PLANKTON
SAMPLER

COUSTEAU-Underwater house

Its cover illustrated not with a building but with a computer loom,[1] in December 1966 *Archigram* no. 7 claimed to be the issue that went "Beyond Architecture" (figure 3.1). And, Peter Cook warned in his editorial, "There may be no buildings at all in *Archigram* 8." In the event, *Archigram* no. 8 did carry a few drawings and plans of things that approximated buildings, but it was clear that brutalist concrete mass, or mass of any kind, had no part to play in the construction of the future.

In *Archigram* no. 2, Timothy Tinker had asked "Ten Questions in Search of an Answer," to which *Archigram* sought answers during its subsequent editions. "As in politics," ran one of Tinker's questions, "can we learn the lessons of the twenties and thirties and start our thinking from where they left off, not from where they began?"[2] Here Tinker appeared to correlate the rise of the stiff "White Architecture"[3] in the twenties and thirties with the rise of totalitarian systems of social organization. Confining both to history, Tinker introduced an all-encompassing notion of freedom that would finally find its terminology in the lexicon of keywords introduced by *Archigram* nos. 7 and 8, among which was *indeterminacy*.[4] *Archigram* no. 8 proffered: "Oxford Dictionary definition: INDETERMINACY: 'Not of fixed extent or character, vague, left doubtful.' Archigram usage: Of varying evaluation. Not one answer. Open-endedness."[5]

Archigram's philosophy of "indeterminacy" brought to a head a long-running, rarely mentioned conundrum of modernism. Modernism is a contradictory idea, inasmuch as the word "modern" implies something that is bang up to date and still in formation, whereas the suffix "ism" implies the opposite, a doctrine, a codified method, a style.[6] *Archigram* would ensure that the "ism" would instead stand for a continual state of becoming, the design of the ever new.

The commitment to indeterminacy addressed a horror with stasis that accompanied Archigram from the outset. The first two *Archigram* newsletters agitatedly drew

ARCHIGRAM SEVEN BEYOND ARCHITECTURE

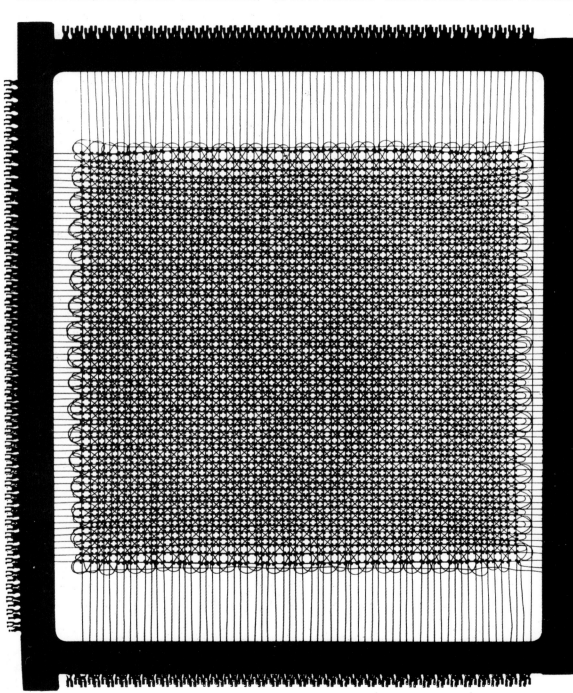

attention to the living, organic properties of the projects they showcased, then "Living City" advocated a culture of circulation and choice. With each new issue *Archigram* went further in its application of "indeterminacy" to the built environment, championing disposable buildings in its third edition and the joys of designing without gravity in its fourth. When the high water of continually evolving megastructures paraded in *Archigram* no. 5 and plug-inscapes in *Archigram* no. 6 receded, it revealed a world beyond architecture: a sublime world of pure servicing, information, networking, transience.

This chapter inspects the design tactics the Archigram group deployed to cope with indeterminacy, and begins by sketching in the cultural background to the mission. Archigram and its allies responded to a great and bewildering amalgam, a backlog of ideas that, if often imprecise or applied out of context, had nonetheless reached a critical mass: interrelated notions of extension, simultaneity, relativity, libertarianism, expendability, organicism, and cybernetics.[7]

One of the more esoteric modernist debates of the 1950s (and 1960s, when it was picked up in conceptual serial art) had asked whether a composition is ever complete. The designs of Mondrian and Mies van der Rohe implied infinite extension, it was suggested: many of Mondrian's orthogonals did not stop short of the canvas but pointed to the space outside; Mies's partitions hovered in space above potentially infinite grids, as though in temporary formation.[8] In 1951, the prominent British architect Richard Llewelyn Davies offered to release Mies from his presumed frustration by proposing an "endless architecture," a design method making use of modular elements repeated in a building to suggest imminent extension. Llewelyn Davies and John Weeks, who can be credited with bringing the word "indeterminacy" into architectural discourse, went on to apply the principle to their design for Northwick Park Hospital (1961–1974), its rhythms generated by load and function, its wings rudely finished in anticipation of addition.[9]

This additive mode of indeterminacy was intriguing but probably a little clunky for Archigram's taste. Likewise, Britain's widely admired postwar CLASP prefabrication system, used mainly for school building, was in theory infinitely extendable

through the addition of construction elements, but hardly emitted the broiling energy Archigram wanted to see in architecture. Early observers of modernity, from Marx to the futurists, considered the nature of the modern world to be of "dynamism" wrought by mechanization, economic liberalization, social upheaval, and new insights into the physical world. The representation of this modernity could only be captured through *simultaneity*. In *Vision in Motion* (1947), László Moholy-Nagy was determined that an understanding of the dynamics of modernity, of "technology-in-flux," be inscribed in the design syllabus as "a conscious search for relationships—artistic, scientific, technical, as well as social" in "the flashlike act of connecting elements not obviously belonging together," believing that "if the same methodology were used generally in all fields we would have *the* key to our age—*seeing everything in relationship*."[10] The pages of *Archigram* were pervaded by a similar vitality of simultaneity.

In the 1950s, the art of Jackson Pollock, Jasper Johns, and Robert Rauschenberg suggested another spontaneous, informal spirit. At Black Mountain College in North Carolina in the 1940s, Rauschenberg, the composer John Cage, and choreographer Merce Cunningham developed indeterminate structures for artistic events. In 1966, various American strands of indeterminate play coalesced as Experiments in Art and Technology, Inc. (EAT), an organization counting among its members Rauschenberg, Cage, and their sometime Black Mountain colleague Buckminster Fuller. From his new base in New York, Archigram's Warren Chalk helpfully provided EAT's full address to those readers of *Architectural Design* in 1970 wanting to produce their "own scene machine today,"[11] and in much the same way the Archigram group imagined a "scene machine" of its own: a continuous creative recomposition of architecture, a lived and playful process configured by the user.

The theoretical ambivalence of modernism, its tension between the spontaneous and the contained, had only gone generally unnoticed this long because of its skillful resolution in the actual buildings of "modern masters" like Le Corbusier, who could create the illusion that walls had dropped by providence into perfect position on the plan.[12] The practice of modern architecture was, secretly, intuitive. In May 1957, John Summerson

3.1 *James Meller, cover of* Archigram *no. 7, December 1966:* Archigram *moves "beyond architecture," hoping to find through the continual recalculations performed by a computer loom an alternative to the permanent spatial choices recorded by buildings.*

came to the assistance of those cohorts of architects who could not attain the apparently effortless intuition of the masters, nor form a methodology from the tangle of theories and manifestos the masters left behind. In "The Case for a Theory of Modern Architecture," an address delivered to the RIBA on receipt of the Gold Medal,[13] Summerson arrived at his theory of "the programme" so as to fulfill the conceptual void at the heart of modernism, "its lack of a communicable rationale once the masters had departed."[14] Summerson cut the Gordian knot of modernism: "Prior to 1750, the prime principle of unity in architecture was the received paradigm of ancient precedent—a classically ordained source of unity that in the twentieth century has come to be progressively displaced, as a principle or order, by the socially determined programme."[15]

Under Summerson's rubric, buildings would be formed by social requirement. Peter Cook's AA tutors, Arthur Korn and John Killick, agreed. "Our authority today sounds perhaps mundane and uninspiring" Killick confessed. "It consists of what can only be summed up in that rather flat word—the programme."[16] This procedure, however, still bore a terrible weight for the architect charged with divining the social will and translating it into built form.[17] Surely, reasoned Archigram, it would be simpler to hand the control levers of the environment straight over to society, and let people determine forms and spaces directly. Apart from which, the moment one made a commitment to an architectural program, everything was frozen—the architectural solution (the building) and the social desire that had brought it into being, which might be nothing more than a passing fad. The program was just another sort of idealism. The imperative for Archigram's generation was to create "open ends"[18] (as an editorial of *Archigram* no. 8 phrased it), an architecture that expressed its inhabitants' supposed desire for continuous change. Architecture, Cook wrote in 1970, "can be much more related to the ambiguity of life. It can be throw-away or additive; it can be ad-hoc; it can be more allied to the personality and personal situation of the people who may have to use it."[19]

This acceptance of uncertainty kept architecture in step with advanced practices elsewhere in culture. Science itself had become a less certain affair since Heisenberg's 1927 discovery of the uncertainty principle (also known as the indeterminacy principle). In physics, uncertainty was a result of the inability to simultaneously determine all the natural variables of a system. The philosopher Karl Popper imported ideas of the indeterminate from the scientific sphere into the political. Once regarded as an inconvenience to the rational functioning of society and space, human variables offered a new challenge for the progressive architect—something, indeed, of a maxim in the wake of Popper's seminal books, *The Open Society and Its Enemies* (vol. 1, 1945; vol. 2, 1966) and *The Poverty of Historicism* (1957),[20] just as Western intellectuals and artists were frantically disengaging with the excessive order of scientific Leninist Marxism (retroactively tainted by Stalinism). The attempts by the masters of political philosophy (Plato, Hegel, Marx) to find plans within human history was, Popper argued, immoral, intellectually dishonest, and counterproductive. In its place Popper proposed a pragmatism of social openness, democracy, and criticism, managed at most by medium-term social engineering.

As Archigram put it in 1966, "buildings with no capacity to change can only become slums or ancient monuments."[21] Programmatic modernism seemed ever less suitable to postwar liberal democracies,[22] and its abandonment helped to rupture CIAM, the guiding body of modern architecture until the 1950s. Thanks in particular to the work of the Smithsons and their colleagues in Team 10, modernists were forced to consider, however superficially, how human communities might *actually* function, rather than how they *should* function. Cook's sometime tutor John Voelcker concisely summarized the issue in Team 10's Draft Framework for CIAM in 1956, contrasting the 1920s thinking of Bauhaus director Walter Gropius with the 1950s thinking of Team 10's Jacob Bakema: "To oversimplify, the idea of 'social responsibility' (Gropius) was directive, 'Moral Function' (Bakema) is libertarian in that the onus placed on the architect is to seek out the existing structure of the community and to allow this structure to develop in positive directions. Induction instead of deduction."[23]

In fact modern architects had long harbored a latent libertarianism in their designs. Sir Andrew Derbyshire, recalling his experiences as a mature architectural student at the AA in the

1950s, candidly admits, "we were very interested in anarchism, which was a bit of a contradiction, I know"—this from one of the leaders of a "second generation" of modernists who had striven to make of modernism a rulebook and who had believed passionately in the benevolent power of planning to reconstruct people's lives.[24] Relative permissiveness was further inspired by existentialism, that most pungent of intellectual movements in the immediate postwar period, which brought with it the insistence that life is negotiated, not preprogrammed. This was partly translated into demands for spaces that allowed for human *encounter* as well as segregation of function,[25] concerns that were elevated to the status of a full politics by Henri Lefebvre, the situationists, and Herbert Marcuse in their war with the cheerless, exploitative rationalization of everyday life. No less influential was the "common-sensical" tone of Jane Jacobs's *The Death and Life of Great American Cities,* her defiant 1961 celebration of the messy pluralism of the American city "as found," unsullied by master plans.[26]

After Jacobs, Archigram (at the "Living City" exhibition) conceived of the environment being determined by the competition between lifestyles, accommodating unruly consumerist appetites and subcultures. In the 1920s, the white austerity of modern architecture promised economy in an age of scarcity; and by the 1950s, modernist economies of scale were finally being realized in the white and gray system-built estates and blocks, just as rationing was being lifted[27] and the West was emerging into the colorful world of plenty. An architecture of strictly finite means was being provided, it seemed to Archigram, to an economy with no apparent limits. It made no sense. "You can roll out steel— any length," wrote David Greene in *Archigram* no. 1, sounding like an advocate of Llewelyn Davies's "endless architecture" until he came to less conventional building materials: "you can blow up a balloon—any size" (the plastic-and-aluminum U.S. satellite balloon Echo 1, launched in August 1960, had a cool one-hundred-foot diameter), "you can mould plastic—any shape . . . you can roll out paper—any length."[28]

Two economics of indeterminacy became apparent in the fifties and sixties, one judicious, the other playful. Buckminster Fuller's indeterminate architectural "kit-of-parts" (such as his

geodesic dome system) redistributed the world's finite building resources more equitably, whereas certain *followers* of Fuller like Archigram (which showed the geodesic dome airborne on the cover of its third, "Expendability" issue; see figure 1.29)[29] urged redistribution through a feeding frenzy of plenty, individuals playfully demanding ever more from their community stores. Prophets of scarcity and plenty alike were prompted by deprivation, Buckminster Fuller's in Depression-era America,[30] Archigram's in postwar austerity. Yet the argument given in *Archigram* no. 3 was that expendability offered the only realistic cue for the future of modern architecture, a departure from the "doing the most with the least" crusade about to be relaunched by Fuller's World Design Science Decade, but in accordance with trends elsewhere in the Western economy.[31]

Almost without realising it, we have absorbed into our lives the first generation of expendables . . . foodbags, paper tissues, polythene wrappers, ballpens, E.P.'s . . . also with us are the items that are bigger and last longer, but are NEVERTHELESS planned for obsolescence . . . the motor car . . . and its unit-built garage. Now the second generation is upon us . . . the London County Council is putting up limited-life-span houses. THROUGH AND THROUGH every level of society and with every level of commodity, the unchanging scene is being replaced by the increase in change of our user-habits—and thereby, eventually, our user-habitats. . . . We must recognise this as a healthy and altogether positive sign. It is the product of a sophisticated consumer society, rather than a stagnant (and in the end, declining) society.[32]

Expendability was analogous to the healthy life-and-death cycle of the natural organism. Organicism had long lurked as the repressed alternative to the mechanistic, rationalistic discourse dominating modernism,[33] and was championed in the first edition of *Archigram*. Organicism was the byword for managing an architecture-in-change, offering the best of both worlds—"natural" order and "natural" laissez-faire.[34] In this way, proponents of the organic felt, architecture would emulate the continually evolving and growing human communities it served.[35] Organic architecture related parts to the whole—the nut and bolt to the structure, the neighborhood to the city, the individual to the collective. By 1970, Peter Cook felt that buildings and planning would benefit from an animal integration—connected and jointed like vertebrae, flesh, organs, skin, and digestion.[36] In the wake of interest in cybernetics, famously defined in 1947 as the comparative scientific study of "control and communication in the animal and the machine,"[37] Cook may have been speaking more than metaphorically. If it was true that the principles of control are common to both inorganic and organic systems, inorganic architecture could operate as an extension of its organic users, each man and woman in turn a nerve ending in the social body.[38]

How else, other than through computer-based cybernetic technology, could the desires of every citizen be respected, tracked, and met? Archigram's "scene machine" would be advocated not as an indulgence to the democratic, consumer economy, but a necessity. The architect, MIT's Nicholas Negroponte claimed in 1970 (quoting another advocate of machine management), "is forced to proceed in this way . . . because watching each sparrow is too troublesome for any but God."[39] The game of architecture could begin: "architecture," Negroponte added, "unlike a game of checkers with fixed rules and a fixed number of pieces, and much like a joke, determined by context, is the croquet game in *Alice in Wonderland,* where the Queen of Hearts (society, technology, economics) keeps changing the rules."[40] Game theory offered a way of theoretically accommodating the desires of more than one "player" in a system. (At "Living City," Archigram compared urban life to a game subjected to chance; see figure 2.16.)[41]

All this assumed that players were operating strategically and rationally, a theoretical shortcoming compounded by the practical problem of primitive predictive computational technology. In other words, the "emergent situations" arising from human foibles looked set to be a persistent problem.[42] Undeterred, Archigram architects were resolved to make architecture sympathetic to emergent situations: while all sorts of sciences and rationales could be corralled to validate Archigram's case for indeterminate architecture, the details rarely detained their pursuit of impromptu pleasures. As Chalk once put it, "the

knowledgeable and apparent sincerity of the glum venture into systems and methods dispels the gleeful enjoyment one can have with meaningless conversations, irrational gestures, jokes and giggles."[43]

Archigram could hear how players improvised within a system when listening to jazz music's transformation of themes. Slipping onto the record turntable the ventures into "free jazz" of the sort featured in "Living City," Archigram could marvel at the extreme meltdown of themes, genres, and musical techniques.[44] Chalk took the title of his open letter to David Greene, "Ghosts," published in *Archigram* no. 7, from the most played number of radical jazz saxophonist Albert Ayler (figure 3.2).[45] Ayler's music sounded chaotic, *was* nearly chaotic, but it was not chaotic; it was music, it was bliss. Architecture might achieve something similar.

FROM THE MEGASTRUCTURE TO THE KIT-OF-PARTS

In his *Come-Go* collage for "Living City," Peter Cook pasted a photograph of a typical American city street lined with vaguely International Style blocks (figure 2.11). "This sort of environment can never be the answer," he wrote, arrows pointing to the blocks. "And it isn't even good technology."[46] Yet the International Style represented modern architecture. If Archigram was to have any credibility, it would have to present the public with another sort of modernism, one as plausible in its rationale as the International Style, and preferably one validated with as impressive a historical lineage. As a counterpoint to mainstream modernist monumentality, Archigram and its allies pieced together an architecture of indeterminacy from some of the more peripheral practices of modern architecture.

Architects should not be building neat partitions, Archigram reasoned, but joining up space and freeing motion. "FLOW?" asked Greene impatiently in *Archigram* no. 1, "water flows or doesn't or does/flow or not flows."[47] Tony Garnier ensured a clean flow of goods and bodies around his classic Cité Industrielle (1917), *Archigram* no. 5 reported, and the best postwar experimental work, like the Smithsons' Sheffield University project (figure 1.16) and Walter Pichler's city study (which had recently arrived from Austria), did the same.[48] The linear city

3.2 *Warren Chalk,* Ghosts, Archigram *no. 7, December 1966: Chalk reveals the images cinematically turning over in his mind as he contemplates a trajectory for architecture, and buildings do not predominate. Le Corbusier's Ronchamp chapel and Mies van der Rohe's Fifty-by-Fifty House project of 1950 are reproduced no bigger than some Bauhaus chairs, a radio telescope, a rotoscope, a car, and Brigitte Bardot. Presiding over the ensemble is radical jazz saxophonist Albert Ayler.*

concept—an invention of the late nineteenth century, revived in projects by Le Corbusier and the constructivists in the 1920s and 1930s[49]—combined qualities of extension and communications simultaneously,[50] stretching new cities along highways and railways. It was rediscovered in Cook's Plug-In City (figure 1.3) and in Cedric Price's Potteries Thinkbelt (1964),[51] one drawing of which showed architectural units being loaded onto trains for distribution through the network.[52]

Yet even "flow" seemed rather deterministic, channeling movement and matter like a river or a tree trunk rather than randomizing it.[53] A semilattice could be seen in Plug-In City's elevations and cross sections, conjoining criteria laterally as well as hierarchically, an idea that would receive a popular theoretical grounding in the 1965 essay by Christopher Alexander, "A City Is Not a Tree."[54] At this point, the megastructure still appealed to Archigram as a way of "framing" (making architectural sense of) the expendable, transient functions of the city. "UNIVERSAL STRUCTURE Can at once GALVANISE and DISCIPLINE a growing city," read a headline in Archigram no. 5. Architecture had somehow to accommodate the "greater number" of postwar mass

society.[55] Since 1958, Yona Friedman's Groupe d'Etudes d'Architecture Mobile had been exploring the potential for three-dimensional urban infrastructure, and Japanese metabolist architects, such as Arata Isozaki and Noriaki Kurokawa, also saw in giant frame systems the means to a seamless, accelerated socio-architectural organicism: "we are trying to encourage the active metabolic development of our society through our proposals."[56]

Frames inevitably rooted activity and locked in their inhabitants, however, and in his 1964 critique of metabolism Peter Smithson revoked his adherence to the clustered megastructure. Experimental architecture was itching to break away from the great singular solution and unity, he thought: "One should be free to opt out, or to work in ways that might in the long run redirect the economy." He invoked Popper's vision: "That would be a real open society."[57] Universal structure, it was true, could only ever offer *relative* permissiveness, like the variable apartment designs of Le Corbusier's iconic Unité d'Habitation.[58] Superstructures benignly framed and dwarfed the individual to the point that the appearance of a plucky little "Moorish" apartment in Le Corbusier's drawing of the gargantuan Algiers scheme of 1931 was a cause for celebration. Moshe Safdie's sensational 1967 Habitat complex for the Montreal Expo accommodated a "greater number" and avoided the cagelike overtones of the frame, but nonetheless it depended upon mutual structural support for its corbeled cells (figure 3.3). The defining challenge for Archigram became to break the unwieldy, static support to which architecture, from house to megastructure, was addicted. And that would require architects to abstain from big, sculptural compositions.

In the mid-sixties Archigram's attention shifted from the slumbering megastructure to the kit-of-parts festooning it. Alongside "clip-on" (Reyner Banham's terminology)[59] and "plug-in" (Cook's), the addition to the Archigram lexicon of the terms "kit" and "kit-of-parts"[60] further enabled the group to speak of architecture not as fixed form but as a set of provisional relationships between components. Banham's mind had turned to kits when he started researching the unsung architectural heroes of air-conditioning components and suspended ceilings in the late sixties. Less prosaically, this intrigue with the gaps, joints, and

3.3 *Moshe Safdie, Habitat modular dwelling system, Expo '67, Montreal, 1967. Archigram/Taylor Woodrow's submission for a central tower at the Montreal Expo was not accepted (figure 1.6), but the Expo did build Safdie's celebrated "indeterminate" megastructure.*

connections of architecture had parallels with the structuralist approach to cultural and literary criticism. Archigram's was also a procedure analogous to the way words were set at liberty from language by the futurists and, subsequently, by the "Living City" exhibition.[61]

Thus it was that *Archigram* no. 5, the "Metropolis" issue, also featured a page of "Underwater Hardware," a collection of Jacques Cousteau-style *capsules trouvées* to be enjoyed alongside the giant city structures (figure 3.4). By the next issue, Warren Chalk's definitive Archigram capsule, the Capsule Home, was

prefixed "Plug-In" to give it continuity with Cook's own mega-structure (figure 1.9), though it was depicted surviving without the mother ship; a year later and David Greene's Living Pod had decisively shaken loose (figure 3.5). Breaking with the megastructural service frame or stem, the "ephemeralization,"[62] dispersal, and mobilization of architecture marked an important juncture in the story of "disappearing architecture."[63]

Archigram enthusiastically recovered precedents for the production and distribution of architecture as flexible, techno-logically advanced, and engineered kits-of-parts. Le Corbusier,

3.4 *Warren Chalk,* Underwater Hardware, Archigram *no. 5, November 1964. Viewed as part of its general program, Archigram's interest in capsules signaled a shift in direction from megastructures to movable structures. Seen from the perspective of architectural aesthetics, meanwhile, Archigram was discovering machine form under the sea just as surely as Le Corbusier did when he showed architects pictures of ships on the surface.*

though, fearing that cultural and technological conditions in France were not ready for a general implementation of "the engineer's aesthetic" (and preferring in the meantime to explore "machine form" through masonry and whiteness), did still deliver to the 1937 Paris International Exposition a translucent, tented Pavillon des Temps Nouveau held in place by steel cables and pylons.[64] The merging of architecture and industrial design had been implicit since Le Corbusier had demanded a "machine for living in," which Archigram now delivered, provocatively taking the master's advice literally: "A house will no longer be this solidly built thing which sets out to defy time and decay . . . it will become a tool as the motor car is becoming a tool."[65]

Nonchalant flexibility presumed lightness and the ready availability of off-the-rack components. Complete kits had been in development since the nineteenth century and later drew inspiration from the serial production techniques found in the American automobile industry, but they lay largely dormant.[66] War was a major spur to progress. The British military gained something of a knack for assembling kit structures, from the lightweight steel Nissen hut (mass-produced from the First World War on)[67] to the use in World War II of prestressed concrete, cement, woodchip panels, and even lightweight concrete shells reinforced with fabric, techniques directed after the war toward the housing shortage. Ron Herron encountered military prefabrication during his National Service in the Royal Air Force.[68] The Bristol Aeroplane company, where Reyner Banham was apprenticed, produced a total of 54,000 light-alloy AIROH (Aircraft Industry Research Organisation on Housing) houses, designed during the war by an industry task force.[69] Riveted together and wired as a loom, with circuits completed by plug and socket attachments, an AIROH house could be delivered on four lorries (a conveyance method demonstrated in Archigram's Instant City, 1968) and was intended to be produced at a rate of one every twelve minutes. After the termination of the Emergency House Building Programme killed off the AIROH house, architectural interest in prefabrication shifted to multistory heavy concrete systems, and Archigram's enthusiasm for the prefab was all the more contrary given their rather disparaged reputation during the postwar years. The Terrapin bungalow of

1948, an aluminum-skinned "expando" designed to retract into single box shape for towing,[70] was featured in *Archigram* no. 3 and was a concept revived by Webb's Drive-In Housing (1966; figures 3.6, 3.7).

The designers Jean Prouvé in France and Buckminster Fuller in America also recommissioned wartime technology for peacetime ends, using redundant aircraft production lines and war-enlarged supplies of light alloy, steel, and skilled labor to produce emergency dwelling units and other kit houses.[71] Fuller returned to a kit-house concept, which he had first explored in the Dymaxion House project of 1927, but failed to find its

3.5 *David Greene, Living Pod project, model, 1966. With the Living Pod, Greene modified his 1962 Spray Plastic Housing project to craft a free-roving exploratory house inspired by the Lunar Modules that NASA was preparing for a moon landing. "Probably a dead end," wrote Greene with typically scathing self-criticism, yet it vividly staged a moment in Archigram's quest for nomadic architecture. Psychologically it posed some interesting conundra too: the occupant was to occupy a womb, a burrow, in wide-open spaces and water, and the realistic detailing of the model created the illusion of a prototype.*

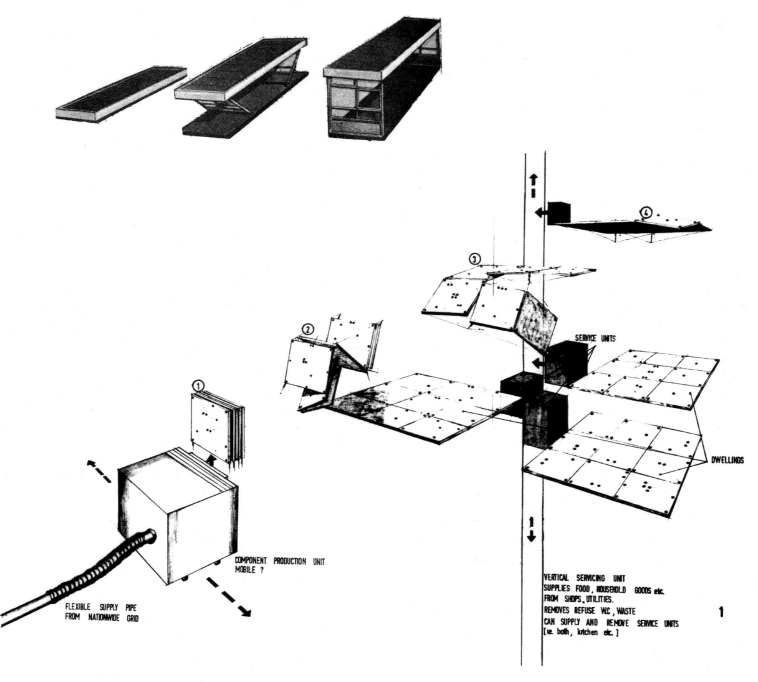

3.6 *"The erection sequence of a 'Terrapin' structure" (Terrapin bungalow of 1948), Archigram no. 3, August 1963. In shifting the paradigm of architecture from the sculptural to the portable, Archigram had to assemble a canon of designs previously considered nonarchitectural, and frequently hailing from a decade regarded as a bleak one for architecture (and humanity)—the 1940s.* **3.7** *Michael Webb, House Project (Drive-In Housing project), perspective of erection sequence, Archigram no. 5, November 1964. With "nonbuildings" such as prefabricated shelters and caravans reappraised, Archigram designers applied their tenets to the challenge of architectural indeterminacy.*

projected one-hundred-million-dollar start-up costs (figure 3.8).[72] Fuller's short-lived WICHITA House (1946), though having less immediate impact upon housing than even the British AIROH, was a still more sophisticated design intended for production at a rate of a thousand per week on Beech Aircraft Corporation production lines, with all its components fitted within a reusable stainless steel cylinder for shipping.[73] It boasted two bathrooms at a time when more than a third of American homes had no piped sanitation, and just as the bathroom was becoming the paragon of postwar discourses on hygiene.[74] Systems building, the daydream of the functionalists of the thirties, steadily gained acceptance after the war as a possible option for efficiency and economy, and in certain systems components could be scrambled to create indeterminate outcomes. Thus Konrad Wachsmann, whose space-frame system was based upon standard joints and connectors, collaborated with former Bauhaus director Walter Gropius in 1942 to promote their Packaged House System.

3.8 *R. Buckminster Fuller, Dymaxion House project, model, 1927, with its inventor. Archigram was separated from one of its greatest forebears by a shared ethos, one might say: Buckminster Fuller had espoused the economics of lightweight component architecture; Archigram pursued its pleasures. The little female occupants recline with a similar ease, however (compare figures 1.9, 3.19).*

But there was an urge among the Archigram generation to move beyond this legacy. There was, in particular, a "strong moralist approach"[75] adhering to kit buildings, stemming from their association with wartime expediency, excessive reverence for the production line, and the quest for the universal joint— a colorless "one-size-fits-all" ethos that had acquired "almost fetishistic overtones."[76] Ethically and aesthetically, Archigram regarded strictly modular building systems as a mixed blessing, partly an overstated "*demonstration*"[77] of prefabrication that might be better combined with other building elements or tacked onto structures already in situ. Archigram increasingly focused upon an eclectic, ad hoc approach, demonstrated in Herron's 1968 Tuned Suburb (figure 3.9) and Cook's Cheek by Jowl high street conversion of 1970.[78] "The successive structuring may be architecturally inconsistent but socially and economically a much simpler job. . . . This is much closer to industrial design and has to involve quite precise operations," Cook believed.[79] Modularization smacked of standardization,[80] when what the postwar public wanted was *choice*. Prefabrication was an unwelcome reminder of the years of austerity during those of plenty. Archigram unashamedly pursued the quality that had been frowned upon by ascetic high modernism: "Comfort: rich and warm. . . . The broad instinct for well-being. . . . It is interesting that the most impressive modern architecture is often accused (by lay people) of being 'uncomfortable.'"[81]

And then there was that feeling, loudly declaimed by *Archigram* no. 1, that the "decaying Bauhaus image" had become "an insult to functionalism,"[82] a stylistic repertoire barely relevant to the materials, techniques, and imperatives of a new age. The Bauhaus in its functionalist phase had come quite close to an engagement with the techniques of industrial production, with Marcel Breuer's steel panel system of 1925 and Gropius's 1927 panel system at Dessau, but over the long term the Bauhaus was lured away by formal considerations. As Buckminster Fuller explained in a letter to the Independent Group's John McHale in 1955, dismissing any connection between his work and Bauhaus doctrine, "the 'International Style' brought to America by the Bauhaus innovators demonstrated fashion-inoculation without the necessity of knowledge of the scientific fundamentals of structural mechanics and chemistry."[83]

Archigram recalled functionalism's origins as the pragmatic nineteenth-century accompaniment to a rapidly industrializing world, seemingly undistracted by manifestos and building codes and aesthetics: "blokes that built the Forth Bridge," Greene wrote, "THEY DIDN'T WORRY."[84] "By comparison, today's architectural experiments seem tentative and prescribed, despite the far-reaching values they claim," Cook later added.[85] The functionalist origins of the modern movement were well documented—acknowledged, of course, in such standard textbooks as Nikolaus Pevsner's *Pioneers of Modern Design* and Sigfried Giedion's *Space, Time and Architecture*. There was a modification, though, in the attitude with which these foundations were rediscovered by the new generation of architects and historians. For Pevsner, engineering served as a source of "ideal" unornamented modern form. Giedion's history too melded the raw inventiveness of Victorian engineering into the planar surfaces of the International Style. What fascinated Archigram's generation were the eccentric, proactive qualities of engineering, the way in which the nineteenth-century exhibition structures (Paxton's 1851 Crystal Palace in London, Eiffel's tower and Dutert and Contamin's Galerie des Machines in Paris in 1889) were conceived as kits-of-parts, temporary and "live."

Dutert's Galerie, for example, was "live" thanks to the hinges at the apex and bases of its inclined arches that permitted the entire structure to move imperceptibly, while its mobile viewing platform rolled spectacularly. (Cook lamented the way travelators, electric cars, and robots had been abandoned as mere world's fairs novelties.)[86] The Crystal Palace and Galerie des Machines served as magnificent "sheds," spatial enclosures amenable to indeterminate activities: an "invisible," background architecture that put *life* at center stage. This approach to construction was endowed with what Giedion wrote of as "the curious association of an unmistakable grandeur with a certain gentleness."[87]

Avowedly utilitarian shed architecture made regular repeat appearances in postwar British architecture: in Basil Spence's

3.9 *Ron Herron,* Tuned Suburb, *montage, 1968. Kit architecture, but not standardized architecture: when Archigram's prefabricated units arrive in a composite British street, it is the vernacular houses—not the pipes, bubbles, and gantries—that appear homogeneous. Words like "exchange" and "responsive" are on hand to affirm the freedoms imparted by the kit to the youthful residents in the foreground.*

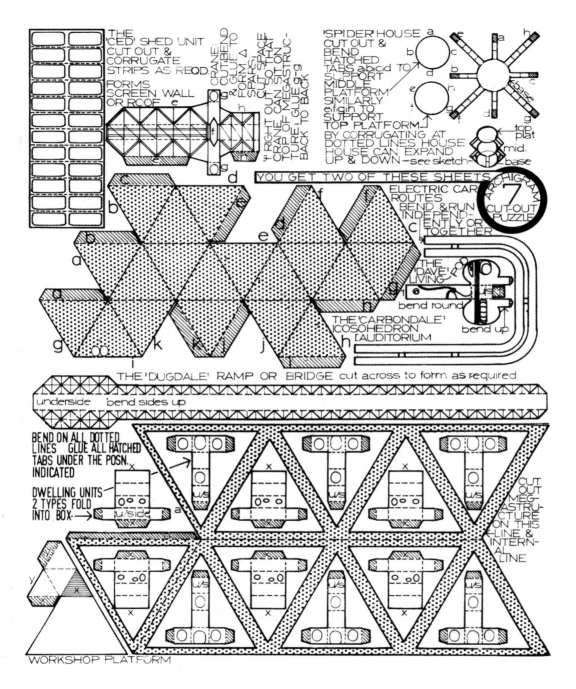

THE 'CED' SHED UNIT CUT OUT & CORRUGATE STRIPS AS REQD

FORMS SCREEN WALL OR ROOF e

CRANE: CUT.BEND & GLUE TO FORM △ SPARS. CUT SPACE SO THAT "F" RIGHT OUT CRANE CAN SIT ON TOP OF MEGASTRUC-TURE. GLUE g-g BACK TO BACK

'SPIDER' HOUSE a CUT OUT & BEND HATCHED TABS a,b,c,d TO SUPPORT MIDDLE PLATFORM SIMILARLY e,f,g,h TO SUPPORT TOP PLATFORM. BY CORRUGATING AT DOTTED LINES HOUSE CAN EXPAND UP & DOWN —see sketch—

top plat
mid.
base

YOU GET TWO OF THESE SHEETS

ELECTRIC CAR ROUTES BEND & RUN INDEPEND-ENTLY OR TOGETHER

ARCHIGRAM 7 CUT-OUT PUZZLE

THE 'DAVE' LIVING — bend round

THE 'CARBONDALE' ICOSOHEDRON AUDITORIUM

bend up

THE 'DUGDALE' RAMP OR BRIDGE cut across to form as required

underside   bend sides up

BEND ON ALL DOTTED LINES GLUE ALL HATCHED TABS UNDER THE POSN. INDICATED

DWELLING UNITS 2 TYPES FOLD INTO BOX→

CUT OUT MEG-ASTRUC-TURE ON THIS LINE & INTERN-AL LINE

WORKSHOP PLATFORM

3.10 *Archigram, Cut-out Puzzle, Archigram no. 7, December 1966. The cutout constructor kit allowed readers to create and rearrange Archigram's architectural vision on a desktop. Included were Tony Dugdale's Ramp/Bridge unit, a Cedric Price shed, a Peter Cook crane, an expanding house by Michael Webb, a David Greene Living Pod, a Buckminster Fuller icosahedron geodesic auditorium, and two generic types of dwelling units with a triangular truss megastructure to support them.*

Sea and Ships Pavilion at the 1951 Festival of Britain; in the Fun Palace project by Archigram's friend Cedric Price (1961, collaborating with Joan Littlewood, figure 1.30); in Ron Herron's Oasis project (*Archigram* no. 8, 1968, figure 4.20) and in Renzo Piano and Richard Rogers's Pompidou Center (1971–1977, figure 4.19), which looked as if it had been assembled from the cutout kit-of-parts supplied with *Archigram* no. 7 (figure 3.10)—not entirely a coincidence, since a designer of the *Archigram* kit, Tony Dugdale, also became a member of the Pompidou team. In addition to Dugdale's Ramp/Bridge unit, *Archigram* no. 7's cutout constructor kit included a "Shed Unit" (of the sort Cedric Price used in the Fun Palace), a crane from Plug-In City, a "Spider House" (so-called because of its expanding form and design by Mike "Spider" Webb), a track for electric cars and a platform (items retrieved from the world's fairs), a little David Greene "Living Pod" supplemented by two generic "Dwelling Units," a Buckminster Fuller icosahedron geodesic auditorium, and, to underpin everything in case it was needed, a "Megastructure," notably reduced in bulk by means of triangular trusses.[88]

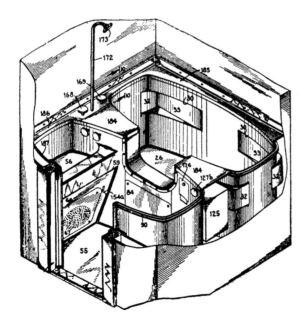

Moving away from these grander structures, the kit-of-parts concept came to its full flowering with quieter proposals by Archigram that set out to "dematerialize" or "uproot" architecture and enclosure. Preferred components shrank in size, rigidity, and resistance, moving from the "kit" through the model of the "pod" to the use of pressurized air. "The vision of the helicopter with the dome dangling beneath it" (reproduced on the cover of *Archigram* no. 3; see figure 1.29) "still summarises the whole point of minimal effort for maximum effect," wrote Cook.[89] Believing that technology increasingly delivered "more for less," the dome's designer Buckminster Fuller had long espoused "ephemeralization" as a shorthand for the ceaseless pursuit of more performance for less weight and material. His archetypal "kit-of-parts," the geodesic dome (under development since the 1940s), acquired iconic status, with 12,000 in use by 1970[90] and with its patent drawings widely reproduced.

The drive "beyond architecture" concentrated interest in consumer durable kits that were self-contained, transportable, interchangeable, and expendable.[91] In short, architecture would become more like a refrigerator, car, or even a plastic bag than an immovable monolith. Fuller again offered paradigms. The radicalism of his Dymaxion House of 1927 (figure 3.8) was not confined to its suspended mast structure: it was, in effect, a large labor-saving device of huge appeal to the Archigram generation, designed to recirculate and package liquid and solid waste, to automatically launder soiled clothing before packing it away again, and to dust and vacuum itself. The free-planned interior space was demarcated by storage units and its lightweight furniture was supported by air. It promised comfort. Fuller's Dymaxion bathroom (1936–1938)—a prefabricated, fully functioning chunk of house (figure 3.11)—increased its currency in avant-garde circles when it inspired the full-size House of the Future by Alison and Peter Smithson (1956, figure 1.28).

The vision was of the works-straight-out-of-the-box, self-contained architectural unit, the mass-produced "capsule" or "pod." As with "flowers in a bowl; caravans on a site," Cedric Price declared in *Archigram* no. 2, the point was to design complete units capable of reorganization, carried by the whim of

3.11 *R. Buckminster Fuller, patent drawing of the Dymaxion Bathroom, 1938. An interchangeable, ruthlessly efficient housing module, the Dymaxion Bathroom found form as if through its rejection of styling—leaving the Smithsons and Archigram to eke out its latent chic (compare figures 1.28, 4.2).*

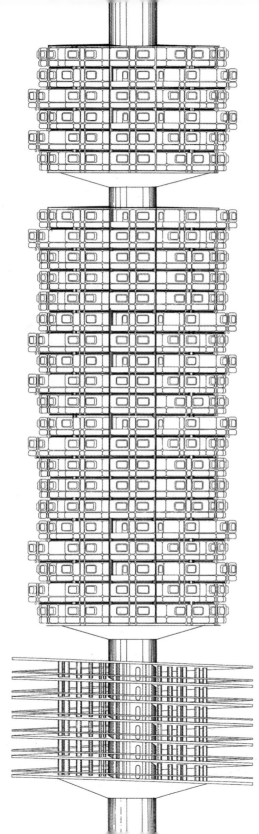

the owner-operator. "It is easier to allow for individual flexibility than organisational change—The expendable house; the multi-use of fixed volumes; the transportable controlled environment."[92] Archigram was on the lookout for prototypes—the fiberglass Monsanto House at Disneyland (1954–1957), the prefabrications of Arthur Quarmby and Ionel Schein,[93] the "expressionist" use of plastic by Pascal Hausermann.[94] Portable temporary cabin accommodation was an increasingly common sight in Britain, especially at building sites, after the introduction of the Portakabin in 1961.[95] Warren Chalk's 1964 vision of capsule living *stacked* into towers proved particularly compelling (figure 3.12), adopted in turn by Kisho Kurokawa, whose capsules became known to Archigram through the pages of *Architecture d'Aujourd'hui* as "the ones to beat," reaching a zenith in his startling Nagakin Capsule Tower of 1970–1972 (figure 3.13).[96] In the interim Nicholas Grimshaw, a contributor to *Archigram,* had a real pod building of his own, the bathroom tower at a student hostel in Paddington, west London (figure 3.14), devised in 1967 with Terry Farrell (who had long harbored ambitions for the sorts of design promoted in *Archigram*).[97] The pods still suckled a common core, yet the bulk was greatly reduced from Plug-In scales of megastructure, and Farrell and Grimshaw had succeeded in making an *existing* nineteenth-century building more *serviceable,* grafting a prosthesis onto the "living body" of the city.

When the mass-produced unit was so irresistibly logical, why had it not succeeded in transforming architectural production so far? Archigram faced the paradox that the search for an architecture that imitated consumer products was being killed by the market. Working with Alex Gordon and partners in 1964–1965, Dennis Crompton was employed on a prefabricated scheme, the IBIS (Industrial Building in Steel) project. Cook ascribed its demise to the same factors that militated against Fuller's Dymaxion concepts (but which would change come the day that white heat ignited the construction industry): "a basic economic equation (which means that it is only viable if it captures a high percentage of the national housing market). This, along with the basic threat which a new technology presents to the building trade, remains a central problem."[98] Like Fuller, Archigram shifted justification for ephemeralization from the market to a still more imperative-sounding logic of "survival," of a race to provide an expanding population with a universal standard of living.

Archigram borrowed the Fullerine rhetoric of "survivalism," even though Fuller was troubled by the finite supply of global resources while Archigram believed in plenty. "Archigram thinks that architects should stop making bigger and better boxes and get down to the real business of architecture today which they think is survival," the 1966 BBC film on the group explained. "Archigram sees that the ideas and techniques we need for this survival are already in existence in the tremendous backlog of ideas and invention deriving from the military, aerospace and

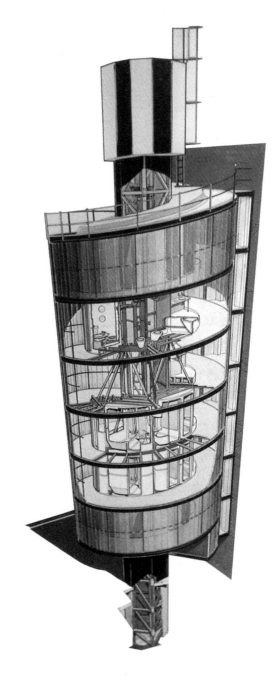

3.12 *Warren Chalk, Capsule Homes: Tower, elevation, 1964. The vision that heralded what was to become a reality (compare figure 3.13), if not in Archigram's own hands: Chalk cantilevered his cabins from a core and, true to Archigram planning principles at the time, ensured that car parking was available below.*
3.13 *Kisho Kurokawa, Nagakin Capsule Tower, Tokyo, 1970–1972. In the early 1970s, Japanese architects began to build structures of the genus that had been merely ruminated upon by* Archigram. **3.14** *Farrell/Grimshaw Partnership, Bathroom Service Tower, Student Hostel, Paddington, perspective elevation cutaway, 1967. The Bathroom Service Tower negated bathroom waiting time for residents of the attached student dormitories by lining Buckminster Fuller-type bathroom units down a spiral ramp (a form seen too at the base of Chalk's Capsule Tower, figure 3.12). It was one of the most competent and logical renditions of* Archigram's *premises.*

electronics industries."[99] Perhaps survivalist rhetoric was made more credible by Cold War conditions. (In 1968 David Greene became a registered fallout shelter designer.)[100] Design for survival was fresh in the minds of older Archigram members. "The first half of the Forties," Chalk and Herron explained in an edition of *Archigram* given over to a wartime decade that the postwar era preferred to forget, "saw a great inventive leap made out of necessity for survival . . . the technology, the laminated timber or geodesic framework of an aircraft, the welded tubular construction of a bridge, the air structure of a barrage balloon, and much more, filtered through to colour our attitudes and disciplines today."[101] Geodesics, tubular trusses, barrage balloons, and even gun emplacements[102] became part of Archigram's iconography (figure 4.13).

Archigram found architectural potential in each technology as it was announced. Gasket windows were borrowed from cars and British Railways;[103] new industrial processes and systems were translated into fiendishly complex architectural superstructures such as Webb's 1966 Drive-In Housing (figure 3.7). To the extent that the self-contained architectural "pod" took its inspiration from the motor vehicle and from the exploration of outer space,[104] it was an example of what Martin Pawley (a contributor to *Archigram* no. 5) would later claim as "technology transfer," the process whereby techniques and materials developed in one field are adapted to serve in others. *Scientific American* was read to hasten the transfer,[105] and *Archigram*'s publication of the technical goodies that it had come across tempted architects into uncharted waters. As part of a list of "phenomena for now," *Archigram* no. 6 explained that "the existence of the pocket tape recorder has the same meaning for us as the tower crane." "Sony TV now available in UK, weight 9 lbs, 9 ounces," the magazine went on, illustrating it as proof of the new "economy of means," merging issues of scarcity and portability. Two issues later *Archigram* had found a pair of sunglasses with a radio and earpiece discreetly built in—"Radio Gonks are real!" it exclaimed, as if proving the viability of Cook's own project for "Info-Gonks" featured in the same issue (figure 3.15).

The *Archigram* magazine posed, to some extent, as one of those "transfer agents" whose responsibility would be to "stimu-

late, accelerate and promote valid technology transfers through overt organized programs," as the 1967 US National Academy Report on the process said. The Report went on to place technology transfer within the enterprise culture that Archigram was trying to foster: "New technological ideas are transferred and implemented by persons—*not* by reports—and for persons to do this effectively, they must operate in an environment that is conducive to a new-enterprise generation."[106] Cook echoed the sentiment in *Archigram* no. 8: "By 1967 Archigram will have been outbursting for some six years. The Littlewood/Price Fun Palace will be three years old, the light pencil even older. . . . There is a choice of at least five British airhouse manufacturers. But where have we actually got?" He urged architects to "get in there with . . . the electronics engineers, the hydraulics engineers, the biophysicists, the programmers, the indiarubber manufacturers, the shipbuilders-turned-capsulebuilders."[107] The invitation was barely acknowledged outside student circles.[108] Archigram was having to fight a rearguard action against brutalism, whose rough-hewn, low-tech concrete monumentality was now widely adopted in the building industry.

Not that *Archigram* itself tarried for long talking with hydraulics engineers, biophysicists, and the like; its job was to inspire its readers to do so. As Cook later tacitly admitted, there was a borrowing from the glamour of advanced technology as well as its necessity: "It was . . . the space race which inspired Warren Chalk to call his prefabricated dwelling unit a 'capsule,'" Cook recalled of Chalk's standard-of-living package that came complete with TV, extractor, kitchen, an intriguing antigravity pad, soft floor, zip-out screen, service sockets, and WC (figure 1.9). "That this particular piece of design was to do with production, expendability, extendibility and consumer association cannot avoid the contention that to name it 'capsule' at that point in time (1964) was highly evocative, even if the unit itself does not actually have to look like a capsule."[109] And there was too a *romance* of "Man in his container on the edge,"[110] an architectural equivalent of the survival pods used to explore space and other hostile environments (the Arctic, the deserts, and the sea), placing occupants beyond the far reach of civilization. Archigram's designs had ever less to do with life support, and

3.15 *Peter Cook, Info-Gonks project (educational TV, glasses, and headset), montage and photograph of the designer wearing a mock-up, 1968. A decade after the popularization of transistor radios, the continued miniaturization of consumer electronics encouraged Archigram's quest for a new type of personal architecture: reception of one's environment could be modified more readily than the environment itself. The headset is for "educational" purposes, affirming Archigram's closer allegiance to modernist progressivism than to psychedelia.*

PLUG IN YOUR HOME NODE
HIGHLY SERVICED FREE TRAILER FRAME: STAK-UP
FREE TIME NC
TRAILER CAGE
RON HERRON-ARCHIGRA
JUNE 1967

3.16 *Ron Herron,* Free Time Node: Trailer Cage, *montage, 1967. Nomadic life was a major motif in Archigram renderings of the late sixties, an ideological blend of fifties beat and sixties rock festival, Native American and pioneer American, space exploration and caravaning. Here, Herron services free spirits with a substructure, funnels, chutes, tarpaulins, and lattice- and concertina-framed marquees; and an architectural language materializes—the campers blithely unaware that they are being provided with the most radical architectural visualization since El Lissitzky, the Vesnin brothers, and the comrades of revolutionary Russian constructivism.*

ever more to do with lifestyle in offbeat locales. Banham showed that the availability since the early 1950s of "plug-in," domestic, self-contained air-conditioning units[111] had facilitated free movement beyond benign habitats. "For anyone who is prepared to foot the consequent bill for power consumed," Banham remarked in *The Architecture of the Well-Tempered Environment* (1969), "it is now possible to live in almost any type or form of house one likes to name in any region of the world that takes the fancy."[112]

Archigram no. 8 offered "The Nomad" as the central character in its story of the new architecture. He or she was equipped with versions of the car and caravan. The Airstream caravan, pictured in 1959 by Alison and Peter Smithson as an "embryo appliance house,"[113] was stacked by Ron Herron into the neutral service frame of the multistory car park in his Free Time Node: Trailer Cage of 1967 (figure 3.16). This admission of the lifestyles of the leisured Airstream Club on the one hand and the indigent poor on the other acknowledged a housing trend: by mid-decade, one in six single-family dwellings in the US were classed as "mobile,"[114] many of them already plugged into service lines, and *Trailer Life* magazine projected the immanent arrival of city-center, high-rise trailer parks.[115] The effects of rising car ownership, previously pondered in "Living City," remained an observable fact through which *Archigram* could rethink architecture. "The car is useful for the game of freedom," *Archigram* no. 8 announced. "This is the attraction of the car-as-satellite-of-the-pad [like Michael Webb's 1964 Drive-In Housing, figure 3.7]. Next the car becomes its own pad. Next the pad itself takes on the role of the car. It divides and regroups." Archigram picked up stones and watched the nuclear families beneath scurry away: "The status of the family and its direct connotation with a preferred, static house, cannot last."[116] Archigram began to conceive of the car "as a mobile piece of furniture,"[117] plugged in, perhaps, to robotic servicing (figure 4.3). Webb and Cook made the electric car a focus of their work at Hornsey College of Art so that personal transport could be domiciled as furniture, divested of its internal combustion, separate garaging, and sovereignty in the street.[118]

The car and caravan nevertheless retained the trappings of opaque enclosure. It was soon time to move beyond. In a series of publications, Reyner Banham tried to revive an enthusiasm for servicing that he felt had been prematurely wrapped up in 1948 by Giedion's *Mechanization Takes Command*, which, magisterial though it was in its attention to everyday life, had neglected even to discuss the impact of the elevator on building and urban design.[119] In the later sixties, the advent of tensile and pneumatic structures theoretically permitted ever more diaphanous, amorphous enclosures and disappearances of structure, coupled with ever more powerful servicing. As Banham asked in "A Home Is Not a House," 1965, "When your house contains such a complex of piping, flues, ducts, wires, lights, inlets, outlets, ovens, sinks, refuse disposers, hi-fi reverberators, antennae, conduits, freezers, heaters—when it contains so many services that the hardware could stand up by itself without any assistance from the house, why have a house to hold it up?"[120]

For those objecting that monumental architecture had its own raison d'être as tectonic expression, there was always the authority of the early moderns to fall back upon: Adolf Loos's admiration for the craft of the American plumber, or the futurists for whom servicing was a vital form of expression. But, in truth, the sort of monumental servicing shown in the drawings by the futurist Antonio Sant'Elia of around 1914—and revived to some extent by Louis Kahn's Richards Laboratories (1961), its stacks and shafts removed to corner towers—was not quite what interested the avant-garde of the later 1960s. To return to the organicist metaphor, the body/architecture analogy was the one that captured Archigram and its colleagues: enclosure and servicing as lightweight, antimonumental skin and guts. Geodesic "skin" appeared repeatedly in Archigram work, on Webb's Sin Centre (1959–1963, figure 1.15) and Cook's Montreal tower (1963, figure 1.6), to give a couple of examples. And with the introduction of stretched plastics, architecture could become properly fleshy, as Frei Otto showed the world in 1967 with his West German Pavilion at Montreal.

Otto bestrode two schools, that of tension structures like the one at Montreal, and that of pneumatics.[121] Pneumatic structures were collated by Price for *Archigram* no. 6, where the Pentadome, sequence photographs for the CidAir airhouse, and Victor Lundy's pavilion for the US Atomic Energy Commission were affirmatively stamped "FACT."[122] Ron Herron followed suit in the same edition with his Cardiff Airhouse. Pneumatic techniques had been understood since at least the Second World War but were considered extra-architectural until the 1960s, used for warehouses and temporary shelters. Suddenly they matched the mood of high-performance minimalism—and offered amorphous sources of form diametrically opposed to planar International Style and brutalism.[123] The avant-garde pursued both official sanction for pneumatics (Frank Newby and Cedric Price finding government sponsorship for the 1971 book *Air Structures*)[124] and adoption from the counterculture, demonstrating the way-out, womblike comforts of the "Pneu World."[125]

But Archigram strove constantly toward further dematerialization,[126] toward "the notion of an ultimate in skins: a membrane which is not there. The skin which can be seen through; the skin which can be parent to all within; the skin which can be regularized; the skin which can be treated as an environmental totality."[127] It was an aspiration for immateriality traceable to those futurists and expressionists who had been entranced by plate glass. In *Glas im Bau und als Gebrauchsgegenstand* (1929), by Archigram's friend Arthur Korn, glass was hailed as "an independent glass skin" permitting "the denial of the outer wall that for thousands of years had to be made of solid materials. . . . It is there and it is not there. It is the great mystery membrane, delicate and strong at the same time."[128] Very early on in Archigram's history, Greene's Seaside Entertainments Building (1961, figure 1.14) had transplanted the state described by Korn into an era of nylon, foam, and plastics consumables. With Webb's Cushicle/Suitaloon (1966), as the membrane is pushed out by its occupant "we get close to something very like man-as-a-bat where the skin of the enclosure is dependent upon a system of vertebrae that respond very directly to the nervous system of the person within";[129] the architectural "skin" was now proximate to the body's skin (figures 3.17, 3.18). Webb was soon toying with the eradication of any impermeable barrier, turning

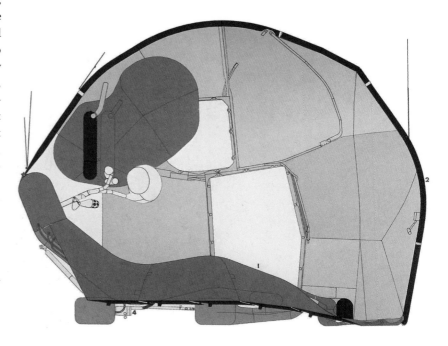

3.17, 3.18 *Michael Webb, Cushicle opened out and in use, section, 1966; and Dave Inside Suitaloon, section, 1977–2004. As portable as a hefty haversack, the Cushicle (air CUSHion VehICLE) was designed as an armature unfolding to provide many of the amenities of the contemporary living room, including television; the Suitaloon was an add-on shell, inflated by the Cushicle to the size of a small room to accommodate its Michelangelesque occupant. The combination offered a variant to Greene's Living Pod (see figure 3.5) or the traditional tent, and it is difficult to envisage its use in an urban setting: Archigram had started to wander open country.*

DAVE INSIDE SUITALOON

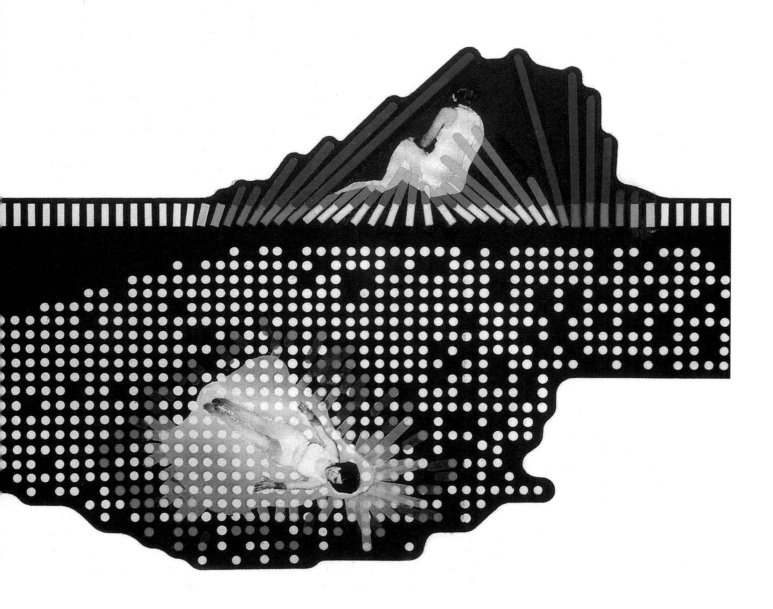

3.19 *Michael Webb,* Magic Carpet and Brunhilda's Magic Ring of Fire, *montage, 1968, redrawn 2004. Possibly the most "immaterial" solution Archigram found to the problem of cosseting the body, Webb's client is here supported by jets of air. The machine's name implies that its user can safely experience the sacrificial pyre of Brünnhilde from Richard Wagner's opera cycle* The Ring of the Nibelung. *Webb's irreverent misspelling of Brünnhilde's name drew on a style of sixties English humor popularized by the Establishment Club and Monty Python.*

toward pressurized air as the medium for his *Magic Carpet and Brunhilda's Magic Ring of Fire* (1968, figure 3.19): "The hovercraft principle in reverse. Tubes blow air at varying pressures to maintain the body in a prone position or to raise it through sitting to the vertical. The tubes can pivot to maintain the body in a static position or to rock it; they can also eject gases for a static or moving enclosure."[130]

This paring away at the "architectural interface," this search for an architecture of instant response so that architecture would be the body's pleasure, not restraint, agreed with Archigram's dismissal of any absolute conceptual boundary between organic and nonorganic systems. "Why People Robots and Trees?" Chalk asked of the title of one of his essays. "It is difficult to separate them, they can be seen to be the same."[131] Archigram was reaching out toward the most active, immaterial, and indeterminate architecture conceivable, a continuous realm of biological-electronic control systems.

SYSTEMS

Less tectonic than its megastructures, less provocative than its inflatables, *Archigram* quietly contemplated the intangible frontier of systems control, variously sounding cautious, euphoric, and resigned to its onset.[132] "Automation affects our way of thinking rather than doing," repeated Archigram's 1966 film as a mantra for the postindustrial mind.[133] The Second Machine Age was beginning, Reyner Banham believed, "with the current revolution in control mechanisms"[134] poised to automate production systems under the direction of computers, removing routine intervention from human operators. *Archigram* no. 4 approvingly noted that the "Recurrent theme in SPACE COMIC universe is mobile computer 'BRAIN' and flexing tentacles."[135] Banham made no mention at this moment of the word computer—so recent was the currency of the word that *Archigram* no. 5 spelled it differently[136]—but the year of *Theory and Design*'s publication also saw the launch of the Digital Equipment PDP-1, the first commercially available transistorized computer.[137]

"For Archigram," the 1966 film announced, "gadgets are less important than the new ability to understand and control a hundred or a thousand different things, all happening at once."[138] Archigram believed it stood at a historical crossroads. "Hitherto individual technologies had impinged separately on society," historian Arthur Marwick explains, charting the impact of technology upon the landscape, work, leisure, and education of Britain since the eighteenth century; "now the concept of one unified technology, based on what its apostles called 'the systems approach,' was beginning to influence every aspect of social organization."[139] Similarly, as Robert Boguslaw put it in a 1965 examination of systems and their social ramifications, *The New Utopians,* "our concern is not with toys, gadgets, or advertising copy versions of a housewife's paradise filled with automated dishwashers and potato peelers. Large-scale industrial, military and space systems are the new utopias that the age of computers has thrust upon us."[140] Archigram subscribed to what Boguslaw skeptically described as the "utopian renaissance"[141] founded upon large-scale command/control systems.

Like the *Archigram* magazine itself, systems theoreticians tried connecting disparate organizations, projects, and intellects.[142] Archigram was a "think tank"[143] unshackled by any one specific agenda except the application of technology to living. For at least one member of Archigram, Ron Herron, systems thinking came naturally; a veteran of the Berlin airlift, he had firsthand experience of one of the exemplars of system design, air traffic control, of which the sophistication at Heathrow was cited in Archigram's 1966 film. Archigram had an empathy for the systems ideal. The principles of "flow" and "organicism," held dear by Archigram, were intrinsic to system design.[144] Archigram's intrigue with the systems concept emerged from their love of adaptable kits: *Archigram* first illustrated the systems idea by reference to a George Nelson Unit House of 1957, presented as the last stage in the sequence of dematerializing architecture on a page in issue no. 3 in 1963: "Bathrooms, bubbles, systems, and so on." And the principle of diversity *Archigram* brought to its evaluation of prefabricated modules, kits, and joints would remain good for electronic control systems: no single system would dominate. Each system would have to evolve[145] to manage "emergent situations," not "established" ones.[146]

In Archigram's world, situations would be most rapidly emergent when they were at their most playful. The moving panel skins of Webb's deliriously complex Rent-a-Wall scheme of 1966 (figure 3.20) would permit the occupant to "change the atmosphere from one of Arabian Nights to Bauhaus simplicity."[147] This was not the managerial-rationalist world envisioned by most systems designers, but one containing so many simultaneous fantasies that nothing less than highly advanced control systems would cope. Webb believed that the systematization of the entire environment would permit the creation of "anything" space, and his 1964 House Project (later known as the Drive-In Housing project, 1964–1966, figure 3.7) was "a preliminary study in the design of automated instructional, servicing and dismantling techniques applied to a large building development," composed from three types of component manufactured from plastic on site: main supporting structural components, floor space panels, and service units (kitchens, bathrooms etc.), the space broken up by free-plan panels, like a pop reworking of Gropius and Wachsmann's General Panel principle.[148]

Archigram's self-styled eccentricity shared affinities with the boffin subculture of systems design. (Boguslaw likened systems design to the crank cartoon world of Rube Goldberg, and the Archigram group drew comparison to Goldberg's British counterpart, Roland Emmett.)[149] But the embrace of systems was not just frivolous; the systems ideal offered a consummate coordination of resources. "We accept the complications thrown up by every aspect of human needs, technological function and environmental control," read Archigram no. 2's "Group statement" in 1962. "Our job is to co-ordinate them as parts of a complete statement to fuse every aspect into a positive related whole."[150]

Coordination-as-design was best demonstrated in William Busfield, Dolan Conway, and Tony Dugdale's Medikit project, published in Archigram no. 9, 1970 (figure 3.21). "Seen against massive population expansion and unprecedented advance in bio-medical and communications technology the pre-Christian concept of 'hospital' becomes increasingly irrelevant," the designers believed. "Medikit is a series of inter-related systems of communication, data-processing, mobile equipment, temporary and/or adaptable enclosures. . . . All the component systems, available by mail order catalogue or through our own staff can be used separately, together or in tandem with your present hospital buildings." Medikit employed ideas of effective time management (the importance of which was often propounded by Cedric Price): "The Medical service given for most in-patient maladies often requires no more than one hour of each day. How long before architects realize that the in-patient day represents a problem in the design of leisure/recreation facilities?" Holistic design would be the acme of experimental architecture: "the situation which can be called experimental will be strategic as well as operational," Cook claimed; "it will involve the design of the process, its economics and its marketing potential as much as the beauty of its detailing."[151]

A metaphor from computing caught the mood. The distinction between the enclosure of space and the operation of space could be compared to that between hardware and software. Archigram no. 8 explained the hardware/software metaphor:

> This oversimplification has the air—and necessity—of rhetoric at a particular moment in history. It is in fact very parallel to Futurist [or] Machine architecture rhetoric. Hardware has limitations. Software is being pitched against it in order to expose [the] architect's continued complete hang up on hardware. On[c]e the thing has coole[d] off [a] little we can get on with linking the two together as response systems. Electronics and the unseen motivation. Deliberate visual contras[t] of the "HARD" e.g.: Monument, New York, wall, machine, metal, plastic, etc: Against "Soft" e.g.: programme, wire, message, instruction, graphic synopsis, equation, mood, abstract."[152]

This line of reasoning wasn't entirely an idiosyncrasy of the Archigram circle. In Architectural Forum in 1966, Edgar Kaufmann Jr. called for an architecture of "serviced situations": "technology is increasingly immaterial, it is increasingly electronic, less mechanical, and the net result is that the imagery of technology readily eludes the designer. . . . The future of design

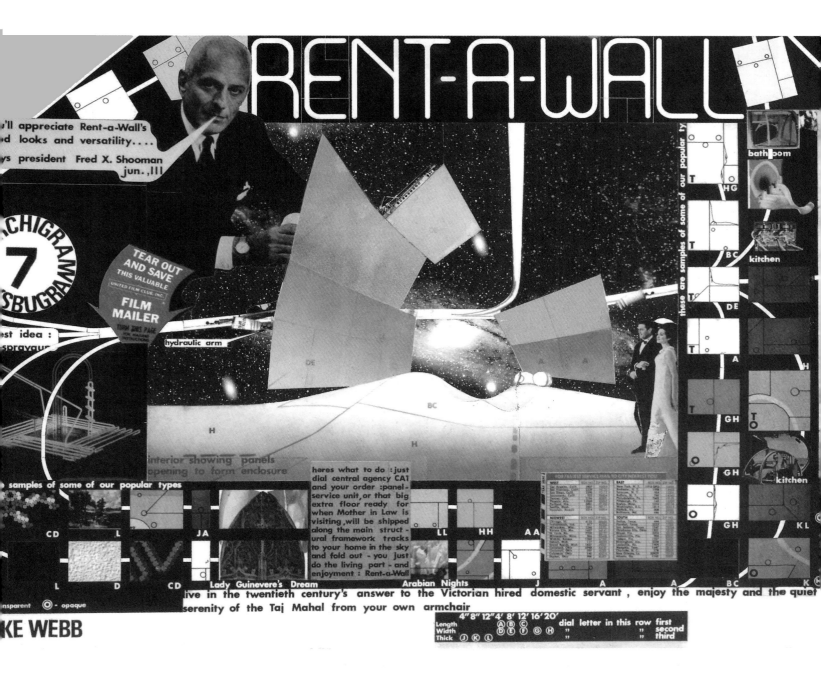

3.20 *Michael Webb, Rent-a-Wall collage for* Archigram no. 7, *1966, redrawn 2004: Speaking through avatar Fred X. Shooman Jnr. III, Webb fantasizes about the future of leased, mail-order architecture to suit the fickle consumer mood. Webb's affectionate spoof of American junk mail is attributable to his relocation to the United States.*

lies in *situation design* and not in production design; products merely implement the situations."[153]

Little wonder that Archigram was so impressed by the transition made by Arata Isozaki in the robotic Theme Pavilion environment he installed within Kenzo Tange's Festival Plaza at Expo '70 in Osaka (figure 3.22). Within a decade, the public would become familiar with the concept of industrial robots, but at this stage Isozaki and Archigram needed to illustrate the difference between machine "slaves" and the "Robbie the Robot" figures of fifties sci-fi. Like Archigram, Isozaki had moved from the concrete megastructure to pure servicing, from hardware to software, but with such audacity. Archigram's Osakagram, a collage of promissory notes shown at Osaka, paled in comparison to the actual delivery of the systems. Isozaki's two giant robots manipulating seating units, gantries, screens, cameras, lights, and enclosures as a controlled unitary system would be imitated in Archigram's own stab at a real large-scale environment, the Monte Carlo project (c. 1969–1973, discussed in chapter 4).

The *potential* of Archigram's projects as the bases for new systems of environmental control had nonetheless been spotted long since, no doubt by Isozaki himself, who hung the Osakagram like a calling card from Archigram in the roof space of the Theme Pavilion.[154] As if egging one another on in the realization of a cybernetic city—always feasible in theory, rather improbable in practice—cybernetic architect Nicholas Negroponte cited Archigram's Plug-In prefabs as the sort of architectural hardware that could be handled by his software.[155] A vision of the cybernetic city of control and communication was contained in Dennis Crompton's 1964 diagram of a Computer City (figure 1.10), and was brought to life in Archigram's 1966 film.[156] "The activities of an organised society occur within a balanced network of forces which naturally interact to form a continuous chain of change. . . . The sensitised net detects changes of activity, the sensory devices respond and fe[e]d back information to program correlators."[157] Computer City regulated the feed and return of traffic into the metropolitan pressure area (a corollary of Plug-In City's Maximum Pressure Area, figure 1.8); as Peter Hall explained with enthusiasm in the book *London 2000*, published the year before, "since 1955, advances in electronics have

3.21 *William Busfield, Dolan Conway, and Tony Dugdale, Medikit project (detail),* Archigram *no. 9, 1970. Disarmingly, the Medikit team propose delivering a hospital through the same mail-order arrangement commended in Webb's Rent-a-Wall scheme (in figure 3.20). The business technique of outsourcing is here anticipated by* Archigram's *conjecture that architecture is a process before it is a plastic art.* **3.22** *Kenzo Tange, Festival Plaza, housing two Entertainment Robots by Arato Isozaki, Expo '70, Osaka. The 1970 Osaka exposition astonished visitors by assembling the architectures suggested in* Archigram's *drawings: Tange's space frame and crumpled, plug-in-style arena housed Isozaki's kinetic structures. Archigram's plans for a comparable Entertainments Centre at Monte Carlo, devised the same year (figures 4.25–4.32), were stillborn.*

made it possible to 'meter' the movements of all vehicles . . . this technique would provide a complete system of traffic control."[158] The "printout" alongside Computer City showed the enormous range of functions being simultaneously monitored in the effort to maintain an urban homeostasis: temperature, transport, goods supply, craneways, levels of self-sufficiency, population, plug-in infrastructure ("ADD CORNER SHOP TP8C FLOOR LEVEL L OVER X POINT 37 CAP 112"), birth rate/death rate, food supply, consumption, recreation, and power supply, among others. "The complex functioning of the city is integrated by its natural computer mechanism," Crompton explained, making an explicit link between the organic and inorganic functioning of his city. "The mechanism is at once digital and biological, producing rational and random actions, reactions and counter-reactions. The computer programme is a conglomeration of rational reasoning, intuitive assumption, personal preference, chance, sentiment and bloody-mindedness which is assimilated and interpreted," he added, describing a "humane" system sympathetic to indeterminate, emergent situations.[159]

Cybernetic architectural visions responded to the "nerve ending" of each citizen, the systems themselves "sampling the environment for cheers and boos," as Negroponte suggested.[160] But a ghost in the machine might be required to coordinate its multifarious systems. Would design decisions be reached by some sort of central planning agency monitoring feedback? Negroponte wondered.[161] For the time being, Archigram and its acquaintances were prepared to make a compromise with such centralized power. In the groovy projection of consumer advocacy (c. 1969) by architect-critic Charles Jencks, for example, the "CIA FBI Pentagon etc. switch to handling relevant information," a utopian role that might have surprised intelligence officers midway through the Vietnam conflict.[162] Webb's "CA1" centralized agency for the Rent-a-Wall scheme, reported in *Archigram* no. 7, was a private outfit: "Here's what you do: just dial central agency CA1 and your order: panel service unit, or that big extra floor ready for when Mother in Law is visiting, will be shipped along the main structural framework tracks to your home in the sky and fold out—you just do the living part."[163]

It made sense to those without a knee-jerk reaction against technocracy. In the late 1960s in the United States, computer networking was directed and funded by the Pentagon's ARPA-NET program, and more than fifty-eight commercial time-sharing computer systems were available, using General Electric and IBM hardware systems. It would make still more sense once something like a household-access Internet service was made available. In Britain in 1967,

The Postmaster General said that within the next 30 years . . . nearly every householder will be linked to a local and national communication network which will enable them to do the following things: control his central heating while away from the house by commanding over the telephone; watch children, etc., with the aid of a TV "eye" while out shopping or at a party; shop without moving out of the house with the aid of a computer; pay for commodities throughout a computer link; receive confirmations and news by teleprinter; consult the local library for information through a picture phone. In fact, new soft transportation technology will give a hitherto unknown degree of freedom.[164]

The service arrived at about the time that the postmaster general predicted, while the architecture meant to accompany it remained in a futurological waiting room.

In the later 1960s, Archigram became preoccupied with this connection point between the system and system user—the interface, the most delicate of architectural boundaries. Cook's Info-Gonks (figure 3.15) reduced the material bulk and physical separation of the interface as the equipment was placed on the user's head. His *Metamorphosis* drawings (figure 3.23) traced and projected this formal development: "1968 straight bits 1970 bending and sophisticating 1975 loosening 1980 and becoming almost ethereal 1985." "Greater number," he felt, meant "mass produced parts used with spirit—which means that a system can be bent—and the parts slowly but continuously evolving— a sensory and responsive rôle and it all gets clearer as it gets nearer the minds within."[165] Minds could be wired together and space dissolved: Herron's associate Barry Snowden contributed

to *Archigram* several projects that explored the use of study stations,[166] such as the Mobile Action Terminal Extension (*Archigram* no. 9), promising the "death of the commuter, the office" (figure 3.24).[167]

Communication, always a central concern of modernism, became an ecstatic condition in Archigram, the breakdown of the architectural interface tantalizingly close in cybernetics, experiments with computer-aided design, and a welter of communications theory. "We are constantly revising the total structure of 'interface,'" *Archigram* no. 8 believed, imploring "if only

we can get to an architecture that really responded to human wish as it occurred, then we would be getting somewhere. . . . Robots, enclosures, facility-machines. Man/machine interface. Information feedback results in environment change."[168] In communications technology Archigram hoped to find the means to engineer the mental, emotional, and associational situations once explored by "Living City." Cook felt that the only drawback to Archigram's own Audio-Visual Jukebox (1969, figure 3.25) was that the programs it showed would be preselected: eventually, he explained, viewers would mix the programs for

3.25 *Archigram,* Instant City: Audio-Visual Jukebox, *montage, 1969. In a social space reminiscent of a diner, youth club, or record store, one pneumatic corner of the Instant City finds young people hanging out with fully enclosed headsets enjoying the audio-visual show.*

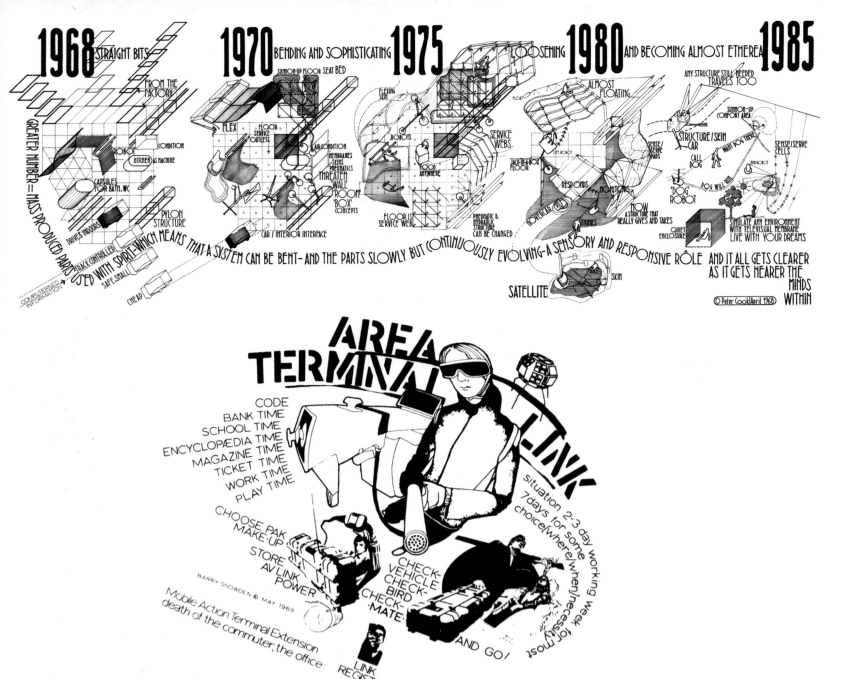

themselves.[169] What Marshall McLuhan anticipated with media, and Timothy Leary engineered through hallucinogens, Archigram hoped to do with architecture: adjust environmental perception. Webb in 1968 proposed "a cavity wall which changes its visual, thermal and insulative properties by means of fluids, gases and silver crystals."[170] In a similar vein Herron proposed the Holographic Scene Setter (1968) and Enviro-pill (1969). "Great . . . switch on the people/turn on the crowd/bring in the whole scene . . . turn off the ceiling."[171]

The ninth and final full edition of *Archigram* was the culmination of trends that had been bubbling under since 1961 (figure 3.26). No. 9's "fruity" interest in gardening had a lot less to do with the ecology movement, in whose direction it nodded (a packet of seeds included with every copy), than with the group's ongoing interest in organicism, cybernetics, and the paring away of the interface. Here, no membranes, nor even computer interfaces, but sensitized plants would detect the gardener's desires. "Not only are the larger problems of Ecology a current conversation," *Archigram* explained in its editorial, "but this arises at just the time when one can see a foolishness in the traditional separation of equipment, facilities, shelter, response-mechanisms."[172]

There was something disturbing about this *1984*-ish evocation of a listening environment, of its attempt to make the environment into a system (rather than insert a system into the environment),[173] and the subsequent collapse of differentiation between the organic and inorganic. Herron provided an interface with services through an Electronic Tomato (a guise for his Manzak personal robot concept of 1969). Greene provided a Bottery, a robotic menagerie illustrated on the cover of *Archigram* no. 9 by Tony Rickaby who explained, "it's all there, moving, changing and sometimes real" (the dog was robotic), "WORK LEISURE HOBBY ENVIRONMENT EARTH . . . losing their identities together in the tangle of OUTGROWTH."[174] This was the ultimate in the organic idea, a joyous fusion of architecture with nature that an enthusiast for precedent could trace back to Louis Sullivan and Frank Lloyd Wright. "WE ARE FOLLOWING OUR DREAMS YET FURTHER," Cook explained at what was nearly the end of the line for the Archigram vision, "and seeing

3.26 Tony Rickaby, Outgrowth, *cover of* Archigram *no. 9, 1970. This illustration of David Greene's "bottery" concept was inspired by the launch of a consumer robot, the Mowbot automatic lawn mower, and by an outdoor leisure market equipped with portable televisions and cool-boxes. It promised an end to the environmental despoilment wrought by buildings, delivering via discreet servicing networks and disguised interfaces the environmental comforts traditionally associated with houses.*

now a gentler softer and more tantalizing environment," as the group moved "into areas where machines and natural forms are together. . . . The Futurist gear of Plug-in-City was necessary at the time, in order to make the statement that 'Architecture does not need to be permanent.' Later this can be simplified to 'Architecture does not need to be.'"[175]

BEYOND IDEOLOGY

Philosophically, two things are striking about the move "beyond architecture." One is the ambition to transcend all social convention (including politics and conflict) through relentless cybernetic modification. The second is the likelihood that, pitched in opposition to the supposed idealism of mainstream modernism (in which pure form was the realization of a social program), the indeterminists were straying into idealism themselves—a belief in the purity of a constant functional "becoming." "In systems of planning," announced *Archigram* no. 8, "we are reaching a point where the statement 'the software' is sufficient to organize the right (control of/positioning of) arrangement of an environment."[176]

Archigram placed the brave new world of systems at the service of Beat lifestyle. Was a cybernetic "control-and-choice" model of the environment capable of guaranteeing participation for all, and could it, in Archigram's phrase, lead toward an "anarchy city"?[177] "Anarchy" is a word commonly corrupted in the English language into a byword for chaos. In this sense, it was barely applicable to Archigram's designs, which set out to *manage* change. The tension between the "anarchy" of modernity and its "management" by modernism, remarked upon at the top of this chapter, would remain at the heart of Archigram schemes like the 1967 Control and Choice project: Cook and Herron's space frame of servicing delivered "as and when needed" through a "tartan grid"[178] of tracks (figures 3.27, 3.28).[179] As its name implied, Control and Choice wrestled with "the inevitable paradox between the *anarchic* and *free* nature of a responsive mechanism for the support of individual people, and the logic of *optimization, standardization* and economics which imply a *control* over what can be supplied for human needs."[180] As *Archigram* saw the conundrum facing the technological beat, "the implication that the whole surface of the World can give equal service is possibly pointing to the time when we can all be nomads if we wish," then immediately qualified the suggestion, explaining that "at the same time the network of support (even if 'soft'—like radio) is still there to be escaped from. At the moment the situation is open-ended."[181]

Archigram sensed the political tribulations of indeterminacy, then; yet its cybernetic projects smiled with an innocent air of political neutrality. This probably derived from Daniel Bell's much-read 1959 study *The End of Ideology: On the Exhaustion of Political Ideas in the Fifties,* which predicted that social decisions would be directed increasingly by local technical-economic factors, not by universal humanist belief systems.[182] In *Archigram* no. 8 Alan Stanton explained the rationale for his "Self-structuring system" thus:

The affluent society[183] *has rejected social and ideological determinism. Technological innovation has allowed the individual to demand and get what he wants. Designers must look to technology as a basis for determinism. For long enough the consumer has been demanding choice in everything he buys. We, as designers, must cash in on this. It's a kit-of-parts, if you want the sociology bit there's an off-the-hook programme. It's up to you.*[184]

The proposal that freedom would be experienced by uninhibited button pushing was contentious even at the time.[185] *Archigram* no. 7 published a cutting by Brian Haynes from *Woman's Mirror,* a popular magazine that was sympathetic to Archigram's work: Haynes explained to wary readers that "in 1966 the range of choice we have in the ordering of our lives is very limited. In 2000 it will be almost total. We shall be entirely responsible for ourselves. In 1966 we may doubt we want this degree of choice. In 2000 we shall see this doubt as that of a slave, freed but asking that his manacles be put back on."[186] Assurances that rational and plentiful distribution would supersede politics prompted critics to recall the warranties issued by Saint-Simon and Comte in the previous century.[187] And critics remembered a fallacy of the vision: commitment to

change unconstrained by the dynamics of political interaction was itself a powerfully ideological stance, probably concentrating power in the hands of technicians avowedly indifferent to ideological constraint.[188] *Archigram* was untroubled: "Indeterminacy is not immoral," *Archigram* asserted, "it is a-moral. . . . There is only really a rule-for-the-job-at-a-moment-in-time."[189]

Thus indeterminacy writhed between left and right. *Archigram* relived Karl Marx's awe at modernity as if from a bourgeois standpoint. Marx:

Constant revolutionizing of production, uninterrupted disturbance of all social relations, everlasting uncertainty and agitation, distinguish the bourgeois epoch from all earlier times. All fixed, fast-frozen relationships, with their train of venerable ideas and opinions, are swept away, all new-formed ones become obsolete before they can ossify. All that is solid melts into air, all that is holy is profaned, and men at last are forced to face with sober senses the real conditions of their lives and their relations with their fellow men.[190]

Archigram:

Whether Religion, Formula, Ideal, Thesis-Antithesis . . . if we really believe that change is for the good, it may imply change in what we believe in. . . . The analogy must be widened to include all parts of a system as being in an evolutionary state. . . . The ability to change is a characteristic of our time. The restructuring and continuous revaluation of things that were reliable, sacred, hierarchic, acknowledged is something that we learn to live with.[191]

Since the industrial revolution, the Western middle class had consolidated itself, geographically and ideologically, within choice urban and suburban residences, close to centers of production and information. By sacrificing this dwelling to indeterminate nomadics, was *Archigram* adapting the middle class to globalization, or liquidating it?[192]

Archigram's sponsorship of obsolescence and deregulation was correspondingly ambiguous politically, pairing antiestab-

lishment overtones with the libertarian dream of the right.[193] Opening boutiques and record labels, zipping around in cars: this was the unconstrained enterprise celebrated by "Living City," and such a potent demonstration of the desire to *participate* in culture that the traditional leftist maxims of orderly solidarity seemed backward. Enterprise spurned the central planning of the Eastern bloc and the tired administration of the welfare state; it challenged class distinction and establishment clout. Pop's automatic obedience to the impulses of popular taste was daring to the point of provocation.[194]

Further to the unanswered questions regarding indeterminacy's politics were the threats it might pose to qualities of "place." As it dispensed with the treatises on "place," written as recently as "Living City" (figure 2.18), Archigram proved unnervingly true to its own maxim of "continuous revaluation of things that were reliable, sacred, hierarchic, acknowledged."[195] Cook admitted that the group's 1967 Control and Choice proposal anticipated the findings of Herbert Gans in *The Levittowners* published the same year,[196] which "accelerated the disintegration of faith in the notion of the intense, piled up,

3.27, 3.28 *Peter Cook and Ron Herron (design), Warren Chalk (drawing), Barry Snowden (drawing, model-maker), David Harrison, David Martin, Simon Connolly, Johnnie Devas (assistant model-makers), Control and Choice Housing study, representing Great Britain at the Paris Biennale, 1967. Throbbing architecture: the build-ing's skin ripples as its gristle of platforms expands and contracts according to the hipster needs and whims of its curiously traditional-looking couples and families.*

dense city" since it "showed that (contrary to fashionable architectural thinking) people actually enjoyed the spread-out suburban environment, and that the mediocrity of the buildings did not worry them."[197] What mattered more to people, Cook now argued, was the convenience of the "unseen networks"[198] of servicing provided by miniaturization, transistorization, and built-in lighting and plumbing in prefabricated units. The city's dense physical presence and carefully honed spaces were replaced by multiplied *fairly significant moments in time*. "This small instant village," Greene explained of part of his Bottery project, "will only exist in the memories of the people that were there and in the information memory of the robot. An invisible village. An architecture existing only in time."[199] If the vision was indebted to Buckminster Fuller (especially the "4D" time-based designs from around 1928, "Lightful" buildings airborne and connected by radio),[200] it also refigured Mies van der Rohe's "less is more" aesthetic, using space-time as a medium: "we get caught up in an abstract delight in the 'nothingness' architecture that this suggests," Cook confessed.[201]

Cedric Price likewise vehemently opposed attempts to design "place." "It is interaction, not place, that is the essence of city and city life," Price wrote in *Archigram* no. 7. "Just as the U.K. is becoming capable of providing an even-spread of invisible servicing, ranging from unemployment offices to natural gas, major current planning proposals with their emphasis on locational concentration seem geared to overload and invalidate such servicing."[202] Price turned to the new American sociology of Melvin Webber that implied urban society is governed less by space than by the "invisible" formation of "interest groups." In the age of the telephone, photocopier, and freeway, many social activities did not require special building provision or symbolic representation. From 1968, Archigram members' personal experiences of Los Angeles, a city introduced to them in accounts by Webber and Banham, provided decisive evidence that culture did not require major spatial/physical concentration. It lent credence to a line of thinking about the subcultural social organization of the city that could be traced from Banham's "The City as Scrambled Egg,"[203] to the "Living City" exhibition,

to Warren Chalk's suggestion that the city revolved around "clans" bound only by "participation."[204]

By the later editions of *Archigram,* its original organizing figures of "place" and "organism" were looking slightly moribund, the threads of civilization in its visions sometimes so baggily woven as to make even labels like "system" and "network" appear nostalgic for cohesion. Archigram's prophecies of a loose-fit society were increasingly detached from the eager connectedness contemporaries saw being generated by technology. "Greece has done it again!" declared Sigfried Giedion in the Delos amphitheater in July 1963,[205] where Constantin Doxiadis had gathered together eminent intellectuals to think laterally about the "network society." But Greece had done little for Archigram, which did not admire the stability of the Greek orders even at a distance; and if it felt affection for the ancient Greek invention of democracy, Archigram was drifting away from the broad humanist legacy. The Delos delegates and the field of ekistics founded by Doxiadis demonstrated that human dwelling was being revolutionized by networks of traffic, aerodynamics, telecommunications.[206] In a less methodical fashion, *Archigram* understood this too, but was ever less disposed to shore up human-to-human contact or plot any more patterns in the effort to make modernity meaningful. Archigram was becoming disinclined to make an unknown and, it increasingly suspected, unknowable world visible and "designable." Price called Doxiadis a "folk-utopian."[207] Media guru Marshall McLuhan was at Delos, looking for his euphoric "global village" of continuous media presence, but David Greene and Archigram eventually contented themselves with their "small instant village"[208] existing only in local memory. Buckminster Fuller himself was at Delos, recruiting curators for a unitary world bound by measured resources, but Archigram was getting engrossed in servicing, consumption, gratification—in hedonism.

At the Archigram-convened Folkestone Conference in 1966, Banham and others nearly sold their audience on the benefits of a placeless *architecture autre*—an "other architecture" evangelically beyond architecture (figure 4.12). But ultimately the Folkestone congregation, brought up in the belief that architecture nurtured community (preferably physical, not virtual communities), harbored reservations. As Robin Middleton (who had known the nascent Archigram in its Euston days) reported for *Architectural Design*,

> *Architects of the future might not be concerned with enclosure[209] at all, or at least not built up enclosures. We could all be floating around in weatherproof space suits, taking "shots" for our feeding or any other physical or mental stimulus that we might require. Somewhere though there would still have to be a horizontal plane, demarked with neon lights if you like, but in some way suggestive of a* place *where we could work out our feelings of community.[210]*

The most impassioned response to Folkestone came in Ruth Lakofski's "open letter," published as a chilling postscript to Middleton's digest.

> *The new will not contain houses, nor yet the city hall. And I'm afraid the new romantic "places" with their visual barriers— hoardings one year, neon the next—will fall quietly by the wayside. . . . Because just as surely as in our new hypodermic world we can have our "shot" against the rain, so we can have our "shot" against contact—all physical contact. For we have the picture-telephone, the closed circuit telly, and the schools of the air. No need to get together for the no-food food. And when at last we have the no-sex sex—a "shot" too perhaps in the dark—we will have cut the natal cord and we shall be free.[211]*

Without doubt, the methods of indeterminacy were culturally ruthless: deprived of the reassurance of habitual spaces, experiences, symbols, and ways of life, people would be *forced* to reinvent culture from scratch. Place would be discovered as found in nature, not prepackaged by design.

The result, Archigram and its associates believed, would be an accelerated social heterogeneity, reversing the well-meaning homogenization with which modernist architectural planning had been saddled. Placeless indeterminacy initiated the search for, and cultivation of, ways of living that were ever more "authentic"

and joyful. In the process, earlier preferred types of model citizens imagined by architects—modernism's "humanist" and "organization man"[212]—were jettisoned by the "individualist." Architecture would do more than serve individual desire: it would actively cultivate it. In an Archigram audiovisual presentation of 1970, repressed, middle-aged suburbanite Norman Jones, married with children, expressed fulsome thanks to Michael Webb's Dreams Come True Inc. for selling him a new custom lifestyle, which as a side effect also released him from architecture's "crushing impact upon human beings."[213] Webb's graphic depiction of joyous intercourse between two wearers of his Suitaloon (1967, figures 3.29, 3.30) similarly illustrated how individuals might be at liberty either to associate with others or to secede from enforced architectural community into a private cocoon.

Here was something reminiscent of Jean-Jacques Rousseau's call back to the good life, a gentle return to wild.[214] Archigram accessorized the drop-out nomadism that began with the beats in the 1950s and carried through with the counterculture of the 1960s and 1970s. Midway through Archigram's Instant City project (c. 1968–1970)[215] for a troupe of "infotainment"-laden trucks and airships (figures 4.1, 4.21, 4.39), the appearance of countryside rock festivals looked like life imitating art. (Mark Fisher, an Archigram-tutored student at the AA, went on to become the preeminent designer of mobile architecture for rock concerts.) A taste for adventure that could no longer be satisfied plugged-in to fixed community would be supported by items from the 1966 Archigram catalogue, such as David Greene's Living Pod (figure 3.5) and Michael Webb's Cushicle (which shrank a fully equipped building into something like a hefty haversack; figure 3.17). Inspired by heroic efforts to inhabit alien environments at the poles and in outer space, this gear seemed a touch overengineered for deployment in Archigram's arcadian dioramas, although the environmental hardships of the Woodstock festival of 1969, bailed out by supplies flown in by the army, indicated the festival's need for decent kit and better systems.

The potential market for the Archigram lifestyle was broader still: Cook straightforwardly located his 1971 Hedgerow Village in "Quietly Technologised Folk Suburbia," snug in the countryside,

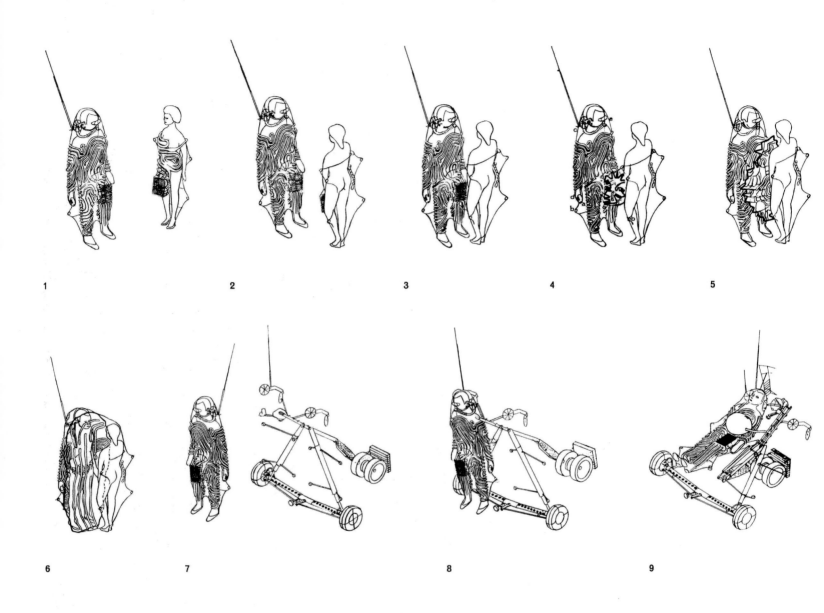

3.29, 3.30 *Michael Webb, Suitaloon, mergence sequence, 1967; Dave and Pat, montage, 1977–2004. In line with the era's sexual liberation, sexuality became a topic pertinent to Archigram's interest in "skin" architecture. Here, a woman joins a man at his Suitaloon bachelor pad, an expanding, possessive second skin inspired by space suits; gregariousness and introversion was a consistent tension in Archigram designs. Stage 6 of the 1967 drawing is depicted in close-up in the later work.*

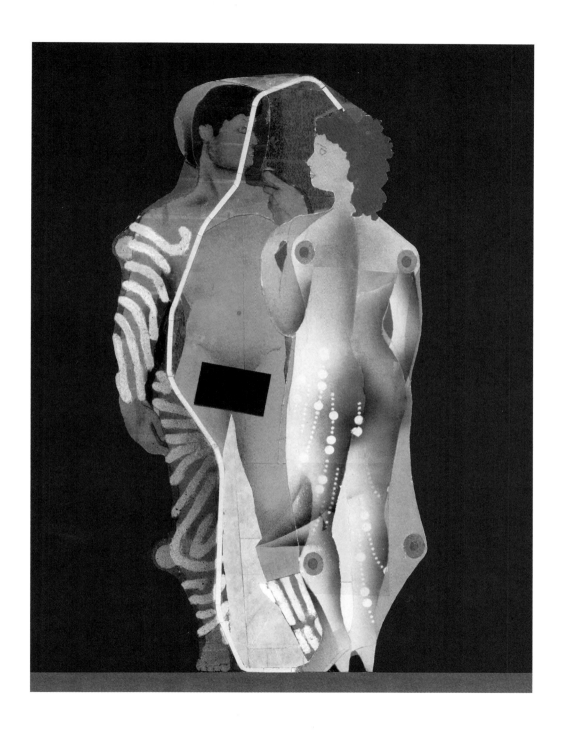

a Frank Lloyd Wright Broadacre City adapted to Middle England (figure 3.31). Archigram's version of nature was a woodland campsite, seen in scenarios like Greene's Logplug and Rokplug (1969), a frighteningly discreet servicing of countryside electrical hookups for voyagers without recreational vehicles (figure 3.32), and Cook's Nomad (1968), an adventure in the grass for an Action Man figurine. "A standard-of-living package (the phrase and the concept are both Bucky Fuller's) that really worked might, like so many sophisticated inventions, return Man nearer to a natural state in spite of his complex culture," Banham wrote to American readers in 1965. "This argument implies suburbia which, for better or worse, is where America wants to live . . . an extension of the Jeffersonian dream."[216]

The technique was to affect a *feeling* of the democratic good life rather than worry about absolute political or spatial freedom.

Freedom need be little more than an electronic illusion. "It might be possible," systems critic Robert Boguslaw skeptically mused on the future of technology, "to modify existing needs for travel and new sights by developing elaborate simulations of green fields, fresh breezes, and quaint people within the confines of the individual home."[217] In *Archigram* no. 9 Cook talked excitedly and enigmatically about a Room of 1000 Delights:

> *The power of the mind has always ranged further than the limits of environment. What is a room? . . . The "container" was a central defining device in the game of architecture. What can it do for you? It can act as a host to the emblems and devices that realise some of your dreams. Now our dreams happen through wires and waves and pictures and stimulant. The interface is between the unlike and the unknown the real and the unreal.*[218]

3.31 *Peter Cook,* Towards a Quietly Technologised Folk Suburbia, Hedgerow Village *project, montage, 1971. One of Archigram's pastimes was to draw out the latent naughtiness of that most conservative of artforms, architecture, and of its middle-class patrons: this time, Cook cross-programs suburbia and wild camping, while a resident sweeps the grass. The gently surreal quality of the scene is aided by the play of pictorial spaces, the painted axonometric of Cook's partitions set against flatly photographic pastoral backdrops.*

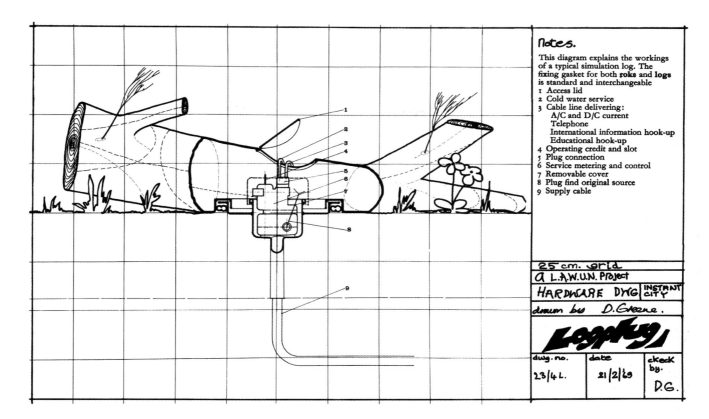

notes.
This diagram explains the workings
of a typical simulation log. The
fixing gasket for both **roks** and **logs**
is standard and interchangeable
1 Access lid
2 Cold water service
3 Cable line delivering:
    A/C and D/C current
    Telephone
    International information hook-up
    Educational hook-up
4 Operating credit and slot
5 Plug connection
6 Service metering and control
7 Removable cover
8 Plug find original source
9 Supply cable

25 cm. grid
a L.A.W.U.N. Project
HARDWARE DWG   INSTANT CITY
drawn by D. Greene.
Logplug
dwg. no.	date	check by.
23/4 L.	21/2/69	D.G.

THE AESTHETICS OF INDETERMINACY

Mainstream modernism invited observers to contemplate the fixed and ideal architectural object.[219] By contrast, Archigram promoted architecture as a complex, dispersed serviced situation, completed only by the active involvement of the observer; in a fully functioning cybernetic environment, in fact, the architecture could become the observer of its human subject. This was the intention. But indeterminate, situational architecture became aestheticized, replacing modernism's dominant aesthetic of fixity. Beauty was perceived in process. Archigram's investigation into cybernetic systems, for example, took pleasure in animation: *Archigram* no. 8 described cybernetician Gordon Pask's dancing robotic mobiles as "An Aesthetically Potent Social Environment," effectively declaring vested interests in art as well as group action.[220] Archigram sincerely wished to initiate "event-spaces" peopled with alternative modes of living, but this ambition transmuted into double representations— images of simulations. And Archigram found architectural form despite the superficial formlessness of indeterminate architecture: whatever the threat to effect the disappearance of architecture, the technical detailing of servicing components was of acute visual interest to Archigram.

Officially, Archigram broke with a "decaying Bauhaus legacy" that had dragged modernism from technology into form, but in practice the distinction between the Bauhaus and Archigram was not so absolute. If the Bauhaus *abstracted* technological forms into architecture, Archigram perceived formal qualities in technology as found. Archigram showed the forms to other architects and demonstrated how to *reassemble* the forms as kits, the very formal articulation of which was their indeterminate

3.32 *David Greene, Logplug project, section, 1968. Greene disguised the terminals of his service networks as natural features, preserving the illusion above ground of an unspoiled idyll. Essentially a serious proposition (utility companies came under increasing pressure to conceal their lines of distribution, and conservationist groups such as the Sierra Club worried about the effects of mass leisure upon natural beauty), Greene nonetheless presents it as a parody of drawing office conventions, flora drawn freehand and free-floating upon the Cartesian grid.*

arrangement; the autonomy of each component spared complete submission to a "higher" visual scheme. In devising a new aesthetic, Archigram architects became "form givers," a slightly unexpected role but historic nonetheless: Archigram is an indisputable source of the new modernism known as high-tech. And Archigram discovered a different typology of techno-form to that used in the 1920s (ships, silos, aircraft, standardization, and so on). Archigram saw beauty in the unheroic, partially hidden technologies of the late twentieth century—air-conditioning, refineries, engines, portable televisions, camping equipment, things made of plastic and nylon, cellophane bags, gaskets, connectors, cables, networks. Archigram was updating the modernist inventory; "we are not trying to make houses like cars, cities like oil refineries, even if we seem to be," Warren Chalk once explained. "This analogous imagery . . . will eventually be digested into a creative system."[221] Archigram recognized formal power in the very antiforms with which Buckminster Fuller tried to repel architectural form, and stepped in to avert aesthetic disaster: Archigram was needed, Peter Cook later claimed, because in their own house Mr. and Mrs. Fuller had failed to prevent "double beds heading for arced walls at high speed."[222]

With the intellectual authority of Banham's *Theory and Design in the First Machine Age* tucked under their arms, the experimental architects of the 1960s officially set out to recuperate the flagging energies of modernism, choosing to sacrifice form to imminence. Services bristled, pneumatics generated wild forms, color-coded components dazzled, stoked by the acid visions that seeped through the arts in the mid-sixties. But, Banham admitted in 1966 about the technological apparitions of Archigram and its kind, "the level of relevance is often only that of form-fondling, round-corner styling, art-work and paint-jobs. It is often more than that, but even if it *were* purely visual and superficial, that would not in itself be contemptible. It does still matter to people what buildings look like."[223] By the late 1960s, Banham was actually backing away from claiming too much for the technological imperative in modern architecture, noting in *The Architecture of the Well-Tempered Environment* (1969) "the avidity with which Modernists, from Le Corbusier

to the fantasists and visionaries of the nineteen-sixties, have stolen forms from other technologies—and hence too the inevitable disappointments when those forms proved neither to guarantee nor even indicate significant environmental and functional improvements over what the older technology afforded, because this was merely that older technology dressed up in borrowed clothes."[224]

There was no doubting that the spatial arrangements and mechanisms of servicing could be used for decorative rather than functional effects. Banham described Bruno Taut's own house in Berlin, 1932: "More than anything else, Taut uses his colours to draw attention to his mechanical equipment."[225] It sounded a lot like the color-coding of Herron's 1972 *Tuning London* series of collages (figure 3.33), in which the architect iconoclastically returned to his own South Bank Complex with a vivid appliqué of hanging gardens, screens, and temporary structures similar to those considered by Renzo Piano and Richard Rogers at the concurrent Beaubourg development. Herron's were necessary to visually animate what was quickly perceived as a gray brutalist monolith, pepped up by the Arts Council in 1970 when it commissioned Philip Vaughan and Roger Dainton's Neon Tower on the roof of the Gallery.

In amplifying Louis Kahn's distinction between servant and served components, Archigram architects and their likeminded colleagues learned to *symbolize* process. "Will 'servant spaces' be the next form of decoration?," Independent Group architect Colin St. John Wilson was moved to ask in reaction to Kahn's Richards building.[226] "Have to do something about these," said Philip Johnson, as he crushed in his fist the balsa wood service towers—similar to those of Cook's 1961 Pressed Metal Student Housing (figure 1.27)—on the scheme of about the same date produced by Richard Rogers and Norman Foster when they were studying at Yale.[227] The irony was that Kahn had wished not to express servicing in his building but to stop it contaminating the interior space.[228] "Simply by being built," Banham reckoned, however, "it legitimised, so to speak, a number of ideas about exposed services that had been floating about in that underground world of student projects and forgotten competition entries"[229] in England, notably the Smithsons' Sheffield scheme of 1953 (figure 1.16)[230] and Michael Webb's Furniture Manufacturers Building (figures 1.11, 1.12). Marco Zanuso's Olivetti factory of 1964, with its clip-on exposed air conditioners using hollow tubular girders as ducts, further differentiated the permanence of structure and the supposed transience of services.[231] And whatever its monumentality, one of the best-known exposés of visible servicing remained for some time to come Chalk, Herron, and Crompton's South Bank Centre, with its separately articulated service and air ducts (figure 1.23). Banham suspected that adverse reaction to the building had less to do with its incidental functional problems, like down drafts, and more to do with its appearance, symbolic as it was of an ongoing revolution in modern architecture and environmental servicing.[232]

Banham described the South Bank Centre's disposition as "romantic" and "picturesque"[233] (a year earlier, he had warned that the English picturesque tradition was always waiting, as he put it, to take its revenge).[234] Archigram's drawings looked lush when compared, for example, to the generally spartan and diagrammatic renderings of Cedric Price, who was otherwise in sympathy with Archigram's cybernetic ideal (figure 1.30). Cook admitted in his 1970 book *Experimental Architecture* that English design experiments were "overlaid with a less than rational tendency toward the picturesque."[235] Cook could see such tendencies in his own work, stressing "the deliberate *varietousness* [sic] of each major building outcrop" in his Plug-In City drawings (figure 1.3): "This city was not going to be a deadly place of built mathematics."[236]

3.33 *Ron Herron,* Tuning London's South Bank *(detail), montage, 1972. Compare with figure 1.24: if the South Bank Centre's impulsive massing had tried to portray a sense of activity, visitors had not generally chimed with it, and in any case Ron Herron's restless imagination would not spare even his own buildings. He returns with a fresh battery of pop devices, admirably unsentimental about his earlier work though perhaps nostalgic for the fading of swinging London.*

Archigram had not cynically used indeterminacy as an algorithm to generate a picturesque aesthetic. In fact, two other interpretations of Archigram's work indicate that the group recognized the problematic interrelationship of the ethics and aesthetics of indeterminacy. It will be seen in a moment that some members of Archigram were trying to kill off visual representation and end the contrivance of style for good. Other members, meanwhile, may have been trying to capitalize on the representational aspect of indeterminacy in order to *merge* the aesthetic with the ethic: when the transient processes of modernization were made visible, the processes would become knowable and enjoyable to architecture's clients.

Even as Archigram announced the disappearance of architecture, in its own projections architecture appeared more profuse than ever—growing, fleshy, luminous, moving. The picturesque traditionally contrived landscapes and cityscapes to induce in observers certain emotional responses, and it looked as though Archigram had ingeniously reversed the procedure, imagining plug-inscapes *produced* by positively charged emotions and their concomitant activities. Were the scenes real, the residue of merrymaking would have become part of the information loop, feeding back the state of play to potential participants. Archigram's picturesque demonstrated flows and processes—and *potential* flows and processes—that otherwise eluded representation. The aesthetics of flowing water had an architectural ancestry from Venice to Fallingwater; architects had revealed the flow of air by flags, weather vanes, and Corbusian funnels. Flows of events, on the other hand, had been more difficult for architecture to depict; the empty space of the city square waiting to be filled with the festive crowd had about it a melancholia unsuited to Archigram.

Flows of information were still more elusive for the architect to present, more so with the steady obsolescence of spinning magnetic tapes and flashing lights, as bits of information proceeded around computer circuits as silently as books stood shelved in a library. "This," warned the archdeacon in Victor Hugo's *Notre-Dame de Paris,* pointing to a Gutenberg book, "can kill that," indicating his church, the great Book of God.[237] But books did not kill buildings, and against the odds Archigram

found a narrative role for architecture in the era of transistorized and wireless information devices too.[238] The architect did not, after all, need to follow monumental architecture into extinction, but could be retained to situate terminals, style interfaces, reveal networks, and package events.

The formal-symbolic properties of indeterminate architecture were probably inescapable,[239] and the architects of indeterminacy repeated the formal idealism of architecture in the very attempt to kill it off. Ethically *and* aesthetically, indeterminacy was leading back to idealism. "If Fuller's philosophy rests on the idea of an 'unhaltable trend to constantly accelerating change,'" wrote architect-critic Alan Colquhoun in 1962, taking on Banham's and Archigram's idol Buckminster Fuller, "he nonetheless, in the Dymaxion House project as in the domes, presents a final form—the image of a technique which has reached an optimum of undifferentiation."[240] And Colquhoun furthermore warned of a latent idealism residing within the very functionalism that underwrote indeterminacy, in which "the architect acts as midwife, as it were, to the forces of nature and bears witness to its hidden laws. He performs no specifically 'artistic' acts, since he is merely the medium through which the technique becomes substantiated," such that architecture would be "not an artifact apart from other artifacts."[241]

Archigram clung to the hope that functional process would short-circuit a conundrum of modernism and "destroy the

3.34 *Archizoom Associati, No-Stop City: internal landscapes, diorama, 1970. The diorama made by the Archizoom group—its name descended from Archigram's— contrived to be stunning and banal simultaneously, part of a critical investigation in Italy into the architecture and ideology of pop.*

dichotomy of the mechanical and the spiritual, of determinism and free will" in, as Colquhoun chided, "a rejection of mediate steps between man and the absolute."[242] Mediate steps were being shed all the time by the most radical thinkers of the Archigram group, Warren Chalk and David Greene. Partly under the influence of Victor Burgin with whom he was teaching at Nottingham, Greene turned to conceptual art, the writings of Joseph Kosuth and Sol LeWitt in particular, for the authority to cease production of drawings and concentrate entirely on concepts of process and system.[243]

There was a clear analogy to be drawn between systems theory and conceptual art's fascination with the serial growth of an idea; Italian conceptual architecture started to parody the resemblance, as architectural concepts were allowed to spawn autonomously in the Continuous Monument and No-Stop City literary/collage projects by the Superstudio and Archizoom groups (1970, figure 3.34).[244] And as the Italians showed, systematic attempts to facilitate spontaneity resulted in structures so unrelenting that they represented anything but a withdrawal of architecture—"the brutalisation of local space," as architect and historian Kenneth Frampton put it.[245]

The lesson Greene took from conceptualism, however, was to cease the quest for some pure and infinite architecture and focus the designer's mind upon the *limitations* of architecture. Greene saw this as the logical outcome of the statement about the rain in Oxford Street made at "Living City": "why draw if rain is more important than architecture?"[246] Greene's tougher approach threatened to undermine the graphic splendor and visual feasting upon which Archigram's empire had been built. As Kosuth was putting it, the visual presentation of experience had in any case been made redundant by the very excess of modernity in which Archigram partook:

> *man in even the nineteenth-century lived in a fairly standardized visual environment. . . . In our time we have an experientially drastically richer environment. One can fly all over the earth in a matter of hours and days, not months. We have the cinema, and colour television, as well as the man-made spectacle of the lights of Las Vegas or the skyscrapers of New York City. The whole*

> *world is there to be seen, and the whole world can watch man walk on the moon from their living rooms. Certainly art or objects of painting and sculpture cannot be expected to compete experientially with this?*[247]

So drawings and building projects began to disappear from Chalk's and Greene's work as they embarked upon the tabula rasa of free-form architectural *thinking,* the purest sort of architectural idealism.

Idealism, that is, in the sense of a turn toward ideas rather than the attainment of perfection. If anything, the intellectual restlessness of Greene and Chalk in particular lent the later Archigram an introspective, even unsettling tone; Greene accepted LeWitt's instruction of 1969 that "irrational thoughts must be followed absolutely and logically."[248] "Architecture is probably a hoax, a fantasy world brought about through a desire to locate, absorb and integrate into an overall obsession a self-interpretation of the everyday world around us," Chalk wrote in an open letter to David Greene in 1966 (figure 3.2).[249]

Idealism veered toward relativism, even dystopianism during Greene and Chalk's inexorable erosion of certainty. Truth, language, and value were all assumed to be relative: "the essence of the process of understanding, the informed overview, unfortunately renders attitudes, beliefs, enchantment, myths, all equally right, all equally wrong," Chalk wrote in the early seventies.[250] The wider *intellectual* transition from structuralism to poststructuralism seemed to be coinciding with Archigram's abandonment of *architectural* structure.[251] The group's later musings courted a final standoff with positivism:

> *The deficiency of words, symbols and visual information is that they cannot communicate experience from one person to another. We can agree to agree, but there remains only mutual incomprehension. You only know what you like or what you know. Yet still there is that desperation of trying to communicate. To reach some understanding of one another's experience and preconceptions we must submit cause and effect to a higher contradiction. We must construct a living paradox which is able to recognize conflict without emotion.*[252]

Humanistic belief in a meaningful culture and its distinction from nature—in the capacity of human beings to make sense of the world and to share that sense with one another, in the very integrity of the human being itself—collapsed in Greene's contribution to the Popular Pak, distributed with *Archigram* no. 8 in 1968, as he succumbed to visions of "Capsulised freak out/Metal to rubber of asphalt ribbons plugged into Vietnam." "In the '20's," he pondered,

> it was all happening on the assembly line. They all got high on industry, liners and Socialism.
> That's all dead, the action's moved on into the delicately tuned transister
> teeny-bopper ears to the highway, K.S.C. [Kennedy Space Center?], the paper packed fizz champagne of the age.
> Coca-Cola, and the magic minds of white-shirted identity-carded men with checkout clip-boards plugged into plasticised cybercircuits.[253]

Particularly disquieting was that Archigram obtained at least as much antihumanist corrosive from the American military-industrial complex as from the Franco-German left. It was as though Archigram had bypassed the political engagement of the sixties, hurtling the group straight from the pop irony of the fifties into the postmodernism of the seventies. As Greene worked through the implications of the zeitgeist, all of human culture, physical and metaphysical, energetic and economic, became compressed into a single layer, a proto-postmodern servicing nexus:

> The organic birth-death-life-earth-heaven-God is no longer valid. Shit. Amplification: 1. It's all service. . . . You merely: take it away, eat it, drive it, fuck it. Scene: religion, parkland, hamburgers, the pill, rentaplane, artmobile, beach, ice, cleanery, tissue, Plug in to any or all. Switch on and be serviced. Finished, full, switch off—doesn't matter because: 2. It's all the same.[254] The joint between God-nodes and you, eat-nodes and you is the same. Theoretically, one node could service the lot. . . . God-burgers, sexburgers, hamburgers. The node just plugged into a giant needery. You sit there and need—we do the rest! . . . Doesn't really matter any more about hierarchy or value systems. Make your own. No need is more important than any other. Wipe your nose, Bach, smell a flower. Plug in and turn on. Because: 3. it's all artificial anyway. . . . The pill and the plastic liver have ended the concern that we are all part of some wonderful inevitable natural process[255]

—succeeding, in that last line, to the ultimate posthumanism, the cyborg, where design and servicing enter the body. The fundamental nonhumanism of systems design[256] was coming a little too close for comfort in Archigram's work, and critical reactions against it will be examined in the final chapter.

4

—

THE ZOOM WAVE

ARCHIGRAM'S TEACHING AND RECEPTION

should Archigram remain a footnote in architectural history, or did it have more than an esoteric effect on the practice and understanding of architecture? It certainly wanted to. Archigram saw its magazine and its attendant symposia as a way of gathering up and encouraging radical architectural ideas both from Britain and around the world. Archigram was a bid to create an avant-garde "school," inspired by the renewing force of the group's drawings. Behind the vaudeville, Archigram was a surprisingly earnest endeavor.

The publication of the "Zoom" edition in 1964 (figure 1.31) established *Archigram* as the leading architectural avant-garde journal and bequeathed a useful general-purpose word to the lexicon of Archigram studies. "Zoom" was a word that became the shorthand for Archigram's composite beliefs in pop, the future, technological innovation, enterprise, indeterminacy, and hyperfunctionalism. Zoom was also the *transmission* of those energies: zoom entailed communication with the general public, with an "invisible university" of architecture students at different establishments, and indeed between members of the Archigram group who, following the disbandment of the Taylor Woodrow Design Group, were usually dispersed geographically and professionally, even after the Archigram Architects office opened in London in 1970. While the Archigram group itself had become effectively closed to new members, zoom was a movement into which other designers could be coopted and it was a beacon to light their path. The broadcast of zoom would be achieved not in a deadly didactic fashion but by more seductive strategies—above all through images.

Archigram architects had, after all, first become known to one another through images, found in the architectural competitions considered to be the best source of new talent (see figures 1.17–1.20).[1] Archigram's exceptional graphic ability permitted the group to communicate virtually nonverbally. "SEE THE ARCHIGRAM EXHIBITION," *Archigram* no. 5 urged, as though rounding up visitors for a circus sideshow, "see much bigger than we dare publish the strange and exotic animal-form buildings . . . see the world of zoom."[2] Archigram assumed the adage that architects learn through images to be true; as Geoffrey Broadbent acknowledged in 1973, "they communicated with an international audience, irrespective of verbal language and at this level, too, they were a part of the Swinging London much as Mary Quant and the Beatles were."[3]

The drawings were sufficiently defined, then, that they could be "zoomed in" upon and explored in detail. A headlong rush, these were not the conjectural sketches typical of avant-garde fellow travelers like Yona Friedman, Constant, or Eckhard Schulze-Fielitz, who invited their audiences to mentally complete the missing specifications. Attention to the structural detail of their imaginary world, Peter Cook and his colleagues felt, was Archigram's competitive advantage when envisaging the future.[4] And yet Archigram did not provide (at least in the published material) what architects conventionally regard as "details"; there were no exploded diagrams of joints, sections through floors, particulars on materials. Archigram was enjoyable for the lay reader. Despite Archigram's rhetoric of technology transfer, the magazine carried little of the technical marginalia found in its own progeny like Clip-Kit and Utopie, and in parallel ventures like Cedric Price's Air Structures.[5] Objections to this oversight would have only impeded Archigram's new architecture. Where technological means were not yet available, it was incumbent upon Archigram's readers to demand or manufacture them.

Even so, Peter Cook later protested, "85% of Archigram projects are immediately buildable using current techniques. Indeed, we were (and are) often irritated by so-called 'ideas' architecture that is buildable by an indefined but all-purpose material."[6] Archigram projects were labeled; they illustrated procedures, and showed every window and every pod. But then, so did the projects of questionable plausibility emanating from science fiction and space agency public relations. Models, improvised in the grand tradition of the British garden shed, furthered the Archigram venture. Like something from the biography of Marcel Duchamp (whose perspectives and peep shows Michael Webb's work sometimes resembled), Webb's

model of the Sin Centre became legendary, its first manifestation supposedly destroyed by an accident on the London Underground; that Webb dismissed this episode as apocryphal only deepened the enigma of the Sin Centre model, reincarnated as if in defiance of the project's censure by examiners for inadequately expressing the structural forces running through its decks.[7]

Mock-ups gave Archigram members a break from the detailing of site work and the turnover of studio teaching.[8] By assembling images, Archigram magazine was providing 1960s architects with a sorely needed source of inspiration. In 1965, Reyner Banham ascribed the power of Archigram to its ability to offer a vision of the future: "we don't want form to follow function into oblivion." Engineers and others working for real with the new technologies may very well have found Archigram unconvincing, Banham conceded, "but practically everyone concerned with architecture as constructed form (including plastics engineers) over-responds to the plug-in vision."[9] He claimed it as the most effective image of an architecture of technology since Buckminster Fuller.[10]

"Archigram's technological and science fiction fantasies do not represent real knowledge about the environment or technology any more than Art Nouveau is a source of botanical insights," argued writer Philip Drew in 1972, before qualifying his bluntness: "Archigram's accumulation of a large body of pattern material inspired by contemporary experience provides an important source of patterns for use by designers seeking to make the leap from programme to form."[11] By putting inspirational images into circulation, Archigram offered a service comparable to Owen Jones's Grammar of Ornament of 1856, Le Corbusier's L'Esprit Nouveau in the 1920s, and the inventories of things seen by Alison and Peter Smithson and Charles and Ray Eames.[12]

Archigram seemed to work out its ideas in public,[13] and publicity would remain the group's lifeblood. Archigram was scolded by its critics for its image-consciousness, but the cultivation of image was a conscious tactic in Archigram's work. Archigram's communicative excess highlighted the moribund condition of conventional architectural communication in the lecture room, planning office, and architectural newspaper. Archigram's uncritical espousal of image was intended to liberate the architectural imagination, bypass the didactic "good design" tastes of the architectural establishment, and, if possible, appeal directly back to the public through mass media.

Modern architecture, Archigram realized, was created as much through magazines, exhibitions, and competition entries as on building sites. And since modernism had always prided itself on being transnational, the image was the prime means for an international communication, all the more so in the age of color photographic slides (offered for sale in *Archigram* no. 7), direct selling, the color magazine, and television. "From around 1830 onwards," wrote Banham in his 1966 article "Zoom Wave Hits Architecture," "architects designed for their fellow-professionals and a blind public. The telly and the proliferation of colour-journalism has altered all that by creating a more visually sophisticated public."[14] Emulating the 1962 coup scored by director Ken Russell and the pop artists with the documentary film *Pop Goes the Easel,* in 1966 the BBC produced Archigram's noisy televisual manifesto, screened on BBC2 the following year,[15] its staccato commentary tapping out Archigram's beliefs about architecture and our way of life.

Archigram's message was urgent (streaming out of the ARCHItecture teleGRAM). Banham and Archigram, it appears, believed that in an age of accelerating mechanical reproduction, images would put pressure on the actual built environment. By inference, the architect could legitimately work in two dimensions, as if this was the truly operative realm of the contemporary world—the realm where the real decisions were made, to be executed in three dimensions sooner or later. The ideological power of representation was recognized in a series of contemporaneous books—Daniel Boorstin's *The Image* (1963) sounded an early alarm, and by the time Marshall McLuhan published *Understanding Media* (1964) and *The Medium Is the Massage* (1967), representation was credited as a key mechanism of Western society. With Guy Debord's *Society of the Spectacle* (1967), representation, indicted as the advanced organization of capital,

was elevated to the political realm. If Archigram members read these texts, they generally disregarded critical implications for Archigram's own procedures of representation—"How to Get Involved Without Understanding McLuhan" was one guide written by Warren Chalk;[16] David Greene's adjournment on drawing may have been the exception. Instead, *Archigram* demonstrated its comprehension of media processing by parodying genres, from the children's comic (*Archigram* no. 7's "cut-out puzzle," for example) to the adult news digest (*Archigram* no. 9's "cover and story by Tony Rickaby," as though the Bottery wasn't pure invention)—all very pop (see figures 3.10, 3.26).

Archigram's publicity architecture was the product of a whole social tenor of the period. Aspiring, glamorous, and self-promotional, it offered architects a taste of the *Blow-Up* lifestyles being enjoyed by London's media industry (featured in Antonioni's 1967 feature film of that name). The *Sunday Times Colour Magazine* recognized in Plug-In City, which it published in September 1964 (figure 1.8), the sort of statement about swinging Britain that was establishing the magazine as the definitive popular guide to lifestyle and ideas.[17] The seven-figure-circulating *Sunday Times Colour Magazine* was a world away from the introvert black-and-white stuffiness of the professional architectural magazines, with their outlook of authority and responsibility.[18] Archigram went for middlebrow media, finding in the stylish, well-designed, popular, consumer-driven magazine an analogue for its own architecture. Archigram wanted to make architecture as desirable as a consumer product. Coverage of Cook's Blow-Out Village and Cage Housing followed suit in a 1966 edition of *Woman's Mirror.* In 1970, the *Daily Express Colour Supplement* felt able to report the immanence of Archigram's Instant City as a matter of fact (figure 4.1).[19]

Archigram was not being passively swept along on waves of publicity. Archigram turned "media" into an architectural medium. Michael Webb, curious to learn whether it was possible to sell a wall as if it was a motorboat, aped advertising's powers of persuasion in the Rent-a-Wall collage of 1966 (figure 3.20). It exaggerated the reality of architecture as a business, increasingly sleek in the hands of the big postwar commercial practices.

Tomorrow's postcard — fantasy fast becoming fact!

Electronic information board   Restaurant and cabaret   Dancing   Exhibition and play area   Light/sound response tents

A city of fun in one wrapper

By NORMAN LUCK

ENTHUSIASM for those magical two weeks by the sea starts with those with whom the heavens open and you are sent scurrying for a tea shop on the promenade.

Several cups of tea later it is still pouring down and the children are getting restless. Is this your idea of holiday bliss?

Now the planners have an answer to all this. They have dreamed up an "Instant City" — an entertainment packed idea shrouded entirely by a vast polythene-type wrapper.

Like a giant travelling circus it transforms a rain-drenched holiday resort into a swinging holiday playground overnight.

The vast city can be sited anywhere. Survey teams have visited Bournemouth and St. Helens tooling reaction and finding out just how they tick.

LIVE CABARET

Huge pneumatic tents, towering gantries and batteries of microphonic equipment mobilised to a fleet of 20 or 30 lorries arrive in the town.

In rain or shine the "plug-in" city will operate like a sixteenth-bus-fair offering nightclub entertainment, live cabaret, computerised bingo, exotic restaurants, and free variety shows from a giant stage.

With blazing neon, heating, and multi-coloured advertising gantries which will act as windbreaks, the new holiday scene would rival even Las Vegas.

MORE ADVANCED

Even more advanced plans for the "Instant City" cater for your everyday needs. Shopping is made easy by calling at a luxurious electronic supermarket.

Dial out your list on a video-link with the "warehouse" and in the time it takes you to drink a

They're digging in Monte Carlo next year . . .

HOW WOULD you fancy a beach paradise where at the flick of a dial you can get anything from a suntan to an ice-cold drink or a 'phone link to tell the folks you have arrived safely? This is what they are starting on in Monte Carlo next year and it could happen in Britain.

The resort of the future could be a sophisticated electronic holiday playground complete with a thermostatically-controlled climate.

LAST WORD

An all-in holiday by computer will be the last word in luxury — with out moving "of the beach."

Holiday breakfasts will advertise your own 3 yards-square plot of grassy beach with a robot "beach attendant", at your finger tips.

If you have an ambition to learn, visit the student centre where by computer-cramming a working knowledge of French can be yours in three days.

Everything is possible in the "Instant City" according to the planners. And they hint "this is only the start."

ultra-violet heat lamp on your beach canopy can be programmed to vary if the sun gets too hot or the weather turns cloudy. Telephone? Dial into the national network. Television? your favourite programmes are yours for the asking.

COMPUTER

The secret of it all is the giant underground computer which obeys your every command. You hire a holiday pack — a gadget which looks like a parking meter — and plug it into a service hole on your plot.

A touch of sunburn? Dial up some soothing lotion. A slight ache? Programme the computer and a relaxing massage will be at your service through a special vibrator attachment.

The seven men of Archigram Ltd — all lecturers in architecture — formed themselves into a partnership eight years ago with the idea of "tuning up" Britain.

Their futuristic plans have already won them a 10,000 dollar - a - year research grant from the Graham Foundation in Chicago.

IDEAS

And still the ideas are flowing.

Planners are even working on wonders under the beach. Walk a few yards from your rented plot to a concealed escalator and you are whisked 100ft below ground into a mammoth leisure emporium. Nothing, it seems, is impossible.

WHAT THEY SAY . . . THE MEN WHO DREAMED IT ALL UP

DENNIS CROMPTON, 35, lecturer at the Architectural Association, London: "Holidays in the future will be taken all the year round. With climatic adjustment and better resorts the individual can expect better service."

MIKE WEBB, 32, lecturer at Virginia Polytechnic Institute, South Carolina, USA: "We are heading for an age when the system will adapt to the individual. The time will come when people will take their holidays at work."

COLIN FOURNIER, 25, lecturer at the Architectural Association, London: "Computer science will bring changes in the type of holidays people take. The mass appeal of the service should keep costs within reason."

PETER COOKE, 34, lecturer at McGill University, Montreal: "Individuals will become flexible and could favour spending their leisure fortnight at home — as long as the feeling of having had a holiday is experienced."

WARREN CHALK, 42, lecturer at the Architectural Association, London: "The future holds a chance that traditional holiday resorts by providing better hardware. Bigger and better Blackpools do not make better holidays."

DAVID GREENE, 33, lecturer at Nottingham School of Art: "I think holidays of the future will not be devoted to providing only the essentials. More and added by electronic science go through the motions of a holiday."

RON HERRON, 39, lecturer at the Architectural Association, London: "Seaside resorts is the next step. You will be able to stay at home and added by electronic science go through the motions of a holiday."

And there's more coast to coast fun and action on the inside pages

---

DAILY EXPRESS

NOT TO BE SOLD SEPARATELY

EXPR
COLO
TODA

THE ALL-IN HOLIDA

Television screens   Balloon tower   Ice rink   Musicdome   Show-ring   Revolving bars

Don't hunt for the sun, just dial it!

By NORMAN LUCK

THIS COULD be your holiday of the future. Half of it is fact already.

The "Instant City" (shown across the two pages of this Express Holiday Special) could be put up at Blackpool, Bridlington, Scarborough or any of our major coastal resorts — in fact surveys have already been carried out to test the effect on Bournemouth.

On the right is the fact. At least it will be fact in 1971 when it gets its first showing at Monte Carlo.

This is the "holiday pack" — a gadget that works like a parking meter. All you do is plug it into a plot of land that you rent and luxury is at your fingertips — without even moving off the beach.

PRAISED

These ideas have been dreamed up by a group of young architects in London — Archigram Ltd — who won an international competition organised by the Principality of Monaco to "tune up" the resort.

Their success has been praised by the Royal Institute of British Architects. A spokesman said: "We find this success of the Archigram group a very encouraging pointer.

"For such a young and adventurous group the Monaco project should prove to be a particularly rewarding challenge."

ENJOY EVERY DAY OF YOUR HOLIDAY WITH THE EXCITING DAILY EXPRESS

4.1 *"The All-In Holiday," Daily Express Colour Supplement, 27 July 1970. The middlebrow British Daily Express was one of several newspapers to give its readers a taste of Archigram's media-friendly avant-gardism. Here the* Express *features one of the group's major projects, Instant City, in which blimps and trucks deliver temporary, high-life entertainment even to the most dormant of communities. The vision edges closer to realization with the Monaco project featured at lower right (compare figure 4.26).*

When *The Sunday Times Colour Magazine* returned to Archigram in 1965,[20] it was to sponsor an audacious turn in Archigram's sales technique: a mock-up of a Plug'n Clip unit (reworking the capsule concept) that was put on display at Woolands store in London (figure 4.2). Woolands was the first of the traditional Knightsbridge department stores to react to the trendsetting King's Road and Carnaby Street boutiques;[21] in return for exhibition space, Archigram brought another futuristic vision to Woolands, and the attention of *Sunday Times* readers. Two years later the direct competitors of Woolands and the *Sunday Times* recruited youthful consumers the same way, when the august Harrods store displayed the "Living 1990" diorama commissioned from Archigram by the *Weekend Telegraph Magazine* (figure 4.3).[22]

From the start, with "Living City," exhibition projects constituted a mainstay of the group's realized work, not a sideline.[23] Such opportunities had been seized by modernist pioneers in the past. "Living 1990" at Harrods more modestly offered an insight into new patterns of habitation that Le Corbusier had set out to achieve with the Pavillon de l'Esprit Nouveau (1925). Archigram's skill at creating exhibitions entailed a synonymity between display design and architectural design, Cook and Herron's Instant City projects looking very much like traveling shows. The group's expertise in exhibition design became recognized by external clients. The Central Office of Information employed Archigram for its exhibit at the Louvre in 1970, and in 1973 Herron and Crompton created a permanent exhibit for Malaysia at the Commonwealth Institute (figure 4.4).

Spectacular and live kits for exhibitions allowed Archigram to move from reproduction to small-scale construction. Nonetheless the Archigram group seemed content, most of the time, to stick to images: images that referred to themselves rather than buildings built or seriously projected, images whose prime aim was to shock conservative observers of architecture and delight others, images that promoted the group. The paring down of Archigram's architecture to an image threatened to emaciate its intellectual reputation in the process. Alternatively, it could be recognized as a logical outcome of Archigram's "dematerialization" of architecture, and as a strategy that

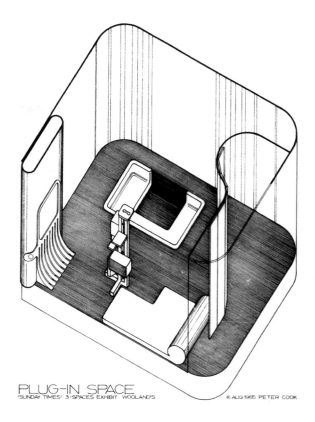

PLUG-IN SPACE
'SUNDAY TIMES' 3-SPACES EXHIBIT WOOLAND'S   © AUG 1965 PETER COOK

4.2 *Peter Cook, Plug'n Clip room set, Woolands store, London, axonometric, 1965. Archigram's simple, clip-together living room, descended from Buckminster Fuller's Dymaxion Bathroom (figure 3.11), lent the nineteenth-century Woolands department store a boutique chic.* **4.3** *Archigram, "Living 1990" display, Harrods store, London, 1967. Archigram's public relations momentum was maintained by the "Living 1990" installation at Harrods, a mocked-up pied-à-terre maximized for comfort and convenience by featuring instant and disposable food and clothing, two robot servants, retractable and inflatable furniture, and a "hoverchair" (whereby personal transport was coopted as furniture).*

would be deployed by an ensuing generation of postmodern architects and urbanists.

Zoom imagery represented modernity even more dynamically than the "vision in motion" that had thrilled modernist audiences in previous decades.[24] "Vision in motion" was ultimately determined by a nineteenth-century mechanical tempo; zoom valued the "postindustrial" tempo of information technology, television, consumerism, and jet travel. Archigram's efforts to respond to a quickening cognitive pace joined those of Le Corbusier and Charles and Ray Eames. "Living City" was unfavorably compared to Le Corbusier's light/sound show for the Philips pavilion at the Brussels world's fair in 1958,[25] where five hundred visitors at a time (duly ejected at the end of the ten-minute show) had been subjected to careening images ranging from concentration camps to cinema monsters to Le Corbusier's own designs, set to music powered by four hundred amplifiers.

Le Corbusier wished to create a "coherent whole"[26] in his *Poème électronique,* and the Eameses carefully studied methods of sequencing between seven screens for their best-known presentation, *Glimpses of the USA,* shown in Moscow in 1959, so as to maintain a rhythm without overwhelming the viewer.[27] But in light and sound shows like *Beyond Architecture,* assembled from 640 slides at the Oxford Museum of Modern Art in 1967, Archigram wanted to *deluge* the audience (figure 4.5). Martin Pawley recalls the atmosphere at the tenth-anniversary performance of Archigram's prepackaged lecture, the *Archigram Opera,* in the cramped lecture hall of the Architectural Association: "May 8 1975. 5pm. The biggest audience for a lecture at the AA for a long time. . . . The opera, a production that had once seemed extravagant when it used two slide projectors, now boasts a tower of stacked tables and a battery of six or eight, plus tape players, mixers and king-size speaker cabinets." And then the *Opera* explodes to a soundtrack by Pink Floyd, the zoom band of choice—two of its members had been student architects, and as the technical designer for Hornsey College of Art's Light/Sound Workshop, Dennis Crompton worked with Pink Floyd at a 1967 festival in Brighton.[28] Crompton again bombards the audience with images of Archigram's personnel, heroes, sources, and visions: "It is impossible to take notes after 10 or 20 minutes.

The noise, the people, the agony, the ecstasy, the overwhelming impression. The heat. It is a solid hour before the slides and music let up and an intermission is called."[29]

It was a visual-architectural stream of consciousness. In a 1973 edition of the *Architectural Association Quarterly,* Geoffrey Broadbent (given to the precise semiological disassembly of architectural communication) likened Archigram's shows to "that curious gobbledygook which so appeals to disciples of Fuller, Soleri and other visionaries." Nonetheless in the confession that followed, Broadbent confirmed the power of such poetics in inspiring students, which was one of Archigram's aims in doing its thinking in public, through teaching, images, and journalism.

4.4 *Dennis Crompton and Ron Herron for Archigram Architects, "Instant Malaysia" exhibition at the Commonwealth Institute, London, 1973. Archigram Architects after* Archigram *had ceased publication: slick, professional design with a flair for image, and looking for opportunities to innovate. The supergraphics led the visitor to a sealed capsule in which the heat and humidity of the tropics could be artificially experienced.*

With disarming frankness, Broadbent compared Archigram mode to the worst lecture that he himself had ever given, which

burbled on in this vein. Yet the organiser told me afterwards, "They loved it, thought it very profound. They'd understood every word of your previous lectures, and thought you were patronising them." One could never accuse Archigram of that. Few people, outside the charmed circle of architects and students, could even begin to understand their recent exhibition at the ICA [1972]. But they were cheered up by the graphics. No need for Archigram to salute respectfully in the direction of Roy Lichtenstein,[30] he should have been saluting them.[31]

In 1974, the latest theories from the "charmed circle" were committed to the screen once more, the stream of images now running at speeds too great to be assimilated by the viewer, and set to the hip jazz-funk of Curtis Mayfield and Herbie Hancock. The effect, however, had moved from euphoria to contemplation. The cool rush of American architectural transience was interspersed with a quiet "Moratorium on Buildings," carried out by David Greene's 1974 teaching unit from the Architectural Association and videotaped around the environs of Bedford Square.[32] The shift in mood reflected more than Greene's personal introspection. It suggested that Archigram's love affair with the image had caused an ambiguous relationship with

4.5 Archigram, Beyond Architecture, *poster, Oxford Museum of Modern Art, 1967. The publicity for Archigram's road shows forewarned of the sorts of images that would deluge the visitor—pictures of* Archigram *magazine, hovercraft, Cook's Plug-In City, Webb and Greene's Thing, and diving bells.*

actual buildings. Archigram's images were a sort of architecture—that of a perpetually deferred alternative state, as if the ultimate outcome of zoom would be a virtual architecture beyond the media of concrete and paper alike. "The printed page is no longer enough: ideas and situations now involve movement and sequences that need film, colour, magnification and explanation in length: magazines will dissolve into hybrid networks of all media at once," *Archigram* no. 7 announced.[33]

By the mid-seventies, Archigram's work really had left the realms of habitable architecture to become pure imagery. During the interval of the 1975 showing of the *Archigram Opera*, Peter Cook began "circulating through the audience like an old pro," "a bunch of Magic Markers in his hand"—those fat, color-filled bullets, recent additions to the Archigram arsenal that zoomed up the drawing process like Zip-a-tone had done a decade earlier.[34] Cook was ready to fill the remaining couple of hours of the evening by drawing until "the paper screen is in shreds, multicoloured sketched to pieces." Martin Pawley saw the future of Archigram: "There will be no more blowtorch engineering or modern masters. Archigram has been outside the air-raid shelter of art history for long enough. . . . For just as old Archigram was to Zoom, so will new Archigram be to the gallery circuit."[35] Cook indeed had opened a gallery, Art Net, as the Archigram office prepared to wind down.[36]

Certainly, Archigram's pictures are "artistic" to the point that it is possible to describe their stylistic development. The technical illustration/comic strip manner of around 1964 (for instance, figure 1.10) evolved with the introduction around 1966 of Archigram's characteristic collage method (for instance, figure 3.16). Collage affected the pictorial space of Archigram's pictures, which now played with the collision of flatness and depth to create hallucinatory, surreal illusions (for instance, figure 3.31). The multiple viewpoints afforded by the pictorial space also implied a simultaneity of events, reinforced by the increasing narrative content of the pictures,[37] texts weaving through the architecture with the urgency of a thirty-second advertisement slot (for instance, figure 3.27). "Bandwidth" was further filled out with intense coloration by 1968–1969—maroon, scarlet, yellow, and fuchsia capturing the psychedelic hour

(for instance, figure 4.37). The artist Tony Rickaby was hired to assist with Archigram's renderings (see figures 4.29, 4.32).[38] The borders, sweeps, and stenciling of Archigram's work in the late sixties picked up the art nouveau and art deco revivals fashionable among London's boutiques.[39] Collage's share of the picture surface now equaled that of architectural drawing, inviting a cast of ecstatic baby boomers to enjoy Archigram's equipment and screens that projected the multichannel imagery of the McLuhanite global village. A monitor in one typical Archigram piece of 1968, Herron's *Urban Action—Tune Up,* was screening the Beatles's *Yellow Submarine* movie of the same year, tacitly acknowledging the curious stylistic parallels between the two (figure 4.21).

ARCHIZONES

The bombardment of images was ethical, in a way: if the architectural establishment wasn't prepared to give new audiences new ideas, *Archigram* was. Zoom was getting a sluggish response from established British architectural journals, and self-promotion took up the slack. No sustained attention was paid by the major journal, the *Architectural Review,* until 1973, some four years after Archigram had made the transition to working architectural practice, and six years after even the *Royal Institute of British Architects Journal* had registered the existence of the domestic avant-garde.[40] *Architectural Design,* which would prove to be Archigram's greatest platform, and which in its relaxed page design from the late 1960s to the early 1970s distantly echoed *Archigram,* waited until November 1965 before publishing a landmark survey of Archigram projects.[41]

And *Architectural Design* was always regarded by the schools and profession as a suspiciously bohemian journal anyway, appealing to a foreign as much as a domestic readership.[42] *Archigram*'s audience was, likewise, international as much as it was domestic, and the territorial spread of the zoom gospel can be charted. With Archigram's success touring the "Living City"[43] and *Archigram Opera* began the long run of exhibitions and conferences that spiraled ever further afield, with the Control and Choice stand at the 1967 Paris Biennale, the Soft Scene Monitor for Oslo in 1968 (figure 4.6), the Milanogram at the 1968 Milan

Triennale (until the show's disruption), and the Osakagram at Osaka's Expo '70. Osaka, a confluence of metabolism and Archigram-primed pop/populism, was the spectacular crest of the zoom wave, a capsule-, inflatable-, and robotic-filled page from *Archigram* made real: whatever the modesty of the Archigram group's direct contribution at Osaka,[44] *Archigram* the magazine had been effective in conveying zoom globally (figure 3.22). In 1964, *Archigram* no. 5 printed cuttings about itself from Sweden, Italy, and France;[45] thereafter publications about *Archigram* hugely proliferated, reaching as far as Japan in 1967, Cuba in 1969, and the Soviet Union in 1970.[46] In 1964 it was already finding an international distribution through bookshops in Paris, Chicago, Los Angeles, Helsinki, and Stockholm;[47] by 1965 it was

advertising its price in francs and cents as well as sterling, boasting David Greene as its "American editor"; and four years later it had found distributors in New York, Berlin, and Florence.[48] Mainly through contacts in schools of art and architecture worldwide, the handmade *Archigram* magazine soared from an initial distribution of about two hundred copies to a thousand with the "sci-fi" hit *Archigram* no. 4, then kept climbing, "1500, 2500, 4000 to a giddy 5000,"[49] all completely sold out until the ninth edition, which suddenly saw *Archigram* remaindered.[50] This major print presence was consolidated through mass-marketed books: Peter Cook's *Architecture: Action and Plan* (London and New York, 1967, reprinted Milan and Tokyo, 1969) and *Experimental Architecture* (New York and London, 1970). The group's "retrospective," *Archigram,* was published in 1972.[51]

Zoom had been greatly inspired by North American culture, yet its reception back across the Atlantic was inconclusive. "It is no accident," *Archigram* no. 9 admitted, "that so many Europeans (such as all the contributors to this Archigram) have been inspired by the experience of the United States. It is still a place where things are done—not just talked about."[52] In 1965, Minneapolis-based *Design Quarterly* provided the first platform for Reyner Banham's "A Clip-On Architecture," an apologia for Archigram-type architectural indeterminacy, consolidated by Archigram's own "History of Clip-On" in *Architectural Forum* that November.[53] Banham had arrived in Chicago the previous year carrying in his luggage six copies of *Archigram*'s "Zoom" edition for general distribution (see figure 1.31),[54] and, beginning in 1965, every member of the group except Crompton taught in the United States during Archigram's heyday, notably at Virginia Tech and the University of California, Los Angeles.[55] US coverage of the group had started in 1964 in New York's *Architectural Forum*,[56] then under the editorship of architectural critic Peter Blake: "Archigram struck and the world hasn't been the same since. I took off for Cape Kennedy."[57]

Blake did not however take many Americans with him. Archigram was not American; Archigram had a *perception* of America, at least until its members belatedly visited and resided in the place. The same had been true for members of the Independent Group, some of whom (Colin St. John Wilson, Alison and Peter

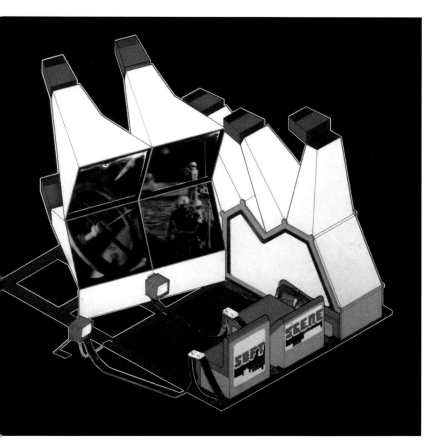

4.6 *Peter Cook and Dennis Crompton for Archigram, Soft Scene Monitor (axonometric), Oslo, 1968. Like Le Corbusier and Charles and Ray Eames, Archigram investigated a "media architecture" in which space was less made than represented, through images and information.*

Smithson) were not even particularly enthused when they returned home. "Americana" was more pungent when distilled through European and Japanese newsstands, cinemas, and television sets. The costs of the American consumer economy, meanwhile, were partly hidden from British observers honeymooning with the United States's mobile lifestyle. "The trouble with Reyner Banham is that the fashionable sonofabitch doesn't have to live here," complained one Los Angeles critic about Banham's delight in the city in 1972.[58] Archigram's elation in the work of the American Buckminster Fuller, and in the American culture of expendability, was regarded as a little bizarre by American architects searching for monumental expression.[59] Since Adolf Loos and Erich Mendelsohn, it had often taken a European eye to discern the "poetry" of American technology; latterly, the air-conditioning units and aluminum-paneled trucks were of greater interest for visitors than for residents of the States.[60] Demarcation between "architecture" and "engineering" ensured the post-Archigram high-tech style a low-key reception in the United States in the 1970s and 1980s.

Peter Blake nonetheless alerted American architect John Johansen to zoom iconography "and *his* life was changed a bit too."[61] Explicit visual references to zoom architecture appeared in Johansen and Ashok Bhavnani's Mummers Theatre, Oklahoma City, 1966–1970, looking like a cross between the South Bank Centre and Ron Herron's Walking City (figures 1.22–1.26 and 1.32), its elements connected by a mixture of ramps and tubes, the "provisional" quality of metal decking and diagonal connectors juxtaposed with the monumentality of reinforced concrete "pods" (figure 4.7). The "color-coded" exterior in its green parkland setting also recalled Archigram's vision of the building as a machine on the move; in detail, the design anticipated the flexibility pursued by Archigram at Monte Carlo (discussed below), with seating, lighting, and entry/exit points readily rearrangeable. An early advocate of a participatory architecture exceeding the "social norm," Johansen was already of a mind with the indeterminists, associating his architecture with "uncertainty" and "relativity."[62]

Johansen espoused his beliefs in *Perspecta,* the student magazine of the Yale architectural school, a centre for initial

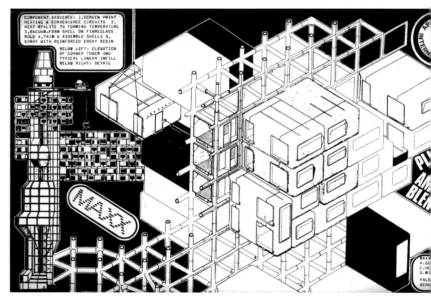

4.7 *John Johansen and Ashok Bhavnani, Mummers Theater, Oklahoma City, 1966–1970. Had the South Bank Centre (figures 1.22–1.26) been designed just a few years later, this is what it might have looked like, the concrete mass lightened by color, metal decking, and flying walkways in the manner of the later Archigram. Instead it fell to Johansen and Bhavnani to adeptly convey the sensation of a building and its users on the move.* **4.8** *Arthur Golding, Craig Hodgetts, and Doug Michels (Yale School of Art and Architecture), Maxx project,* Archigram no. 7, December 1966. *This scheme was derivative of* Archigram's *from 1964, but was supplied with a short technical description more typical of Yale than* Archigram. *Its key significance, however, is as evidence that* Archigram's *ideas were being picked up in the United States, planting a seed for American experimental architecture.*

to work out . . . the fantasy . . . of the Dome. This was going to be a great geodesic dome on top of a cylindrical shaft . . . the dome would have a great foam-rubber floor they could lie down on. Sunk down in the foam rubber, below floor level, would be movie projectors, video-tape projectors, light projectors. All over the place, up in the dome, everywhere, would be speakers, microphones, tape machines. . . . People could take LSD or speed or smoke grass and lie back and experience what they would, enclosed and submerged in a planet of lights and sounds such as the universe never knew.[66]

Reminiscent in its formal description of Cook's Montreal Tower of 1963 (figure 1.6), something of the Kesey vision would be mocked up in Archigram's "Living 1990" diorama (figure 4.3), complete with its cushioned floors, and then reoriented toward the West Coast "heads" scene by Ron Herron in 1968–1969 with the Holographic Scene-Setter and Enviro-Pill. The multimillion-selling *Whole Earth Catalog,* published out of Santa Cruz by Prankster associate Stewart Brand, promoted Archigram in 1971 as "the 'Captain Billy's Whiz Bag' of architecture, with lots of imitators by now and still no equals."[67]

In 1967, Warren Chalk became a visiting lecturer at the University of California, Los Angeles (UCLA),[68] where he was joined in the winter of 1968–1969 by Ron Herron and then by Peter Cook. Archigram acolytes soon sprang up around the Department of Urban Design at UCLA (figure 4.9). "Envirolab" and "Chrysalis"—centered around British visiting students Denny Lord, Chris Dawson, Alan Stanton, and later Mike Davies, "cronies and ex-students of [the] Archigram Group"—became Archigram's "US Associates,"[69] creating Mylar domes for the artists collaborative Experiments in Art and Technology (EAT) at the Pepsi Pavilion at Expo '70,[70] and for the 1970 movie *Myra Breckenridge.* Envirolab's designs for mobile audiovisual units around Los Angeles, realized as a Video Van lending out motion picture gear free of charge,[71] added detail to a vision of the Instant City that Archigram taught at UCLA, backed by the funding and prestige of Chicago's Graham Foundation.

Archigram members were teaching at UCLA alongside Arata Isozaki (see figure 3.22), which epitomized the international

American interest in Archigram on the East Coast. In 1967, a briefing on "Amazing Archigram" erupted across the usually tidy pages of *Perspecta,*[63] after the Maxx project—"plug-in American blend"—was submitted by Yale architecture students Arthur Golding, Craig Hodgetts, and Doug Michels to *Archigram* no. 7 (figure 4.8).[64] Michels became a founding member of the group Ant Farm, at the forefront of American experimental architecture from 1968.[65] Ant Farm set up base in San Francisco and zoom too gravitated to the West Coast, which was exactly where it needed to be, integral to the general remaking of culture fueled by the student and acid revolutions.

Swinging British pop culture and the West Coast dropout scene made for a surprisingly good match. Archigram's drawings imported the psychedelic colors and lettering of an acid melee, also intent upon "electrifying" the environmental experience. Among the acid ventures of Ken Kesey and the Merry Pranksters, recorded by Tom Wolfe, was their ambition, around 1965,

4.9 *Denny Lord, Chris Dawson and Alan Stanton, "Envirolab" (detail),* Archigram *no. 9, 1970. In this publicity flier, Envirolab, an Archigram spinoff working in southern California, demonstrate a greater interest in technological experimentation than in drawing and modeling, connecting the zoom dream to actual architectural practice. Nonetheless, in such collages Goldie Hawn became the counterpart to the French female icons starring in drawings earlier in the decade (compare figures 2.17, 3.2).*

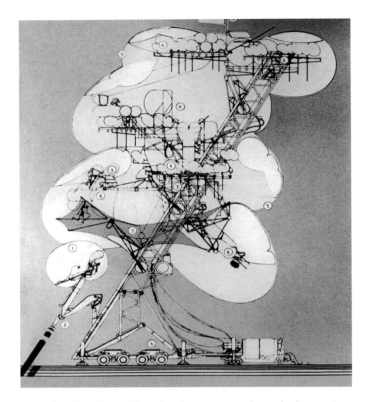

cross fertilization of ideas by the avant-garde in the late 1960s. The raison d'être of the *Archigram* magazine had been to act as a clearinghouse for progressive ideas and projects, and the interchange started to feel tangible, following the Archigram personnel themselves and allies such as Cedric Price and Reyner Banham. All were increasingly sought after as lecturers on the international circuit, facilitated by the decreasing costs of commercial jet aircraft travel. Archigram attracted an exceptional following in Germany and Austria; in 1971, the group's Adhocs (Addhox) Gallery in Covent Garden hosted the first showing in Britain of Coop Himmelblau,[72] the radical Archigram-influenced Austrian practice founded by Wolf D. Prix and Helmut Swiczinsky in 1968 (figure 4.10). Like virtually every progressive architect visiting Britain from overseas, Prix and Swiczinsky passed through the Architectural Association, effectively the hub of Archigram's international network.[73]

For *Archigram,* the world was divided into "Archizones," each region allocated a number (figure 4.11).[74] *Archigram*'s enthusiasm for the work of other architects demonstrated the group's largesse, certainly, but it pointed also to a desire to make the world of experimental architecture into another system of sorts, a network (to exploit one of the group's favorite words), an alternative circuit to the "drearies" of the modernist establishment.[75] Archigram energetically pursued contact with other experimental architects worldwide. *Archigram* no. 5 tapped into visionary urbanisms from across Europe (Yona Friedman and Paul Maymond from France, Hans Hollein and Walter Pichler from Austria, groups from the schools of architecture in Rome and Geneva) and from the United States (Paolo Soleri and the Arcosanti project). Whether the magazine was in personal contact with all of those designers who were listed as its "contributors" was unclear,[76] though Archigram's determination to physically reveal an international network of the avant-garde had become pressing by its magazine's sixth issue in 1965, when it decided to offer "a new service by which we hope to make known the names of such architects, particularly for the benefit of itinerant students."[77] In common with what seemed to be the magazine's usual editorial style,[78] the list of names was gloriously misspelled, but included Eckhard Schulze-Fielitz and Frei Otto from Germany, Joseph Weber from Holland, Pascal Hausermann, Ionel Schein, and the Groupe Architecture-Principe (Claude Parent and Paul Virilio) from France, and, from Czechoslovakia, the "Continualism" group.[79]

The identification of "Archizones" suggested Archigram's anxiety to comprehend its own position on the international stage. Perhaps Archigram needed to ascertain that it was at the centre of the activity (in conjunction with Reyner and Mary Banham's convivial "salon" across the road from *Archigram*'s "office" in Aberdare Gardens).[80] The Archigram network was the next step from Team 10's loose organizational structure (which had in turn superseded the caucus of CIAM); *Archigram* no. 7 tellingly superimposed a map of the Archigram nexus upon "the architectural network of Team 10."[81] Like Team 10, Archigram never hinted at collaboration with its confederates, confining itself to mutual moral support.

4.10 *Coop Himmelblau, Cloud, 1968. Austrian architecture in the late sixties was most cognate with the British scene gathered around Archigram, and it was, if anything, more extreme. If Archigram's thinking had its principal roots in the fifties (blending pioneer modernism with popular taste and the growth of leisured mass society), Austrian architecture smacked more of sixties radicalism, destabilizing spatial use, testing the body, liberating the psyche.*

Archigram became preoccupied instead by the *variants* of avant-gardism, differentiating the "brands" competing in the marketplace of experimental architecture, and some "competitors" detected a race to have "the first man into the bubble" among several goals.[82] Browsing Scandinavia, *Archigram* no. 9 found choices for the architectural future that ranged from the place making of Christian Norberg-Schulz ("despite [the] creepiness of [his] theories") to activities in Aarhus which, the magazine noted with equal skepticism, were "rather more flower-power than extremely activist."[83] *Archigram* meanwhile admitted to a jocular rivalry with work from Austria. Austria had been enjoying a powerful avant-garde revival of its own since the late fifties, with which Archigram established a lasting affinity: "those darned Austrians: they're great. . . . They are far more cynical and frustrated than (say) the young English. But also by comparison, they articulate this by powerful images, fleshy design and really imaginative ideas." Cook, intrigued by group dynamics, identified Hans Hollein "at 35 the daddy of it all," and monitored Walter Pichler, Raimund Abraham, Friedrich St. Florian, the Graz group, Zünd-up, Haus-Rucker-Co, and of course Coop Himmelblau.[84]

Architecture d'Aujourd'hui and its British correspondent, Claude Parent, were among the first to appreciate that extraordinary things were happening across the Channel, and it was only with considerable effort that experimental French groups like Utopie would feel able to emerge from Archigram's shadow.[85] In 1965, Archigram accepted Claude Parent and Patrice Goutet's invitation to participate in their "Exploration du Futur" exhibition at Arc-et-Senans, and the compliment was returned (or perhaps the initiative regained) the next year, when Archigram invited Parent to address its own exhibition and gathering of the avant-garde at Folkestone (figure 4.12).

The ingenious choice of venue for the 1966 Folkestone conference was both cosmopolitan (it permitted easy access to delegates from Continental Europe) and deeply provincial, an unremarkable English seaside town with its overtones of cheerfulness, middlebrow taste, and transitoriness. "The core of Folkestone," *Architectural Design*'s correspondent, Robin Middleton, noted, "is a gathering of streets at the port. The nucleus

4.11 *Archigram, "Archizones,"* Archigram *no. 9, 1970. Archigram* mapped the international "interchange" of experimental design—intelligence preparing *Archigram's footsoldier readers to take on the world of architecture.*

of this cultural centre is the fish and chip shop, the lights of the Manhattan Amusements, the Clarendon Arms and two coffee bars, one Greek, the other Spanish."[86] If zoom could reach here, it could surely reach anywhere.

The Folkestone conference was hosted by Archigram on 10–11 June at the New Metropole Arts Centre, which had taken "Living City" a few years earlier. Typical of the emphasis upon learning, and sponsored by Archigram's old sparring partner, the British Architectural Students Association (BASA), it was billed as a "student conference,"[87] and most of its five hundred delegates were indeed students, with more than twenty from the "New Bauhaus" of the Hochschule für Gestaltung (HfG) at Ulm, still more from the Ecole des Beaux-Arts in Paris. It was unequivocal evidence of some sort of "zoom wave," speakers setting out the wares of the avant-garde for perusal by a predominantly student consumer. When—since the early meetings of Team 10, and before that, the meetings of CIAM—had architecture witnessed such a gathering of its avant-garde? With the numbers of continental delegates apparently matching those from Britain, the sense of national competitiveness at Folkestone was palpable (apparent too in Banham's hectoring of the French): the surprise delivery of a model Living Pod from David Greene, then teaching in the States, "was a tremendous uplift to the London contingent" (figure 3.5).[88]

The conference was to be an International Dialogue of Experimental Architecture—"IDEA" for short, a nicely corny pun, appropriately printed in computer-style typography. "Anyone, almost, is welcome,"[89] it was promised, in keeping with the emergent sense of sixties cultural inclusiveness. Some "totem figures" failed to show,[90] but the guest list was a remarkable one nonetheless: Cedric Price and Arthur Quarmby joined the English delegation of Archigram and Banham; Yona Friedman, Ionel Schein, Paul Virilio, and Claude Parent traveled from France, Joseph Weber and Hans Hollein from Rotterdam and Vienna. Anthony Gwilliam and James Meller were there to propound Buckminster Fuller's World Design Science Decade, while Gustav Metzger's presence indicated the interest being taken in experimental architecture by "a whole gallimaufry of poets, painters and producers."[91] Exhibits were received from

Frei Otto, Eckhard Schulze-Fielitz, the Japanese metabolists, and Paolo Soleri.[92]

There were moments of melodrama. Having built up anticipation by arriving twenty minutes late, Reyner Banham entered, dressed in pop/boffin mode, wearing an anorak with pens in the arm pocket and a chestful of badges (one of which instructed the observer to "take it"), to announce the death of architecture.[93] The atmosphere was less than harmonious, indicating initial shortcomings in the zoom revolution. Despite the recollections of some that at Folkestone it "was possible to enjoy architecture and not treat it as a moral crusade,"[94] Hollein, for his neoclassicism, "was not surprisingly dubbed Fascist by Jos Weber,"[95] but then so was Ron Herron as he lectured on his completely unclassical Walking City (figure 1.32): "cries of 'Fascism, war machine, totalitarian,' etc. were heard."[96] Like Herron, Hollein had been circulating a "war machine" image since 1964, in the form of his famous aircraft carrier collage. The intention of the utopian architects of course was to rewire the hardware of war for peaceable ends[97]—the Thames Fortresses, a likely inspiration for Herron's Walking City,[98] had just been taken over by a pirate pop music radio station (figure 4.13).[99] Whatever fascination military technology held over the architects, all were horrified at the prospect of unleashing it in anger, the Walking City giving faceless technology loveable, googly-eyed countenances.[100] Claude Parent endured still worse heckling than Hollein and Herron, barracked by students who gave him the Nazi salute, whereupon he declined to speak again in England for another

4.12 *Archigram, flyer for the Folkestone conference, New Metropole Arts Centre, 1966. Reminiscent of the transnational campaigning of the interwar modern movement, Archigram's Folkestone conference also explored national variations in architectural taste. Above all it aimed to mobilize student opinion.* **4.13** *Shivering Sands Fort, Thames estuary, Whitstable, Kent, 1943. The Thames Fortresses are the most frequently cited source for such Archigram images as Herron's Walking City (see figure 1.32), but the noble warring that excited Archigram's members as boys was menacing to their baby-boomer students.*

thirty years.[101] Perhaps Archigram's lesson of student rebellion had been learned so well that Archigram and its constellation was already being perceived as "establishment" itself; Cook was slow-handclapped from the stage.[102] Grievances were allowed to pivot around the techno-libertarianism of the 1960s neo-avant-garde that was exemplified by Archigram. It came as an upset to a group genuinely fond of the student cohort.

EDUCATION

As Folkestone showed, Archigram remained true to its origins in student dissent and retained its key audience in the student body, to whom Archigram architects acted as young, charismatic dissidents. Cultivating the antiestablishment reputation of 1960s youth, Archigram regarded the student not as an empty vessel to be filled with knowledge, but as an active agent of change. *Archigram* the magazine served as the underground literature of the student corps, invisibly networking the architectural schools. The neo-avant-garde role of Archigram thereby extended beyond the production of images and ideas about buildings to a critique of architecture as a discipline, hijacking the schools to train acolytes through whom Archigram might produce architecture vicariously.

Solidarity with architectural students was important for the very distribution of *Archigram*. Supplementing the skeleton chain of booksellers carrying the magazine, it was distributed by a network seemingly modeled on samizdat; "Archigram can also be bought from students at most schools of architecture in the U.K.," claimed *Archigram* no. 6 in 1965; according to *Archigram* no. 8 in 1968, the magazine was available "from schools of architecture in most countries." "Zoom wave hits architecture," declared critic-historian Reyner Banham to readers of *New Society,* in his 1966 assessment of the impact of *Archigram* and other architectural "protest magazines"[103]—from Regent Street's *Polygon* in the mid-fifties to Bristol's *Megascope* (launched 1964) and the Architectural Association's *Clip-Kit* (launched 1966 with Peter Murray as its editor, formerly of *Megascope,* and the secretary of BASA who organized the first meeting between Archigram and students in 1965).[104] "Zoom rave hits Bristol," declared *Archigram* no. 6, depicting architecture students wearing "Zoom"

T-shirts and playing on swings to commemorate a lecture visit to the city from Peter Cook (figure 4.14). "Zoom nympholets of our architectural schools are determined to extrude ideas," declared the pop journalism of *Megascope* as a rationale for its launch, damning the academic or bureaucrat that would dare get in the way of the architectural space age.[105]

"Schools of architecture are dead!" exclaimed a 1966 *Megascope* editorial in typical zoom mood, before reviewing the first five editions of *Archigram*. "New thought, new ideas are squashed by the stranglehold of RIBA external examiners and anaemic teaching staffs."[106] "There is only one 'school' capable of . . . deal[ing] with the problems facing architects," BASA's president Patrick Hammill commented in *Archigram* no. 9 in 1970, articulating a common complaint about the isolation of individual schools, "that's an openended network of all the schools."[107] The bases of this further "network" in the UK were duly mapped out as "Archizone 1" (figure 4.15), the first in the series of zones that stretched as far as Archizone 11 (figure 4.11), founded upon the efforts of the Australasian Architecture Students' Association to set up an independent school of architecture as a free

4.14 *Archigram,* "Zoom Rave Hits Architecture," Archigram *no. 6, November 1965. Like a surreal scene from a new wave movie, "playpower" erupts through an architecture school when an* Archigram *editor visits.*

4.15 *Archigram, "Archizone 1: United Kingdom,"* Archigram *no. 9, 1970. Archigram's map of Britain linked schools of architecture as though they were nodes in a unitary network, student cohorts poised to overturn monumental practices of architecture.*

university, following a schism with the Royal Australian Institute of Architects in 1963.[108]

The Archizone would be formed through shared resources, itinerant lecturers, and talking shops. In 1967, for instance, *Archigram* no. 7 advertised meetings with students at Glasgow, Bournemouth, and Leicester, as well as one that would bring together students from the AA and the Ecole at Lyons.[109] Peter Cook went to the trouble of designing "The Box," a cheap audio-visual teaching unit that would also record responses and pass them on around the circuit of schools.[110] In *Archigram* no. 9, fellow traveler Cedric Price outlined the idea of an Architectural Schools Network he called Polyark.[111] "However repressive the school is, it cannot stop Archigram, AD etc. coming through your letterbox," *Archigram* no. 9 assured students who still felt cut off from the revolution. "It cannot easily stop your Union and BASA getting AD (or any other) topics discussed by the same people circuited round," giving as its example the "2000+ Conference" held by the school in Liverpool, a "3 day jamboree made up from what looked like 'Architectural design' [sic] faculty (Archigr., ARse [Architectural Radicals, Students and Educators], [Cedric] Price, [Richard] Rogers, [Rupert] Spade &c)."[112]

Zoom was nevertheless patchy in its distribution. Precisely because zoom remained firmly outside the RIBA-enforced core syllabus of British architectural education, it was possible to be an architectural student in Britain in the mid-sixties and to have next to no idea what Archigram was or what it stood for. It is difficult to imagine how the Leicester school received Archigram's road show in 1967 and David Greene as its fifth-year master two years later; as recently as 1965, its first-year students were being taught the orders in the manner of the Beaux-Arts.[113] "School least heard of awarded to Brighton, and all of 52 miles away,"[114] sneered *Archigram* from its London base in 1970, frustrated in its promotion of a united front of schools working as a single Archizone.

The uneven reception of zoom in the schools can be seen by thumbing through *Megascope*. Its 1966 "Schemes" section reproduced a range of zoom-style schemes; yet Arthur Quarmby conveyed to *Megascope* the struggle to promote new thinking at the chalk face of teaching. It was in the face of "the strangle-hold of the RIBA on schools like Bradford," where he had recently taught, that Quarmby had led students there in the creation of a parabolic pneumatic polythene dome.[115] Wanting to report an architectural revolution, *Megascope*, like *Archigram*, was actually ferreting out the particular, the fringe, instances of potential. Elsewhere, the avant-garde flair of zoom failed to overturn disinterested rationalism in its various guises. Some students, for example those at London University's Bartlett School swayed by lecturer John Christopher Jones's "Design Methods," disregarded zoom as lacking substance. Jones's lofty, professional approach could hardly be more different from zoom: Design Methods "teaches design as a series of logical decisions and not 'inspired flashes,'" wrote Jones in a 1969 comparison of his own Bartlett School with the AA and Regent Street Polytechnic nearby.[116]

"By turning out a 'professional product' schools are perpetuating the traditions of the first machine age,"[117] *Megascope* argued in 1966, pledging itself to the zoom paradigm shift of a "second machine age," forecast by Reyner Banham in *Theory and Design in the First Machine Age* (1960). The frontispiece of *Megascope* reprinted the iconic picture of Banham on his mini-Moulton bicycle with a speech bubble: "I take it as a good sign that an increasing number of students are flunking out of architectural schools in disgust of what they are being taught there. I take it as a hopeful sign that the next generation recognise that architecture is too important to be left to the architectural profession."[118] It was questionable, however, whether zoom's alternative of fun, freedom, and untried future technologies could make major inroads into the execution of architecture. Zoom's kit-of-parts epistemology, physically reflected in the loose assemblages and multiple formats that characterized *Clip-Kit* and *Archigram* nos. 7 and 8, made an uncertain basis for developing curricula. This apparently utopian phase of teaching and learning came at the risk of directionless, unlimited freedom. "Do I have to do what I want to do again today?" one student wrote on a wall at the AA school at the peak of Archigram's influence there.[119] Led out by Timothy Leary, Herbert Marcuse, and the like, this was the era for radical experiments with the structure of learning and its teacher/student interaction; Peter

Cook believes he may have infringed RIBA rules by working alongside his fifth-years on their diploma projects.[120] If Archigram's fraternization fell short of outright *political* radicalism (indeed, many radicalized students turned against Archigram's political liberalism), it expressed a solidarity with students—their numbers exploding with the introduction of mandatory study grants in the U.K. in 1962—as agents of long-lasting change.

Peter Cook typified the absorption of Archigram members in architectural education; entering Bournemouth college at age sixteen, he was almost continually in architectural school, first as a student and then as a teacher, and during his brief spell as an employee of James Cubitt he incurred the wrath of his employer for sitting on too many architectural juries.[121] Salaried employment in the big offices was thought to take architects "off the scene."[122] Ron Herron, the Archigram member most consistently engaged in mainstream practice after the Taylor Woodrow period, still taught regularly.[123] "Those who can, teach, those who can't, build," Alvin Boyarsky would later quip of the post-Archigram culture over which he presided at the Architectural Association.[124] The passion for architectural education broadened into a commitment to learning of all kinds. A host of projects from the *Archigram* stable imagined the widening of adult access to education by dissolving any spatial boundary between learning and living, such as Barry Snowden's study stations, Peter Cook's Info-Gonks of 1968, and David Greene's Invisible University of 1971 (figures 3.15, 3.24, 4.34).[125] The mood was reflected by Archigram acolytes such as Nicholas Grimshaw (figure 3.14) and friends who, as students of the AA, spurned attendance at Bedford Square itself, campaigning instead for its decentering through information technology.[126]

Rebuffing the authoritarian overtones of the traditional master/pupil teaching relationship, Archigram members cultivated something more like the connection between a rock band and its fan base; for the *Archigram Opera* presentation of 1975, "all the Archigram principals have had themselves photographed in the style of album covers: one is out in the Mohave desert in Western boots; another on the Las Vegas strip; a third astride a motorbike; a fourth in close-up sports aviator shades."[127] The rock band image was inspirational. C. Ray Smith, charting the roots of postmodernism in America, noted the number of experimental architects who, inspired by Archigram,

devised names for their groups and their workshops as if they were ball teams or rock groups: Ant Farm, Southcoast, Onyx, Truth Commandos, Intangible, Elm City Electric Light Sculpture Co., The Grocery Store, Zomeworks, Kamakazi Design Group, Mind Huns, Space Cowboys, All Electric Medicine Show, Crystal Springs Celery Gardens, Crash City, Archi-Week, Globe City, Hog Farm, and Peoples Architecture.[128]

The blurring of master/pupil distinctions was evident as student projects began to appear in *Archigram* and as students taught by Archigram members entered into the Archigram fold itself. In a photograph in *Architectural Design* of "The Archigram Family: November 1970," the office team included young architects working on the project to zoom-up Cook's home town, the retirement resort of Bournemouth (Colin Fournier, Janet Sacks, Diana Jowsey, Margaret Helfard, Bobby Wilson), and architectural enfant terrible Piers Gough ("who'd dropped in for tea").[129] Archigram's "junior team"—Fournier, Ken Allinson, Bernard Tschumi, and artist Tony Rickaby among others—were similarly featured in the *Archigram Opera* of 1975.[130]

The subsequent fame of many Archigram students and apprentices suggests an afterlife for the "zoom academy." In their study of architectural education, Mark Crinson and Jules Lubbock have found that "young teachers . . . have used the schools to develop new ideas and even to form embryonic practices amongst their most talented students,"[131] and that "the schools became a kind of architectural laboratory where Brutalism, non-plan, Archigram, post-modernism and deconstruction could all be fashioned without incurring the costs of actual building, often a decade or more before they appeared on the streets."[132]

FROM GRAY TO ELECTRIC

At the outset of her own ascent to architectural fame, Zaha Hadid attended the 1972 summer school held at the Architectural Association. She was too new to "the scene" to recognize

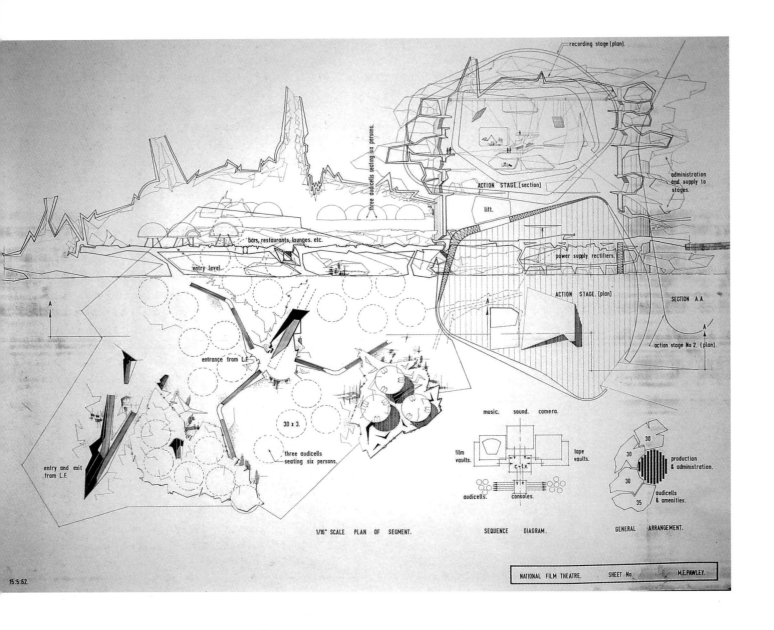

4.16 *Martin Pawley, National Film Theatre project, section and plan (detail), Architectural Association fourth year, 1962. Pawley's frenzied design, drawn with a mountainous section and cellular plan overlapping, was a cauldron of individual audiovisual booths, experimental building materials, and theoretical technology. An activist for "progressive" architectural education, Pawley went on to become a contributor to* Archigram *and a prominent architectural commentator in his own right.*

the portraits of Archigram members and other stars of experimental architecture depicted on the "commemorative stamps" issued by the Summer Session. The stamps, she recalls, looked like "Blackpool memorabilia,"[133] a seaside iconography close to the heart of Archigram. The postage system analogy, like the design of Summer Session timetables as London Transport Underground maps, likely alluded to the "connections" afforded by "underground" culture, and Summer Session materials were bundled—indeterminately—into plastic bags. Hadid's experience was of the Architectural Association in the twilight of what Peter Cook fondly called its "Electric Decade."

If there was a zoom wave, then its headquarters were at the Architectural Association. Every one of Archigram's members taught there, as well as Cedric Price, with more or less regularity, in the 1960s and 1970s.[134] So profound was the AA's absorption of Archigram that the 125th Anniversary Exhibition for the School in 1973 was undertaken as an Archigram project. Moreover Archigram, the AA, and *Architectural Design* (which championed the "zoom wave" through the editorship of Monica Pidgeon and the hidden hand of Archigram's promoter, Theo Crosby) mutually promoted one another, creating a new circuit for progressive and "international" notions. "The [AA] culture became more and more externalised," Cook claimed in the mid-seventies. "*Architectural Design* became England's most potent educator . . . it began to bring word of young guys arguing and designing . . . the Culture of Bedford Square . . . and the AA became almost synonymous with *AD* . . . much to the annoyance of other English schools."[135]

Archigram had to carve out its own niche at the AA. A discussion in the AA magazine *Arena* in 1966 concluded that *Archigram* was "neither with it nor sick but sad,"[136] and in the "jungle" that was the AA,[137] with no official syllabus for its teachers to follow, the teaching of Archigram members was left to compete with that of other tutors. Archigram took advantage of the AA's traditional tolerance of new ideas and trends, of which brutalism had been the most recent. Yet even the verve of brutalism, the most dynamic strand of British architecture in the 1950s, was fading in the AA of the early 1960s, due not least to the brutalists' own unspoken "call to order."[138] An ethos of a "straight,"

"architecture-as-service" mode of design had meanwhile been imported by those "clean-shaven"[139] AA tutors influenced by the HfG in Ulm on the one hand and the United States's Skidmore, Owings and Merrill on the other, bolstered, Cook claimed, by the theoretical work of Alan Colquhoun.[140] Colquhoun was joined at the AA by the likes of Patrick Hodgkinson in his belief that modern architecture had to realize its destiny as a methodology. "This project cannot be considered as architecture as the external skin does not express the interior functions, and that is the purpose of Architecture,"[141] announced Hodgkinson in a magnificently dismissive crit of a 1965 housing scheme by third-year student John Frazer, who appeared to have grasped Archigram's kit-of-parts principles with aplomb.[142]

In 1962, Martin Pawley, who transferred to the AA for his fourth year, following his expulsion from the Oxford School of Architecture, submitted a project for the National Film Theatre that was quite as outlandish as anything that had yet appeared in *Archigram,* a technical tour de force permitting visitors seated in private "audicells" to watch the contents of the film archive on demand (figure 4.16).[143] Cook—the "new, spotty juror" and little more than a year out of school himself—felt his impotence, unable to intervene in Pawley's derisory reception. For Cook, this confirmed that something was going wrong at the AA. Cook and David Greene had already written to the *Guardian* newspaper[144] when they first heard that Pawley, with three fellow members of the so-called "Progressive Architecture Movement," were being "slung out of the Oxford School of Architecture for (apparently) making progressive architecture!"[145] And now that the Progressive Architecture Movement had found its way to the most progressive school in the country, its members were dismayed to discover that they were merely "a spark of fire in a grey atmosphere. Five years earlier the AA would have offered the [National Film Theatre] scheme tolerance . . . even encouragement, and a more appropriate critical scrutiny instead of pique. What had happened? How had the early sixties become so grey?"[146]

Pawley's work, with its crystalline enclosure and an abstract landscape, was the last stand of 1950s British expressionist tendencies, now rapidly fading into memory, that *Archigram* no. 1

had set out to revive. Cook returned to the AA from Taylor Woodrow in 1964, aged 27, to become deputy fifth-year master on the strength of Plug-In City, published seven weeks earlier in the *Sunday Times Colour Supplement* (figure 1.8). However sensational it may have seemed to readers of the *Sunday Times*, Plug-In did not look much like serious architecture to the AA class of 1964.[147] By the following year, however, Cook detected "electricity in the air" again at the AA. Martin Godfrey's fifth-year Battersea Urban Renewal Scheme—the "Battersea finger" megastructure[148]—expressed its functions with abandon in a picturesque, brutalist massing of terraces and services (figure 4.17). Complete with transport interchanges, it was indebted to Archigram's projects, and Cook embraced it as if was his own: "it took up the entrails forgotten since 1960—the wrapping of rooms round streets, streets round air, air funnelling through wrapped ducts and tanks and glass and ramps and . . . so much. Heady stuff again. The finger disintegrating . . . withering towards an English park. Oh joy!"[149] A reciprocal relationship was developing: student schemes like Godfrey's would be featured in *Archigram* (no. 6, 1965) as "Newcomers," while successive AA student projects during the coming years were reworkings of those latest schemes featured in *Archigram*. This was zoom education in action, as Archigram architects worked to stay a step or two in front.

THE "SERVICED SHED"

In 1972, ground was broken at the plateau Beaubourg in Paris for the building that would represent the apogee of zoom architecture: the arts center and library by Renzo Piano and Richard Rogers known as the Centre Pompidou. In the 1960s, Piano and Rogers's design ideas had moved in a similar trajectory to those of the Archigram architects. Piano was a student of Louis Kahn and friend of Jean Prouvé (a member of the jury for the Beaubourg competition).[150] Rogers's melee ran parallel to Archigram's. Rogers graduated from the AA in 1959, less than a year before Cook, and went on to tutor at the AA and at Regent Street. He was exposed to practically identical debates and tutors, most particularly John Killick and Peter Smithson. Rogers shared a platform with Archigram on the BASA confer-

ence circuit—frustrated like Archigram with the condition of architectural education, challenging RIBA elitism, and propounding educational visions comparable to those of Archigram.[151] His choice of name for the 1963 practice he formed with Norman Foster,[152] "Team 4," implied an avant-garde succession to Team 10 even more explicitly than did Archigram. Like Archigram, Team 4 projected a pop group image of fashionability, youth, and mystique.[153] Rogers would later employ architects trained by Archigram members at the AA and UCLA.

Team 4's 1967 Reliance Controls building in Swindon represented the truest manifestation so far realized in Britain of the "serviced shed" idea that was engulfing studios at the AA, where the frame was designed as neutrally as possible so as to nurture permutations of modular architectural elements slotted inside (figure 4.18). Team 4 split soon after the completion of Reliance,

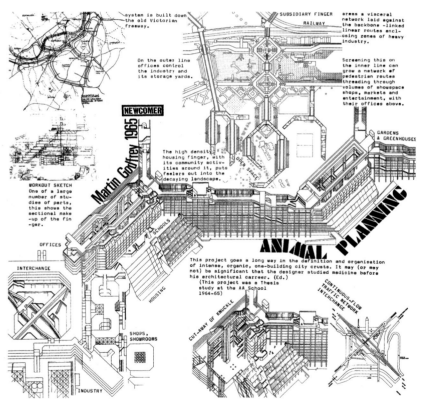

4.17 *Martin Godfrey, Battersea Urban Renewal Scheme (Urban Finger), axonometric, Architectural Association fifth year, 1964–1965,* Archigram *no. 6, November 1965. At the end of his first full year teaching at the AA, Peter Cook believed that the project put together by Martin Godfrey was evidence of a student resurgence. It was, in effect, a solidified, monumental Plug-In City with "picturesque" massing and vertebral joints in its plan.*

but from then on the preeminent model for indeterminate, flexible architecture was established as the impersonal, rectangular envelope assembled from prefabricated parts creating a free plan. Reliance looked somehow innocent and natural—like a "lost vernacular," in the opinion of the *Financial Times*[154]—and seemed all the more persuasive for the way it could incorporate plug-in/clip-on additions: the glazed side of the Reliance building could either face a courtyard or plug in to additional adjoining units.[155]

Nonetheless the work of Piano and Rogers was much less known than Archigram's when in 1971 they jointly bid, in partnership with structural engineers from the Ove Arup office, for one of the biggest architectural prizes since the Second World War (figure 4.19). As the names of the winning architects of the Beaubourg competition were read out to the jury, which had

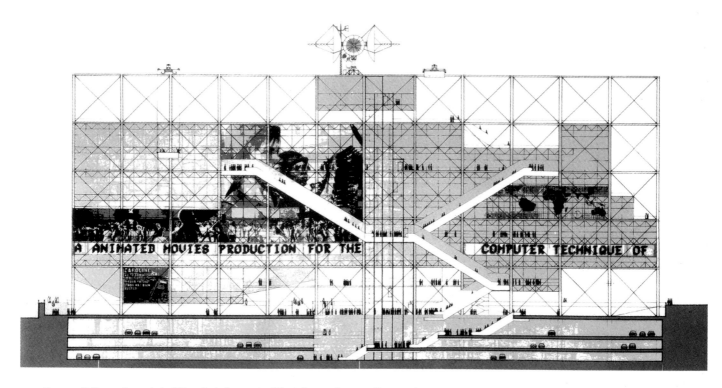

4.18 *Team 4, Reliance Controls building, Swindon, 1967. "Sheds" were theoretically appealing to progressive young British architects because they repudiated formalism and concentrated upon function. In reality, shed designers could not avoid questions of style and symbolism even if they wanted to, and this is no less the case with the "California cool" of the Reliance Controls building (an exemplar of shed design) than with the steaming energy of the Fun Palace (figure 1.30) and the picturesque fertility of Herron's Oasis (figure 4.20).* **4.19** *Piano and Rogers, competition design: west elevation (showing information wall), 1971, for Centre Georges Pompidou, Paris, 1971–1977. The Pompidou Center triumphantly summarized the "zoom" stream of modern architecture and was thus a vicarious achievement of Cedric Price and Archigram; it was a Fun Palace and an Instant City—indeterminate, superserviced, media-saturated, pop, popular. Unequivocally, however, it was Piano and Rogers who leapt the void separating zoom from built structure.*

judged the entrants anonymously, there was a baffled silence, relieved only by mention of the name Arup.[156] That Piano and Rogers's entry proposal was appreciated by the jury is surely tribute in part to the "zoom wave." Just as Piano and Rogers knew the work of Cedric Price and Archigram, jury member Philip Johnson (for one) was familiar with Archigram's relentless quest for an architecture of pure servicing.[157]

Significantly, though, the jury found the understatement of Piano and Rogers's Beaubourg renderings reassuring. In this, the Piano and Rogers presentation was quite distinct from Archigram's typically hot imagery; "the deliberate dryness of the drafting"[158] was reminiscent instead of Cedric Price, and it was Price's Fun Palace project that was the most significant inspiration for Beaubourg as a whole (figure 1.30). In accordance with Price's and Littlewood's vision, Beaubourg was to be a rectangular, gantried, excellently serviced support for continuous, improvisatory cultural situations, without which the structure would assume virtually no form and enjoy no raison d'être.

But when the elevations of Beaubourg are read, it is difficult to spot any key concept or formal device not already present in Ron Herron's own "serviced shed" reworkings of the Fun Palace, the Oasis and Instant City projects of 1968–1969 (figures 4.20, 4.21). The Oasis drawing depicted a cross-braced frame of pylons and gantries (crashing through old monoliths like the Smithsons' Economist Building), suspending semi-external walkways, its cranes and bulging accoutrements a little more "picturesque" than those proposed for Beaubourg, but nonetheless broadly rectangular in outline until it junctured with a cylindrical section connected by wormlike plug-ins, the whole ensemble raised on pilotis as Piano and Rogers originally wished their building to be. Servicing, of which there is plenty in Herron's schemes, is naturally left exposed, as Piano and Rogers chose to do too (in distinction to the increasingly "zipped-up" and "tailored" work of Norman Foster). Herron even posted his work with the sorts of buzzwords that resurfaced in Piano and Rogers's Beaubourg pitches—"choice," "respond," "indeterminate"—and the similarities between the two schemes were underscored when the drawing was held up in front of the building in a 1980 Arts Council film.[159]

In the *Urban Action—Tune Up* Instant City collage (figure 4.21), Herron's selection of keywords became still more suggestive of the world of Beaubourg. As if anticipating the first line of Piano and Rogers's competition entry, which so struck the jury—"We recommend that the Centre Beaubourg be developed as a 'Live Centre of Information' covering Paris and beyond. Locally it is a meeting place for the people"[160]—Herron promoted "zerox" (sic), "information screen," "community educational servicing," "CCTV," and "audio visual library" as vital components of urban tuning. The information screens were inspired by Piccadilly and Times Square, with antecedents in Oscar Nitzchke's unbuilt 1932–1935 Maison de la Publicité (projected for the Champs-Elysées and replete with cross-braced external gantries and permanent rooftop crane).[161] To illustrate such screens, Herron helpfully pasted his collage with magazine photos and lettering, a technique redeployed in the Piano and Rogers drawing.

4.20 *Ron Herron, Oasis, montage, 1968. Crashing the salon of typical and exemplary postwar architecture—from the Smithsons, Safdie (see figure 3.3), Le Corbusier, SOM, Lasdun, Mies van der Rohe, Goldberg, Tange—Herron's Oasis prepared the public for buildings composed (like figure 4.19) not of walls and cubic volumes but of open frames, interchangeable units, and visible ducts.*

4.21 *Ron Herron for Archigram, Instant City project:* Urban Action—Tune Up, *montage, 1969. When the* AA/UCLA *Chrysalis group joined the Piano and Rogers team in Paris, this was likely the type of scenario, drawn by Herron at* UCLA, *that it hoped to erect on the Beaubourg piazza: retractable pylons, spotlights, Frei Otto-style tarpaulins, capsules, and (foremost) video. A new dot matrix display provides text bulletins, and among the feature presentations is* Yellow Submarine *with its Archigram-style capsule. The Beatles themselves play a concert on the stage provided by Herron;* Instant City *is in effect an early touring rock show.*

The screens were never installed as envisaged by the Beaubourg team, but they had come pretty close to getting risqué zoom imagery and messages flashing at the heart of one of the world's great cities. As it stood, the Piano and Rogers team managed to erect the *monument* to the zoom wave, the biggest and best shed ever, "where it's at," to quote Cook's generous assessment, "a well equipped hangar."[162] This, needless to say, was the unequivocal achievement of the Beaubourg design team. Archigram was famous for the exquisite detailing of its drawings; but in the offices on the banks of the Seine, the detailing of massive spans and of cast and centrifugally spun steel columns was going on for real, thrashed out between the offices of Piano and Rogers and Arup.[163] There was nothing in *Archigram* to guide the Beaubourg team once it had passed the concept stage. Beaubourg

was not the only homage to the Price/Archigram pop shed; at Aachen University, for example, Weber, Brand and Partners pressed on from 1969 to 1986 with their Faculty of Medicine, another striking essay in ductwork, color coding, and indeterminate frames (maneuvered into the classical symmetry enjoyed in German and Austrian circles). The only Beaubourg-style project that Archigram realized for itself was on a micro scale— the Adventure playground at Milton Keynes (figure 4.22), built mainly to the design of Ron Herron in 1972, with the color-coded iconography of roller doors and funnels that became so familiar with the completion of Beaubourg five years later.

So Archigram and their associates were destined to work vicariously in the creation of the greatest and most ambitious of zoom buildings, by informing the thinking behind Beaubourg

4.22 *Dennis Crompton and Ron Herron for Archigram Architects, Adventure Play Centre, Calverton End, Milton Keynes, 1972. The industrial components, the color coding, the funnels, and the fun provided an appetizer to the Pompidou Center, though the burial of the building indicated Archigram's desire to prevent architecture from making more than a moundlike imprint upon the landscape.*

HAVING A LOVELY TIME WITH THE LADS

HAVING A LOVELY TIME AT MONTE CARLO

and by having a hand in the training of no less than four key members of the design team, including Tony Dugdale (with whom Rogers had lectured at Cornell) and Chris Dawson.[164] Dugdale and Dawson had completed pioneering work on "well-serviced sheds" at the AA in 1966 and 1967, respectively, and in Cook's opinion remained among the most incisive thinkers about the concept at a time when it became "a mere panacea for an 'anything goes' level of thought. The AA school produced some real shockers."[165] Rogers called Dugdale because he needed 150-foot spans at the Pompidou, exactly the same span that Dugdale had projected "in all directions"[166] for his space-framed Learning Shed project at the AA, and included, in miniature cutout, as part of *Archigram* no. 7's self-assembly "kit of parts" (figure 3.10).

BEYOND THE SHED

Visiting the Pompidou Center with a film crew shortly after its opening, Archigram and Cedric Price were impressed—"ostensibly it appears to be an Archigram building," said Herron[167]— but the group could not help finding it "too consistent,"[168] as if the frame had come to dominate the disparate activities it was meant to facilitate. "Someone either designs a building to move or does not design a building to move," said Price. Greene pointed to a nearby crane—"much more dynamic."[169] "Our friends Archigram and Cedric Price are right" conceded Renzo Piano, admitting that it had become a prestige monument, "it's not very dynamic."[170]

A year before Piano and Rogers's Beaubourg submission Cook, Crompton, and Greene had sensationally landed their own ill-fated shed (of sorts), won in a competition organized by the Principality of Monaco in 1969 (figures 4.23, 4.24). They were assisted by youngsters Ken Allinson and Colin Fournier, and by the highly regarded consulting engineer Frank Newby, who had previously diverted himself working with experimental projects such as the Price/Snowdon Aviary at London Zoo (1961) and the Price/Littlewood Fun Palace.[171] The success of the submission ostensibly occasioned a shift in the Archigram group's core business from agitprop to architectural practice: the Archigram Architects office opened in London in 1970,

4.23 *Archigram Architects (Peter Cook, Dennis Crompton, Ron Herron, partners), Monte Carlo project postcard, 1970. Terminating publication of the* Archigram *magazine shortly after winning the competition for a new entertainment center in Monte Carlo, Archigram opened an office in London and printed postcards of ongoing projects, both conceptual and those slated for production.* **4.24** *Archigram Architects (Peter Cook, Dennis Crompton, Ron Herron, partners), Monte Carlo project postcard, 1970. The Monte Carlo design combined Archigram's past explorations of mechanical entertainments and the "instant city." Thus the motif of the seaside was to prove consistent in Archigram's work from beginning to end.*

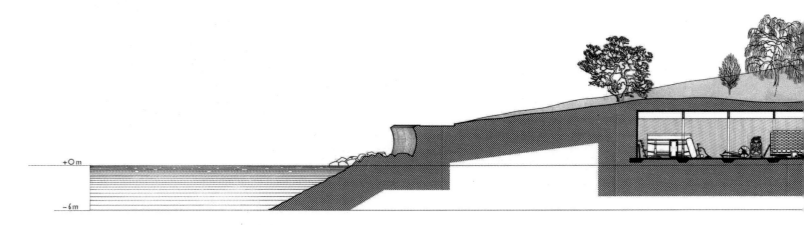

COUPE

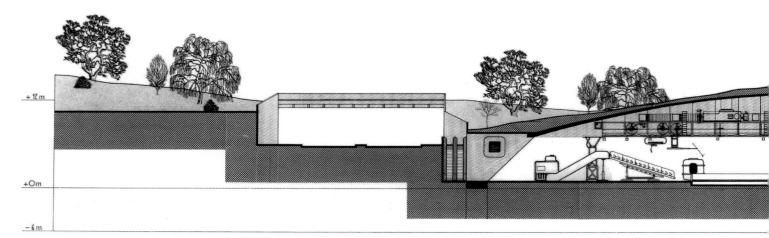

COUPE

moving to a five-story Covent Garden building in 1971 and adding its Adhocs (Addhox) Gallery (see frontispiece).

The brief for an "edifice polyvalente" at Monte Carlo, requiring a single building for a variety of entertainment and sporting functions, had been echoed in the Beaubourg competition announcement.[172] The crossovers were probably not coincidental. Judges for the Monaco Entertainments Centre included Ove Arup, whose business partner Edmund Happold persuaded Piano and Rogers to enter the Beaubourg competition; Happold

had in the past worked with Frei Otto, another Monte Carlo finalist.[173] What was so radical about the solution at Monte Carlo, though, and contrasted so strongly with Piano and Rogers's Beaubourg, was Archigram's decision to invert the serviced shed, burying it beneath the site (a plot of reclaimed land—a scruffy park—on the seafront, figure 4.25). The resulting scheme was a circular forum (a shape recommended by Newby in preference to a rectangle for its stability). Actually, it was a covered pit; monumentalism had disappeared once and

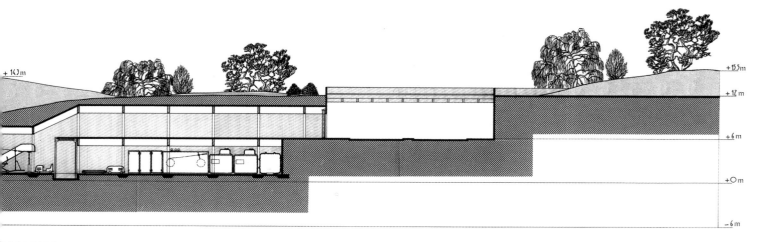

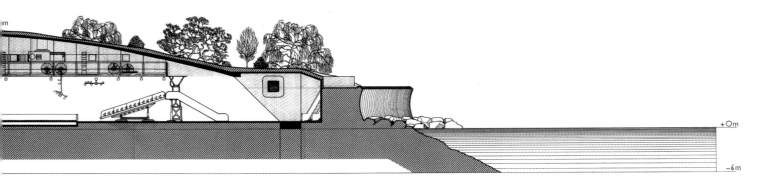

for all, and even the curvature of the dome, a mainstay of traditional architectural form, was obscured by a suspended gantry. Here was the attempt to *build* beyond architecture. "Instead of creating a complex architectural sculpture that would etch a stunning silhouette against the background of the blue Mediterranean, they decided to dig a hole and pull the earth back over it," Banham explained in 1970.[174] This shallow dome of post-tensioned, reinforced concrete beams—a subterranean Jahrhunderthalle brought alive by activity alone—was

no more than half the project: servicing had an equal if not higher priority.

Monte Carlo was a chance to test the "robot" principle that was given central importance during the preceding couple of years by Greene in particular. Indeed, the team initially hoped to use Greene's 1968 Rokplug and Logplug devices in the park at Monte Carlo, and the idea survived the move underground because surface "features" were devised by Greene. Instant City-type paraphernalia—headphones, sunshades, and compressed

4.25 *Peter Cook, Dennis Crompton, Colin Fournier, Ron Herron, Diana Jowsey, and Frank Newby for Archigram Architects, Monte Carlo project, sections, 1970. Barely interrupting the descent of the Monte Carlo shoreline to the Mediterranean, a shallow dome (to be engineered by Frank Newby) and entrance lobby were to be slipped beneath a public park. A catwalk and open arena completed the permanent elements of the design: though integral to the architectural assembly, the seating, escalators, stage, and booms could be wheeled away.*

4.26 *Archigram Architects (montage by Ron Herron), Monaco Entertainments Centre project: surface view with enviro-plug, 1969. Graphics worked hard at Archigram's Monte Carlo, here presenting the added-value "features" devised for the original competion entry by David Greene and derived from his 1968 Rokplug and Logplug devices (see figure 3.32). Public entertainment (headphones, sunshades, compressed air, periscopes) would be provided for users of the park above the new Archigram arena, promoting organized and spontaneous events concurrently.*

air for inflatables—were to be at the disposal of the park's users, and periscopes would peep through "golf holes" into the auditorium below (figure 4.26). Within the auditorium, the servicing solutions were much like those installed at Osaka's Expo '70 by Arata Isozaki (figure 3.22)—movable staging and seating, light towers, gantries, and bolt-on capsules: a big kit-of-parts (figures 4.27–4.33). It was the perfection of this kit-of-parts that Archigram believed would make or break the success of the Monte Carlo building, "insisting that in the elaboration of their working contract the study of the equipment must proceed in parallel with the study of the architecture and at the same level of detail."[175] Banham went further, pointing out that in the long term, this architecture of perpetual becoming, of event rather than form, needed *management,* "someone with a Diaghilev flair," to realize the building's potential: "Monaco in the hands of an unqualified pilot would just be a complete waste of three million quid."[176]

The issue of the budget was itself interesting—according to one acoustic expert at the time, Archigram's £3million/$6million estimate represented a £5million/$10million shortfall.[177] But the robots may not have been as complex as Archigram's own description of Monte Carlo as "a giant cybernetic toy" (reviving the byline for the Fun Palace, figure 1.30) made it sound.[178] Very likely, the robots would have been assemblages of existing technologies already available in theater design, television studios, concert halls, and sports stadia. Archigram was assured by French designers that a great deal of the equipment was already being incorporated into French auditoria design, and a 1971 progress report on Monte Carlo featured equipment as mundane as capsule WCs (figure 4.33).[179] The escalation in cost was due in part to the Principality's extension of reception areas adjoining the arena, creating budget difficulties at the same time that the Principality lost duty revenues from France (1973).[180]

Even so, this exploration of an architecture in pure becoming was undoubtedly close to the edge of viability, hatched near the sincere but oddball robotic and inflatable projects of Archigram's AA students—the scheme was initially devised in a studio belonging to the AA, and the Monte Carlo design team included recent graduates from the school.[181] Pneumatic structures, which came out of the AA studios in a steady stream, epitomized zoom's last push to make the architectural interface yield before the inflexible reality of current building technology set in. The feasibility of inflatable architecture was as uncertain as its rationale. Inflatables attained a high profile and an embryonic authority at Expo '70, notably in the pavilions for Fuji (Yutaka Murata) and the United States (Davis, Brody and Associates). But small-scale thrill seeking was the chief motivation for young pneumatic architects, longing for spatial reorientations and a new intimacy with materials. These were promised in 1965 by Reyner Banham, caught wearing only his beard (and François Dallegret's body) in the Un-House project.[182] Banham and Dallegret's cool collage was misleading, however, as zoom architects soon discovered when they sweated it out in the impermeability of real pods. A sort of romanticism about the new architectures had overtaken common sense, particularly in the use of inflatables. In the early stages of Piano and Rogers's Beaubourg project, drafting was executed in a pneumatic hut: "The architects put up with it, because it was an inflatable, by the Seine. The engineers thought the architects were out of their minds—it had no charm for them; it was just too hot."[183]

The prophets of modernity accepted their sufferance during zoom's experiments in living. When Archigram's UCLA associates Chris Dawson and Alan Stanton established their radical architectural practice in 1968 (joined the next year by Mike Davies, fresh from the AA), they named it Chrysalis, after the natural exemplar for an "architectural interface"—a second skin—and gamely attempted to live in experimental structures in the frazzled atmosphere of the California desert, playing with the immateriality of thermal barriers and light.[184] In 1968, Davies conducted preliminary meetings with Richard Rogers on the potential of jointly developing the work on inflatables. All three members of Chrysalis headed back to Europe and were put in charge of Beaubourg's "non-programmed" activities.[185] Dynamic structures on the Beaubourg piazza, it was believed, would activate the spontaneous, interactive life of the Center, excluded from the brief and the final design but held dear by Rogers.

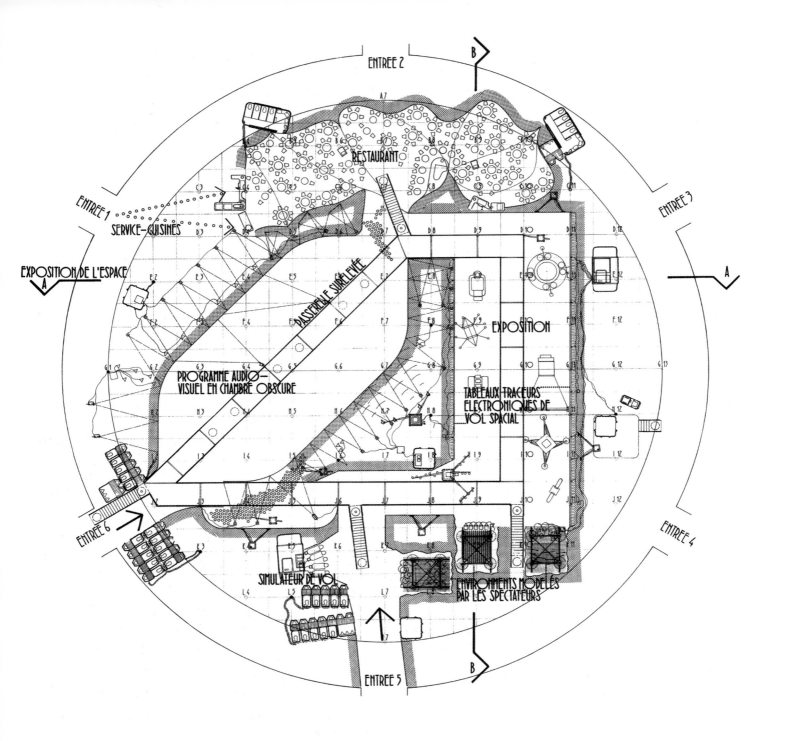

ENTREE 2

B

ENTREE 1

SERVICE-CUISINES

RESTAURANT

ENTREE 3

A

EXPOSITION DE L'ESPACE

A

PASSERELLE SURÉLEVÉE

EXPOSITION

PROGRAMME AUDIO-
VISUEL EN CHAMBRE OBSCURE

TABLEAUX TRACEURS
ELECTRONIQUES DE
VOL SPACIAL

ENTREE 6

SIMULATEUR DE VOL

ENVIRONNEMENTS MODELÉS
PAR LES SPECTATEURS

ENTREE 4

B

ENTREE 5

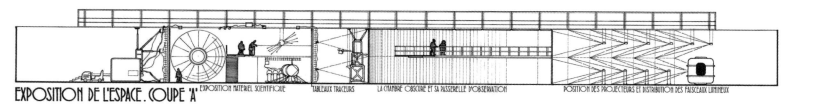

EXPOSITION DE L'ESPACE. COUPE 'A'   EXPOSITION MATERIEL SCIENTIFIQUE   TABLEAUX TRACEURS   LA CHAMBRE OBSCURE ET SA PASSERELLE D'OBSERVATION   POSITION DES PROJECTEURS ET DISTRIBUTION DES FAISCEAUX LUMINEUX

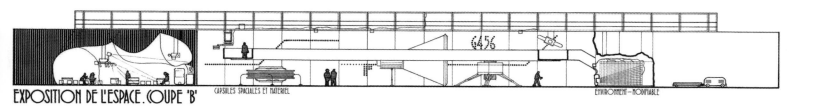

EXPOSITION DE L'ESPACE. COUPE 'B'   CAPSULES SPACIALES ET MATERIEL   ENVIRONMENT – MODIFIABLE

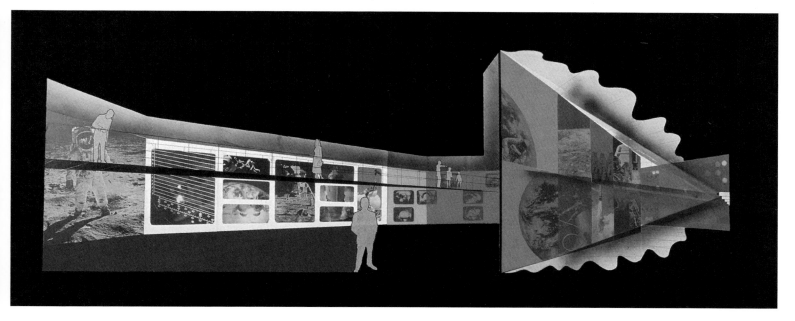

4.27, 4.28, 4.29 *Peter Cook, Dennis Crompton, Colin Fournier, Ron Herron, Diana Jowsey, and Frank Newby for Archigram Architects, Monaco Entertainments Centre project: plan, sections, and montage (by Tony Rickaby) of the arena arranged for a space exhibition, 1970.*

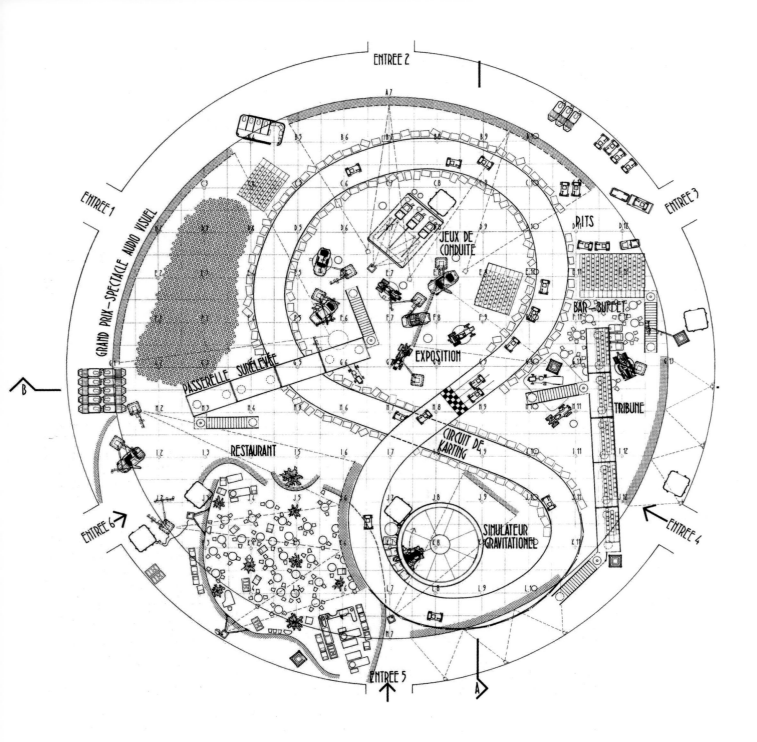

ENTREE 2

ENTREE 1

ENTREE 3

ENTREE 6

ENTREE 4

ENTREE 5

GRAND PRIX – SPECTACLE AUDIO VISUEL

JEUX DE CONDUITE

PITS

BAR-BUFFET

EXPOSITION

PASSERELLE SURÉLEVÉE

TRIBUNE

RESTAURANT

CIRCUIT DE KARTING

SIMULATEUR GRAVITATIONEL

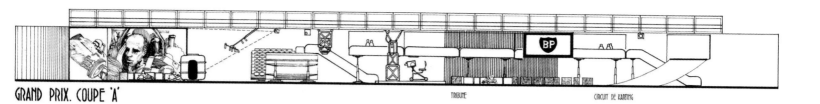

GRAND PRIX. COUPE 'A'   TRIBUNE   CIRCUIT DE KARTING

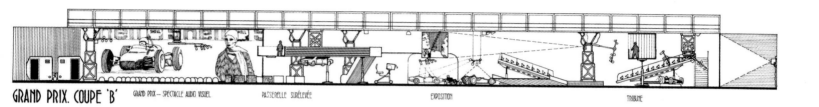

GRAND PRIX. COUPE 'B'   GRAND PRIX — SPECTACLE AUDIO VISUEL   PASSERELLE SURÉLEVÉE   EXPOSITION   TRIBUNE

4.30, 4.31, 4.32 *Peter Cook, Dennis Crompton, Colin Fournier, Ron Herron, Diana Jowsey, and Frank Newby for Archigram Architects, Monaco Entertainments Centre project: plan, sections, and montage (by Tony Rickaby) of the arena arranged for a kart race, 1970. The circular arena at Monaco was a single-minded purging of form that foregrounded events.*

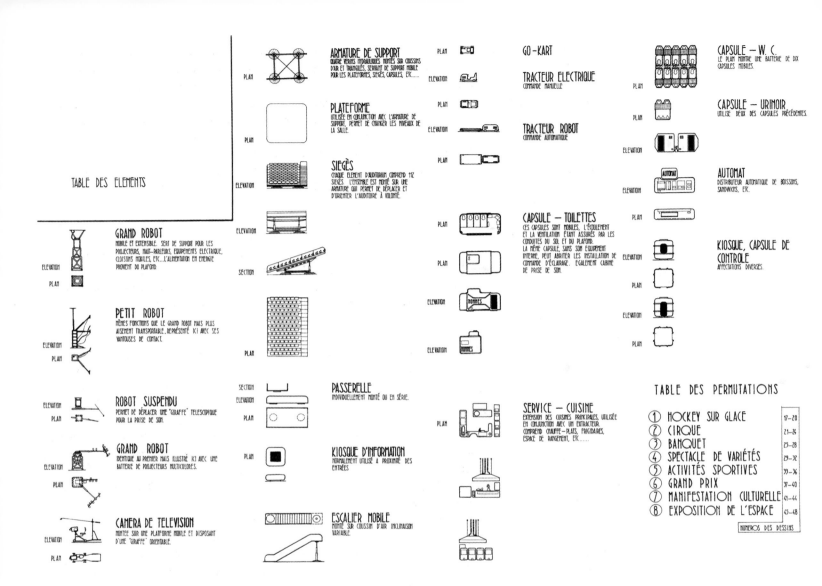

4.33 *Peter Cook, Dennis Crompton, Colin Fournier, Ron Herron, Diana Jowsey, and Frank Newby for Archigram Architects, Monaco Entertainments Centre project: kit-of-parts for the arena, plans and elevations, 1970. Archigram held steadfast to the conventions of architectural representation in its Monaco progress report, offering plans, sections, and elevations to depict apparatus such as robots, vending machines, portable toilets, and tractors that might not have qualified as architecture at a different time or in a different place.*

Chrysalis had been unusually committed to turning zoom images into three-dimensional reality, selling inflatable domes through *Playboy* magazine[186] and proving, with the 140-foot mirror dome fabricated with EAT, David Greene's insistence in *Archigram* no. 1 that a balloon could be blown to any size.[187] But at Beaubourg, the real-life experimental laboratory of zoom, the design team's energies were gradually diverted toward the detailing of the main Beaubourg megastructure.[188] The tyranny of the hard architectural interface survived, because for the moment it was the only architectural technique that the architects and engineers and clients could deal with. Zoom had been performing the same maneuvers as early modernism, creating images and prototypes with only a conjectural relationship to building technology as it existed. The engineers' report for Piano and Rogers's Beaubourg had the honesty to admit that the building would take more time to complete than that allowed by the client timetable, and it somehow disappeared from the submission, perhaps removed by a juror sympathetic to the scheme.[189] Archigram Architects, who initially assumed that the organizers of the Monte Carlo competition had invited them to participate simply to confer an avant-garde credibility, found themselves abruptly presented with the prospect of making the scheme work.

"Their certainty in those days was unbounded," Martin Pawley recalled in 1975 of Archigram's halcyon days. "Verging occasionally on the Monty Pythonesque . . . they did their best work at one of those times when visionaries believed that what they had drawn and described had really happened. They were of course aided in this belief by critics who . . . believed equally strongly that only their opposition stood between the Archigram blueprint and its realisation."[190] Critics openly queried the purpose of the zoom pursuit, however; in 1973, *Building* magazine's reviewer Michael Cassidy, previewing Archigram's latest exhibition at the ICA (marking Cook's appointment as ICA director), found only inventive solutions to "a host of problems that don't exist."[191]

THE "INSTITUTIONALISATION OF INNOCENCE"

Zoom's optimism was all the more remarkable now that technological modernity numbered among its attainments the Holo-caust, Hiroshima, deforestation, and the prospect of nuclear Armageddon. Zoom faced technophilic quandary with each succeeding year of the sixties, as the degradation in Vietnam of the most technologically sophisticated army ever fielded coincided with the sublime feat of Apollo 11. Prior to zoom, modernists tended to bind the unpredictable Prometheus of technology ever further into formal, monumental structures. Zoom modernists, on the other hand, barely wavered in their faith in technology as liberator. "Technology is morally, socially and politically neutral, though its exploitation may require adjustments of social and political structures, and its consequences may call moral attitudes into question," Banham announced in 1962 in his quest "Towards a Pop Architecture,"[192] and it would be many years before he admitted to his naiveté on the issue.[193]

AA tutor Fred Scott recalled the perversely arcadian atmosphere of his school in the later sixties as the libertarian, techno-utopian spell of Archigram and its allies took hold:

It was a peculiarly agreeable time, remarkably free of argument, seeing as it did the architect's role as supplying choice, as an alternative to resolving conflicts in a world rich in possibilities. . . . Designing was considered to be an activity freed from pre-conceptions of form, style or morality . . . this commitment seemed in many ways to be an institutionalisation of innocence, and because of its assumption of the impartiality of technology, designing became an unimpassioned cool activity, of which it was meaningless to ask to whom in particular it was being useful.[194]

The "institutionalisation of innocence" would barely falter at the AA until the early seventies, despite the assault upon techno-liberalism originating in antiwar, anticapitalist, feminist, ecological, and race emancipation movements. The Folkestone Conference showed in 1966 that the reception of Archigram's techno-pop libertarianism was turning sour. The British sixties as a whole was corrupted that year by the cooling of white heat confidence during Wilson's second term, and the transition from pop affluence to alternative orders and drugs.[195] Such an *Archigram* stalwart as *Architectural Design* feared zoom's loss of innocence: "System builders, throw-away utopians and plug-in idealisers will continue the trend to a worsening environment until man has to resort to artificial stimulants."[196] The transition from utopian to dystopian in the mid-sixties was apparent in television, film, and even the boys' comics that had once supplied Archigram with an iconology: the comic strips' cast of evildoers—big corporations, rogue scientists—were now as likely to come from Earth's military-industrial complex as from outer space.[197]

Somehow, Archigram insulated itself from the devastating ecological and social critiques of (American) capitalism, like Rachel Carson's *Silent Spring* (on pesticide pollution) and Michael Harrington's *The Other America* (on the persistence of widespread poverty), both published in 1962. Archigram had even remained separate from the new environmentalism at the AA, nurtured by Paul Oliver, who published his *Shelter and Society* in 1969, a celebration of environmentally sensitive vernacular and indigenous architectures.[198] This state of affairs can be attributed in part to the AA's culture of inclusivism that permitted, even encouraged, seemingly contradictory points of view to be taught under the same roof. AA environmentalism and zoom appeared at the time to have as much in common as in opposition, emerging from a joint rebellion against the AA's measured drawing program in the early 1960s.[199] Primarily, both camps felt that architectural crisis originated in centrally administered programs such as the British town-planning and mass-housing schemes. Archigram's solutions were more obviously technological, Oliver and others espoused a return to a vernacular that bordered on the primitivist, but the two tendencies appeared to be in concert. Technology, geodesics, cybernetics, squatting, local-level action—these were seen as mutually supportive to those at the AA who "were concerned to close the gap between the changing needs of society and the capacity of the built environment to respond to them," as Oliver put it,[200] noting too the nonpartisan admiration for the United States as a space of liberty "where a man . . . [can] build himself a house of his own with the minimum of official interference."[201]

Devising a "primitivist" style, influenced by the land art movement which had been gaining momentum since the mid-sixties,[202] *Archigram* extended an olive branch to environmen-

talists toward the end of its publication run. "We are entering primitive heterogeneity," Greene noted in 1972, criticizing those architectural solutions that "ignore the sociological paradigm of the natural environment."[203] His 1971 Invisible University, composed from scrub, paid homage to non-Western vernaculars, which Greene credited as the most architecture needed (figure 4.34).[204] Provided, that is, these vernaculars were linked to an electronic service network, and that the creators of indigenous architecture were plugged in to Western software. "Here is an aborigine," Greene observed in an essay of 1971, collaging onto the illustration a television into which the Aborigine was now made to peer (figure 4.35).

Does she, like the guerrilla, have something to tell us about our situation? Her technology was primitive but her lifestyle was complex, full of valuable myths and fantasies and she lived with her environment, not parasitically upon it. Our architectures are the residue of a desire to secure ourselves to the surface of the

4.34 *David Greene, illustration for "Imagining the Invisible University,"* Architectural Design, *April 1971. Still absorbed by the possibility of making architecture tread more lightly upon the earth (see figure 3.32), David Greene assimilated non-Western vernacular architectures (otherwise incompatible with Archigram's high-technology bravura) and land art.*

planet . . . our anchors to the planet, like the aborigine's, should be software, like songs or dreams, or myths. Abandon hardware, earth's-surface anchors. Electric aborigine makes for the moratorium on Buildings.[205]

In 1972 Greene juxtaposed a picture of a mud-hut-dwelling family with one of an astronaut wielding a cine-camera:[206] "boy meets girl" read the caption, capturing the "one world" euphoria of the moment when astronauts first captured images of the Earth (figure 4.36).

But of course Greene's caption glossed over the often rapacious nature of technology transfer from the West ("boy") to the South ("girl"). The illimitable extension of technology suggested an odd politics of development, at once demanding the justice of even global development while extending the imperialism of Western technocratic values. "There is the real opportunity," Cook contended in *Experimental Architecture*,

that the underdeveloped countries may by-pass the whole nineteenth-century hang-up which other environments have had to contend with. It is not only possible but advisable for these countries to go direct to the most advanced technologies which are appropriate. The image of the mud-hut with television teaching could be repeated in many other fields.[207]

The campaign against underdevelopment took a Buckminster Fullerine turn, extending inward to the "developed" world itself: "survival is not just a pleasant, sophisticated and well-heeled pursuit. The edge exists elsewhere," like "in the more desperate parts of Glasgow, Brussels or Marseilles. . . . The real experiment is going on where inventors, designers and 'activators' are working together."[208]

Archigram's heart was in the right place, but many "activators" preferred to think small, in the terms of an "appropriate technology" suggested by E. F. Schumacher.[209] Archigram's selective reception of environmentalism only added to the impression that they were stuck in a high-technology rut. "Ecology—there, I've said that word—is a social problem," Chalk announced to the AA Summer Session in 1970, shortly after twenty million people had taken to the streets to demonstrate in favor of Earth Day.[210] "We have been told so by *Time, Life, Newsweek, Look* and the Nixon administration. . . . Well. Our very survival depends on an ecological utopia, otherwise we will be destroyed." Chalk was sounding unconvinced. "This technological backlash we are experiencing must be fought with a more sophisticated technology, a more sophisticated science. . . . If we are to prevent eco-catastrophe it can only be done by more sophisticated environmental systems, not by dropping out."[211] As it happened, the seventies did not witness

4.35 *David Greene and Mike Barnard,* The Electric Aborigine, *montage, 1971.* **4.36** *David Greene,* Boy Meets Girl, *montage, 1972. Ever well-intentioned and ever provocative, at the beginning of the 1970s Archigram uneasily negotiated an entente between its own technocratic-consumerist principles and the ecological-countercultural reaction to them. The results could be both paternalistic and poetic, imagining the exchange of non-Western existential values in return for industrial knowledge.*

the end of the world, but, with the declining esteem of the nuclear industry and the advent of the 1973 energy crisis, neither did this decade heavily reinvest in technocratic consumerism. Archigram Architects was no better positioned to escape the ensuing economic downturn than any other architectural office, hastening the company's demise after the Monte Carlo site was sold off to private developers.

If *Archigram* responded to ecological critique by adjusting its iconography, its response to feminist critique did not even stretch to that. Progressive observers were offended by Archigram's tendency to decorate its collages with "dolly-bird" pictures of young, pretty, passive women collected from clothes catalogues, magazines, and advertisements. Banham invited viewers to believe that the potent union of women with machines was without significance, solemnly explaining that that was simply how the women appeared in the pictures that Archigram cut up (as when garnered from the sort of men's magazines that Banham admitted to finding meritorious, one might wonder): "nothing could more neatly illustrate the dangers of mistaking a piece of British graphic opportunism for an ideological programme."[212] Of Archigram's huge output, only a fraction used overtly sexist imagery (perhaps a dozen pieces), and it was consistent with the prevalent standards of sixties advertising, film, and the avant-garde. Unfortunately, it might also have appeared consistent with an adolescent worldview; Martin Pawley recalls how, having "dug deep into the roots of the Modern Movement . . . Mendelsohn, Scharoun, the Taut brothers, the Constructivists, De Stijl," the slides in the *Archigram Opera* turned to "the real sources of their inspiration; pictures from magazines of zeppelins, submarines, spacecraft, molecules, transistors, girls."[213] Delegates to the 1966 BASA Conference were met by "girls in black fishnet stockings and red T-shirts bearing the words ARCHIGRAM across them."[214] Reviewing *Archigram* in the *Whole Earth Catalog* in 1971, Stewart Brand's impression was of guys trying a little too hard to shock— "dream architecture, joke architecture, blasphemy architecture, science fiction architecture, adolescent wet dream architecture, leather architecture. Sin. Fun. For a while."[215]

It was not as though Archigram fell into obvious traps, like juxtaposing images of dominant men alongside quiescent women. Indeed, the group's tendency toward colorful loveliness can be credited with breaking the "tough" masculine conventions of hard-edged, black-and-white, geometric renderings that dominated modernist architectural drawing. This certainly was the effect for instance of the *Archigram* compendium's 1972 cover (designed by Diana Jowsey, one of several female assistants at Archigram Architects) and the floral extravagance of Archigram's "Palm Tree" submission for the Monte Carlo Summer Casino competition (1971, figure 4.37). Yet something willfully unreconstructed persisted in the "institutionalisation of innocence." The way Archigram Architects pandered to the taste of client Rod Stewart was knowingly absurd, presenting a pouting and suggestively crouching Ali McGraw in the foreground of the drawings for the rock star's new swimming pool enclosure (figure 4.38). It was 1972, too late in the day to be written off as a naive product of the swinging sixties. Archigram's presentations were "fun," depending upon the predilections of the viewer, but perhaps just too *reflective* of commercial and sexist imagery, comparing unfavorably even to the witty irony of the Independent Group.

4.37 *Ron Herron, Dennis Crompton, Warren Chalk, Ken Allinson, and Colin Fournier for Archigram Architects, "Palm Tree" scheme for the Monte Carlo Summer Casino competition, montage, 1971. In relating the "general ambience" of a seasonal casino for Monte Carlo, the Archigram group's usual gantries and trusses are overtaken by a "feminine," pink-tinted floral haze attracting Monaco's wealthy residents to the betting chips like bees to pollen.*

4.38 *Ron Herron and Dennis Crompton for Archigram Architects, pool enclosure for Rod Stewart, Ascot, montage, 1972. Archigram's neatly tailored "shed" for a rock star's swimming pool is packaged here as a fantasy, one man to five women, including a model coopted for experimental architecture, film star Ali McGraw.*

4.39 *Peter Cook, Instant City: typical nighttime scene, montage, 1968. Instant City entertainments roll around the clock for the brief period of its existence, images and text blown aloft by pneumatic tubes and dangled from balloons. Ambiguous perspectives, puzzling shapes, and "all-over" composition convey the vibrancy. In all, it is not the sort of scene normally associated with the political upheavals of 1968. Some attendees bear a resemblance to Archigram members appearing incognito.*

Archigram could appear unable to think outside its James Bond fascination with gadgets and the technological extension of the individual's power. "Freedom for Women" read a headline on the "Emancipation" section of *Archigram* no. 8, the magazine's sole direct reference to women's liberation. And there the reference ended; the woman illustrated, wearing the Info-Gonk and Handi-Pak, was being emancipated by zoom appliances. The attempt made in the same feature to theorize "emancipation" in terms of class fell back yet again to gadgets and consumption. "This is the crux of the matter: in the past the indulgences of the mind and intellect (as applied to artefacts) was the privilege of the rich. . . . It is now reasonable to treat buildings as consumer products, and the real justification of consumer products is that they are the direct expression of the freedom to choose."[216]

In short, Archigram sought a constituency of young, liberated, high-libido consumers—male or female. They congregated in Archigram's collages, joined in the Monte Carlo renderings of 1969 onward by older men *and* women who remained beautiful because of their evening-dressed wealth (figure 4.37). Mostly absent was anyone working, elderly, ordinary (even the Smithsons' collages were more inclusive than that, with "authentic" people joining Monroe and DiMaggio in the Golden Lane collages), or non-Caucasian. The whiteness of so much Archigram imagery (except in reference to jazz) was all the more puzzling given that the hip attitudes into which Archigram plugged and the inclusive overtones of "Living City" (figure 2.17) had origins in black culture. So the issue of representativeness successively went beyond gender to encompass age, class, and race. True again, this was how the models emerged out of the catalogues, but the meeting of the fashion catalogue with Archigram design was not accidental. "GLAMOUR": the word is suspended in midair in Cook's Instant City collage of 1968 (figure 4.39). While Instant City surely drew inspiration from the community activism of the sixties, Archigram swept aside the make-do dowdiness of much local-level activity; as Herron set about "tuning London" in 1972, it was to sustain the ebbing energies of swinging London (figure 3.33).

The "direct action" in Herron's images belonged to a different era from that actually being effected by squatting and riots in London's Notting Hill and Brixton, or even by the celebrated 1968 sit-in at Hornsey College of Art where Archigram members taught.[217] More critical investigation into the pop landscape hailed instead from younger designers of the late sixties and early seventies, such as the Italian radical architecture groups Archizoom and Superstudio (both founded in 1966) reacting to images from Archigram and the metabolists (figure 3.34). The Italians satirized pop in the "Superarchitecture" exhibitions of 1966–1967—"Superarchitecture is the architecture of super-production, of superconsumption, of superinducement to consumption, of the supermarket, of Superman, of super-high-est gasoline. Superarchitecture accepts the logic of production and consumption and makes an effort to demystify it."[218] And they variously replaced indeterminism with overdeterminism, or overdeterminism with indeterminism, in each case exploring the degrees to which architecture and capital can liberate the social body. The Italians found few solutions in Archigram's tangled robotic paraphernalia.[219] "In place of the myths peculiar to the design of the sixties, based on flexibility, unit assembly and mass-production," Archizoom's Andrea Branzi recalls, "the [Italian] avant-garde proposed unitary objects and spaces that were solid, immobile and aggressive in their almost physical force of communication."[220]

For many designers, the ten-day occupation of the Milan Triennale of 1968 by anarchists and students was a consciousness-raising affair. Archizoom (its very name an homage to Archigram) and Japanese architect Arata Isozaki (then working in a robotic/electronic idiom very close to Archigram) were both signatories of the occupation agreement,[221] but the upheaval did not apparently politicize another exhibitor at the show, Archigram. Prior to its destruction, exhibitors at the Milan show had undertaken to respond to the theme of mass society, of "greater number," and David Greene took the cue to ease himself into a mock-up of Webb's Cushicle Inflatable Suit-Home (figures 4.40–4.43).[222] As individuals were pampered, Archigram intimated, the well-being of the "greater number" was being served too.

Archigram tried to look relaxed riding the political changes, sharing an increasingly crowded platform of architectural

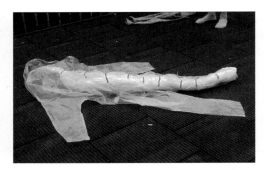

4.40, 4.41, 4.42, 4.43 *Archigram, Inflatable Suit-Home (suit made by Pat Haines and worn by David Greene), Milan Triennale, 1968. A working mock-up of Michael Webb's Suitaloon (figure 3.18) represented Archigram's response to the problems of mass society at the 1968 Triennale. The show was occupied and trashed by protestors shortly after.*

activists and willing to maintain a dialogue with radicals. "I don't know how Ron's Tuned Suburb grabs you," Cook reached out in 1970 to the editors of *ARse* ("Architectural Radicals, Students and Educators or whatever you want to call us").[223] "Perhaps it is a symbol of capitalist attitudes: the dangling of consumer-goodies to bolster up middle-class tat: and thereby stave off the real problem."[224] Yes, Cook was well aware of the shifting sands of student opinion, as close by as the AA itself, where *ARse* was edited,[225] featuring Cook on the cover of its May 1970 issue presenting the Monaco scheme to a board of plutocrats, Greene, Crompton, and Herron in impassive attendance (figure 4.44). But Cook was at pains to explain why he believed that architecture was an alternative to political radicalism, not a reaction to it: "I think that we share many objectives: particularly when it comes to action: humanitarian or physical."[226]

At the turn of the decade *Archigram* in effect deferred to the student body as the harbinger of change, while barely disguising its irritation with student opinions that it could no longer mold and with which it could not always empathize. Cook, writing on the cusp of the seventies, seemed to sense the end of an era. "1970: Good Luck from Archigram," the group magnanimously wished in greeting cards to fellow travelers and occasional foes such as Utopie (figure 4.45)[227] and *ARse*, as everyone braced themselves for a decade that promised to be a payback period for the excesses of the sixties, with none of its pleasures.[228] The 1970 installation of Edward Heath's Tory government in Britain confirmed that the sixties had ended culturally as well as temporally. "The seventies will be shit!" David Greene told the young architect Will Alsop on New Year's Eve, 1969.[229] "One is also aware of time passing and a basically crummy situation (by our way of thinking—a basically evil one by yours)," Cook told *ARse*. "There are then two strategies. We can go on irritably, because we are aware of mutual inconsistency; or we can jostle each other towards the action."[230] This "jostling" became *Archigram*'s final major project, as if in a bid to leave a legacy by galvanizing a student movement. For all of its own rhetoric against architecture, *Archigram* was largely bemused by young radicals' scathing criticism of architecture's institutional collusion with capitalism. "The objective is quite sharp: to get things moving

4.44 *ARse*, "Archigoon Wins at Monte," cover of ARse, no. 3, London, May 1970. Archigram *spawned many little magazines of architecture, some of which were politically militant by the late sixties and early seventies. Here* ARse, *in Oedipal mood, reacts to the news that Archigram have won the Monte Carlo competition (cf. figure 4.25).* **4.45** *Archigram, New Year's card to Utopie, 1970. A token exchanged through the experimental architecture network, demonstrating Archigram's largesse to its critics.*

by the collective effort and dynamic will of everybody who might read *Archigram 9*," enthused *Archigram* no. 9, launching a "Questionnaire":

Its background arises out of the many conversations which the Archigram Group and their friends and colleagues have in the architecture schools . . . if only these separated strands could be related and brought together there might be a very powerful, AND EXPLOSIVE statement to be made. . . . The more replies we get and compute together the more powerful is the mandate to do something about it. We shall print the questionnaire in AD, the BASA AJ supplement and anyone else's magazine that will print it.

Archigram acknowledged students as the "revolutionary" force, as did the new left, though it would be a mistake to think of *Archigram* as being *of* the new left. Archigram tried to prevent ZOOM's "contamination" by politics. What credibility Archigram still enjoyed at the end of the sixties derived from the reputation it had already accrued as part of an earlier "alternative" culture. It still qualified for the checklist of sources for an alternative society issued by the direct action group Friends of the Arts Council Co-operative (formed summer 1968),[231] and Jeff Nuttall's classic 1968 apologia for the sixties, *Bomb Culture*, contained the very mandate for Archigram's macho vision of a "revolution" managed by virile technologies:

Can we devise a fine architecture of ecstatic muscle and musical light? Can we apply a quivering phallic strength to our civic organization and our economy? . . . Let us take down our improvisations so that they can be perfected by skilled interpreters. . . . Let us build adventures, environments, mazes and gardens we can walk in and be reinformed continuously of our fine vitality. Let us turn away from the contemplators and listen to the architects, the activists, the engineers, the Archigram Group with their Plug-In City scheme, Cedric Price the Fun Palace designer . . .[232]

But events suddenly moved on after the autumn of 1967, when Nuttall wrote these closing paragraphs to his book,[233] and Plug-In seemed less pressing than the explosive street actions of 1968. In France, the students and architects who received a large 1969 AA delegation of fifth-years and staff "were irritated by the relaxed 'cool' of the AA students and their apparent lack of political involvement; their visitors were surprised by the Parisian militancy."[234]

The "cool" started to crack. "We suspect that there is many a bourgeois waiting to creep out from behind the barricades. Prove us wrong. Go on. Somebody," begged *Archigram* no. 9. "We have been to those congresses . . . where there are cries for Marx and the Mercedes is parked around the corner . . . where there are cries for Revolution . . . and then a return to the drawing board where the 'people's housing' is still an architect's elitist notion of what-the-people-should-have."[235] *Archigram* was referring obliquely to the French groups Architecture Principe (founded by Claude Parent and Paul Virilio) and Utopie. Launched in 1966 at the Ecole des Beaux-Arts in Paris through inspirations close to Archigram's—"the infuriating stupidity of the school. We dreamed of nothing more or less than to change the sclerotic world of architecture"[236]—*Utopie* magazine was powerfully influenced by *Archigram* and was in turn courted by London. In a sense, *Archigram*'s hunch was correct; by 1969, Utopie's architects Jean Aubert, Jean-Paul Jungmann, and Antoine Stinco were indeed drifting back into more traditional practice, but not before propagating radical ideas hailing from Henri Lefebvre and the Situationist International, imported into Utopie's thinking by theorists in the group including Jean Baudrillard and Herbert Tonka.[237] In 1967, *Utopie*'s founders Aubert, Jungmann, and Stinco submitted pneumatic structures for their diplomas as a test of the deeply establishment Ecole des Beaux-Arts. For the Utopie group, pneumatica assumed an ideological ideal—spontaneous structure in the hands of "the people"—and the Utopie group figured that the only obvious avant-garde space still unoccupied by Archigram was that of coherent theory and explicit social rationale.[238] Only after this groundwork was complete, Utopie believed, was a socially valid architecture possible. French radicalism made Utopie deride Archigram liberalism.

Despite their considerable resilience, by 1970 the maulings received by Archigram were bound to leave them a little bruised and suspect of "radicals." In April 1969, Archigram attended the congress Utopia e/o Rivoluzione at the Polytechnic of Turin, an auspicious gathering that also included Superstudio, Archizoom, Soleri, Yona Friedman's Groupe d'Etudes d'Architecture Mobile, and Utopie. Utopie were by this stage in particularly combative mode. "At a colloquium called 'Utopia [and/] or Revolution,'" Utopie's Herbert Tonka has extravagantly recalled of the ensuing lock-in, "we wrapped a number of shitheads in toiletpaper. We held the whole conference hostage for several hours with a leftist group called the Vikings. The cops showed up with submachine guns, etc. . . . Archigram was there; Archigram was on the wrong side, that of the hostages, not of the hostage-takers."[239] Tonka, clearly, had had enough of Archigram's refusal to come off the political fence or publish its reasoning for regarding design as autonomous from ideology; indeed, Archigram's aversion to "theory" per se, wherever possible positing the image in its place, smacked of agency for the capitalist "society of the spectacle." *Archigram* no. 8, the most theorized of the run, was far from leftist. The time had come to reestablish the connection of the avant-garde with antibourgeois revolution.

Although the younger groups often demonstrated a capacity for organization and output that rivaled Archigram's,[240] Archigram had a tendency to dismiss it as gestural.[241] Gestures were of no interest to Archigram: they wanted to see the *projects* for change. *Archigram* no. 9 cursorily reviewed the astonishing 1968 collapse of the Ecole des Beaux-Arts and rise of the revolutionary Unités Pédagogiques, merely concluding that "the Utopie Group still form the principal articulation of the May architects," presumably because their designs (pneumatic architecture) could be appreciated with or without the proletarian gestures they were meant to convey. *Archigram* deigned to "glance at Italy, where architecture schools remain only intermittently open. One problem (to an Englishman) is the multiplicity of layers of thought, attitude or nuance that are indulged in. To us, there is too much posturing and then a return to a nice bit of styling: SOONER OR LATER SOMEONE WILL HAVE TO DEFINE THE PROBLEMS: AND THEN *DO SOMETHING*."[242]

Faced with political criticism, Archigrammers had a tendency to assume the guise of realism and pragmatism about the motors of change, leaning upon a tradition in liberalism—"since we are English, we are most attracted to the characteristically Anglo-Saxon tactic of infiltration as contrasted with the characteristically Latin emotion which demands confrontation."[243] It was, moreover, a liberalism that bordered upon the libertarian—"Archigram's politics are the politics of people . . . not a conveniently abstract notion of 'the people' but a constantly evolving view of real situations . . . where the people are the essential ingredient of a dynamic state"[244]—and, more precisely, the rightward techno-libertarian. "When the busts are chosen for the staircase at Bedford Square to commemorate the heroes of the last decade," Fred Scott suggested in 1972, shortlisting a libertarian canon for the AA, "among the more obvious candidates included should be Daniel Bell, author of the *End of Ideology,* and Karl Popper, author of the *Open Society and Its Enemies,* executed, I would suggest, in a bio-degradable material; Ezra Pound, in a more durable material for saying 'make it new,' and a space left where Henry T. Ford's bust would have been, had one been done, for his observation on antiquity."[245]

DEZOOMING THE AVANT-GARDE

Not until Greene's 1974 Archigram/AA film *Warren, I Remember Architecture Too* (produced with Mike Mires) did a note of despondency enter the group's work, Greene comparing architects to butchers. Another witness in the film described his experience of working for the borough of Camden in north London, realizing that he was just a name on the borough payroll, struggling to recall his purposes for entering the profession, pondering his once-held belief that Camden could be the microcosm of ideal order in the universe. By this time, the Camden of borough chief architect Neave Brown was an anomaly, the bold megastructure of the Alexandra Road Housing Scheme (1961–1979), for example, just surviving the crash in esteem for modernist public housing in Britain.

In the early seventies backlashes against "thinking big," "plenty," and the "architecture of technology" inevitably eroded interest in Archigram's vision, just as surely as it did that of mainstream modernism. There was little likelihood of architects adopting the advanced building technologies proposed in *Archigram* while those deployed in the field were woefully unproven or disproven. The investment made by the Greater London Council into the sorts of plug-in, gasket-sealed techniques promoted in *Archigram*—such as plastic bathroom units, fiberglass cladding, and gasket-seal windows—looked like the start of a new era (figure 4.46), but it was the beginning of the end.[246] The collapse in east London in May 1968 of the Ronan Point flats, erected by a subsidiary of the Archigram architects' former employer Taylor Woodrow using a Danish building system, finished public receptivity to architectural mass production.

But because *Archigram* had itself helped catalyze opprobrium for mainstream modernism, always figuring out what could come after the concrete and the housing estates, it maintained a splendid isolation from the agonies that modernism was undergoing generally. Indeed its pragmatic design methods could be claimed as contextual (possibly conservationist) in outlook. The group was rather postmodern in certain respects, such as the emphasis it laid upon choice and the deemphasis of architecture's moral-political mission. Still, it was nowhere near postmodern enough to stay at the leading edge of the 1970s: *Archigram* had little interest in history; after "Living City," it abandoned the city; its response to "theory" was confused.

As far back as 1966 at Folkestone, when the zoom wave should have been at its zenith, Archigram and Reyner Banham must have already suspected that architects were everywhere foreclosing the modernist project before it had reached its "logical" conclusion of *architecture autre*—an architecture of pure, ecstatic servicing. In America, supposedly the natural home of technological indeterminism, Charles Moore and Philip Johnson were advocating history, form, erudition, and artistic intuition at the expense of the purely modern, and at just that point, in 1966, the Museum of Modern Art itself published Robert Venturi's *Complexity and Contradiction in Architecture,* the summary of such reactionary heresies. In Italy, architect Aldo Rossi was modifying his rationalist sensibilities, arguing in his *Architettura della città* (again published in 1966) for the careful matching of modern architecture with the existing typologies of the "architecture of the city." In Venturi's and Rossi's wake, "place-making" with piazzas, pitched roofs, classical rhythms, vaults, and mortar started nudging aside the flyaway balloons and rivets of the avant-garde vision.

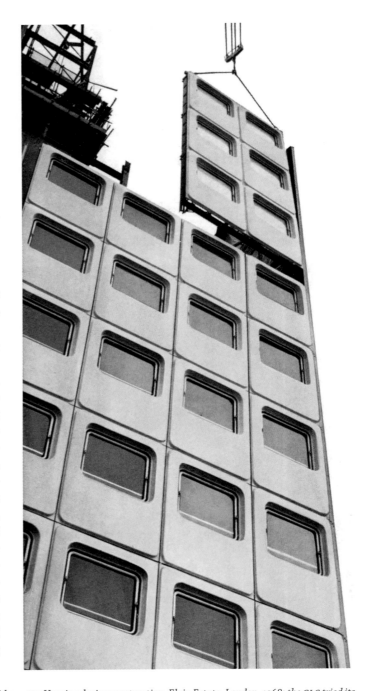

4.46 *Greater London Council Architects' Department, section leader J. W. Davidson,* SF1 *Housing during construction, Elgin Estate, London, 1968: the GLC tried its hand at the "plug-in" plastic units and fiberglass cladding promoted through* Archigram *by some of its former employees four or five years earlier (and which more distantly recollected experiments such as Harrison and Abramovitz's Alcoa Headquarters, Pittsburgh, 1951–1953). But the techniques were similar to system building, which was quickly diminishing in reputation, and they received little further development within the public sector.*

It was with some relish that Banham taunted detractors of zoom with the news in 1970 that Archigram had won the Monte Carlo competition:

"Come-uppance" was the word that sprang to the lips of the world's wisecrackers. Said one, in my hearing, "So it's goodbye to all that plug-in crap, now Archigram have got to design a real building like the rest of us." Of course, it's people like him, who unthinkingly equate "visionary" with "impracticable," who get architecture a bad name.[247]

The sun was nevertheless setting on zoom. Ironically, Archigram's reputation as the leading avant-garde in architecture ended not with Monte Carlo (which it might otherwise have done, a move from paper to construction on the one hand, a colossal test of its competence on the other) nor with student-driven radicalism, but with the general return of the architectural radicals of circa 1968 to "professionalism," to the practice of building. The Pompidou Center, inspired by a heady combination of Fun Palace, Archigram, and the direct democracy of '68, ultimately captured the monumental vision of a zoomed-up French state. Even within the radical teaching units of the dismembered Ecole des Beaux-Arts, the ambition of some students to earn professional qualifications in 1971 had to be policed with increasing violence, hard-liners adopting the example of the rioting students of Yale in 1968 by burning down the school office.[248]

The switch from unbridled optimism about radical architecture to a suspicion of it was one of the signal qualities of postmodernism. The American postmodernists Robert Venturi and Denise Scott Brown, criticizing the misapprehension that architecture can or should change the world through ruthless modernization, were already disavowing the pretensions of the avant-garde in their teaching seminars at Yale in 1968 (which would lead to publication of their seminal *Learning from Las Vegas*, written with Steven Izenour in 1972). Archigram found the work going on under Venturi and Scott Brown overly precious: "Yale students," *Archigram* no. 9 reported, "study their own new cultures (Las Vegas or Cape Kennedy) with an archness befitting Inigo Jones treading the pavements of Rome: relaxedness, the real clue, is missed."[249] For her part, Scott Brown had critically reviewed the zoom wave in her 1968 article "Little Magazines in Architecture and Urbanism."[250] In *Learning from Las Vegas*, Venturi, Scott Brown, and Izenour held up Archigram and its world of zoom as a modernist bogey whichever way they looked at it. "The megastructure has been promoted by the elaborate journalism of groups such as Archigram who reject architecture but whose urban visions and mural-scale graphics go beyond the last, megalomaniac gasps of the late Beaux-Arts delineators."[251]

Scott Brown implied that Archigram paid attention to the detailing of images at the expense of detailed thinking; zoom was an admiration of American technological/consumerist form without an attendant understanding of the social, economic, political, psychological, or even technological forces that created it. "Someone in *Archigram*," Scott Brown suggested in didactic tone,

should find out why the prefabrication of housing in America has been a failure in spite of massive inputs of government money. . . . The prefabs, since their savings were related to only half the cost of the house (almost half the house cost in a single house goes into on-site work), were not able to bring about significant cost reductions. Levitt, by owning or controlling enough components of the building industry to ensure rationalization of the construction process from manufacture to the elements of delivery and erection, was able, without going to car bodies or plastic capsules, to produce the best value housing in America.[252]

In fact, the massive infrastructure of Plug-In (figure 1.3) was a proposition to ameliorate the cost of the site work, though how it would be funded was part of the Archigram mystery; perhaps it was to have been the ultimate manifestation of the British mixed economy, a public infrastructure with private infill. Whatever, a pragmatically inclined Scott Brown was unimpressed, arguing that total flexibility demanded excessive redundancy—space and services lying around on the off-chance that they were wanted. Archigram was allowed no "get-out": the group's drive "beyond architecture" was described not as a liberation but as nihilism:

> No architecture is not the answer to too much architecture. . . . The world science futurist metaphysic, the megastructuralist mystique, and the look-Ma-no-buildings environmental suits and pods are a repetition of the mistakes of another generation. Their overdependence on a space-age, futurist, or science-fiction technology parallels the machine aestheticism of the 1920s and approaches its ultimate mannerism. They are, however, artistically a dead-end and socially a cop-out.[253]

It was a quirk of fate that the criticism making Archigram into an anachronism at the beginning of the 1970s should be articulated by architects working from a comparable standpoint of "popularity." Venturi and Scott Brown were Americans, yet did not welcome Archigram's homage to the United States; Archigram's approach was disparagingly likened to the "latter-day mass-pop cultural-object wonder, à la Tom Wolfe."[254] Venturi and Scott Brown were, like Archigram, admirers of the Smithsons, and they chastened Archigram in the way one might have expected from the Smithsons themselves: Archigram stood accused of designing neither for the Smithsons' "ordinary person" nor for Venturi and Scott Brown's Levittowner, but for their own superconsumer.

As the initiative gravitated toward the United States, the neo-avant-garde itself acquired an air of professionalism. No more "little magazines," chaotically produced and distributed, left exposed to critique by poor theorization and cursory acknowledgments of history: step forward Venturi's sleekly produced *Complexity and Contradiction,* all its words typeset on a letterpress, with its pictures seated in straight lines. Step forward, too, the formidably titled *Oppositions,* launched in 1974 by Peter Eisenman et al. from the Institute for Architecture and Urban Studies in New York, written through with a sophisticated theorization that interrogated architecture before it presumed to tune society.[255] The cost of this professionalism and critical rigor was, Archigram felt, the *pleasure* that pop had introduced into architectural production: "Archigram says love our pictures, not our words . . . Archigram is not about Derrida but the staccato of ideas."[256]

The meeting of Continental theory with American gravitas in the 1970s left zoom out of the circuit.[257] American architectural criticism acquired a consistently severe tone. "As the Modern Movement died in 1939," Eisenman wrote in a 1975 *Oppositions* editorial, "so too did this neo-functionalism of Archigram die in 1968."[258] Eisenman now declared a "Post-Functionalism,"[259] an autonomy that validated the rise of the New York Five (Eisenman, Michael Graves, Charles Gwathmey, John Hejduk, and Richard Meier). Avant-garde architectural drawing in the 1970s depicted buildings as apparitions from a netherworld, not a home appliance catalogue. Archigram may not have seen the need for "ideology," but the New York Five also jettisoned hope of global renewal by architecture. They concentrated instead upon what they knew modern architecture to be capable of—local form—reworking the achievements inherited from Le Corbusier and Terragni in which Archigram had become largely uninterested. The handover of initiative was observed by the senior critic-historian Colin Rowe, whose foreword to *Five Architects* in 1972 added Archigram to the memorial roll-call "of fractional style phases; the cult of townscape and the new empiricism, Miesian neo-classicism, neo-Liberty, the New Brutalism, Team X, the Futurist Revival, Archigram, in terms of which involutions any consideration of architecture in the 1970s must be based."[260] And Peter Cook, indefatigably networking the avant-garde (with or without *Archigram*), hosted an exhibition of the New York Five at his own Art Net gallery in 1975.[261]

CONCLUSIONS

The introduction to this book suggested the plot of Archigram's adventure. It remains for these conclusions to speculate why sales of *Archigram* faltered before that adventure had ended.

By 1972, Robert Venturi and Denise Scott Brown could no longer take Archigram seriously (though their murderous engagement with it suggested that, on another level, they did): "Archigram's structural visions are Jules Verne versions of the Industrial Revolution with an appliqué of Pop-aerospace terminology."[1] Three years later, Martin Pawley was rearranging the observation to show how serious Archigram had been (thereby recognizing that Archigram hadn't been taken seriously), hoping to persuade readers of *Oppositions* that Archigram stood for "an existential technology for individuals that the world will, in time, come to regard with the same awe as is presently accorded to the prescience of Jules Verne, H. G. Wells, or the Marquis de Sade. Futile to complain (as many do), 'But they never *build* anything.' Verne never *built* the *Nautilus,* Wells could hardly drive a car, and the Marquis de Sade?"[2]

Some will today favor Pawley's defense, and others will concur with Venturi and Scott Brown's prosecution, for exactly the same reasons that observers were split about Archigram's worth at the time. Archigram successfully restored avant-gardism in the expectation of giving modernism a new lease of life, placing technology center stage again—and these reasons for saluting the group were and are reasons why it was also spurned. Archigram generously made touch papers that could reignite the *image* of the architectural profession—but for many, it *does* matter that architectural projects yield to acceptable built results, or at least look plausible.

If the Monaco Entertainments Centre had been built—and it might have been, since it was detailed by Archigram Architects and its Parisian consultants over a period of four years, with fruitless monthly site visits—Archigram's place in history would be fundamentally different.[3] It would be less fantastic and it would be narrower, since the tendency would doubtless be to read *Archigram* magazine as the herald for Archigram buildings, rather than as the prophet of architectural possibilities. Structures completed by the Archigram office between 1972 and 1974—the Play Centre for Calverton End in Milton Keynes, the swimming pool and kitchen block for Rod Stewart at Windsor, and the "Instant Malaysia" installation for the Commonwealth Institute, London—have not affected the perception of Archigram as unbuilt and utopian.

Even such "soft-centered" buildings slightly conflicted with the ultimate logic of *Archigram*'s move "beyond architecture," and by the late sixties it was possible to distinguish those members of Archigram determined to build from those who would prefer a "moratorium" on buildings and even drawings of buildings.[4] Ron Herron relinquished a senior post at the major Los Angeles architectural office of William L. Pereira Associates so that he could work at Archigram Architects alongside the other company partners, Peter Cook and Dennis Crompton, while Warren Chalk, David Greene, and Michael Webb were less involved with the new practice.[5] Built or unbuilt, all members agreed that the purpose of architecture was to serve as an event. That belief had arisen for them at a certain historical moment, known as "the Sixties." Perhaps it was better that the Archigram legacy lived on in the drawings and concepts of ecstatic social intercourse, rather than be stillborn in neutral serviced sheds of obsolete, cutback seventies technologies.

AHEAD OF THE FUTURE

In the meantime, the world that Archigram was trying to address with its zoom gospel moved on, and Archigram's core messages were found increasingly invalid. Even its old adversary, mainstream modernism, was forced into retirement by social and political changes and by its own hubris, packing up work on the housing projects and city center comprehensive redevelopments, leaving Archigram not so much triumphant as alone. What hadn't so much killed mainstream modernism was Archigram, which dreamed that the architectural "establishment"—the heads of the large public offices, the big architectural practices, and the RIBA—would wither away after zoom was adopted by the student body and public.

One of Archigram's accomplishments had been to reorient architecture toward changing social and ideological patterns, recognizing that individualism and consumerism were the prevalent postwar European and American social movements. Socialism had earned a tenured place in mainstream European politics, and radicalism made impressive breakthroughs, as in 1968, but the collectivity and state control that informed the ideology of modernism from the 1920s to the 1950s generally lost their allure. This Archigram acutely perceived.

So zoom went headlong into the world of mass consumption. A pitfall was that zoom simply exchanged one definition of the architectural clientele (the collective masses) for another (the consumer masses). This meant that shoals of people fell through Archigram's net, from the disadvantaged of the inner-city poor to the pioneers of the environmental frontier; Archigram, whatever its humanitarian compassion, seemed still less relevant outside the West.

Moreover, Archigram may have got ahead of actual consumer desire. Archigram assumed that consumers wanted architecture to be provided to them in much the same way as the cars, motorboats, and televisions for which they undoubtedly yearned. It was true that, in its windswept housing projects and civic centers, mainstream modernism had inadvertently deprived its clientele of a sense of place and control. Archigram set out to offer an alternative, but by dissolving place into a nexus of servicing points joined by free-roving human receptors, it too threatened to dissolve place and spatial ownership. Archigram sought the solution to modernism's shortcoming in making modernism more extreme; the appetite, postmodernists were discovering, was for the opposite.

It was as if consumers relished the contrast between stasis and ephemerality. More people flew, and chose fixed and concrete points in space as their destinations. Consumers continued to discriminate between their houses and their caravans; they distinguished homemaking from package holidays, souvenirs from consumer durables, and separated their emotional attachment to dining tables from their lack of sentiment for kitchen gadgets; the ceremony of drawing the curtains was not to be the same as switching off the television. It was, perhaps, as liberating for people to not think about architecture as it was for them to be preoccupied by its continual rearrangement. These oddities and hierarchies of living were somewhat disregarded by zoom. Not that Archigram underrated the sophistication of its prospective clients. Archigram foresaw a world of genial consumers venting their creativity through architecture. But in the late twentieth century consumers veered ever more toward the bottom line of equity in their houses, and do-it-yourself (which certainly embodied physical interaction between occupants and buildings) actually recovered the *traditional* techniques of the building trade, serving the dictum of frugality rather than plenty.

In the decades after the sixties, architecture learned the trick of looking solid while actually being pretty easy to put up and take down, gamely housing rapid turnovers of information terminals and personnel. Typical postmodern steel frame office blocks of the eighties, lightly clad with rusticated panels and held aloft by hollow cement Tuscan columns, were Archigram-like illusions, aside from their rejection of modernism's industrially derived aesthetic. With remarkable prescience, Archigram had risen to meet the challenges mounted to the fixed edifice of architecture by late capitalist economies. But social mobility and capital flows did not annul the dictation of ground plans by land ownership, utilities, and roads. Nor did capital wash away discrepancies in opportunity between classes, regions, races, and genders, or liquidate a third of the working week. In other words, the social and economic conditions for total zoom never quite came to fruition.

REMOTE CONTROL

Some of this may be clearer with hindsight, though a number of observers at the time found Archigram irritatingly remote from pressing social issues. This book has pointed to Archigram's "indeterminism" as precisely the feature that made it momentous to the history of the avant-garde, but this needs to be weighed against the cost to Archigram's long-term credibility. "The movement that *Archigram* 1 was preceding must be noted for its lack of precision on the theoretical side," noted the otherwise devoted *Megascope* (itself hardly weighty) in 1966.[6]

Though Warren Chalk and David Greene promoted a more reflective approach for Archigram, it remained somewhat inscrutable, and unacceptably hedonistic for the new left–influenced "commitments" of a late-sixties/early-seventies student caucus. Archigram's disinterest in the precise relationship between its technical vision and attendant politico-economic mechanisms, initially part of its futurist charm, finally stranded the group in a semitheorized limbo, too antithetical to positivism to subscribe wholeheartedly to technocracy or systems theory, still less Marxism, yet hesitant about the emergent structuralist and poststructuralist ideas that countered positivism. Archigram came to regard theory not as a vehicle by which to transport its bliss to others, but as a contaminant through which spoilers might break up Archigram's party.

More architectural ideas were ever Archigram's recourse, yet in the early 1970s the keynote Italian critic Manfredo Tafuri was arguing that architectural practice was merely a superstructural phenomenon of bourgeois society and could thus be nothing better than a bourgeois implement of repression. If this was true of architecture generally, Tafuri indicated, it was true too of its avant-gardes—even more so of those like Archigram that disregarded self-reflexive theory. Their experiments were only so many futile aestheticizations of the conditions of postwar mass consumer culture, which swamped attempts at meaning with a flood of consumer goods. Hence, Tafuri's argument followed, the desperate gestures by an avant-garde like Archigram, embracing formlessness and indeterminacy in an effort to make sense of the conditions from which it was created, desirous to be swept along by the tide and speak the same language. "The formlessness," explained Tafuri in 1974,

> no longer generates anxiety once it is accepted as linguistic material. . . . And vice versa: language can speak of the indeterminate, the casual, the transient, since in them it greets the advent of the Whole. Yet this is but an endeavour to give a form of expression to the phenomenon of *mass consumption. It is not by chance that a great many of such celebrations of formlessness take place under the banner of a technological utopia. The ironic and irritating metaphors of the Archigram and Archizoom groups, or*

Johansen's and Gehry's notion of architecture as an explosion of fragments . . . have their roots in the technological myth. Technology can thus be read mystically, as a "second nature." [7]

Archigram tackled the symptoms of a dying modernism more directly than the reasons why modernism was dying. This was masked by celebration—"designing for pleasure, doing your own thing with the conviction that comes from the uninhibited exercise of creative talent braced by ruthless self-criticism . . . because it's so rare it's beyond quibble," Reyner Banham claimed of Archigram in 1972.[8] In other words, Archigram's internal criticism allowed the group to pay little heed to external critique, and artistic impulse alone could provide a rationale if society and architectural practice could not.

The Situationist International, another "last avant-garde" with which Archigram had a passing acquaintance, can serve as a reference point in evaluating Archigram's ideology. As it too responded to the supreme currency of the image in a world devoid of meaning beyond consumption, the ultraleftist Situationist International chose to produce theory and tactics rather than more images. The situationists wanted to lead the world beyond spectacle, and the consequences of failure, they believed, would be a future of unobstructed economic flows, everyone a pure consumer, the entire material world functioning as commodity.

Archigram *did* care about people: its assertion of choice over prescription was a major advance upon mainstream modernism. Archigram envisaged emancipation through the architectural equivalent of fridges and cars and kits that made everyone an architect. Let the workers have the fridges and cars they produced, the situationists concurred. Consumption, however, would not liberate workers, the situationists added; liberation would arrive with the realization that commodities don't really satisfy human needs.[9]

POSTMODERN MODERNISM

In the immediate aftermath of the sixties, both the left's anticapitalism and Archigram's supermodernity looked problematic to an architectural profession with newly downsized ambitions, making its way with an (initially) low-key, piecemeal, "postmodern" stance. That Archigram was a last stand for heroic modernist renewal made it no less consequential to postmodernism, however.

Indeed history validated the claims of both the situationists and Archigram. To some extent the events in Paris in 1968 underscored situationist rage, and then, with the onset in the 1970s of capitalist-fueled postmodern culture, Archigram's go-with-the-flow ethos began to look far-thinking after all. Archigram's world was both a stage behind and a stage beyond that of the situationists; former Utopie member Jean Baudrillard, rescinding situationist-inflected Marxism to become a voice of postmodernism, began writing in the "take it away, eat it, drive it, fuck it"[10] vein of late Archigram. The situationists and Archigram also shared rediscovery, after two or three decades sitting on file, by students attracted to the sixties not only for its retro appeal but also for its path-breaking encounter with techno-cultural democracy.

In addition to sparking the high-tech testimonial buildings of the seventies, Archigram contributed to low-tech postmodern sentiments. It celebrated the untidy heterogeneity of the city, it enjoyed the vulgarity of popular culture. Its very manner was of postmodern inconsistency, by turns cheering and disavowing architecture. It recognized that architecture *is* a consumer product; it accelerated that condition, then contrarily dissolved the central object of the property-owning democracy, the fixed abode with investment value.

The dissent at the core of Archigram's pedagogy, so apparent in the cocktail shaken by early editions of *Archigram* and at Archigram's 1966 Folkestone conference, again made it a herald to the emergent, pluralist, postmodern atmosphere. Reluctantly acknowledging students' widespread rejection of technology as the universal panacea for social and architectural ills, in the late sixties and early seventies zoom teaching criteria were adjusted to the "pluralistic situation."[11] The liberalization of the architectural syllabus in the last quarter of the twentieth century can be traced back to zoom, if not exclusively to it. Treating every student as a rock star, zoom recognized as many different autograph styles as there were performers.

So nebulous and multifarious are Archigram's consequences that they have about them a maddening inescapability. Rem Koolhaas, no Archigram devotee but carrying the rock star charisma of an AA zoom graduate, confesses to the indelibility of that period on his thought processes: "there have been no new movements in urbanism since Team 10 and Archigram."[12] Successive cohorts of architectural students on the verge of inventing media-, kit-, and event-based design find themselves looking back to an earlier moment.

TOUCHDOWN

The nuances and contradictions running beneath the shimmering cartoon surface of Archigram were its undercurrents of consequence. Archigram, the group and the magazine, must be integral to accounts of the avant-garde, and to the chronicles of modernism, postmodernism, architectural education, and urban design. *Archigram* published the most extreme portfolio to have issued from architects since the halcyon interwar years of Le Corbusier, Russian constructivism, and Buckminster Fuller.

The sober evaluation (perhaps the postrationalization) of something rustled up for pleasure is the peculiar burden that here befalls architectural history. Archigram appropriated the forms of popular culture (the funny images, the snap-together language, the indifference to referencing) so that it could intervene in weighty matters about architecture's purpose. *Archigram*'s papery discoveries can now offer witness in questions of architectural representation, the prevalence of historicism, the architectural control of space and society, the relationship of architecture to environmental design and culture at large, and the state of architectural technology. Though its members generally opted to design with ink on paper, not with the light pen and computer, Archigram forewarned the profession that information technology would likely change architecture formally and programmatically. (Philosophical and artisanal, in many ways Archigram was more deeply traditional than the mainstream of bureaucrats that it wanted to supersede.)

What remained compelling about Archigram's work for progressive architects was the possibility of an architecture without architecture, organizing experience without incarcerating it. This then would be an architecture to parallel other modern instruments for the organization of spatial experience—the reproduced image, the telephone, the computer—delicious in their flows and fast edits but incapable alone of sustaining human occupation. Archigram's work (and in this it was aided by its noncommittal politics) has resonated too with the dream of escaping the conventions of space, as it is organized around the clutches of the market, the family, the state, and other hegemonies exposed in the celebrated late-twentieth-century treatises of the new left, Foucault, Deleuze, and Guattari.

Archigram asserted the importance of the "event" of architecture, that quality which design now readily acknowledges, and paradoxically Archigram's event-based architecture left a legacy to architectural aesthetics. Indeed, Archigram's memorandum on the pleasures of the ephemeral and the poetry of contemporary technology became visible in countless buildings of the late twentieth century, Ron Herron Associates' Imagination Headquarters in London (1989) an exemplar of the style, its silicon-coated fabric roof stretched on tensile connectors between an Edwardian school and its neighbor, as if provisionally.[13]

Nevertheless, one studies Archigram because it is symptomatic of the architectural condition, not because it is exemplary of architectural production. Archigram's greater vision of a world emotionally redeemed by technology slipped from its control and degraded over ensuing decades into the syrupy marketing favored by the telecommunications, airline, and computing industries, while habitable, private, itinerant machines emanated solely from the car showroom. In one of the last pieces he wrote on behalf of Archigram, Chalk dutifully reiterated the group's ultraoptimism, but the title of the 1969 article hinted at the creeping banality of technology: "Owing to Lack of Interest, Tomorrow Has Been Cancelled."[14] In the Archigram retrospective of 1972, Chalk recalled the moment when he realized that the space age was losing thrust:

> David Greene, Spider Webb and I clamoured ecstatically over the rocket support structures at Cape Kennedy. I visited the NASA control centre at Houston and later witnessed the second Surveyor (manless) moon landing on the monitors at the Jet Propulsion Laboratories in Los Angeles, collecting small fragments of the moon surface. But it was an omen. The technician assigned to me, sitting in front of a bank of 39 close-circuit TV monitors of the lunar operation, was in fact watching the Johnny Carson Show on the fortieth.[15]

NOTES

PREFACE

1 For many years the best readily available source-book for Archigram was that edited by Archigram itself: Peter Cook, ed., *Archigram* (London: Studio Vista, 1972, subsequently reprinted). This was supplemented in 1994 by Archigram Archives' splendid small survey *A Guide to Archigram 1961–74* (London: Academy), which included essays by Pascal Schöning and Herbert Lachmayer suggesting lines for the theoretical interpretation of Archigram's work, expanding upon the largely technological-determinist tenor of earlier British commentators such as Reyner Banham and Martin Pawley. 1994 also saw the publication of the Pompidou Centre catalogue *Archigram*, ed. Alain Guiheux (Paris: Centre Georges Pompidou, Collection Monographie), which accompanied an Archigram exhibition; similarly, in 1997, the Kunsthalle Wien published the proceedings of *Archigram: Symposium zur Ausstellung*, ed. Eleonora Louis et al. (Vienna: Ritter Verlag). Ian Jeffrey's insightful "Young British Architects," in David Alan Mellor and Laurent Gervereau, eds., *The Sixties: Britain and France, 1962–1973* (London: Philip Wilson), also appeared in 1997. A valuable "companion volume" to *A Guide to Archigram 1961–74* was produced in London in 1998, when Archigram Archives published *Concerning Archigram*. This latter volume contained the excellent essay by Barry Curtis, "A Necessary Irritant," which placed Archigram in the context of British cultural history. Hadas Steiner has related Archigram to various scientific discourses: see "The Permanence of Impermanence," in Patrizia Bonifazio et al., eds., *Tra guerra e pace* (Milan: Franco Angeli, 1998), and "Off the Map," in Jonathan Hughes and Simon Sadler, eds., *Non-Plan* (Oxford: Architectural Press, 2000), chapters that drew upon research for her Ph.D. dissertation, Massachusetts Institute of Technology, 2001 (sooner than preempt material which might yet be published from this dissertation, the present book consults only that work by Steiner which is in print). The award to Archigram of the Royal Gold Medal prompted such commentaries as Sam Jacob's "Der Futurismus von Archigram," *Arch +*, no. 164–165 (April 2003), pp. 96–101, which wittily reaffirmed the "Englishness" of Archigram.

2 See Simon Sadler, "Open Ends: The Social Visions of 1960s Non-planning," in Hughes and Sadler, eds., *Non-Plan;* "Archigram and Technocracy," in *Universal versus Individual: The Architecture of the 1960s, Conference Proceedings 2002* (Jyväskylä: Alvar Aalto Academy, 2002); "The Brutal Birth of Archigram," in "The Sixties," *Twentieth Century Architecture*, no. 6 (London: Twentieth Century Society, 2002); "The Invisible University," *arq (Architectural Research Quarterly)* 6, no. 2 (2002); "Portrait of the Architect as a Young Man," *Art History* 26, no. 3 (2003); and "New Babylon versus Plug-in City," in Martin van Schaik and Otakar Máčel, eds., *Exit Utopia: Architectural Provocations 1956–76* (Munich: Prestel, 2005).

3 See <http://www.wmin.ac.uk/sabe/page-497>. This memorable description of the perennial inaccessibility of Archigram's archival material reiterates the one given to the author by Dennis Crompton, London, 29 May 2000, and accordingly only publications by or in collaboration with Archigram Archives appear to reference that material by Archigram not yet in circulation. Meanwhile the archive of Reyner Banham pertinent to the period studied in this book was largely destroyed during the relocation of the Banham household to the United States in 1976 (interview with Mary Banham, London, 28 April 1997), and Taylor Woodrow Construction, the sometime employer of members of the group, is unable to trace the relevant archive (e-mail, 4 October 2003).

4 Dennis Crompton is preparing a new title, *The Archigram Files*, for Monacelli Press.

5 Given the uneven accessibility of primary evidence, readers might beware the increased risk of minor errors in dates and attributions, even where the Archigram and Herron Archives have endeavored to cross-check them.

INTRODUCTION

1 David Rock, "Citation for Royal Gold Medal 2002," Royal Institute of British Architects, London, 20 November 2002, reprinted <http://www.architecture.com/go/Architecture/Also/Awards_311.html>.

2 "A Comment from Peter Reyner Banham," in Peter Cook, ed., *Archigram* (London: Studio Vista, 1972), p. 5.

3 Martin Pawley, "Peter Cook—Archiman or Anarchist?," *Building Design,* 15 May 1970, pp. 6–7.

4 Archigram Architects, postcard, 1970, in the archive of Tony Rickaby.

5 James Cubitt quoted in Reyner Banham, "Stocktaking," *Architectural Review,* February 1960, reprinted in Reyner Banham, *Design by Choice*, ed. Penny Sparke (London: Academy, 1981), p. 48. Cook and Greene worked at Cubitts between 1960 and 1962. See Peter Cook, "The Beginning," in Dennis Crompton, ed., *Concerning Archigram* (London: Archigram Archives, 1998), p. 15.

6 See Sam Jacob, "Der Futurismus von Archigram," *Arch +,* no. 164–165 (April 2003), pp. 96–101, for an articulation of this argument.

7 Dennis Crompton, address at the Archigram symposium, Cornerhouse, Manchester, 9 February 1998.

8 "Let's Give a Big Hand," *Archigram* no. 8 (1968), n.p.

1   A NEW GENERATION: ARCHIGRAM'S FORMATION AND ITS CONTEXT

1 Peter Cook, "Archigram, the Name and the Magazine," *Perspecta,* supplement no. 11 (1967), reprinted as "Some Notes on the Archigram Syndrome," in Archigram, ed., *A Guide to Archigram 1961–74* (London: Academy, 1994), p. 25.

2 See Theo Crosby and John Bodley, eds., *Living Arts,* no. 2 (London: Institute of Contemporary Arts and Tillotsons, 1963), p. 120.

3 "The Month in Britain," *Architectural Design,* November 1961, p. 431.

4 See Alison and Peter Smithson's famous survey, "The Heroic Period of Modern Architecture," *Architectural Design,* November 1965, p. 587ff.

5 The idea that architects were broadly divided by generation was popularized by Philip Drew's classic survey, *Third Generation: The Changing Meaning of Modern Architecture* (New York: Praeger, 1972), and by the Smithsons (see, for instance, Alison Smithson, ed., *Team 10 Meetings* [New York: Rizzoli, 1991]).

6 John Summerson, *Ten Years of British Architecture 1945–55* (London: Arts Council of Great Britain, 1956), p. 6.

7 To put the style in context, the architects at the Festival of Britain were countering the preponderance of the dreary neo-Georgian style that had so far easily satisfied straitjacket London building codes, and was an approved style of the LCC as late as 1951. See Royston Landau, *New Directions in British Architecture* (London: Studio Vista, 1968), p. 27. In the meantime, it had been left to other programs, such as those in inner-city boroughs like Finsbury or the famous school-building projects of Hertfordshire, to set the pace for modern architecture in Britain.

8 The "picturesque" was energetically promoted by *Architectural Review*.

9 Summerson, *Ten Years of British Architecture*, p. 8. The Festival of Britain was reminiscent of the 1930 Stockholm Exhibition.

10 Even "second generation" sympathizers like J. M. Richards had felt forced to announce "The Failure of the New Towns" (*Architectural Review*, July 1953)—due, he said, to an excessive reliance on garden city models.

11 Cedric Price, "Activity and Change," *Archigram*, no. 2 (1962), n.p.

12 Cedric Price, in *Megascope*, no. 1 (1964), n.p., cited in Denise Scott Brown, "Little Magazines in Architecture and Urbanism," *Journal of the American Institute of Town Planners* 34, no. 4 (July 1968), p. 227. Price's jibes were aimed at the *Architectural Review*'s delight in "picturesque" detailing.

13 The "domesticated" modernism that developed in Britain, using Scandinavian, Soviet, and vernacular inspirations, became known variously as "new humanism" and "new empiricism," depending on the political hue of the architects. See, for instance, Reyner Banham, "New Brutalism," in Vittorio Lampugnani, ed., *The Thames and Hudson Encyclopaedia of 20th Century Architecture* (London: Thames and Hudson, 1986), p. 247.

14 See, for instance, Anthony Jackson, *The Politics of Architecture: A History of Modern Architecture in Britain* (London: Architectural Press, 1970), pp. 200–201.

15 Thomas Sharp, "Planning Now," *Journal of the Town Planning Institute* 43 (1957), pp. 133–136, quoted in Jackson, *The Politics of Architecture*, p. 201.

16 Thomas Sharp, "Failure of Planning," *Sunday Times*, 9 August 1964, p. 10, cited in Jackson, *The Politics of Architecture*, p. 201.

17 Peter Cook, "Plug-In City," *Sunday Times Colour Magazine*, 20 September 1964.

18 See Reyner Banham, *Megastructure: Urban Futures of the Recent Past* (London: Thames and Hudson, 1976).

19 The linear city concept was revived by the Russian NER group in the 1920s. For a brief discussion see William Curtis, *Modern Architecture since 1900*, 3d ed. (London: Phaidon, 1996), pp. 252–253.

20 My thanks to Tim Benton for drawing my attention to Mendelsohn.

21 The lattice structure almost certainly drew from other sources, most recently Konrad Wachsmann and more distantly Alexander Graham Bell, whose astonishing triangulated space-frame tower of 1902 was featured in a book known to Archigram, Wachsmann's *The Turning Point of Building* (1961; see Peter Cook, "The Electric Decade: An Atmosphere at the AA School 1963–73," in James Gowan, ed., *A Continuing Experiment: Learning and Teaching at the Architectural Association* [London: Architectural Press, 1975], p. 138), and in Archigram's "Living City" exhibition of 1963. For discussion of these "network structures," see Mark Wigley, "Network Fever," *Grey Room*, no. 4 (Summer 2001), pp. 83–122.

22 Peter Cook, *Experimental Architecture* (London: Studio Vista, 1970), p. 77. Archigram's principal source of information on Japanese developments was Günther Nitsche's "The Metabolists of Japan," *Architectural Design*, October 1964, May 1965, May 1967. Charles Jencks recalls meeting Kisho Kurokawa and Hans Hollein at a Team 10 meeting in 1966, and finding that "young people were not very much admired in those days." Charles Jencks, introducing Kisho Kurokawa, Architectural Association, 19 June 1997.

23 See Kiyonori Kikutake, Kisho Kurokawa, Fumihiko Maki, and Masato Otaka, "Metabolism 1960—A Proposal for New Urbanism" (1958), manifesto delivered to the 1960 World Design Conference, reprinted in Kisho Kurokawa, *Metabolism in Architecture* (London: Studio Vista, 1977), p. 27. For an account of metabolism, see Cherie Wendelken, "Putting Metabolism Back in Place: The Making of a Radically Decontextualized Architecture in Japan," in Sarah Williams Goldhagen and Réjean Legault, eds., *Anxious Modernisms: Experimentation in Postwar Architectural Culture* (Cambridge, Mass.: MIT Press, 2000), pp. 279–299.

24 See Reyner Banham, *The New Brutalism* (London: Architectural Press, 1966).

25 My thanks to Barry Curtis for first drawing my attention to this. J. Stanley Matthews, "An Architecture for the New Britain: The Social Vision of Cedric Price's Fun Palace and Potteries Thinkbelt," Ph.D. dissertation, Columbia University, 2002, p. 113, also finds the formative impact of Meccano.

26 This is an allegation raised ("Desert Island Discs," BBC Radio 4, 24 June 2001) by Nobel laureate chemist Professor Sir Harry Kroto (b. 1939)—of the same generation as Archigram, and sharing its passion for graphic design and Buckminster Fuller geodesics. Meccano was patented by Frank Hornby in 1901; the current Lego stud-and-tube coupling system was patented in 1958.

27 Published in *Archigram*, no. 7 (1966), n.p., reprinted in Cook, *Experimental Architecture*, p. 106.

28 Archigram, dir., *Archigram*, BBC Productions, 1966.

29 Dennis Crompton and Peter Cook, in lectures at the Archigram symposium, Cornerhouse, Manchester, 9 February 1998, suggested that Computer City and Plug-In City were directly linked.

30 See Mark Crinson and Jules Lubbock, *Architecture, Art or Profession? Three Hundred Years of Architectural Education in Britain* (Manchester: Manchester University Press, 1994), passim.

31 In 1960, 63 percent of architecture students were still being trained at art and technical college. MARS had long targeted entry into the profession through pupilage (pupils would qualify by taking the RIBA's external exams) as an obstacle to architecture as a modernist research discipline. The Department of Architecture at Bournemouth College of Art (where Peter Cook trained) became a victim of this shift in the late 1960s, closed down by the RIBA's Board of Education because the Department tended to provide coaching for the external exams rather than for full-time study. Barry Curtis, "Archigram—'A Necessary Irritant,'" in Dennis Crompton, ed., *Concerning Archigram* (London: Archigram Archives, 1998), p. 33, emphasizes that a new generation of architects were recipients of educational grants and public-sector employment.

32 See Lionel Esher, *A Broken Wave: The Rebuilding of England 1940–1980* (London: Allen Lane, 1981), p. 66.

33 Archigram, "The Archigram Group," in Peter Cook, ed., *Archigram* (London: Studio Vista, 1972), pp. 140–141.

34 Dennis Crompton and Peter Cook, talk at the Cornerhouse, Manchester, 9 February 1998.

35 Reyner Banham, in Denis Postle, dir., *Beaubourg: Four Films by Denis Postle,* Tattooist International for the Arts Council, 1980.

36 Beat writing was a particular favorite of David Greene.

37 Jackson, *The Politics of Architecture,* p. 179.

38 "No Future in the Town Hall," *Architectural Review,* no. 138 (1965), p. 245, cited in Jackson, *The Politics of Architecture,* p. 192. Indeed the culture of architecture as a selfless, relentless public service, under siege by building targets, shortages, and politics, wore down even the key names of the architectural establishment, with Leslie Martin, Stirrat Johnson-Marshall, Richard Llewelyn Davies, and Robert Matthew all among those who sometime abandoned the LCC for private practice. See Tim Benton, "The Housing Question: The Exemplary Case of Roehampton," in *Rassegna,* issue "The Reconstruction of Europe after World War II" (1993), p. 33, n. 13.

39 The first editions of Archigram were printed on a Roneo. Peter Murray emphasizes the importance of offset lithography to the little magazine revolution (including such titles as *Oz*). Peter Murray, at Archigram World Rally, University of Westminster, 19 November 2002.

40 Richard Sheppard, "Review of the Work Submitted for the Prizes and Studentships, 1961," *RIBA Journal,* March 1961, pp. 174–175, quoted in Jonathan Hughes, "1961," in Louise Campbell, ed., *Twentieth-Century Architecture and Its Histories* (London: Society of Architectural Historians of Great Britain, 2001). The following year the RIBA called in the police to control crowds gathering to hear Louis Kahn deliver the RIBA's annual discourse. See Jackson, *The Politics of Architecture,* p. 192.

41 This was a concept deployed at Kahn's Richards Laboratories, Philadelphia, 1957.

42 This was a bitter comparison to an architect with whom Pevsner had himself initially struggled to come to terms. Gaudí was accepted as a "modern architect" by Pevsner only in later editions of *Pioneers of Modern Design.*

43 Nikolaus Pevsner, "Modern Architecture and the Historian, or, the Return of Historicism," *RIBA Journal,* April 1961, p. 231, cited in Hughes, "1961." The incident was recalled by Michael Webb in a lecture at the Bartlett School of Architecture, London, 23 February 1998.

44 Pevsner, "Modern Architecture and the Historian," p. 238, quoted in Hughes, "1961."

45 James Gowan, "Curriculum," *Architectural Review,* December 1959, pp. 320–321, also cited in Hughes, "1961."

46 Though never as radical as *Archigram,* the *Polygon* magazine enjoyed an "avid student readership" (Brian Hanson, "Polygon," in *Rassegna* 4, no. 12, "Architecture in the Little Magazines" [December 1982], p. 72). The impact of its first couple of editions upon stirrings at the Architectural Association was "critical." Cook, "The Electric Decade," p. 138, n. 3.

47 See George Kassaboff, John Outram, Paul Power, and Ian McKechnie, "Student Section—BASA," *Architects' Journal* 129, no. 3342 (19 March 1959), p. 451.

48 The Editors, "An AJ Student Section," *Architects' Journal* 129, no. 3342 (19 March 1959), p. 429.

49 "AJ Student Section," *Architects' Journal* 129, no. 3342 (19 March 1959), p. 450.

50 John Outram and Wilfred Marden, "The Technology of Change," *Architects' Journal* 129, no. 3342 (19 March 1959), p. 455.

51 M. de Webb, "Furniture Manufacturers Association Showrooms High Wycombe," *Architects' Journal* 129, no. 3342 (19 March 1959), pp. 452–454. Peter Cook recalled the mystique surrounding "de Webb" in his introduction to Michael Webb's lecture at the Bartlett School of Architecture, University College London, 5 December 1996.

52 Archigram, "Archigram Group, London: A Chronological Survey," *Architectural Design,* November 1965, p. 560. The scheme had promptly been published in the *Architectural Review* as well.

53 *Architectural Design* reported that the Furniture Manufacturers Building "was in reality founded on the release of ideas offered by the example and teaching of the Smithsons, Stirling and Gowan, Howell and Killick—all of whom can be traced through to the recently emerged architects who contributed to *Archigram.*" Archigram, "Archigram Group, London: A Chronological Survey," p. 560. And in the opinion of Charles Jencks, "the influence was definitely two-way: 'Howellism,' a sister of 'Bowellism,' gave birth to many buildings based on pedestrian flow and 'the erupted skin.'" Charles Jencks, *Modern Movements in Architecture* (Harmondsworth: Penguin, 1973, 2d ed. 1985), pp. 280–282. The first BASA "Student Section" in the *Architects' Journal* was in fact sponsored by William Howell.

54 Interview with David Greene, London, 1 June 1998.

55 See Jackson, *The Politics of Architecture,* p. 194.

56 See Banham, *The New Brutalism.*

57 Peter Cook, Dennis Crompton, David Greene, Michael Webb, Ron Herron, interview with Philip Mann, London, 1 December 1990. This contrariness was reiterated by Cook in his address at the Architectural Association 150th Anniversary seminar, Clore Management Centre, Birkbeck College, London, 9 July 1997, where he spoke of "hatred" as "a great motivator" for Archigram's work.

58 Cook, "The Electric Decade," p. 138.

59 See Brian Appleyard, *Richard Rogers: A Biography* (London: Faber, 1986), p. 181: "To the Smithsons it was Mickey Mouse architecture. . . ."

60 Michael Webb, lecture at the Bartlett School of Architecture, London, 23 February 1998.

61 Webb's diploma was delayed by Regent Street until 1972, and was finally awarded by a jury upon which Warren Chalk served. The first thesis scheme that Webb submitted, for a research lab, had also failed, and the Sin Centre was substituted, which failed twice more. My thanks to Michael Webb for piecing this story together for me (in conversation, London, 19 November 2002, and in correspondence, 17 August 2003).

62 The Cook/Greene entry for the Berkshire County Offices Competition the following year had a comparable style.

63 Norman Engleback, address to the 20th Century Society's Hayward Gallery symposium, Architectural Association, London, 20 March 1999.

64 See, for instance, their Paisley Technical College and Enfield Civic Centre competition entries, and Chalk's Chelsea College of Advanced Education.

65 In Landau's concise description, Starcross "was a Modern-Movement, classically grouped building complex with Garches-smooth facades"; on the other hand, "it had the current vernacular inverted-L window and used a 'movement organising' concourse bridge, an idea of the Brutalists." Landau, *New Directions in British Architecture*, p. 46.

66 G. E. Kidder-Smith, *The New Architecture of Europe* (Harmondsworth: Penguin, 1962), p. 52.

67 Norman Engleback, address to the 20th Century Society's Hayward Gallery symposium, Architectural Association, London, 20 March 1999. Ordinarily, the LCC's organization permitted its design teams general autonomy (see Landau, *New Directions in British Architecture*, pp. 45 f). Bennett nonetheless added the scheme to his CV in *Who's Who*.

68 Archigram, "Archigram Group, London: A Chronological Survey," p. 560.

69 Engleback joined the LCC office under Leslie Martin in 1950.

70 See Landau, *New Directions in British Architecture*, pp. 31–37.

71 Andrew Saint, address to the 20th Century Society's Hayward Gallery symposium, Architectural Association, London, 20 March 1999.

72 For commentary on the Queen Elizabeth Hall's services, see Reyner Banham, *The Architecture of the Well-Tempered Environment* (London: Architectural Press, 1969), pp. 255–264.

73 As recounted by Peter Cook in an address to the Architectural Association 150th Anniversary seminar at the Clore Management Centre, Birkbeck College, London, 9 July 1997.

74 Norman Engleback, address to the 20th Century Society's Hayward Gallery symposium, Architectural Association, London, 20 March 1999.

75 One rationale for this was the hope that British Rail would build an escalator link. Robert Maxwell, address to the 20th Century Society's Hayward Gallery symposium, Architectural Association, London, 20 March 1999.

76 Edward Jones and Christopher Woodward, *A Guide to the Architecture of London*, rev. ed. (London: Weidenfeld and Nicholson, 1992), p. 258.

77 Norman Engleback, address to the 20th Century Society's Hayward Gallery symposium, Architectural Association, London, 20 March 1999.

78 Warren Chalk, "Architecture as Consumer Product," *Arena: The Architectural Association Journal*, no. 81 (March 1966), pp. 228–230, reprinted in Archigram, ed., *A Guide to Archigram*, p. 92.

79 Andrew Saint, address to the 20th Century Society's Hayward Gallery symposium, Architectural Association, London, 20 March 1999.

80 Ibid.

81 For discussion of the ICA's role in British culture see, for instance, David Mellor, ed., *Fifty Years of the Future: A Chronicle of the Institute of Contemporary Arts* (London: Institute of Contemporary Arts, 1998), and Thomas Crow, *The Rise of the Sixties* (London: Weidenfeld and Nicolson, 1996), chapter 6.

82 It permeated little journals like the ICA's *Living Arts* and the Royal College of Art's *ARK*, but also relatively mainstream organs like the *Architectural Review* (under Banham's contributing influence: see especially the collage of a robot gracing the magazine's May 1957 cover, courtesy of Independent Group member John McHale) and its competitor *Architectural Design* (under Theo Crosby).

83 Chalk and Herron had been party to conversations with the participants of the show, and Archigram's comrade Cedric Price worked there as an assistant to Ernö Goldfinger. See Peter Cook, "The Beginning," in Crompton, ed., *Concerning Archigram*, p. 16.

84 Peter Cook, in an interview with Barry Curtis, 17 October 1990.

85 Alison and Peter Smithson, "But Today We Collect Ads," *ARK*, no. 18 (November 1956), reprinted in David Robbins, ed., *The Independent Group: Postwar Britain and the Aesthetics of Plenty* (Cambridge, Mass.: MIT Press, 1990), p. 186.

86 Alison and Peter Smithson, "The New Brutalism," *Architectural Design*, April 1957, p. 113, quoted in Reyner Banham, *The New Brutalism*, p. 66.

87 Cook, "The Electric Decade," p. 138. Emulating the success of the Smithsons, Cook, Greene, and Webb entered the Ideal Home Exhibition Competition of 1963.

88 "I think we had been at Aberdare Gardens quite a bit before we knew they [the Archigram group] were there, and vice versa, and then Peter Cook began to chase my Peter. And for a long time he didn't respond, and I said wouldn't you like to go over there and see what they're up to? In the end he did and he was bowled over by what they were doing." Interview with Mary Banham, London, 28 April 1997. David Rock also recalls drawing Banham's attention to Archigram: see David Rock, "Citation for Royal Gold Medal 2002," Royal Institute of British Architects, London, 20 November 2002, reprinted <http://www.architecture.com/go/Architecture/Also/Awards_311.html>.

89 Reyner Banham, "The Atavism of the Short-Distance Mini Cyclist," Terry Hamilton Memorial Lecture, November 1963, published in Theo Crosby and John Bodley, eds., *Living Arts*, no. 3 (London: Institute of Contemporary Arts and Tillotsons, 1964), pp. 91–97, reprinted in Banham, *Design by Choice*, p. 88.

90 See Cook, "The Electric Decade," p. 138. "Issues referred to are around Nos. 20–21 (1958–60)." Through Theo Crosby, Archigram also became friendly with pop artist Joe Tilson (see Peter Cook, "The Beginning," in Crompton, ed., *Concerning Archigram*, p. 16).

91 See Curtis, "A Necessary Irritant," in Crompton, ed., *Concerning Archigram*, p. 56.

92 In addition to pop activities of the Independent Group and RCA, the May 1958 Scroope group exhibition at Cambridge School of Architecture had seen the application of pop titles to abstract paintings.

93 Greene was married to a secretary from the RCA, while Cook's first wife Hazel was a painter he had met while studying at Bournemouth College of Art. Gordon Sainsbury, a contributor to the first *Archigram*, also studied at Bournemouth College of Art (like architect Michael Hopkins), and many of the Bournemouth circle had gone on to the RCA. (Interview with Gordon Sainsbury, Cambridge, Mass., 27 April 1998.) The Bournemouth alumni were encouraged by their mentor Ronald Sims, a friend of artist Patrick Hodgkinson, to go to London, rather than the more usual destination of Plymouth. Cook names Sims as one of his great inspirations (Peter Cook, "Statement of Intent," <http://www.riba.org/go/RIBA/Also/Education_2444.html>).

94 Interview with Gordon Sainsbury, Cambridge, Mass., 27 April 1998.

95 See Reyner Banham, "Towards a Pop Architecture," *Architectural Review*, July 1962, reprinted in

Banham, *Design by Choice*, pp. 61–63: "it is anticipated that the cordon-sanitaire between Pop Art and architecture is about to be breached . . . and a Pop architecture emerge about 1966" (p. 61)—though Banham himself actually rejected the prediction. See his 1979 note to the same article (*Design by Choice*, p. 141): "it derived from the insistence of Sir Hugh Casson that the emergence of Pop painting must automatically presage a Pop architecture—a willful transference of Kenneth Clark's views of the Renaissance."

96 Banham, "The Atavism of the Short-Distance Mini Cyclist," p. 87. Note however that Banham differentiated architecture from consumer products, and so his opinions on expendability did not exactly equate with Archigram's; Archigram reciprocally affected Banham's opinions on what a truly pop architecture might be. See Nigel Whiteley, *Reyner Banham: Historian of the Immediate Future* (Cambridge, Mass.: MIT Press, 2002), pp. 170ff., pp. 176ff. For more on expendability, see *Archigram*, no. 3 (1963).

97 Susan Mossman, "World War Two and Polythene Perspectives," "Defiant Modernism" symposium, Science Museum, London, 26 June 1999.

98 Christopher Booker, *The Neophiliacs: A Study of the Revolution in English Life in the Fifties and Sixties* (London: Collins, 1969), p. 132.

99 Ministry of Housing and Local Government, *Homes for Today and Tomorrow* (London: HMSO, 1961).

100 David Greene, writing in Dolan Conway, ed., "Three London Schools of Architecture within Ten Minutes Walking Distance of Each Other," *Architectural Design*, March 1969, p. 142.

101 Cf. Henri Lefebvre's ideas on the social reproduction of space.

102 Peter Cook, address at the Archigram symposium, Cornerhouse, Manchester, 9 February 1998.

103 For a comprehensive discussion of the Fun Palace, and an analysis of background social forecasting, see Matthews, "An Architecture for the New Britain." See also Mary Louise Lobsinger, "Cybernetic Theory and the Architecture of Performance: Cedric Price's Fun Palace," in Goldhagen and Legault, eds., *Anxious Modernisms*, pp. 119–139.

104 Webb's father was an accountant to the regatta, giving the family privileged access to the event, which became a recurrent motif in Webb's work. See Michael Sorkin, "Canticles for Mike," in his *Exquisite Corpse: Writing on Buildings* (New York: Verso, 1991), pp. 203–210.

105 His student colleague Edward Jones commented that "Timothy Tinker's housing thesis at Moldgreen in native Huddersfield characterises and concludes an era; it was Peter Smithson's final year at the AA, Park Hill was nearing completion, the British cinema had discovered the North through 'Room at the Top' and social realism through [Richard Hoggart's] 'Uses of Literacy' (1957) [which] was in paperbacks." Edward Jones, "Housing at Moldgreen," in James Gowan, ed., *Projects: Architectural Association 1946–71* (London: Architectural Association, 1973), p. 53.

106 Arthur Marwick, *British Society since 1945* (Harmondsworth: Penguin, 1996), pp. 60–61.

107 See Michael Young and Peter Willmott, *Family and Kinship in East London* (London: Routledge and Kegan Paul, 1957). The book alerted architects and planners to the shortcomings of isolated housing estates.

108 Cf. Chalk, "Housing as a Consumer Product."

109 Dennis Crompton, address at the Archigram symposium, Cornerhouse, Manchester, 9 February 1998.

110 See Marwick, *British Society since 1945*, p. 69.

111 See "The Month in Britain," *Architectural Design*, January 1962, p. 1. *Architectural Design* described the implications of the program as "odious."

112 Dennis Crompton and Michael Webb, talk at the Bartlett School of Architecture, London, 23 February 1998.

113 John A. D. Palmer, "Introduction to the British Edition," in Robert Goodman, *After the Planners* (Harmondsworth: Penguin, 1972), pp. 25, 26.

114 Part of the Fulham urban renewal study of 1963 (examined in chapter 2).

115 Dennis Crompton and Michael Webb, talk at the Bartlett School of Architecture, London, 23 February 1998.

116 See in particular Peter Cook, *Experimental Architecture* (London: Studio Vista, 1970), and *Archigram* no. 5.

117 In June 1961, Crosby convened the UIA's London Conference on the theme of "The Impact of 20th Century Technology on Architecture." The sessions and exhibits were peppered with old Independent Group regulars and climaxed with Buckminster Fuller's speech on "The Architect as World Planner."

118 See John McHale, introduction to "Universal Requirements Checklist," *Architectural Design*, January 1960, pp. 101–110 and *Architectural Design*, July 1961, pp. 290–327. McHale was shortly to become Fuller's assistant at the University of Southern Illinois. During visits to London, Fuller dined and resided with Magda and John McHale, Mary and Reyner Banham, Gill and James Meller, and Cedric Price (interview with Mary Banham, London, 28 April 1997).

119 Reyner Banham, "Space, Fiction and Architecture," *Architects' Journal* 127 (17 April 1958), p. 559, cited in Graham Whitam, "Science Fiction," in Robbins, ed., *The Independent Group*, p. 62.

120 This account of comics draws upon Mike Catto, "Futures Seen through British Comics," Design History Society Conference "Futures: Visions and Revisions," University of Middlesex, 14 December 1996.

121 "Man, Machine and Motion" correlated with subjects raised during the second round of Independent Group meetings led by Hamilton, Banham, Alloway, and McHale.

122 For interest in the transfer of exploratory technologies, see Warren Chalk, "Hardware of a New World," *Architectural Forum* 125, no. 3 (October 1966), pp. 46–51.

123 Dennis Crompton, lecture at the Bartlett School of Architecture, London, 23 February 1998.

124 A description derived from Catto, "Futures Seen through British Comics."

125 David Walters, "The Architect as Superhero: Archigram and the Text of Serious Comics," *Architronic* 3, no. 2 (1994), paragraph 6 <http://architronic.saed.kent.edu>.

126 Julius Posener, "Les tendances de l'architecture dans le Troisième Reich," *Architecture d'Aujourd'hui*, no. 4 (1936), p. 9, quoted in Leonardo Benevolo, *History of Modern Architecture*, vol. 2 (London: Routledge and Kegan Paul, 1971), p. 553.

127 "Editorial," *Focus*, no. 1 (1938), p. 1.

128 Leslie Martin, for instance, was twenty-six when he became the chair of architecture at the University of Hull.

129 Benton, "The Housing Question: The Exemplary Case of Roehampton," p. 33, n. 28.

130 Peter Cook, *Six Conversations* (London: Academy, 1993), p. 123.

131 This comparison was drawn by Mary Banham. Interview with Mary Banham, London, 28 April 1997.

132 Peter Cook, address to the Architectural Association 150th Anniversary seminar at the Clore Management Centre, Birkbeck College, London, 9 July 1997.

133 An observation made in Brian Hanson, "Il momento inglese," *Rassegna* 4, no. 12, "Architecture in the Little Magazines" (December 1982), pp. 31–40.

134 Archigram, "Archigram Group, London: A Chronological Survey," p. 560. Reynolds died in 1959.

135 *Archigram,* no. 1 (London, 1961), n.p. Lionel Esher recalls that Saul Steinberg's 1950 cartoon of a "graph paper" International Style building was well known (Esher, *A Broken Wave*, p. 67).

136 William Howell, writing in the *AA Journal* 74 (February 1959), p. 218, quoted in Hanson, "Il momento inglese."

137 Between 1960 and 1961, *Architectural Design* regularly filled its "For Students Only" section with "Modular Design Information Sheets." In the *Architectural Review* in 1960 Reyner Banham was moved to indict what he called the "logical Formalist" strain of architecture, beholden to the grid on supposedly pragmatic grounds (see Reyner Banham, "Stocktaking," in Banham, *Design by Choice*, p. 54). For a larger critique of the grid's pretense to objectivity, see Rosalind Krauss, "Grids," reprinted in *The Originality of the Avant-Garde and Other Modernist Myths* (Cambridge, Mass.: MIT Press, 1986).

138 Crinson and Lubbock, *Architecture, Art or Profession?*, p. 148, citing Richard Llewelyn Davies, *The Education of an Architect* (London, 1961), p. 6, and Dean Latourell, "The Bartlett 1969," *AIA Journal,* October 1969, p. 91.

139 The "Palmatic" cradle was a regular feature in *Architectural Design*'s advertising pages in the early 1960s. The cradle mechanism became a permanent fixture at Stirling and Gowan's Leicester University Engineering Building. The in-situ crane became a favorite device of high-tech architects; see, for instance, Richard Rogers's Lloyds Building, London (1978–1986), and Norman Foster's Hong Kong and Shanghai Bank, Hong Kong (1979–1986).

140 Booker, *The Neophiliacs,* p. 41.

141 David Greene, "A Statement," *Archigram,* no. 1 (1961), n.p.

142 Kiesler's importance was emphasized by Dennis Crompton and Peter Cook, Archigram symposium, Cornerhouse, Manchester, 9 February 1998. Ellen Rowley also reminded me of the importance of Kiesler as an avant-garde architect. Kiesler's work would consistently inform Archigram's, as it had—we can speculate—that of the Smithsons (for instance the House of the Future, 1956). Hailing as well from Kiesler (who drew in turn on surrealism) was the oneiric quality of Archigram's work, such as the spongy floors of the "Living 1990" exhibit at Harrods, 1967—possibly borrowed from Kiesler's "Space House" exhibit at the Modernage Furniture Company in New York, 1933.

143 "Decade 1960," in Dennis Sharp, *20th Century Architecture: A Visual History* (London: Lund Humphries, 1991), p. 235.

144 See Arthur Korn and Felix J. Samuely, "A Master Plan for London," *Architectural Review* 91, no. 546 (June 1942), pp. 143–150; the 1944 MARS exhibition, "Living in Cities"; and Ralph Tubbs for MARS, *Living in Cities* (Harmondsworth: Penguin, 1944).

145 See Cook, "The Beginning," in Crompton, ed., *Concerning Archigram,* p. 16.

146 Iakov Chernikhov was a particular influence.

147 Michael Webb, interview at Greenport, N.Y., 3 August 1997.

148 "Futurism and Modern Architecture," *RIBA Journal,* February 1957.

149 The English translation *Fantastic Architecture* (New York, 1962, London, 1963) was by Christiane Crasemann Collins and George R. Collins, the latter also the author of a popular English work on Gaudí, published in 1960. For discussion of the impact of these books see Reyner Banham, "Revenge of the Picturesque: English Architectural Polemics, 1945–1965," in John Summerson, ed., *Concerning Architecture* (London: Allen Lane, 1968), p. 270.

150 Peter Cook, in an interview with Barry Curtis, London, 17 October 1990: "We were very high on imagination," like "Otto Wagner and his lads" in Vienna, "a syndrome which was more than a sum of its parts, like Archigram."

151 Cook, address to the Architectural Association 150th Anniversary seminar at the Clore Management Centre, Birkbeck College, London, 9 July 1997.

152 Mary Banham, speaking at the Archigram World Rally, University of Westminster, 19 November 2002.

153 The "family" metaphor is discussed in Alison Smithson, ed., *Team 10 Meetings* (New York: Rizzoli, 1991), p. 9 and passim.

154 Cook, address to the Architectural Association 150th Anniversary seminar at the Clore Management Centre, Birkbeck College, London, 9 July 1997.

155 An early effort to theorize the organization of the architectural neo-avant-garde can be found in Jim Burns, *Arthropods: New Design Futures* (New York: Praeger, 1972), pp. 9–10.

156 For a report from one of the "Christian Weirdies," see "Andrew Anderson," in *Archigram,* no. 2, n.p. The name was accorded to Quinlan Terry, Andrew Anderson, and Malcolm Higgs by tutor William Howell in a review of school work in the *AA Journal;* their projects evinced a skepticism about modernist technique and ideology (correspondence with Malcolm Higgs, 14 August 2003). Gordon Sainsbury recalls that work submitted to *Archigram* had to fit the increasing "discipline" of its themes (interview with Gordon Sainsbury, Cambridge, Mass., 27 April 1998).

157 Bruno Taut, 24 November 1919, in Iain Boyd Whyte, ed. and trans., *The Crystal Chain Letters* (Cambridge, Mass.: MIT Press, 1985), p. 19.

158 Matthews, "An Architecture for the New Britain," p. 45.

159 The phrase was used, for instance, in Archigram, *Archigram Opera,* 1975 (?) (rescreened at Cornerhouse, Manchester, February 1998).

160 David Greene, lecture on Archigram films, Architectural Association, London, 17 February 1998.

161 An ambition expressed, for instance, in the undated "Turin Shroud" project shown at the exhibition "Archigram," Cornerhouse, Manchester, February 1998.

162 Summerson, *Ten Years of British Architecture*, p. 10.

163 Alison and Peter Smithson, "The Heroic Period of Modern Architecture," including icons from Le Corbusier, Mies van der Rohe, Frank Lloyd Wright, Gerrit Rietveld and the Dutch School, Hugo Häring and Bruno Taut, the Russian constructivists, and Sant'Elia and the Italian futurists.

164 Scott Brown, "Little Magazines in Architecture and Urbanism," p. 223.

165 See Denise Scott Brown, "Learning from Brutalism," in Robbins, ed., *The Independent Group*, pp. 203–206.

166 For an account of the wider urge for "homecoming" within the intelligentsia, see "The 1970s: Bringing It All Back Home," in Marshall Berman, *All That Is Solid Melts into Air: The Experience of Modernity* (London: Verso, 1983).

167 See Archigram, "Archigram Group, London: A Chronological Survey," p. 567. The project was terminated by the suspension of office building in London by the national government (and LCC) in 1964. See Martin Pawley, "Peter Cook—Archiman or Anarchist?," *Building Design*, 15 May 1970, pp. 6–7, and "The Euston Story," *Architectural Design*, June 1966, p. 267. The loss of offices in favor of flats led to a reduction in financial interest. Within a few years "Crosby's initial team had gradually drifted apart. In 1964 he himself felt bound to resign" ("The Euston Story"), as his group was reassigned to demoralizing design-and-build jobs, though other speculative small projects by the Taylor Woodrow team, assembled in 1963–1964, went ahead. I am grateful to Robin Middleton for recollecting the events at Taylor Woodrow (telephone interview, 16 January 2005).

168 This was a feeling expressed for instance in David Greene, lecture on Archigram films, Architectural Association, London, 17 February 1998.

169 Reyner Banham, "Zoom Wave Hits Architecture," *New Society*, 3 March 1966, reprinted in Banham, *Design by Choice*, p. 64.

170 How bohemian and radical Gropius and Mies had been in their day—ensconced within their own curriculum at the Bauhaus—is a moot point.

171 Peter Cook, interview with Barry Curtis, London, 17 October 1990.

172 Conversation with Mary Quant, Milton Keynes, 5 June 1998.

173 Crinson and Lubbock, *Architecture, Art or Profession?*, p. 168. This conclusion is informed of course by hindsight (and a certain antipathy toward the modernist syllabus); participants in modernist sectarianism doubtless sensed what to them were real creative and political differences.

174 Le Corbusier, "Eyes Which Do Not See," in *Towards a New Architecture,* trans. Frederick Etchells, 1928 (rpt. London: Butterworth, 1987), p. 84 (first published as *Vers une architecture*, Paris, 1923).

175 The attitude was inherited from the Independent Group, which was interested in non-Aristotelian logic (sometimes found in science fiction). The Independent Group also imported communications theories that validated freeformed, lateral associations of words, images, and ideas, for instance those of Charles and Ray Eames. The Independent Group further garnered sources for an "indeterminate" aesthetic from D'Arcy Wentworth Thompson and Marcel Duchamp. See Robbins, ed., *The Independent Group.*

176 Similarly, the Independent Group confronted the academy armed with "no single verbalizable aesthetic criterion," which had a certain strategic value, as spokesman Lawrence Alloway admitted in an interview with Reyner Banham, n.d. (c. 1976), *Fathers of Pop*, Arts Council films, 1979 (also reprinted in Robbins, ed., *The Independent Group*, p. 33).

177 Cook, "Archigram, the Name and the Magazine," pp. 22–23.

178 See the description of the group's formation in Archigram, "Archigram Group, London: A Chronological Survey," p. 559. A similar group dynamic operated in the Independent Group.

179 For instance, Cook related, in *Archigram,* no. 7 (1967), n.p., how "suddenly a much bigger conversation looms (one which could not be imagined when we started Archigram, which is more than the sum of its parts)."

180 Booker, *The Neophiliacs*, p. 36.

181 Ibid., pp. 57–58.

182 Archigram members refute accusations that they lacked seriousness, but accept that their use of humor was a defense against the daily grind of architectural practice, and a vehicle for the exploration of problematic issues. Peter Cook and Dennis Crompton, presentation at the Archigram Symposium, Cornerhouse, Manchester, 9 February 1998.

183 *Private Eye* was advertised in the student magazine spun off from *Archigram, Clip-Kit.*

184 Price counted among his close friends key young intellectuals and satirists, such as Jonathan Miller and Eleanor Bron of the "Beyond the Fringe" group; he also enjoyed contacts with a new generation of modernizing politicians on both left and right.

185 The film was also given a cinema release in 1966.

186 Warren Chalk, "The Tiger in the Tank," *Architectural Design,* September 1965, p. 424, reprinted from the RAIC *Journal,* May 1965. Chalk listed the recent attempts to categorize the "fantastic": the "Fantastic Architecture" exhibition at MoMA, New York; "Architectures fantastiques," special edition of *Architecture d'Aujourd'hui,* June/July 1962; Conrads and Sperlich's *Fantastic Architecture,* 1963; and *Archigram,* no. 4.

187 *Architecture d'Aujourd'hui,* "Architectures fantastiques" issue, no. 102 (June-July 1962).

188 John Fowler, "Visionary Architecture," *Architectural Design,* May 1961, pp. 181–182.

189 See, for instance, Graeme Shankland, "What Is Happening in Oxford and Cambridge? Architecture and the New University," *Architectural Design,* January 1960, pp. 85–93; also *Architects' Journal,* 2 and 9 January 1958.

190 Ron Herron, "It's a . . . ," 1972, reprinted in Cook, ed., *Archigram,* p. 137.

191 See, for instance, the linear city models by Team 10 (as featured in *Architectural Design,* December 1962, passim) and the proposal to convert railway lines, "News," *Architectural Design,* April 1963, p. 151.

192 See Hughes, "1961." The rationale of the Garden City and Ville Radieuse was being superseded.

193 See Oliver Marriott, *The Property Boom* (London: Hamish Hamilton, 1967).

194 Sigfried Giedion, *Mechanization Takes Command* (Oxford: Oxford University Press, 1948; rpt. New York: Norton, 1969), p. 715.

195 Ronald Bryden, "Bulge Takes Over," *Town*, 1962, quoted in Booker, *The Neophiliacs*, p. 173.

2 THE LIVING CITY: POP URBANISM CIRCA 1963

1 There were, however, disagreements over "Living City": Michael Webb recalls "suspicions at the beginning that Dennis and Peter were making decisions on our behalf." Herbert Lachmayer and Pascal Schöning, interview with Michael Webb, London, 13 December 1991.

2 See *Archigram*, no. 3 (August 1963).

3 The show occupied the ICA from 19 June to 2 August before touring to Manchester City Art Gallery, the Walker Art Centre, Cambridge, and the New Metropole Arts Centre, Folkestone.

4 Taylor knew Cook when they were students at Bournemouth College of Art. Taylor's "Living City" poster earned a Council of Industrial Design award. Telephone interview with Peter Taylor, 13 November 2002.

5 Foreword to Theo Crosby and John Bodley, eds., *Living Arts*, no. 2 (London: Institute of Contemporary Arts and Tillotsons, 1963), p. 1. I am indebted to Jonathan Hughes for the long-term loan of this journal, which was essential to the research for this chapter.

6 Robert Maxwell, "The 'Living City' Exhibition at the ICA," in Theo Crosby and John Bodley, eds., *Living Arts*, no. 3 (London: Institute of Contemporary Arts and Tillotsons, 1964), p. 99.

7 Charles Jencks, *Modern Movements in Architecture* (Harmondsworth: Penguin, 1973, 2d ed. 1985), p. 291.

8 Constantin Doxiadis, *Encyclopaedia Britannica, Book of the Year 1968*, p. 21, cited in Jencks, *Modern Movements in Architecture*, p. 291. Doxiadis promoted a new science of human settlement called ekistics.

9 "Our exhibition would present the opening phase of our time and record it as we see it now, as did the Esprit Nouveau Pavilion for 1925." Alison and Peter Smithson, "Texts Documenting the Development of *Parallel of Life and Art*," reprinted in David Robbins, ed., *The Independent Group:*

Postwar Britain and the Aesthetics of Plenty (Cambridge, Mass.: MIT Press, 1990), p. 129.

10 Peter Cook, Introduction to Crosby and Bodley, eds., *Living Arts*, no. 2, pp. 68–69. With a critical distance unavailable to the brutalists, Cook conceded that the Festival of Britain "certainly did more to design in Britain than anything a decade before or since."

11 For discussions of the role of the image in brutalism, see Banham, *The New Brutalism* (London: Architectural Press, 1966), p. 61; and Banham, "The New Brutalism," *Architectural Review* 118 (December 1955), p. 361, reprinted in David Robbins, ed., *The Independent Group: Postwar Britain and the Aesthetics of Plenty* (Cambridge, Mass.: MIT Press, 1990), pp. 171–173.

12 Interview with Graham Witham, 10 January 1983, reprinted in Robbins, ed., *The Independent Group*, p. 25.

13 Published in Oscar Newman, *New Frontiers in Architecture: CIAM 59 in Otterlo* (New York: Universe Books, 1961), p. 16, quoted in Joan Ockman, introduction to Joan Ockman, with Edward Eigen, ed., *Architecture Culture 1943–1968: A Documentary Anthology* (New York: Rizzoli, 1993), p. 19.

14 Peter Cook, introduction to Crosby and Bodley, eds., *Living Arts*, no. 2, p. 71.

15 The original intention was to make the structure from still more amorphous spray plastic.

16 Cook, introduction to Crosby and Bodley, eds., *Living Arts*, no. 2, p. 70.

17 Assembly of the structure took longer than expected, and the finalizing of the exhibition was rushed. Telephone interview with Peter Taylor, 13 November 2002.

18 "Swinging London" was officially born in an article of the same title in *Time* magazine, 15 April 1966, although the pace of London culture had been accelerating for some years prior to that.

19 Christopher Booker, *The Neophiliacs: A Study of the Revolution in English Life in the Fifties and Sixties* (London: Collins, 1969), p. 264.

20 "It is absurd," Lawrence Alloway contended, "to print a photograph of Piccadilly Circus and caption it 'ARCHITECTURAL SQUALOR' as Ernö Goldfinger and E. J. Carter did" (in *The County of London Plan*, Penguin, 1945). By 1951, even CIAM had considered repealing its outright condemna-

tion of such environmental noise (see J. Tyrwhitt, J. L. Sert, and E. N. Rogers, eds., *The Heart of the City: Towards the Humanisation of Urban Life* [New York: Pellegrini and Cudahy, 1952]). "In fact," Alloway went on, "the lights of the Circus are the best night-sight in London, though inferior to American displays." Lawrence Alloway, "City Notes," *Architectural Design*, January 1959, excerpted in Robbins, ed., *The Independent Group*, p. 167. The Germans in and around the AA would also have propagated the interest in "LichtArchitektur," developed by the ex-expressionist architects in Germany in the late 1920s. Arthur Korn's book *Glas im Bau und als Gebrauchsgegenstand* (1929) is full of nighttime views of German buildings in the 1920s (by Erich Mendelsohn, Wassili Luckhardt, etc.), a vision that found its way into London with Joseph Emberton's Simpsons facade and the Peter Jones store in the 1930s. Dennis Crompton would also have been familiar with Emberton's Pleasure Pavilion at Blackpool, which projected the silhouettes of members of the public walking on a wobbly surface onto a picture window on the facade. My thanks to Tim Benton for several of these observations.

21 The Flicker Machine was based upon the Flicker Machines developed by Brion Gysin and Ian Sommerville in the early 1960s, and was distantly inspired by László Moholy-Nagy's *Light-Space Modulator*, the 1928–1932 experiment in kinetic/light sculpture that was "rediscovered" by the op art scene in the early 1960s, and by Group 2's rotoscopes at "This Is Tomorrow." The interest in flickering was founded in turn upon the neurological theories of W. Grey Walter: see his *The Living Brain* (Harmondsworth: Penguin, 1956). W. Grey Walter also popularized the computer among the British public, devising the "mechanical tortoise" *Machina speculatrix* for the Festival of Britain. (See Jonathan Benthall, *Science and Technology in Art Today* [London: Thames and Hudson, 1972].)

22 "Movement Gloop," in Crosby and Bodley, eds., *Living Arts*, no. 2, p. 109.

23 Cedric Price in conversation, London, 9 April 1998.

24 As Lawrence Alloway had enthused, "The ride from Chicago's O'Hare airport into the Loop at night is a journey along a noisy, narrow corridor of neon. To the compilers of the *Architectural Review*'s 'Man-Made America' this would be 'unintended squalor,' intolerable to people living the architectural way. In fact, it is one stretch of the lighted street which runs across America. . . . Attempts are now being made to bring within architectural reach much of the pop art that has thrived without being architecture in the qualitative sense of the word." Lawrence Alloway, "City Notes."

25 Published as Sir Walter Worboys, *Traffic Signs 1963: Report of the Committee on Traffic Signs for All-Purpose Roads* (London: HMSO, 1963).

26 "Movement Gloop," p. 109.

27 Robert Freeman, "Living with the 60s," in *Cambridge Opinion*, no. 17 (1959), p. 8.

28 "Gloop 4 Communications in Living City," in Crosby and Bodley, eds., *Living Arts,* no. 2, pp. 106–107.

29 Peter Taylor, "Words at Liberty: Alphabetic communication in the Living City," in Crosby and Bodley, eds., *Living Arts* no. 2, pp. 78–79. A typographic meltdown comparable to that at "Living City" could already be seen in Robyn Denny's well-known 1959 mural at Austin Reed's Store in London's Regent Street. See David Mellor, *The Sixties Art Scene in London* (London: Phaidon, 1993), pp. 42–45 passim. This meltdown had been investigated by Herbert Spencer in his "Mile a Minute Typography," *Typographica,* December 1961, and it was evident too in Edward Wright's mural for Theo Crosby's UIA Conference at the South Bank in 1961. See *Architectural Design,* November 1961, pp. 489–507, photographed for *Architectural Design* by Robert Freeman, whose own mile-a-minute photographic account of London had been published in the first edition of *Living Arts* magazine in 1963 (Robert Freeman, "Comment," *Living Arts,* no. 1 [London: Institute of Contemporary Arts and Tillotsons, Spring 1963], p. 81; see also Mellor, *The Sixties Art Scene in London,* pp. 50–54). Frenetic visual pace was also promoted in the animated films of the 1950s and 1960s hailing from Norman McLaren, Charles and Ray Eames, and Czechoslovakia, manners replicated in Archigram's own film of 1966.

30 The 1959 "Place" show, coordinated by a team that included Rumney, had already demonstrated

at the ICA the potential for an exhibition to operate as a complete, sensorially surrounding environment, like "Living City."

31 See "The Situationists in London" in Guy Atkins, *Asger Jorn* (London: Methuen, 1964).

32 Peter Cook, "Archigram," lecture at the "New Babylon" conference, Faculty of Architecture, Delft University of Technology, 26 January 2000; J. Stanley Matthews, "An Architecture for the New Britain: The Social Vision of Cedric Price's Fun Palace and Potteries Thinkbelt," Ph.D. dissertation, Columbia University, 2002.

33 See letter from Peter Cook to Constant, 20 July 1964, in the Constant archive, the Rijksbureau, The Hague.

34 Conversation with David Greene, London, 24 April 1997.

35 "Situation," in Crosby and Bodley, eds., *Living Arts,* no. 2, p. 112.

36 Ibid.

37 Reyner Banham, "City as Scrambled Egg," *Cambridge Opinion,* no. 17 (1959), pp. 18–23.

38 Freeman, "Living with the 60s," p. 8.

39 This is the situationists' own definition. "Definitions," *Internationale situationniste,* no. 1 (Paris, 1958), cited in Ken Knabb, ed. and trans., *Situationist International Anthology* (Berkeley: Bureau of Public Secrets, 1981), pp. 45–46.

40 "Movement Gloop," p. 109.

41 Guy Debord with Asger Jorn, *Guide psychogéographique de Paris: discours sur les passions de l'amour,* 1956, screenprinted map.

42 Peter Cook, "Come-Go," in Crosby and Bodley, eds., *Living Arts,* no. 2, p. 80.

43 Ibid.

44 Maxwell, "The 'Living City' Exhibition at the ICA," p. 99.

45 Charles Baudelaire, "The Painter of Modern Life" (*Le Figaro,* 1863), in Baudelaire, *The Painter of Modern Life and Other Essays,* ed. and trans. J. Mayne (London: Phaidon, 1964), p. 13.

46 Cook, "Come-Go," p. 80.

47 Ibid.

48 See Theo Crosby, *The Necessary Monument* (London: Studio Vista, 1970). Crosby proposed "Living City" to the ICA, obtained the money for the show from the Gulbenkian Foundation, and edited its publication in *Living Arts* magazine.

49 Peter Cook, introduction to Crosby and Bodley, eds., *Living Arts,* no. 2, p. 69.

50 See Robbins, ed., *The Independent Group,* pp. 142–143.

51 See ibid., pp. 146–147.

52 Four years later, Archigram's "Living 1990" for Harrods, 1967, incorporated apparent references back to Group Two, notably the spongy floor. "At particular points" Archigram's floor could "be made hard enough to dance on or soft enough to sit on" (Archigram, ed., *A Guide to Archigram 1961–74* [London: Academy, 1994], p. 197), while Group Two's floor, when stepped on, emitted strawberry air freshener.

53 In order to attend CIAM 10.

54 See Robbins, ed., *The Independent Group,* p. 142.

55 Cook, introduction to Crosby and Bodley, eds., *Living Arts,* no. 2, p. 70.

56 Cook, "Come-Go," p. 80.

57 Taylor, "Words at Liberty."

58 Sigfried Giedion, *Architecture, You and Me* (Cambridge, Mass.: Harvard University Press, 1958), p. 127. The patriarchal usage of "man" here refers to both sexes.

59 See the summary of CIAM 8, Hoddeson, July 1951, in Tyrwhitt, Sert, and Rogers, eds., *The Heart of the City.*

60 Nigel Henderson's photo-collage *Head of a Man* was the centerpiece of Patio and Pavilion. See too Sarah Williams Goldhagen, "Freedom's Domiciles: Three Projects by Alison and Peter Smithson," in Sarah Williams Goldhagen and Réjean Legault, eds., *Anxious Modernisms: Experimentation in Postwar Architectural Culture* (Cambridge, Mass.: MIT Press, 2000), pp. 75–95, for discussion of the impact of existentialism upon the Smithsons and their friends Paolozzi and Henderson.

61 Cook, introduction to Crosby and Bodley, eds., *Living Arts,* no. 2, p. 71.

62 "The term 'Gloop' was coined to define an area of the exhibition; it derived from the idea of a loop-enclosure of a soft profile and was one aspect of the original intention to build the exhibition structures from spray plastic." "Extracts from *Living Arts* magazine no. 2, June 1963," in Peter Cook, ed., *Archigram* (London: Studio Vista, 1972), p. 20. Hesitation about the meanings of various gloops was still evident in the edition of *Living Arts* magazine that served as the exhibition catalogue. Nine years later, Archigram's own retrospective quietly clarified matters with some deft editorial work on the extracts from *Living Arts*. The sense of confusion may be attributable to the fact that responsibility for the gloops was divided out into separate teams, rather as space at "This Is Tomorrow" was allocated to autonomous groups.

63 "Man," in Crosby and Bodley, eds., *Living Arts*, no. 2, p. 100.

64 Ibid., p. 101.

65 Ibid., p. 100.

66 Frank Lloyd Wright, *The Living City* (New York: Horizon Press, 1958; rpt. New York: New American Library, 1970). The book was a reworking of *When Democracy Builds*, 1945.

67 There is no evidence that Archigram knew this book.

68 Georg Simmel, "The Metropolis and Mental Life," 1902, trans. in Kurt H. Wolff, ed., *The Sociology of Georg Simmel* (Glencoe, Ill., 1950), reprinted in Charles Harrison and Paul Wood, eds., *Art in Theory 1900–1990: An Anthology of Changing Ideas* (Oxford: Blackwell, 1992), pp. 130–135.

69 "Crowd," in Crosby and Bodley, eds., *Living Arts*, no. 2, p. 105.

70 "Situation," in Crosby and Bodley, eds., *Living Arts*, no. 2, p. 112.

71 Ibid. The "distracted" perceptions are reminiscent of the phenomenology of Henri Bergson.

72 Ibid.

73 Jane Jacobs, *The Death and Life of Great American Cities* (New York: Vintage, 1961); for more on the impact of the book, see introduction to Richard T. LeGates and Frederic Stout, eds., *The City Reader* (London: Routledge, 1996), p. 103.

74 William H. Whyte, *The Organization Man* (New York: Simon and Schuster, 1956).

75 Cook, introduction to Crosby and Bodley, eds., *Living Arts*, no. 2, p. 70.

76 See for instance Peter Hall, *London 2000* (London: Faber and Faber, 1963), p. 33: "I wish to argue that London, and its continued growth, are in themselves not necessarily a bad thing. The lay Londoner may think this thesis so obvious as to need no proof. But among professional planners this is not so."

77 Possible sources for "Living City's" thinking about "place" would include Louis Kahn and Christian Norberg-Schulz, inspired in turn by Martin Heidegger (also a source of existentialism). Jane Jacobs had outlined some of the qualities of "place"; Christopher Alexander and Serge Chermeyeff's *Community and Privacy: Toward a New Architecture of Humanism* (1963) indicated new thinking about "pattern language," but may not have appeared in time to influence the exhibition. My thanks to Adam Sharr for discussing with me sources for "place."

78 "Place," in Crosby and Bodley, eds., *Living Arts*, no. 2, pp. 110–111.

79 See Alison and Peter Smithson's CIAM *Grille*, for CIAM 9, 1953.

80 "Place."

81 Cook, introduction to Crosby and Bodley, eds., *Living Arts*, no. 2, p. 71.

82 See Tyrwhitt, Sert, and Rogers, eds., *The Heart of the City*. See also Giedion, *Architecture, You and Me.*

83 Dennis Crompton has suggested Shirley MacLaine as another possible identification for this face.

84 The image also bears a resemblance to President Harry Truman.

85 The bisected face may be Louis Armstrong; I cannot offer an identification for the two female faces.

86 "Crowd," in Crosby and Bodley, eds., *Living Arts*, no. 2.

87 Freeman, "Living with the 60s," p. 8.

88 See "Living City Survival Kit," in Crosby and Bodley, eds., *Living Arts*, no. 2, p. 103.

89 An observation made by Mellor, *The Sixties Art Scene in London*, p. 58.

90 Correspondence with Dennis Crompton, 18 July 2002, confirmed in conversation with Michael Webb and Peter Cook, 19 November 2002.

91 Issues of identity and the body in relation to pop are discussed in, for example, "Bodies and Gender—Heroines and Heroes," in Mellor, *The Sixties Art Scene in London.*

92 On the representation of architects and their practice see, for instance, Andrew Saint, *The Image of the Architect* (New Haven: Yale University Press, 1983); for the British context see, for instance, John R. Gold, *The Experience of Modernism: Modern Architects and the Future City, 1928–53* (London: E & FN Spon, 1997); for discussion of architecture and masculinity (including the role of *Playboy* magazine) see, for instance, Joel Sanders, ed., *Stud: Architectures of Masculinity* (New York: Princeton Architectural Press, 1996).

93 Reyner Banham, "I'd Crawl a Mile for . . . *Playboy*," *Architects' Journal*, 7 April 1960, reprinted in Reyner Banham, *Design by Choice*, ed. Penny Sparke (London: Academy, 1981), p. 130. The Playboy organization's reputation for an urbane modernity would be further consolidated in the UK with the completion of Walter Gropius's Playboy Club in London, 1966.

94 Mailer was heavily critiqued by feminists in the 1970s.

95 My thanks to Alan Powers for reminding me of this connection.

96 My thanks to Ben Highmore for sharing his observations on the theorization of everyday life.

97 Lewis Mumford, "What Is a City?" (1937), reprinted in LeGates and Stout, eds., *The City Reader*, p. 181. My thanks to Ana Bettencourt for drawing my attention to this particular essay.

98 See Eric Mumford, *The CIAM Discourse on Urbanism, 1928–1960* (Cambridge, Mass.: MIT Press, 2000), p. 132.

99 The space pod was provided by Shepperton Film Studio.

100 See figure 103, "Advertisement for Wrapped and Sliced Bread, 1944," in Sigfried Giedion, *Mechanization Takes Command: A Contribution to Anonymous History* (London: Oxford University Press, 1948, rpt. 1969), p. 196.

101 Alloway, "City Notes."

102 Reyner Banham, "The Atavism of the Short-Distance Mini Cyclist," in Crosby and Bodley, eds., *Living Arts*, no. 3, pp. 91–97, reprinted in Banham, *Design by Choice*, p. 87.

103 Le Corbusier, "Letter to CIAM 10," 1956, in Newman, *New Frontiers in Architecture*, p. 16, quoted in Ockman, ed., *Architecture Culture 1943–1968*, p. 19.

104 Banham, "City as Scrambled Egg," insert, pp. 22–23.

105 Warren Chalk failed his medical for National Service. Correspondence with Dennis Crompton, 21 February 2003.

106 Recorded with Don Cherry.

107 Because of Musician's Union restrictions, it was difficult to hear American jazz musicians live in London. Correspondence from Peter Murray, 20 December 2002.

108 Hamilton later titled the image "Self Portrait." See Mellor, *The Sixties Art Scene in London*, p. 142.

109 For a critique of this, see Edward Jones and Christopher Woodward, *A Guide to the Architecture of London*, rev. ed. (London: Weidenfeld and Nicolson, 1992), p. 175. Christopher Woodward had in fact been a member of the Buchanan team.

110 Louis Kahn had long been interested in the idea of "clustering" the city rather than strictly zoning it in the Corbusian manner. In the December 1962 edition of *Architectural Design* devoted to Team 10, Kahn referred to "a place of maximum intensity," which Cook may have translated into the "Maximum Pressure Area" of his Plug-In City (1964).

111 Alison and Peter Smithson, editorial in *Architectural Review*, November 1957, excerpted in Reyner Banham, *The New Brutalism* (London: Architectural Press, 1966), p. 72.

112 Banham, "City as Scrambled Egg," p. 19.

113 Cook, introduction to Crosby and Bodley, eds., *Living Arts*, no. 2, p. 68.

114 For discussion of the Piccadilly controversy, see Jonathan Hughes, "1961," in Louise Campbell, ed., *Twentieth-Century Architecture and Its Histories* (London: Society of Architectural Historians of Great Britain, 2001).

115 The flyover was later removed.

116 See Warren Chalk and Ron Herron, "City Interchange-Project," in Crosby and Bodley, eds., *Living Arts*, no. 2, pp. 72–77.

117 Cook, "Come-Go," pp. 82–83.

118 See Jones and Woodward, *A Guide to the Architecture of London*, p. 303.

119 The Steering Group, "To: The Right Honourable Ernest Maples, MP, Minister of Transport," paragraph 4, in Colin Buchanan et al., *Traffic in Towns: A Study of the Long-Term Problems of Traffic in Urban Areas* (London: HMSO, 1963), n.p.

120 These interests were reiterated in a publication related to research apparently carried out for Buchanan: Brian Richards, *New Movement in Cities* (London: Studio Vista, 1966). The book featured Crompton's Computer City and Chalk and Herron's City Interchange project (pp. 22, 51), and it was probably Cook and Crompton's electric car project at Hornsey College of Art that was referred to on p. 23. Chalk drew up Richards's own scheme on p. 40.

121 Inside slip, Buchanan et al., *Traffic in Towns*.

122 Dennis Crompton concedes the Archigramish feel of parts of the Buchanan Report, though he denies any direct link. The "D. H. Crompton" listed among the Report's authors is no relation. (In conversation, 18 April 1997.)

123 The scheme was commissioned by the Ministry of Housing and Local Government and is discussed below. See Taylor Woodrow Group, *Urban Renewal: Fulham Study. A Pilot Study of an Area in the Metropolitan Borough of Fulham in the County of London Carried Out by the Taylor Woodrow Group at the Invitation of the Minister of Housing and Local Government* (London: Taylor Woodrow Group, 1963).

124 Based on a photograph from *Discovery Magazine*.

125 See figure 58 in Buchanan et al., *Traffic in Towns*, p. 43.

126 See, for instance, "The Report of the Working Group," paragraph 123 et seq., in Buchanan et al., *Traffic in Towns*, pp. 43–47.

127 See The Steering Group, "To: The Right Honourable Ernest Maples, MP, Minister of Transport," paragraph 38, and "The Report of the Working Group," paragraphs 100, 101, in Buchanan et al., *Traffic in Towns*, n.p.

128 See The Working Group, "A Central Metropolitan Block," part four of chapter 3, "Practical Studies," in Buchanan et al., *Traffic in Towns*, pp. 290–299.

129 Buchanan et al., *Traffic in Towns*, paragraph 480, p. 200.

130 See "The Future of the Motor Vehicle," in Buchanan et al., *Traffic in Towns*, pp. 24–25.

131 See Arthur Marwick, *British Society since 1945* (Harmondsworth: Penguin, 1996), p. 117.

132 See The Steering Group, "To: The Right Honourable Ernest Maples, MP, Minister of Transport," paragraph 11.

133 Archigram, dir., *Archigram*, BBC Productions, 1966, and see also Marwick, *British Society since 1945*, p. 118.

134 Chalk and Herron, "City Interchange-Project," p. 73.

135 Hall, *London 2000*, p. 107.

136 The Steering Group, "To: The Right Honourable Ernest Maples, MP, Minister of Transport," paragraph 9.

137 Archigram, dir., *Archigram*, BBC Productions, 1966. The obverse of this is recorded in Arthur Marwick's history of the period: "Mobility, perhaps, was fine for those with cars; for many without, especially in the country areas, there was almost a return to pre-industrial conditions." Marwick, *British Society since 1945*, p. 118.

138 Raymond Williams, *The Long Revolution* (London: Chatto and Windus, 1961), p. 321.

139 The Steering Group, "To: The Right Honourable Ernest Maples, MP, Minister of Transport," paragraph 40.

140 Cook, "Come-Go," pp. 82–83.

141 Richard Hamilton, "Urbane Image," in Crosby and Bodley, eds., *Living Arts*, no. 2, p. 44.

142 "Report of the Working Group," paragraph 437, p. 190. In this instance the Buchanan team was concentrating on driving in LA.

143 The Steering Group, "To: The Right Honourable Ernest Maples, MP, Minister of Transport," paragraph 22.

144 The Hawker Hunter was the fastest jet of its time, and a symbol of Britain having "made it."

145 Lawrence Alloway, "The American Sublime," in Crosby and Bodley, eds., *Living Arts*, no. 2, p. 12. Alloway had been curator at the Guggenheim in New York since 1960.

146 In conversation with Simon Herron, at the Paul Mellon Centre symposium "Special Relationship: American and British Architecture since 1945," Architectural Association, London, 30 October 1998.

147 See "Report of the Working Group," paragraph 424, p. 183.

148 Kristin Ross, *Fast Cars, Clean Bodies: Decolonization and the Reordering of French Culture* (Cambridge, Mass.: MIT Press, 1995), pp. 9–10.

149 Cook, "Come-Go," p. 83.

150 Booker, *The Neophiliacs*, pp. 153–154.

151 Archigram, dir., *Archigram*, BBC Productions, 1966. Archigram's efforts to publicize technological possibilities coincided with popular science offerings from BBC TV, including *Horizon* (1964) and *Tomorrow's World* (1965).

152 Marwick, *British Society since 1945*, pp. 20–21.

153 Booker, *The Neophiliacs*, pp. 148–49, citing *Encounter*, October 1960, n.p.

154 Booker, *The Neophiliacs*, p. 99.

155 Ibid., p. 153. Other "modernizing" publications included *The Observer, Queen*, and *About Town*.

156 For more on these distinctions, see, e.g., Williams, *The Long Revolution*, p. 346.

157 Banham insisted that he was a "scholarship boy" and that "the working class is where I come from." Banham, "The Atavism of the Short-Distance Mini Cyclist," in Banham, *Design by Choice*, p. 84.

158 Williams, *The Long Revolution*, p. 358. Williams further remarked on the differentiation of voting trends emerging between men and women.

159 Booker, *The Neophiliacs*, p. 93. According to Mary Banham (interview in London, 28 April 1997), Ron Herron "was working-class and proud of it; Cockney."

160 Marwick, *British Society since 1945*, p. 44, drawing on the work of Margaret Stacey.

161 Warren Chalk, "Housing as a Consumer Product," *Arena*, no. 81 (March 1966), pp. 228–230, reprinted in Archigram, ed., *A Guide to Archigram 1961–74*, p. 92.

162 Alison and Peter Smithson, "But Today We Collect Ads," *Ark*, no. 18 (November 1956), reprinted in Robbins, *The Independent Group*, p. 186.

163 Archigram, dir., *Archigram*, BBC Productions, 1966.

164 Lawrence Alloway, "The Long Front of Culture," *Cambridge Opinion*, no. 17 (1959), pp. 24–26.

165 Banham, "The Atavism of the Short-Distance Mini Cyclist," p. 87.

166 Taylor Woodrow Group, *Urban Renewal*, p. 20.

167 Ibid., p. 36.

168 Quoted in Michael Webb, "The Notion of Motion," in Dennis Crompton, ed., *Concerning Archigram* (London: Archigram Archives, 1998), p. 103.

169 Hall, *London 2000*, p. 162.

170 See ibid., p. 162. The main problem, Hall felt (p. 164), was "the virtual sterilization of large areas of land immediately around the shopping precincts . . . the desolation of the 'back sides' of central Coventry, or central Stevenage," an error seemingly repeated on the plans for Fulham.

171 Preview of the South Bank Development, *The Guardian*, Friday, 24 March 1961, part reprinted in Crompton, eds., *Concerning Archigram*, p. 32.

172 Cf. Hall, *London 2000*, pp. 162–163.

173 John Adam and Robert Adam, the Adelphi, built on a riverside "deck" near the Strand, London, 1768–1774.

174 Hall, *London 2000*, p. 164. Hall went on to cite "V" solutions at the Barbican and the William Holford plan for the comprehensive redevelopment of Piccadilly Circus. The LCC Architects Department had also projected V solutions for the aborted Hook new town project.

175 See Taylor Woodrow Group, *Urban Renewal*, pp. 52–53.

176 Ibid., p. 46.

177 Ibid.

178 Ibid.

179 Ibid.

180 Booker, *The Neophiliacs*, pp. 198–199.

181 Cf. Yona Friedman's Channel Bridge project, 1963.

182 David Greene and Michael Webb, "Story of the Thing," in Crosby and Bodley, eds., *Living Arts*, no. 2, pp. 92–93.

183 Ibid., p. 92. Kiesler's essays and manifestoes for a "City in Space" originated with his design for the Austrian Section of the Exposition Internationale des Arts Décoratifs et Industriels Modernes, directed by Josef Hoffmann at the Grand Palais in Paris, 1925.

184 "If we were not consumers, but users, we might look at society very differently, for the concept of use involves general human judgements—we need to know how to use things and what we are using them for, and also the effects of particular uses on our general life—whereas consumption, with its crude hand-to-mouth patterns, tends to cancel these questions, replacing them by the stimulated and controlled absorption of the products of an external and autonomous system." Williams, *The Long Revolution*, p. 321.

3 BEYOND ARCHITECTURE: INDETERMINACY, SYSTEMS, AND THE DISSOLUTION OF BUILDINGS

1 The cover of *Archigram* no. 7 was by James Meller.

2 Timothy Tinker, "Ten Questions in Search of an Answer," *Archigram*, no. 2 (1962), n.p.

3 The term was popularized by James Stirling.

4 The word "indeterminacy" first enters the Archigram lexicon in Peter Cook's "A Very Straight Description," *Archigram*, no. 7 (1966), n.p.

5 "Indeterminacy," *Archigram*, no. 8 (1968), n.p.

6 It can be claimed that a defining dynamic of modernism was the dialogue between the *containment* of the new and renewal through *spontaneity*. In *The Painter of Modern Life* (1863) Charles Baudelaire sought a balance between the eternal and the transient, and from then on the dynamic seems to be ever present in modernism, even within its very historiography: Nikolaus Pevsner looked for the immutable rules underlying modernism; while his pupil, Reyner Banham, championed the ephemeral (discussed by Gillian Naylor, "Theory and Design: The Banham Factor," the 9th Reyner Banham Memorial Lecture, Victoria and Albert Museum, 14 March 1997). As Hugh de Cronin Hastings précised Banham's investigation of the conundrum, "Stocktaking": "*Tradition* means . . . the stock of general knowledge . . . which specialists assume as the ground of present practice and future progress. *Technology* represents its converse, the method of exploring . . . a *potential* which may at any moment make nonsense of all existing knowledge . . . even 'basic' ideas like *house, city, building*" (Hugh de Cronin Hastings, foreword to Reyner Banham, "Stocktaking," *Architectural Review*, February 1960, reprinted in Reyner Banham, *Design by Choice*, ed. Penny Sparke [London: Academy, 1981], p. 48). A history of uneasy coalitions between containment and spontaneity can be traced within modernist practice: between rationalism and expressionism at the Bauhaus, or the disputes between functionalism and surrealism in the 1930s, or the way in which Theo van Doesburg felt able to bestride De Stijl and dadaism. The dynamic was even evident in modernism's preferred background music, jazz, with its tension between theme and improvisation. Modernism's accommodation of such a co-nundrum at its core made it a highly resilient and adaptable movement, a fact that had not gone entirely unnoticed. Rudolf Wittkower, Sigfried Giedion, and others variously noted how modernism had absorbed the competing bequests of the classical and the Gothic, creating a relationship representative by extension of the dynamic between closed and open spatial and formal concepts, Dionysian and Apollonian cultures, academic and craft teachings (see Frank Werner, "Constructive, Not Deconstructive Work: On the City of the 21st Century, Remarks on the Recent Work of Coop Himmelblau," in Coop Himmelblau, *Die Faszination der Stadt / The Power of the City* [Darmstadt: Georg Büchner Buchhandlung, 1988], pp. 6–11; and Sigfried Giedion, "Movement," in *Mechanization Takes Command* [Oxford: Oxford University Press, 1948; rpt. New York: Norton, 1969], p. 15).

7 This apparent critical mass of ideas was surveyed at the end of the decade in William Zuk and Roger Clark, *Kinetic Architecture* (New York: Van Nostrand Reinhold, 1970).

8 See Richard Llewelyn Davies [and John Weeks], "Endless Architecture," *Architectural Association Journal,* July 1951, pp. 106–112; see also John Weeks, "Indeterminate Architecture," *Transactions of the Bartlett Society,* no. 2 (1963–1964), pp. 83–106.

9 For further discussion of Llewelyn Davies and Weeks, see Jonathan Hughes, "The Indeterminate Building," in Jonathan Hughes and Simon Sadler, eds., *Non-Plan: Essays on Freedom, Participation and Change in Modern Architecture and Urbanism* (Oxford: Architectural Press, 2000), pp. 90–103.

10 László Moholy-Nagy, *Vision in Motion* (Chicago: Paul Theobald, 1947), p. 68.

11 Warren Chalk, "Trying to Find Out Is One of My Constant Doings," *Architectural Design,* January 1970, reprinted in Archigram, ed., *A Guide to Archigram 1961–74* (London: Academy, 1994), pp. 322–329. In the late sixties EAT was assisted in its work by Envirolab of Los Angeles, a group of Archigram acolytes.

12 In the early 1970s, Kenneth Frampton claimed that Le Corbusier was the only architect of his generation to attend to the dilemma, contrasting him with Mies van der Rohe who, "after a quixotic beginning in which he was to exploit the free plan for its capacity to articulate the rectilinear planes asymmetrically disposed in space," had concentrated on the idealization of the trabeated frame. Kenneth Frampton, "Reflections on the Opposition of Architecture and Building," in James Gowan, ed., *A Continuing Experiment: Learning and Teaching at the Architectural Association* (London: Architectural Press, 1975), p. 110. Alan Colquhoun similarly wrote in 1962 that "Le Corbusier made no claims to be writing a systematic treatise, and it could be that the contradictions in the argument represent a necessary conflict of ideas which can only be resolved in the works themselves—a dialectical sequence the third term of which can only be introduced at the level of symbolic representation." Alan Colquhoun, "The Modern Movement in Architecture," *British Journal of Aesthetics,* January 1962, pp. 59–65, reprinted in Joan Ockman, with Edward Eigen, ed., *Architecture Culture 1943–1968: A Documentary Anthology* (New York: Rizzoli, 1993), p. 344.

13 John Summerson, "The Case for a Theory of Modern Architecture," *RIBA Journal* 64, no. 8 (June 1957), reprinted in Ockman, ed., *Architecture Culture 1943–1968,* p. 233.

14 Brian Appleyard, *Richard Rogers: A Biography* (London: Faber, 1986), p. 87.

15 Summerson's argument as summarized by Frampton, "Reflections on the Opposition of Architecture and Building," p. 107.

16 Quoted in Sherban Cantacuzino, *Howell, Killick, Partridge & Amis* (London: Lund Humphries, 1981), p. 10, and cited in Appleyard, *Richard Rogers,* p. 86.

17 Listening to Summerson's paper, Banham and Smithson had objected that "the programme" does not generate actual forms. See Appleyard, *Richard Rogers,* p. 86.

18 See Archigram, "Open Ends," editorial from *Archigram* no. 8, n.p., reprinted in Archigram, ed., *A Guide to Archigram 1961–74,* pp. 216–222, and in Peter Cook, ed., *Archigram* (London: Studio Vista, 1972), p. 74.

19 Peter Cook, *Experimental Architecture* (London: Studio Vista, 1970), p. 67.

20 Karl Popper, *The Open Society and Its Enemies,* 2 vols. (London: Routledge and Kegan Paul, 1945, 1966); and *The Poverty of Historicism* (London: Routledge and Kegan Paul, 1957).

21 Archigram, dir., *Archigram,* BBC Productions, 1966.

22 See too Barry Curtis, "The Heart of the City," in Hughes and Sadler, eds., *Non-Plan.*

23 John Voelcker, "Draft Framework 5" (for CIAM X), *Arena,* June 1965, p. 13, quoted in Charles Jencks, *Modern Movements in Architecture* (Harmondsworth: Penguin, 1973, 2d ed. 1985), p. 306.

24 Sir Andrew Derbyshire, "Fifties Education: Architecture from a Former Student's Point of View," "AA 50/90" symposium, Architectural Association, London, 16 November 1996. Benjamin Franks has suggested to me that the source of this "anarchism" was Patrick Geddes and Peter Kropotkin.

25 CIAM responded in the late forties and early fifties by paying new attention to the problem of the "Urban Core." See for instance J. Tyrwhitt, J. L. Sert, and E. N. Rogers, eds., *The Heart of the City: Towards the Humanisation of Urban Life* (London: Lund Humphries, 1952).

26 Jane Jacobs, *The Death and Life of Great American Cities* (New York: Vintage, 1961).

27 Building materials rationing was lifted in the UK in 1954.

28 David Greene, "Statement," *Archigram,* no. 1 (1961), n.p.

29 *Archigram,* no. 3 (August 1963).

30 See John Beck, "Buckminster Fuller and the Politics of Shelter," in Hughes and Sadler, eds., *Non-Plan,* pp. 116–125.

31 See Joachim Krausee and Claude Lichtenstein, eds., *Your Private Sky: R. Buckminster Fuller, the Art of Design Science* (Baden: Lars Müller, 1999), pp. 92–93 and passim. The World Design Science Decade, launched by Fuller in 1965, was widely reported in journals such as *Architectural Design,* and was promoted in the UK by proponents as close to *Archigram* as James Meller at its own Folkestone conference (1966).

32 "Discussion," *Archigram,* no. 3 (1963), n.p.

33 For more on organicism in respect to postwar architectural theory, see Barry Curtis, "The Heart of the City"; Reyner Banham, "A Clip-On Architecture," *Design Quarterly,* 1965, reprinted *Architectural Design* 35 (November 1965), p. 534; Sigfried Giedion, *Space, Time and Architecture: The*

Growth of a New Tradition, rev. ed. (Cambridge, Mass.: Harvard University Press, 1967).

34 Curtis, "The Heart of the City," p. 63.

35 Summerson himself recognized the breakthrough, admiring the way in which Bruno Zevi's book *Towards an Organic Architecture* (London: Faber, 1950) had been based "on a social idea and not on a figurative idea." Summerson, "The Case for a Theory of Modern Architecture," p. 232.

36 Cook, *Experimental Architecture,* p. 47.

37 See Norbert Wiener, *Cybernetics, or Control and Communication in the Animal and Machine* (Cambridge, Mass.: Technology Press, 1948).

38 See Giedion, *Mechanization Takes Command,* p. 719. He gave the example of physiology, which was exploring the semiautonomous parts of the nervous system, signaling the developments in the understanding of homeostasis that would lead to cybernetic theory. My thanks to Reinhold Martin for first bringing this path of development to my attention. For more on the origins of ideas on control, communication, and cybernetics, see Robert Boguslaw, *The New Utopians: A Study of System Design and Social Change* (Englewood Cliffs, N.J.: Prentice-Hall, 1965), pp. 31–32.

39 B. Harris, "The Limits of Science and Humanism in Planning," *American Institute of Planners Journal,* no. 5 (September 1967), pp. 324–335, quoted in Nicholas Negroponte, *The Architecture Machine: Toward a More Human Environment* (Cambridge, Mass.: MIT Press, 1970), p. 3.

40 Negroponte, *The Architecture Machine,* p. 3.

41 "Man," in Theo Crosby and John Bodley, eds., *Living Arts,* no. 2 (London: Institute of Contemporary Arts and Tillotson, 1963), p. 100. See too the indeterminate board game illustrating Reyner Banham, Paul Barker, Peter Hall, and Cedric Price, "Non-Plan: An Experiment in Freedom," *New Society,* 20 March 1969, pp. 435–443.

42 See Boguslaw, *The New Utopians,* p. 65.

43 Warren Chalk, "People Robots and Trees," in Gowan, ed., *A Continuing Experiment,* p. 68.

44 "Free jazz" had roots in another Archigram favorite, Ornette Coleman (see Peter Cook, "The Beginning," in Dennis Crompton, ed., *Concerning Archigram* [London: Archigram Archives, 1998], p. 16), and found its greatest exponent in John Coltrane's *Ascension* (1965). Archigram's attention to jazz was as much a matter of intellect (and image) as of taste; some members of the group, notably Peter Cook and Michael Webb, personally preferred classical music.

45 My thanks to Neil Jackson for identifying Mies van der Rohe's Fifty-by-Fifty House project (1950) in this montage. "Ghosts" was first recorded in 1964 on the album *Spiritual Unity.* See "Albert Ayler: His Life and Music" by Jeff Schwartz, <http://ernie.bgsu.edu/~jeffs/ayler.html>, and the chapter on Albert Ayler in Valerie Wilmer, *As Serious as Your Life* (London: Allison and Busby, 1977).

46 Peter Cook, "Come-Go," in Crosby and Bodley, eds., *Living Arts* no. 2, pp. 82–83.

47 David Greene, "Statement," *Archigram,* no. 1 (1961), n.p.

48 "Diagonals and Connections," *Archigram,* no. 5, n.p.

49 The linear city ultimately derived from the inventions of Arturo Soria y Mata in the 1880s: see Françoise Choay, *The Modern City: Planning in the Nineteenth Century* (London: Studio Vista, 1969), pp. 100–101.

50 A point remarked upon by Peter Cook in *Experimental Architecture,* p. 94.

51 See Cedric Price, "Potteries Think Belt," *Architectural Design* 36 (October 1966), pp. 483–497.

52 This was a concept already seen in Moisei Ginzburg's Green Moscow project of 1929–1930, where linear railways fanned out from the Soviet capital carrying, free of charge, movable wooden houses.

53 See Cook, *Experimental Architecture,* p. 101. See also "Universal Structure," *Archigram,* no. 5, n.p.

54 Christopher Alexander, "A City Is Not a Tree," *Architectural Forum,* May 1965, pp. 58–61 (part 1), April 1965, pp. 58–62 (part 2). Ultimately, Archigram steered clear of attempts to find patterned solutions to architecture. In this they adhered to Cedric Price's critique in *Archigram* no. 7 of the urban plan as a two-dimensional diagram (Cedric Price, "Cedric Price," *Archigram,* no. 7 [1966], n.p.). Price (who had met Alexander when they were both studying at Cambridge) described Alexander's reasoning as "puerile . . . a mere mental convenience for an intellectually under-endowed profession." For a survey of pattern language, see chapter 2 of Philip Drew, *Third Generation: The Changing Meaning of Modern Architecture* (New York: Praeger, 1972).

55 "Greater number" was the theme of the 1968 Milan Triennale, to which Archigram contributed. It had been a concern since the late fifties; see, for instance, Ockman, ed., *Architecture Culture 1943–1968,* p. 399.

56 See Kiyonori Kikutake, Kisho Kurokawa, Fumihiko Maki, and Masato Otaka, "Metabolism 1960—A Proposal for New Urbanism" (1958), a manifesto delivered to the 1960 World Design Conference. Quoted in Kisho Kurokawa, *Metabolism in Architecture* (London: Studio Vista, 1977), p. 27.

57 Peter Smithson writing on the Tokyo Bay project, *Architectural Design,* September 1964, p. 479, quoted in Jencks, *Modern Movements in Architecture,* p. 343.

58 For a still more flexible variant on the principle, see also N. J. Habraken's *De Dragers en de Mensen,* 1961 (translated as *Supports: An Alternative to Mass Housing* [London: Architectural Press, 1972]).

59 Banham, "A Clip-On Architecture."

60 The term "kit" was to be found, for example, in Archigram, dir., *Archigram,* BBC Productions, 1966, and in Alan Stanton, "Self-Structuring System," *Archigram,* no. 8 (1968), n.p., and then acquired a new level of authority in chapter 4, "The Kit of Parts: Heat and Light," of Reyner Banham's *The Architecture of the Well-Tempered Environment* (London: Architectural Press, 1969).

61 See Peter Taylor, "Words At Liberty: Alphabetic Communication in the Living City," in Crosby and Bodley, eds., *Living Arts,* no. 2, pp. 78–79.

62 "Ephemeralization" was a term coined in the 1938 edition of Buckminster Fuller's *Nine Chains to the Moon.* See Martin Pawley, *Theory and Design in the Second Machine Age* (Oxford: Basil Blackwell, 1990), p. 9.

63 Indeed *Archigram* contributor Martin Pawley has suggested it is one of the hallmarks of the transition from the First to the Second of the Machine Ages, and tried to outline the importance of technological atomization in his book *The Private Future: Causes and Consequences of Community Collapse in the West* (London: Thames and Hudson,

1973): "The railway train and the cinema of the First Machine Age did not change home life or individual human relationships in the drastically fundamental way that the car or television did." Quoted in Pawley, *Theory and Design in the Second Machine Age*, p. 2.

64 See Charles Jencks, *Le Corbusier and the Tragic View of Architecture* (London: Allen Lane, 1973; rpt. Harmondsworth: Penguin, 1987), p. 163.

65 Le Corbusier, *Towards a New Architecture* (London: Architectural Press, 1947), quoted in Barry Curtis, "A Necessary Irritant," in Crompton, ed., *Concerning Archigram*, pp. 25–79.

66 See, for instance, the two remarkable kit structures by George Fred Keck, the House of Tomorrow and Crystal House, at the 1933 Century of Progress exhibition in Chicago, which were light, steel-framed structures composed from plate glass, sheet metal panels, battledeck steel floor systems (of the sort pioneered by Henri Labrouste at the Bibliothèque Nationale, 1858–1868), and, in the Crystal House, a distinctive exoskeleton space frame that anticipated the Fun Palace and Pompidou Center structures.

67 See Pawley, *Theory and Design in the Second Machine Age*, pp. 78–79.

68 See Curtis, "A Necessary Irritant," p. 53.

69 See Pawley, *Theory and Design in the Second Machine Age*, pp. 79–80.

70 See ibid., p. 81.

71 Ibid.

72 See David P. Handlin, *Amercian Architecture* (London: Thames and Hudson, 1985), p. 214.

73 See Pawley, *Theory and Design in the Second Machine Age*, pp. 80–81.

74 For more on discourses on hygiene, see Arthur Marwick, *The Sixties: Cultural Revolution in Britain, France, Italy, and the United States, c. 1958–c. 1974* (Oxford: Oxford University Press, 1998), and Kristin Ross, *Fast Cars, Clean Bodies: Decolonization and the Reordering of French Culture* (Cambridge, Mass.: MIT Press, 1995).

75 Cook, *Experimental Architecture*, p. 31.

76 Ibid. See too Charles Jencks's summary of the Smithsons' transition from "moralistic" interchangeable panels at Sheffield, 1953 (see figure 1.16) to complex "consumer" panels in the House of the Future, 1956 (see figure 1.28): "opposed to the single joint repeated within the single unit (Gropius) was the particularized joint repeated over many units (Ford)." Jencks, *Modern Movements in Architecture*, pp. 276–277.

77 Cook, *Experimental Architecture*, p. 31.

78 See *Archigram*, no. 9 (1970).

79 Cook, *Experimental Architecture*, p. 115.

80 Ibid.

81 "Comfort," *Archigram*, no. 8, n.p.

82 David Greene, "A Statement," *Archigram*, no. 1 (1961), n.p.

83 Quoted in Reyner Banham, *Theory and Design in the First Machine Age* (London: Architectural Press, 1960, rpt. 1988), pp. 325–326.

84 Greene, "A Statement."

85 Cook, *Experimental Architecture*, p. 11. The admiration for nineteenth-century engineering was probably conveyed to Archigram by architects such as James Stirling.

86 Ibid., p. 119.

87 Giedion, *Space, Time and Architecture*, p. 255.

88 The kit was shown assembled in Reyner Banham, *Megastructure: Urban Futures of the Recent Past* (London: Thames and Hudson, 1976), p. 98.

89 Cook, *Experimental Architecture*, p. 63.

90 See ibid., p. 83.

91 Ibid., p. 103.

92 Cedric Price, "Activity and Change," in *Archigram*, no. 2, (1962), n.p.

93 Featured in *Archigram* no. 3. Schein designed his first capsule for the Exposition des Arts Ménagères in 1955. Schein's Project for a Mobile Library, 1957, offered a clear antecedent for Greene's 1966 Living Pod. See Banham, "A Clip-On Architecture," p. 535, which claims that a clip-on principle was also adopted by a young Belgian, Jacques Baudon, in a competition entry of 1959, "a house-design that added an essential further concept—the connector between the units. Apart from the living-room, which was of totally indeterminate form and construction according to the whim of the inhabitants, each other function—sleeping, bathroom, kitchen—was housed in a separate capsule reached from a corridor-tube made up of standard branching sections," and thus was infinitely extendable.

94 All these examples were noted in Cook, *Experimental Architecture*, p. 59.

95 Portakabins were developed by Donald Shepherd, a construction manager with firsthand experience of temporary accommodation. They became a key element in Cedric Price's Inter Action Centre, Kentish Town, London 1971.

96 Peter Cook, "Capsules, Pods and Skins," in Crompton, ed., *Concerning Archigram*, pp. 80–82.

97 On the Paddington Tower, see Cook, *Experimental Architecture*, pp. 59–61. For information on Farrell's early work, see Terry Farrell, "Hedgehogs and Foxes," in Terry Farrell et al., *Terry Farrell* (London: Academy Editions, 1984), p. 19, as cited in Jonathan Hughes, "1961," in Louise Campbell, ed., *Twentieth-Century Architecture and Its Histories* (London: Society of Architectural Historians of Great Britain, 2001). Farrell and Grimshaw were congratulated in *Archigram* no. 8. Grimshaw had previously been published in *Archigram* no. 6.

98 Cook, *Experimental Architecture*, p. 57.

99 Archigram, dir., *Archigram*, BBC Productions, 1966.

100 See David Greene's curriculum vitae, <http://www.wmin.ac.uk/sabe/index2.asp?page=9>.

101 Warren Chalk, "The 40s," *Archigram*, no. 6 (1965), n.p.

102 The Thames Fortresses were illustrated in ibid., and also in Warren Chalk, "Hardware of a New World," *Architectural Forum* 125, no. 3 (October 1966), pp. 46–51. Artillery bunkers along the Channel coast were already being cited as an aesthetic source of brutalism.

103 "I suspect that the reiterativeness of the rounded corners . . . was as important to the whole Archigram Group, as the preference for Suprematist gambits must have been for the young Russians of 1929." Peter Cook, "In Memoriam Archigram," *Daidalos*, no. 4 (15 June 1982), p. 54.

104 See Cook, *Experimental Architecture*, p. 112.

105 At the Archigram-convened Folkestone conference in 1966, Robin Middleton found that "questioners had all but intimated that our only hope was to stop buying magazines like *Architectural Design* and to subscribe to the *Scientific American*." Robin Middleton, "Folkestone IDEA," *Architectural Design*, July 1966, p. 322. The magazine was also referenced by Cedric Price.

106 Charles Kimball, "Technology Transfer,"

National Academy of Sciences Report, *Applied Science and Technological Progress,* 1967, n.p., cited in Pawley, *Theory and Design in the Second Machine Age,* p. 156.

107 Peter Cook, "Into 1967 YOU YOU YOU IT'S UP TO YOU," *Archigram,* no. 7 (1967), n.p. However, in her review of *Archigram* in 1968 ("Little Magazines in Architecture and Urbanism," *Journal of the American Institute of Town Planners* 34, no. 4 [July 1968], p. 231, n. 20), Denise Scott Brown noted a lack of engagement with the details of technology and systems. "One is surprised to find no mention in their writings of the work of Richard L. Meier; for example, his *Science and Economic Development* (Cambridge: The MIT Press, 1956). One would have thought his notions on the MASL (Minimum Adequate Standard of Living) quite pertinent to the encapsulated society."

108 Pawley, *Theory and Design in the Second Machine Age,* p. 148, argues that just as the "first generation" underestimated the importance of technology transfer to the modern movement, the "second generation" almost entirely ignored it (nylon, carbon fiber, Kevlar, Mylar, Nomex, Teflon, IT, electronic management of building systems, building intelligence).

109 Cook, *Experimental Architecture,* p. 63.

110 Ibid., p. 112.

111 See Banham, *The Architecture of the Well-Tempered Environment,* p. 183.

112 Ibid., p. 187.

113 See Alison and Peter Smithson, "Caravan: Embryo Appliance House?," *Architectural Design,* September 1959, reprinted in Alison and Peter Smithson, *Ordinariness and Light* (London: Faber and Faber, 1970), pp. 114–122.

114 See Melvin Charney, "Predictions for Design," *Landscape,* Spring 1967, pp. 21–24, reprinted as "Environmental Conjecture: In the Jungle of the Grand Prediction," in Stanford Anderson, ed., *Planning for Diversity and Choice: Possible Futures and Their Relations to the Man-Controlled Environment* (Cambridge, Mass.: MIT Press, 1968), pp. 313–326. The statistic dates from 1965. In American usage, "mobile" often designates a factory-made house, brought complete to site, so that mobility is possible but unlikely.

115 See David F. Lyon, "High Rise Mobile Home Parks," *Trailer Life,* October 1964, cited in Melvin Charney, "Predictions for Design," p. 317.

116 "The Nomad," *Archigram,* no. 8 (1968), n.p.

117 Cook, *Experimental Architecture,* p. 119.

118 Cook, "Capsules, Pods and Skins," p. 82.

119 See Banham, "Stocktaking," and *The Architecture of the Well-Tempered Environment,* pp. 13ff.

120 Reyner Banham, "A Home Is Not a House," *Art in America,* no. 53 (April 1965), pp. 109–118, reprinted in Banham, *Design by Choice,* p. 56.

121 Otto was in Cook, *Experimental Architecture,* pp. 50–51.

122 "Current Scene," *Archigram,* no. 6 (1965).

123 See Cook, *Experimental Architecture,* pp. 61–62.

124 Cedric Price, Frank Newby, Robert H. Suan, and Felix J. Samuely and Partners, *Air Structures: A Survey* (London: Department of the Environment / HMSO, 1971).

125 The theme of *Architectural Design,* June 1968.

126 On the concept of "dematerialization" in the arts generally, see Lucy R. Lippard, *Six Years: The Dematerialization of the Art Object from 1966 to 1972* (New York: Praeger; London: Studio Vista, 1973).

127 Cook, *Experimental Architecture,* pp. 51–55.

128 Cited and translated in Banham, *Theory and Design in the First Machine Age,* pp. 306–307. Transparency had also been the ideal demanded in Bruno Taut's *Alpine Architektur* (1919) and in Paul Scheerbart's *Glasarchitektur* (1914).

129 Cook, *Experimental Architecture,* pp. 51–55.

130 Cook, ed., *Archigram,* p. 77. "Brunhilda" is Webb's joke spelling of 1968.

131 Chalk, "People Robots and Trees," p. 68.

132 "It would seem that any acceptance of method or system is still in its infancy. We tend either to see as victim mesmerised by the outrageous demands of facts and figures or to slink uncomprehendingly away depressed and in misery at the lack of firm evidence that could in any way evaluate or prevent embarrassing diametrically opposite or endlessly inventive opinions from fruition." Ibid., p. 67.

133 Archigram, dir., *Archigram,* BBC Productions, 1966.

134 Quoted in Pawley, *Theory and Design in the Second Machine Age,* p. 1, no citation.

135 "Zoom! Space Probe!," *Archigram,* no. 4 (1964), n.p.

136 *Archigram* used the spelling "computor."

137 See Pawley, *Theory and Design in the Second Machine Age,* p. 1.

138 Archigram, dir., *Archigram,* BBC Productions, 1966.

139 Arthur Marwick, *British Society since 1945* (Harmondsworth: Penguin, 1996), pp. 110–111.

140 Boguslaw, *The New Utopians,* p. 5.

141 Ibid., p. 28 and passim. Another example of this was ekistics, launched by Constantin Doxiadis in the mid-fifties; he inaugurated the Athens Technological Institute in 1958 as a research center and architecture school based around the study of global statistics, spatial patterns, and control systems, and hosted annual study conferences. For a discussion of ekistics, and the "networking" context of Archigram, see Mark Wigley, "Network Fever," *Grey Room,* no. 4 (Summer 2001), pp. 83–122.

142 See Boguslaw, *The New Utopians,* p. 34.

143 The archetypal think tank was the RAND Corporation, established in Santa Monica in 1948 to coordinate interdisciplinary research into and systems analysis of military, social, technical, and economic problems.

144 See Boguslaw, *The New Utopians,* p. 30.

145 The problem of "evolutionary design" is discussed in Boguslaw, *The New Utopians,* p. 142.

146 See ibid., pp. 7–8.

147 Cook, *Experimental Architecture,* p. 55.

148 Mike Webb, "House Project," *Archigram,* no. 5 (1964), n.p.

149 See Boguslaw, *The New Utopians,* pp. 7–8; cf. *Ark* no. 42 (1968), in which Chalk and Price "respectively rejected the two poles between which Archigram sought to operate—'a ridiculous Emmett level' and 'dreary Bauhaus logic'" (quoted in Curtis, "A Necessary Irritant," pp. 30–31).

150 This statement was issued by Herron and Chalk, with John Roberts, John Attenborough, and David Curry.

151 Cook, *Experimental Architecture,* p. 33.

152 "Hard and Soft-ware," *Archigram,* no. 8 (1968), n.p.

153 Edgar Kaufmann Jr., "Design, sans peur et sans resources," *Architectural Forum,* September

1966, cited in Pawley, *Theory and Design in the Second Machine Age,* n. 8, pp. 172 and 123–124.

154 The Osakagram was lodged alongside exhibits by Alexander, Safdie, Friedman, and Kurokawa.

155 See Negroponte, *The Architecture Machine,* p. 63.

156 Dennis Crompton and Peter Cook, in lectures at the *Archigram* symposium, Cornerhouse, Manchester, 9 February 1998, implied that Computer City and Plug-In City were directly linked. Crompton had previously investigated the potential for computer-controlled lighting at the South Bank Centre, the top gallery of which was controlled by an electronic eye and blinds (details given in Norman Engleback, address to the 20th Century Society's Hayward Gallery symposium, Architectural Association, London 20 March 1999).

157 Dennis Crompton, "Computer City," *Archigram,* no. 5 (1965), n.p.

158 Peter Hall, *London 2000* (London: Faber and Faber, 1963), pp. 112–113.

159 Dennis Crompton, "City Synthesis," in Crosby and Bodley, eds., *Living Arts,* no. 2, p. 86.

160 Negroponte, *The Architecture Machine,* p. 69.

161 Ibid.

162 Charles Jencks, "Consumer Democracy" collage, c. 1969, in Charles Jencks and Nathan Silver, *Adhocism: The Case for Improvisation* (London: Secker and Warburg, 1972), p. 63. In *The New Paradigm in Architecture* (New Haven: Yale University Press, 2002), p. 203, Jencks claims that the collage was intended as an "ironic critique of the defense department."

163 Michael Webb, "Rent-a-Wall," *Archigram,* no. 7 (1966), n.p.

164 Dolan Conway and Brian Mitchenere, "Computer Community," in James Gowan, ed., *Projects: Architectural Association 1946–71,* AA Cahiers Series No. 1 (London: Architectural Association, 1974), p. 78, citing the *Evening Standard,* 15 June 1967. It was foretold that the GPO Computer grid would be joined by other projects coming on stream, such as the University of the Air (later realized as the Open University) and Educom.

165 Peter Cook, "Metamorphosis," *Archigram,* no. 8 (1968).

166 See also the Lecture Project in *Archigram* no. 8. Study stations were in development in the work of Sol Cornburg; see Sol Cornburg, "Creativity and Industrial Technology," *Architectural Design,* May 1968, cited in Cook, *Experimental Architecture,* p. 82.

167 Barry Snowden, "Mobile Action Terminal Extension," *Archigram,* no. 9 (1970), n.p.

168 "Exchange and Response," *Archigram,* no. 8 (1968), n.p.

169 Cook, *Experimental Architecture,* p. 127. The jukebox concept had also appeared in plans for the Price/Littlewood Fun Palace. See J. Stanley Matthews, "An Architecture for the New Britain: The Social Vision of Cedric Price's Fun Palace and Potteries Thinkbelt," Ph.D. dissertation, Columbia University, 2002, p. 429.

170 Mike Webb, "Fluid and Air-Wall," 1968, in Cook, ed., *Archigram,* p. 76.

171 Ron Herron, "Enviro-pill and Holographic Scene Setter," *Archigram,* no. 9 (1970), n.p.

172 "In This Archigram," *Archigram,* no. 9 (1970), n.p.

173 Cf. Boguslaw, *The New Utopians,* pp. 149–150.

174 Tony Rickaby, "Outgrowth," *Archigram,* no. 9 (1970), n.p.

175 "In This Archigram," n.p.

176 "Hard and Soft-ware," *Archigram,* no. 8 (1968), n.p.

177 Peter Cook, "Control or Choice," *Control,* 1967, reprinted in Cook, ed., *Archigram,* p. 69. Cook also wrote of his Moment-Village ("The Nomad," *Archigram,* no. 8), "Its group-regroup-shift implication suggests that its ultimate might be an anarchy-city or that 'place' exists only in the mind."

178 Compare the "tartan grid" to the plan of Candilis, Josic, Woods with Manfred Schiedhelm and Jean Prouvé, Free University Berlin, 1963–1973.

179 Cf. Webb's Drive-In Housing project, 1964–1966.

180 Cook, *Experimental Architecture,* p. 109. These issues had been raised in Stephen Willats's *Control* magazine.

181 "The Nomad," *Archigram,* no. 8 (1968).

182 Daniel Bell, *The End of Ideology: On the Exhaustion of Political Ideas in the Fifties* (Glencoe, Il.: Free Press, 1959).

183 The phrase derives from J. K. Galbraith's classic *The Affluent Society* (1958).

184 Alan Stanton, "Self-Structuring System," *Archigram,* no. 8 (1968), n.p.

185 See Boguslaw, *The New Utopians,* p. 4.

186 Brian Haynes in *Woman's Mirror,* no citation, reprinted "Into 1967," *Archigram,* no. 7 (1966).

187 See, for instance, Bruce Mazlisch, "Obsolescence and 'Obsolescibles' in Planning for the Future," in Anderson, ed., *Planning for Diversity and Choice,* p. 165; or Jencks, *Modern Movements in Architecture,* p. 72.

188 See for instance Noam Chomsky, *American Power and the New Mandarins* (New York: Pantheon, 1969).

189 "Indeterminacy—Relaxed Scene," *Archigram,* no. 8 (1968), n.p.

190 Karl Marx, *Communist Manifesto,* trans. Samuel Moore, 1888, reprinted in *The Marx-Engels Reader,* ed. Robert C. Ticker, 2d ed. (New York: Norton, 1978), p. 338, quoted in Marshall Berman, *All That Is Solid Melts into Air: The Experience of Modernity* (London: Verso, 1983), p. 95.

191 Cook, "Metamorphosis," n.p.

192 This point adapts an observation made by Volker M. Welter, "Noble Savage or Cosmopolite? Who Is It That Wants to Live Mobile?," lecture at the conference "Where or What Is Home—Mobile Architecture versus Permanent Dwellings," University of California, Santa Barbara, 11 October 2003.

193 Cf. the approximate free market libertarianism adopted by Reyner Banham, Cedric Price, Peter Hall, and Paul Barker in their remarkable *New Society* "Non-Plan" feature of March 1969. For further discussion of these issues, see Hughes and Sadler, eds., *Non-Plan.*

194 "The notion of obsolescence," Bruce Mazlisch, professor of history at MIT, explained to an audience of architects and planners (including Cedric Price) in 1966, "goes against the time sense of both conservatives and liberals . . . and it offends against our hopes of immortality." Mazlisch, "Obsolescence and 'Obsolescibles,'" p. 155.

195 Cook, "Metamorphosis," n.p.

196 Herbert Gans, *The Levittowners: Ways of Life and Politics in a New Suburban Community* (London: Allen Lane, 1967).

197 Cook, *Experimental Architecture,* p. 110.

198 Ibid., p. 124.

199 David Greene, "Bottery," *Archigram,* no. 9 (1970), n.p.

200 See Krausee and Lichtenstein, eds., *Your Private Sky,* p. 80 and passim.

201 Cook, *Experimental Architecture,* pp. 124–125. Cook looked forward to circuitry built into wall panels (panels with built-in plumbing were already available in Italy), and possibly with lighting filaments too.

202 Cedric Price, "Cedric Price," *Archigram,* no. 7 (1966), n.p.

203 Reyner Banham, "City as Scrambled Egg," *Cambridge Opinion,* no. 17 (1959), pp. 18–23.

204 Chalk, "People Robots and Trees," p. 67.

205 Sigfried Giedion, quoted in "Ninth Meeting—July 12, 1963. The Declaration of Delos: Statements and Comments," *Ekistics* no. 16 (October 1963), p. 254; quoted in Wigley, "Network Fever," p. 90.

206 See Wigley, "Network Fever." The Delos Declaration was the culmination of the first ekistics meeting.

207 Price, "Cedric Price," n.p.

208 Greene, "Bottery," n.p.

209 The reduction of architecture to "enclosure" was an intellectual maneuver made (in the wake of Fuller) by Price and Banham.

210 Middleton, "Folkestone IDEA," p. 322.

211 Ruth Lakofski, "Oh, Please, Mr. Banham: An Open Letter to Those Who Were There," *Architectural Design,* July 1966, p. 322.

212 "Organization man" or "Orgman" was identified in Harold Rosenberg, *The Tradition of the New* (New York: McGraw-Hill, 1965).

213 Archigram, *Archigram Opera,* 1975 (?) (rescreened at Cornerhouse, Manchester, February 1998), based on Mike Webb, "Dreams Come True" project, *Archigram* no. 9 (1970), n.p.

214 Rousseau, Robert Boguslaw noticed, "continually plays what we might call a 'good life' rather than a 'freedom' game. The payoff in this game is *not* necessarily freedom; it is something called the good life. Freedom becomes a principle of play." Boguslaw, *The New Utopians,* p. 92, citing Jean-Jacques Rousseau's *The Social Contract* (reprinted Chicago: Henry Regnery, 1954). On the interest in nomadism to postwar architectural culture, see Felicity Scott, "Bernard Rudofsky: Allegories of Nomadism and Dwelling," in Sarah Williams Goldhagen and Réjean Legault, eds., *Anxious Modernisms: Experimentation in Postwar Architectural Culture* (Cambridge, Mass.: MIT Press, 2000), pp. 215–237.

215 From 1969 to 1970, Instant City was funded by the Graham Foundation, Chicago. In an interesting etymological coincidence, in 1969 Fuller wrote to Doxiadis saying that computers will create "instant city." See Wigley, "Network Fever," p. 113.

216 Banham, "A Home Is Not a House," p. 60.

217 Boguslaw, *The New Utopians,* p. 87. In fact, Boguslaw explained that it would be possible to effect technological and environmental changes as alternatives to social commands and prohibitions, for example by modifying the human body, deploying auxiliary equipment, or colonizing beneath the earth or sea—all tactics suggested by Archigram too.

218 Peter Cook, "Room of 1000 Delights," *Archigram,* no. 9 (1970), n.p. Cf. Buckminster Fuller: "A room should not be fixed, should not create a static mood, but should lend itself to change so that its many occupants may play upon it as they would upon a piano." *Chronofile,* no. 36 (1929), quoted in Krausee and Lichtenstein, eds., *Your Private Sky,* p. 111.

219 For further discussion, see for instance Eeva-Liisa Pelkonen, *Achtung Architektur! Image and Phantasm in Contemporary Austrian Architecture* (Cambridge, Mass.: MIT Press, 1996), pp. 13–14.

220 Gordon Pask, "An Aesthetically Potent Social Environment," *Archigram,* no. 8 (1968), n.p. Pask was the cybernetic consultant on Joan Littlewood and Cedric Price's Fun Palace.

221 Warren Chalk, "Architecture as Consumer Product," *Japan Architect,* no. 7 (1970), p. 37, quoted in Drew, *Third Generation,* p. 103.

222 Cook, "In Memoriam Archigram," p. 54. By extension, British high-tech becomes an Archigram legacy if Archigram's aesthetic achievement is foregrounded.

223 Reyner Banham, "Zoom Wave Hits Architecture," *New Society,* 3 March 1966, reprinted in Banham, *Design by Choice,* p. 65.

224 Banham, *The Architecture of the Well-Tempered Environment,* p. 289.

225 Ibid., p. 132.

226 Colin St. John Wilson, writing in *Perspecta 7,* quoted in Banham, *The Architecture of the Well-Tempered Environment,* p. 249, no citation.

227 Norman Foster, lecture at the conference "Special Relationship: American and British Architecture since 1945," Paul Mellon Centre/Architectural Association, at the Architectural Association, London, 30 October 1998.

228 See Louis Kahn, in John Donat, ed., *World Architecture,* no. 1 (London: Studio Vista, 1964), p. 35, quoted in Banham, *The Architecture of the Well-Tempered Environment,* p. 249: "I do not like ducts, I do not like pipes. I hate them really thoroughly, but because I hate them so thoroughly, I feel they have to be given their place. If I just hated them and took no care, I think that they would invade the building and completely destroy it."

229 Banham, *The Architecture of the Well-Tempered Environment,* p. 255.

230 Published 1956, though unlikely to have influenced Kahn.

231 See Banham, *The Architecture of the Well-Tempered Environment,* p. 242.

232 See ibid., p. 264.

233 Ibid., pp. 256–257.

234 The picturesque was a persistent idea in English architectural aesthetics, and became directly linked to Archigram through Reyner Banham's "Revenge of the Picturesque: English Architectural Polemics, 1945–1965," in John Summerson, ed., *Concerning Architecture* (London: Allen Lane/Penguin Press, 1968), pp. 265–273.

235 Cook, *Experimental Architecture,* p. 94.

236 Cook, "Plug-In City," in Cook, ed., *Archigram,* p. 36.

237 "Ceci tuera cela," quoted in Vittorio Magnago Lampugnani, "The Permanent Side: Wishful Thinking about the City of the Telematic Age," in Steven Spier, ed., *Urban Visions: Experiencing and Envisioning the City* (Liverpool: Liverpool University Press and Tate Liverpool, 2002), p. 202.

238 Information flow assumed the same role for Archigram and ekistics as traffic flow had assumed in the Athens Charter (and in "Living City"). See Wigley, "Network Fever," pp. 100, 107, and passim.

239 For instance, Team 10's Shadrach Woods wrote that "a point is static, fixed. A line is a measure of liberty. A non-centric web is a fuller measure." Shadrach Woods, in John Donat, ed., *World Architecture II* (London: Studio Vista, 1965), p. 117, quoted in Jencks, *Modern Movements in Architecture,* p. 344.

240 Colquhoun, "The Modern Movement in Architecture," in Ockman, ed., *Architecture Culture 1943–1968,* p. 344.

241 Ibid., p. 343.

242 Ibid.

243 Greene recalls two texts in particular, LeWitt's "24 Rules for Conceptual Art" and Kosuth's "Art after Philosophy." Interview with David Greene, London, 1 June 1998.

244 These projects could also be compared to "undertaking elaborate rational, logical or mathematical exercises which often are not used or are not useful," a procedure that was known in systems theory as "ritual modeling." See Donald N. Michael, "Ritualized Rationality and Arms Control," *Bulletin of the Atomic Scientists* 17, no. 2 (February 1961), p. 72, cited in Boguslaw, *The New Utopians,* p. 66.

245 Kenneth Frampton, "Reflections on the Opposition of Architecture and Building," in Gowan, ed., *A Continuing Experiment,* p. 112.

246 Interview with David Greene, London, 1 June 1998.

247 Joseph Kosuth, "Art after Philosophy" [pt. 1], *Studio International* 178, no. 915 (October 1969), reprinted in Charles Harrison and Paul Wood, eds., *Art in Theory 1900–1990: An Anthology of Changing Ideas* (Oxford: Blackwell, 1992), pp. 847–848.

248 Sol LeWitt, "Sentences on Conceptual Art," *Art-Language* (Coventry) 1, no. 1 (May 1969), n.p., in Harrison and Wood, eds., *Art in Theory 1900–1990,* p. 837; David Greene, talk on Archigram films, Architectural Association, 17 February 1998.

249 Warren Chalk, "Ghosts," *Archigram,* no. 7 (1966).

250 Chalk, "People Robots and Trees," pp. 68–69. Chalk called instead for something he described as "a fifth dimension" of understanding. This may have been a continuation of a process started by the non-Aristotelians of the Independent Group.

251 British interest in French theory increased in the early 1970s with the publication of papers from the Centre for Contemporary Cultural Studies, Birmingham University.

252 Chalk, "People Robots and Trees," p. 69.

253 David Greene, "Popular Pak," *Archigram,* no. 8 (1968), n.p.

254 This phrase repeated the claim made in *Archigram* no. 2 about the relationship between architecture and expendable goods.

255 Greene, "Popular Pak."

256 See Boguslaw, *The New Utopians,* p. 2. See also p. 159 for the conclusion to Boguslaw's discussion of the contribution made by existentialism to an understanding of systems. "Is there a *fundamental* difference between human beings and lower forms of animals or automatons? Let us remain agnostics on this subject." Critical consideration of Archigram's attempt to negotiate a position for the human subject between a declining urbanism and an ascendant, nonterritorial electronic network was taken up by Jonathan Crary in "J. G. Ballard and the Promiscuity of Forms," *Zone* 1/2 (1986), and subsequently in Felicity D. Scott, "Involuntary Prisoners of Architecture," *October,* no. 106 (Fall 2003), pp. 75–101.

4 THE ZOOM WAVE: ARCHIGRAM'S TEACHING AND RECEPTION

1 For instance, in 1961 Herron, Chalk, and Crompton became known to Cook and Greene via the Lincoln Civic Centre competition and others. On the importance accorded to competitions by "creative" designers, see Lionel Esher, *A Broken Wave: The Rebuilding of England 1940–1980* (London: Allen Lane, 1981), p. 67.

2 Anon., *Archigram,* no. 5 (1965), n.p.

3 Geoffrey Broadbent, "Archijam Tomorrow: What Has Archigram Achieved?," *Architectural Association Quarterly* 5, no. 3 (Autumn 1973), p. 58.

4 This was a point reiterated by Peter Cook, "Archigram," lecture at the "New Babylon" conference, Faculty of Architecture, Delft University of Technology, 26 January 2000.

5 See Cedric Price, Frank Newby, Robert H. Suan, and Felix J. Samuely and Partners, *Air Structures: A Survey* (London: Department of the Environment/HMSO, 1971).

6 Peter Cook, "In Memoriam Archigram," *Daidalos,* no. 4 (15 June 1982), p. 56.

7 Michael Webb in conversation, London, 19 November 2002, and in correspondence, 17 August 2003: Webb does, however, "remember taking the finished model in a taxi from my Highgate home down to the Poly. Every corner the taxi lurched around . . . there was a sickening cracking sound, like a gun going off. By the time Little Titchfield Street appeared the model looked like the victim of a V2 attack." See also Michael Sorkin, "Canticles for Mike," in *Exquisite Corpse: Writing on Buildings* (New York: Verso, 1991), pp. 203–210. A new model of the Sin Centre is now complete.

8 David Greene collages of 1966 put his Living Pod against backgrounds of Piranesi and derelict houses; an assemblage, observes one critic, that permitted the "manipulation of multi levels of urban reality." David Walters, "The Architect as Superhero: Archigram and the Text of Serious Comics," *Architronic* 3, no. 2 (1994), <http://architronic.saed.kent.edu/>, para 11.

9 Reyner Banham, "A Clip-On Architecture," *Architectural Design,* November 1965, p. 535.

10 Ibid.

11 Philip Drew, *Third Generation: The Changing Meaning of Modern Architecture* (New York: Praeger, 1972), p. 102.

12 The Eames show at the Cooper-Hewitt Museum, New York, Winter 1999–2000, related that the Eameses had collated some 260,000 slides.

13 This remains conjectural until all Archigram archives are opened. For a sustained discussion of the relationship between modern architecture and mass media, see Beatriz Colomina, *Privacy and Publicity: Modern Architecture as Mass Media* (Cambridge, Mass.: MIT Press, 1996).

14 Reyner Banham, "Zoom Wave Hits Architecture," *New Society,* 3 March 1966, reprinted in Reyner Banham, *Design by Choice,* ed. Penny Sparke (London: Academy, 1981), p. 65.

15 Archigram, dir., *Archigram,* BBC Productions, 1966; "Newsbit," *Archigram,* no. 7 (1967), n.p.

16 Warren Chalk, "How to Get Involved without Understanding McLuhan," *Architectural Design,* October 1969.

17 Peter Cook, "Plug-In City," *Sunday Times Colour Magazine,* 20 September 1964. Significantly, the

Sunday Times Colour Magazine was launched to handle the demand for color advertising, and its first edition in February 1962 contained a seminal article on Peter Blake, "Pioneer of Pop Art."

18 The main British architectural journals were *Architectural Review* and *Architects' Journal.*

19 Archigram, "The All-In Holiday," *Daily Express Colour Supplement,* 27 July 1970, pp. I–IV.

20 Peter Collins, "Plug'n Clip," *Sunday Times Colour Magazine,* September 1965.

21 See Kate McIntyre, "The Most 'In' Shops for Gear," *Twentieth Century Architecture,* no. 6, "The Sixties" (2002), p. 38.

22 See Drusilla Beyfus, "Flexible Space," *Weekend Telegraph Magazine,* no. 126 (3 March 1967), pp. 22–27. The "Living 1990" exhibit was displayed 3–25 March.

23 Archigram eventually felt trapped in exhibition work. See Martin Pawley, "Peter Cook—Archiman or Anarchist?," *Building Design,* 15 May 1970, pp. 6–7. I am grateful to Chee Kien Lai for sharing with me details of the "Instant Malaysia" installation.

24 See László Moholy-Nagy, *Vision in Motion* (Chicago: Paul Theobald, 1947). This book, like Amédée Ozenfant's *Foundations of Modern Art* (trans. 1952) and Giedion's *Mechanization Takes Command* (1948), fascinated the brutalist/Independent Group set with its juxtaposition of multifarious sources for the modern. See David Robbins, ed., *The Independent Group: Postwar Britain and the Aesthetics of Plenty* (Cambridge, Mass.: MIT Press, 1990), p. 55.

25 See Robert Maxwell, "The 'Living City' exhibition at the ICA," in Theo Crosby and John Bodley, eds., *Living Arts,* no. 3 (London: Institute of Contemporary Arts and Tillotsons, 1964), p. 100.

26 Le Corbusier, *My Work* (London, 1960), p. 186, quoted in Charles Jencks, *Le Corbusier and the Tragic View of Architecture* (London: Allen Lane, 1973; Harmondsworth: Penguin, 1987), p. 164. The music was delegated to Edgar Varèse, the parabolic structure to architect/musician Iannis Xenakis. See Marc Treib, *Space Calculated in Seconds: The Philips Pavilion, Le Corbusier, Edgard Varèse* (Princeton: Princeton University Press, 1996).

27 See Pat Kirkham, *Charles and Ray Eames: Designers of the Twentieth Century* (Cambridge, Mass.: MIT Press, 1995), pp. 320–325. The show was enclosed in a geodesic dome designed by Fuller.

28 Light/Sound Workshop was directed by Clive Latimer; Peter Cook was also a member. See Advanced Studies Group, *K4: Kinetic Audio Visual Environments, West Pier, Brighton* (London: Hornsey College of Art, 1967) (courtesy of Tony Rickaby).

29 Martin Pawley, "Death by Architecture," *Blueprint,* January 1998, pp. 22–24.

30 The group had saluted Lichtenstein in *Archigram* no. 4, the sci-fi/pop edition that began to make the group famous.

31 Broadbent, "Archijam Tomorrow," pp. 58–59.

32 David Greene and Mike Myers, dirs., *Warren, I Remember Architecture Too,* Archigram, 1974.

33 "Network," *Archigram,* no. 7 (1967), n.p.

34 See, for instance, the advertisement for Pentel marker pens in *Megascope,* no. 3 (November 1966), n.p.

35 Pawley, "Death by Architecture."

36 Archigram's first office in 1970 was at 10 Newman Passage, near Tottenham Court Road, before they relocated in 1971 to 53 Endell Street, Covent Garden. Like Archigram's first office, Art Net (West Central Street), launched 1974, was close to the Architectural Association.

37 *Archigram* no. 1 had made extensive use of "narrative" captions.

38 Rickaby first met Cook and Crompton when they were teaching together in the Light/Sound Workshop at Hornsey College of Art, 1967. On the basis of his association with Archigram, he taught at the AA from 1974 (telephone interview with Tony Rickaby, 27 August 2003).

39 For more on British retail style, see McIntyre, "The Most 'In' Shops for Gear."

40 Dennis Sharp, "Forecasting Tomorrow's World," *Royal Institute of British Architects Journal* 74 (December 1967), pp. 537–541. Note however that a brief review of *Archigram* no. 4 was featured as "Zoom Architecture," *Architectural Review,* August 1964, p. 83.

41 Archigram, "Archigram Group, London: A Chronological Survey," *Architectural Design,* November 1965, pp. 559–572.

42 A point made in conversation by Catherine Cook (who later wrote for *Architectural Design*), January 1997.

43 "Living City" toured from the ICA to the AA, Manchester City Art Gallery, the Walker (Arts Council) Art Gallery in Cambridge, and the New Metropole Arts Centre in Folkestone.

44 The diminutive presence of the Osakagram was compounded by the fact that it was not properly wired.

45 Archigram's work entered Scandinavian consciousness in spring 1965 with features in the Stockholm journal *Aftonbladet* and the Helsinki journal *A.* Archigram projects (usually Cook's Plug-In) were examined twice in the Milanese journal *Edilizia Moderna* in 1963, then in 1964 in the journal that had been such an inspiration in the huts at Euston, *Architecture d'Aujourd'hui,* which returned to the group twice more in 1965.

46 See for instance Archigram, "English Architects," *Kenchiku Bunka* (Tokyo), January 1967; *Actualidades Tecnico Cientificas Arquitectura* (Havana), 1969; *Architecture USSR,* no. 728 (Leningrad), 1971.

47 See "Archigram's Self-Ad Bit," *Archigram,* no. 5 (1964), n.p.

48 See *Archigram,* no. 8 (1968).

49 Letter from Peter Cook to the author, 16 February 2004, that dramatically revises earlier estimates (see for instance Barry Curtis, "A Necessary Irritant," in Dennis Crompton, ed., *Concerning Archigram* [London: Archigram Archives, 1998], p. 58 but that correlates with estimates at the time: see "Archigram," *Megascope,* no. 3 (November 1966), n.p.: "Archigram 6 . . . is expected to sell 2000 copies."

50 Dennis Crompton says he was left with stacks of undistributed copies of *Archigram* no. 9.

51 The *Archigram* book was originally scheduled to be published by Faber and Faber and the MIT Press, around 1969.

52 "Archizone 9, North America," *Archigram,* no. 9 (1970). Archigram's influence was already evident in architectural competition entries in the United States: see Reyner Banham, *Megastructure: Urban Futures of the Recent Past* (London: Thames and Hudson, 1976), pp. 102–103.

53 Reyner Banham, "A Clip-On Architecture," *Design Quarterly,* 1965, whole issue, reprinted

Architectural Design, November 1965, pp. 534–535; Archigram, "The History of Clip-On," *Architectural Forum* 123, no. 4 (November 1965), p. 68.

54 Interview with Mary Banham, London, 28 April 1997.

55 First to depart was Greene (to the Virginia Polytechnic Institute in 1965), closely followed by Webb, who later moved to the Rhode Island School of Design in Providence.

56 Peter Cook, "Plug-In City Study," *Architectural Forum,* 8 September 1964. Webb's Furniture Manufacturers Building had already been seen in the MoMA "Visionary Architecture" show of 1961.

57 Peter Blake, "A Comment from Peter Blake," in Peter Cook, ed., *Archigram* (London: Studio Vista, 1972), p. 7.

58 Peter Plagens, "Los Angeles: The Ecology of Evil," *Artforum,* December 1972, p. 76, quoted in Nigel Whiteley, *Reyner Banham: Historian of the Immediate Future* (Cambridge, Mass.: MIT Press, 2002), p. 241.

59 An issue raised at the Paul Mellon Centre symposium "Special Relationship: American and British Architecture since 1945," Architectural Association, London, 30 October 1998.

60 Norman Foster (ibid.) recalls that these were the environmental details that caught his attention on the road with Richard Rogers when searching for buildings by Frank Lloyd Wright. See also Reyner Banham, *The Architecture of the Well-Tempered Environment* (London: Architectural Press, 1969).

61 Blake, "A Comment from Peter Blake."

62 See Charles Jencks, *Modern Movements in Architecture* (Harmondsworth: Penguin, 1973; 2d ed. 1985), p. 204, quoting *Architectural Forum,* January 1966, n.p., and John Johansen in *Perspecta,* no. 7, n.p.

63 Archigram, "Amazing Archigram: A Supplement," *Perspecta* 11 (1967), pp. 131–154.

64 A. Golding, C. Hodgetts, and D. Michels, "Maxx Project," *Archigram,* no. 7 (1966), n.p. The provenance of this project is confirmed by Craig Hodgetts, correspondence, 8 July 2003.

65 See also "Archizone 9, North America."

66 Tom Wolfe, *The Electric Kool-Aid Acid Test* (1968; rpt. London: Black Swan, 1989), pp. 205–206.

67 Stewart Brand, ed., *The Last Whole Earth Catalog* (Santa Cruz: Portola Institute, 1971), p. 89.

68 Estimated date.

69 See "Envirolab," *Archigram,* no. 9, and Peter Cook, "Los Angeles," in Crompton, ed., *Concerning Archigram,* pp. 122–123. Alan Stanton had also worked for Norman Foster.

70 Envirolab's West Coast EAT contacts were David McDermott and Ardison Phillips. Correspondence with Alan Stanton, 19 August 2003.

71 Alan Stanton, Mike Davies, and Chris Dawson, "Envirolab," at Archigram World Rally, University of Westminster, London, 19 November 2002.

72 See Peter Cook, "Addhox," in Crompton, ed., *Concerning Archigram,* pp. 138–139. Note, however, that Coop Himmelblau, *Die Faszination der Stadt / The Power of the City* (Darmstadt: Georg Büchner Buchhandlung, 1988), dates the show to 1972.

73 Nicholas Grimshaw claims that up to four hundred visiting lecturers per year passed through the AA in the 1960s. Nicholas Grimshaw, AA 150th Anniversary lectures, Clore Management Centre, Birkbeck College, London, 9 July 1997.

74 See *Archigram* no. 9, passim.

75 "Let's Give a Big Hand," *Archigram,* no. 8 (1968).

76 Constant was still being sought by *Archigram* no. 6, even though Archigram had earlier attempted correspondence. See letter from Peter Cook to Constant, 20 July 1964, in the Constant archive, the Rijksbureau, The Hague. See also Mark Wigley, *Constant's New Babylon: The Hyper-Architecture of Desire* (Rotterdam: 010 Publishers, 1998), p. 41. In 1966, *Archigram* was also looking for Frederick Kiesler in the United States, Jerzy Soltan in Poland, and, most surprisingly, had still to establish contact with the Japanese metabolists.

77 "Experimental Architects," *Archigram,* no. 6 (1965), n.p. Compare the networking operations of *Ekistics,* which in 1965 referenced Archigram's projects of 1964, and in 1969 published Archigram's Ideas Circus. See Mark Wigley, "Network Fever," *Grey Room,* no. 4 (Summer 2001), pp. 88, 108, and passim.

78 Reyner Banham noted *Archigram*'s relaxed copy editing in "Zoom Wave Hits Architecture," p. 64.

79 A member of the continualists, Dalibor Vesely, would soon arrive in England.

80 The Banhams' open house coffee-and-drinks meetings gained a reputation as an essential "salon" of advanced architectural minds. The Banhams brought their hospitality from Norwich to London, first at Primrose Hill, where they would be joined on Sunday mornings by architects and Independent Group members like James Stirling, Robert Maxwell, Alan Colquhoun, and Colin St. John Wilson. At their new Swiss Cottage home in Aberdare Gardens, they were further joined on Friday evenings by David and Beryl Alford from YRM, Frank and Evelyn Newby, and, eventually, by Peter Cook, who recalled it as "an amazing salon" (Peter Cook, in an interview with Barry Curtis, 17 October 1990) where he encountered Richard Meier, Yona Friedman, Buckminster Fuller, Harry Seidler, and many others.

81 "Networks around the Channel," *Archigram,* no. 7 (1966).

82 Zamp Kelp (of Haus-Rucker-Co), at Archigram World Rally, University of Westminster, London, 19 November 2002. David Greene however does not recall being "in competition" with other groups from Italy and Austria (at Archigram World Rally, University of Westminster, London, 19 November 2002), which suggests different levels of engagement with "the scene" among the members of Archigram and various neo-avant-gardes.

83 "Archizone 3: Scandinavia," *Archigram,* no. 9 (1970).

84 Peter Cook, "Archizone 2: Europe," *Archigram,* no. 9 (1970). Cook had been subscribing to Günther Feuerstein's *Transparente* magazine (Günther Feuerstein, "Visionary Architecture in Austria," lecture at the Bartlett School of Architecture, 9 December 1996).

85 Jean Aubert, in conversation with Tim Benton, Paris, 1998.

86 Robin Middleton, "Folkestone IDEA," *Architectural Design,* July 1966, p. 322.

87 Jencks, *Modern Movements in Architecture,* p. 292.

88 Peter Cook, "Folkestone," in Crompton, ed., *Concerning Archigram,* p. 107.

89 "IDEA—International Dialogue of Architecture," *Architectural Design,* June 1966, p. 312.

90 Middleton, "Folkestone IDEA."

91 "IDEA—International Dialogue of Architecture."

92 See New Metropole Arts Centre, *International Dialogue of Experimental Architecture* (Folkestone: New Metropole Arts Centre, 1966).

93 Martin Pawley, "The 1960s: A Personal Memoir," lecture at Architectural Association, London, 16 February 1998.

94 David Dunster, AA 150th Anniversary lectures, Clore Management Centre, Birkbeck College, London, 9 July 1997.

95 Middleton, "Folkestone IDEA."

96 Jencks, *Modern Movements in Architecture,* p. 292.

97 Cf. Robert Goodman, *After the Planners* (Harmondsworth: Penguin, 1972), pp. 72ff., for a critique of liberal apologies for the military-industrial complex.

98 The scale, color, hydraulics, and gasket windows of giant earth-moving and excavating machines may also have provided inspiration to such projects as Walking City.

99 Warren Chalk, "Hardware of a New World," *Architectural Forum,* October 1966, reprinted in Crompton, ed., *Concerning Archigram,* p. 172.

100 This was an observation made by graduate students in the Department of Art History, University of California, Davis.

101 Claude Parent, "Instability, a Necessity," lecture at the Royal Institute of British Architects, London, 3 February 1998.

102 Martin Pawley, "We Shall Not Bulldoze Westminster Abbey: Archigram and the Retreat from Technology," *Oppositions,* no. 7 (Winter 1975), reprinted in K. Michael Hays, ed., *Oppositions Reader* (New York: Princeton Architectural Press, 1998), p. 433.

103 Banham, "Zoom Wave Hits Architecture," pp. 64–65.

104 *Clip-Kit*'s cofounder was Geoffrey Smyth. Contributions were forthcoming from such eminences as Cedric Price and Michael Webb. Peter Murray had also edited the BASA page in the *AJ,* but was sacked for using it to promote *Clip-Kit* (Peter Murray, at Archigram World Rally, University of Westminster, London, 19 November 2002). BASA sponsored a symposium in November 1965

on "The sociological and other aspects of the plug-in city" at the Building Exhibition at Olympia exhibition hall, where Archigram had designed a stand for Taylor Woodrow.

105 Quoted in Denise Scott Brown, "Little Magazines in Architecture and Urbanism," *Journal of the American Institute of Town Planners* 34, no. 4 (July 1968), p. 225.

106 "Introduction," *Megascope,* no. 3 (November 1966), n.p.

107 "Archizone 1: United Kingdom," *Archigram,* no. 9 (1970). See also Dolan Conway, ed., "Three London Schools of Architecture within Ten Minutes Walking Distance of Each Other," *Architectural Design,* March 1969, pp. 129–164.

108 See "Archizone 11: Australasia," *Archigram,* no. 9 (1970). This was a development hailed by *Archigram* as "AASAZOOM."

109 See Peter Cook, "Into 1967 YOU YOU YOU IT'S UP TO YOU," *Archigram,* no. 7 (1967).

110 Peter Cook, "The Box," *Archigram,* no. 9 (1970).

111 See "BASE" and "International Institute of Design Summer Session," *Archigram,* no. 9 (1970).

112 "Archizone 1: United Kingdom."

113 A point made in conversation in 1995 with Dr. Mike Harrison, an architectural student at the time.

114 "Archizone 1: United Kingdom."

115 "Arthur Quarmby," *Megascope,* no. 3 (November 1966), n.p.

116 John Christopher Jones, in Conway, ed., "Three London Schools of Architecture within Ten Minutes Walking Distance of Each Other," p. 131.

117 "Introduction," *Megascope,* no. 3.

118 Ibid.

119 Fred Scott, "Myths, Misses, and Mr. Architecture," in James Gowan, ed., *A Continuing Experiment: Learning and Teaching at the Architectural Association* (London: Architectural Press, 1975), p. 169.

120 Peter Cook, "The Revolutionary Sixties," discussion at AA 150th Anniversary lectures, Clore Management Centre, Birkbeck College, London, 9 July 1997.

121 Peter Cook, "The Electric Decade: An Atmosphere at the AA School 1963–73," in Gowan, ed., *A Continuing Experiment,* p. 140.

122 Piers Gough, "The Revolutionary Sixties," discussion at AA 150th Anniversary lectures, Clore Management Centre, Birkbeck College, London, 9 July 1997.

123 Of the Archigram members, only Herron remained in consistent practice between the disbanding of the Euston Team in 1964 and the opening of Archigram Architects in 1970, and he retained teaching commitments. In 1965 he and Chalk were briefly in practice together; in 1965–1967 he was an associate of Halpern & Partners; in 1967 he was consultant architect to Colin St. John Wilson, Cambridge; in 1968 in private practice, London; in 1969–1970, Director of Urban Design, William L. Pereira Associates, Los Angeles.

124 Quoted by Dennis Crompton, interview, London, 29 May 2000.

125 See also Archigram's welcome to the Open University: Ron Herron, "It's a . . . ," 1972, in Cook, ed., *Archigram,* pp. 136–137.

126 Grimshaw, "The Revolutionary Sixties."

127 Pawley, "Death by Architecture," pp. 22–24.

128 C. Ray Smith, *Supermannerism: New Attitudes in Post-Modern Architecture* (New York: E. P. Dutton, 1977), p. 25. Another source of inspiration was surely the Merry Pranksters. See Wolfe, *The Electric Kool-Aid Acid Test.* Something of "the scene" can be felt in Jim Burns, *Arthropods: New Design Futures* (New York: Praeger, 1972).

129 Hazel Cook and Jane-Mary Greene are also present; Warren Chalk and Michael Webb are present only as photographic reproductions. The Bournemouth Steps project was presented in a small executive case with baseboard model, photo-collage, slides, and slide viewer.

130 See Pawley, "Death by Architecture."

131 Mark Crinson and Jules Lubbock, *Architecture, Art or Profession? Three Hundred Years of Architectural Education in Britain* (Manchester: Manchester University Press, 1994), p. 1.

132 Ibid., p. 5.

133 Zaha Hadid, "Alvin Boyarsky at the AA," lecture at "Special Relationship: American and British Architecture since 1945," Paul Mellon Centre/Architectural Association, London, 30 November 1998. The sessions had been inaugurated by Boyarsky in 1970.

134 Peter Cook, the only member of Archigram who was a graduate of the school, returned to the AA as a unit master in 1964, and was joined by Ron Herron, who worked as a tutor, the following year.

135 Cook, "The Electric Decade," pp. 143–144 (original ellipses).

136 Francis Duffy, ed., "Some Notes on Archigram," *Arena,* June 1966, p. 172.

137 This was James Gowan's description of the AA. See James Gowan, introduction to Gowan, ed., in *A Continuing Experiment,* p. 16.

138 As Edward Jones remembered of the Residential Teachers Training College, his 1963 fifth-year thesis with Paul Simpson, well known within AA circles, "the early years of the sixties at the AA, very much in the shadow of the preceding Smithsonian era, were characterised by a distrust of the private will to form, a reaction against the preceding imagist phase, and a feeling that pre-architectural factors should be emphasised." Edward Jones, "Residential Teachers Training College, Swindon," in James Gowan, ed., *Projects: Architectural Association 1946–71,* AA Cahiers Series no. 1 (London: Architectural Association, 1974), p. 63.

139 Cook, "The Electric Decade," p. 140. This was a character metaphor: Cook, in fact, was also clean-shaven.

140 Ibid. Colquhoun was nothing if not uniform in his demand for rational consistency; with Peter Cook, he jointly attacked Peter Murray's AA thesis for inserting an internal structure into an inflatable. Peter Murray, at Archigram World Rally, University of Westminster, London, 19 November 2002.

141 Patrick Hodgkinson, "Housing," in Gowan, ed., *Projects,* p. 68.

142 See John Frazer, "Housing," in Gowan, ed., *Projects,* p. 68. In his fourth year (1967), Frazer's Flexible Enclosure System of two geometrical "building block" units rivaled the Fuller icosahedron unit demonstrated in *Archigram* no. 7 the previous year; his fifth-year thesis for an Unfolding Caravan, designed in 1969 over the telephone with Peter Colomb, adopted Archigram's preoccupations with mobility.

143 Correspondence with Martin Pawley, 19 August 2003. When Pawley returned to the AA in 1966, his well-known "Time House" diploma project reversed the NFT's control process, its occupants now the behavioral data recorded by the building.

144 The letter was unpublished.

145 Cook, "The Electric Decade," p. 137.

146 Ibid., pp. 137–138.

147 Peter Cook, discussion at AA 150th Anniversary lectures, Clore Management Centre, Birkbeck College, London, 9 July 1997.

148 Cook, "The Electric Decade," p. 140.

149 Ibid., p. 141.

150 Tim Benton observes that the Pompidou Center's ambition to have its floors raised and lowered upon hydraulic jacks was a principle harking back to Jean Prouvé's Maison du Peuple, Clichy, 1937–1939.

151 See "Richard Rogers," in Conway, ed., "Three London Schools of Architecture within Ten Minutes Walking Distance of Each Other," p. 149. Note too that Rogers served on the jury that awarded Archigram the RIBA Gold Medal in 2002.

152 Like Dennis Crompton, Foster was a graduate of the technologically oriented architecture department of Manchester University.

153 See Brian Appleyard, *Richard Rogers: A Biography* (London: Faber, 1986), p. 109.

154 *Financial Times,* 30 November 1967, quoted in Appleyard, *Richard Rogers,* p. 131.

155 See Appleyard, *Richard Rogers,* p. 129. Richard and Su Rogers's particularly neat development of the idea, the 1968 Zip-Up No. 1 house design for the DuPont House of the Future competition, could expand through the zipping-in of extra "slices" of house.

156 See Appleyard, *Richard Rogers,* p. 165, and Nathan Silver, *The Making of Beaubourg: A Building Biography of the Centre Pompidou, Paris* (Cambridge, Mass.: MIT Press, 1994), pp. 41–42.

157 Philip Johnson gave Hans Hollein a copy of *Archigram* in 1964 (see Hans Hollein, "A Comment from Hans Hollein," in Cook, ed., *Archigram,* p. 6). It is reasonable to assume that other jury members—Jørn Utzon, Jean Prouvé, Willem Sandberg, and Oscar Niemeyer—also knew Archigram's work by this date.

158 Beaubourg Jury Report, 1971, quoted in Silver, *The Making of Beaubourg,* p. 46.

159 Denis Postle, dir., *Beaubourg: Four Films by Denis Postle,* Tattooist International for the Arts Coucil, 1980.

160 Quoted in Appleyard, *Richard Rogers,* p. 166, see also p. 33. See also Piano and Rogers's interim mission statement reprinted in Silver, *The Making of Beaubourg,* pp. 102–105.

161 See Silver, *The Making of Beaubourg,* pp. 32–33.

162 Quoted in ibid., p. 175, no citation.

163 See Silver, *The Making of Beaubourg,* p. 68.

164 For more on the recruitment of Dugdale and Dawson, see Appleyard, *Richard Rogers,* pp. 199ff., and Silver, *The Making of Beaubourg,* pp. 60ff.

165 Cook, "The Electric Decade," p. 143.

166 Tony Dugdale, "Learning Shed," in Gowan, ed., *Projects,* p. 72. After graduation Dugdale carried on investigating the long span with Mike Pearson.

167 Postle, "Beaubourg."

168 Cook, "In Memoriam Archigram," p. 185.

169 Postle, "Beaubourg."

170 Ibid.

171 For more on Newby, see J. Stanley Matthews, "An Architecture for the New Britain: The Social Vision of Cedric Price's Fun Palace and Potteries Thinkbelt," Ph.D. dissertation, Columbia University, 2002, pp. 112ff. The team also included Colin Fournier, Ken Allinson, Tony Rickaby, Diana Jowsey, and Bernard Tschumi.

172 Reyner Banham, "Monaco Underground," *Architects' Journal* 152, no. 35 (2 September 1970), pp. 506–509, reprinted in Archigram, ed., *A Guide to Archigram 1961–74* (London: Academy, 1994), p. 278; cf. Silver, *The Making of Beaubourg,* p. 45.

173 See Appleyard, *Richard Rogers,* p. 154, and Silver, *The Making of Beaubourg,* p. 7.

174 Banham, "Monaco Underground," p. 272.

175 Ibid., p. 280.

176 Ibid.

177 See Pawley, "We Shall Not Bulldoze Westminster Abbey," p. 431.

178 Archigram's 1970 press release re Monte Carlo: "The entire building is seen as a giant cybernetic toy." See ibid.

179 Interview with Dennis Crompton, London,

29 May 2000, during which the 1971 progress report on Monte Carlo was inspected.

180 Ibid. Following the Treaty of Rome, the Principality sold off the site to speculators.

181 See "Monte Carlo—Three Projects," in Crompton, ed., *Concerning Archigram*, p. 132.

182 Banham declined to pose naked for the picture, so Dallegret improvised. Interview with François Dallegret, Architectural Association, London, 26 October 1998. Illustration from Reyner Banham, "A Home Is Not a House," *Art in America*, no. 53 (April 1965), pp. 109–118.

183 Silver, *The Making of Beaubourg*, p. 91.

184 Alan Stanton, Mike Davies, and Chris Dawson, at Archigram World Rally, University of Westminster, London, 19 November 2002. See also Appleyard, *Richard Rogers*, p. 199, and "Chrysalis," *Architectural Design* 43, no. 42 (March 1972), pp. 172–174.

185 Appleyard, *Richard Rogers*, pp. 199–200. The meeting was held with Rogers's partner John Young. Chrysalis also evolved into "Chrysalis Mid West," with a new colleague, Joe Valerio. After working on Pompidou, Mike Davies and Alan Stanton attempted to restart Chrysalis in London with Ian Ritchie while running a unit at the AA (correspondence with Alan Stanton, 19 August 2003).

186 For another example of such enterprise, see Mark Fisher and Simon Conolly, Air Structures Design D.I.Y. Kit, 1970, in Gowan, eds., *Projects*, p. 88. (The date is taken from the drawing rather than the text.)

187 Alan Stanton, Mike Davies, and Chris Dawson, at Archigram World Rally, University of Westminster, London, 19 November 2002. The polyester and aluminum structure was adapted from weather balloons.

188 See Silver, *The Making of Beaubourg*, p. 63.

189 Ibid., p. 43.

190 Pawley, "We Shall Not Bulldoze Westminster Abbey," p. 431.

191 Michael Cassidy, "Space Odyssey on the Rocks: Archigram—Pioneers or Exhibitionists?," *Building* 224, no. 1 (5 January 1973), pp. 43–46.

192 Reyner Banham, "Towards a Pop Architecture," *Architectural Review*, July 1962, reprinted in Banham, *Design by Choice*, pp. 61–63.

193 See Banham's note (1979) to "Towards a Pop Architecture" in Banham, *Design by Choice*, p. 141.

194 Scott, "Myths, Misses, and Mr. Architecture," pp. 168–169. Scott was a fifth-year tutor at the AA from 1967 and, like Crompton and Cook, a tutor at Hornsey College of Art. Something of the atmosphere at the AA is also captured in Patrick Wright, "They Came In through the Bathroom Window: Refounding British Architecture in the Tyneham Gap," *The Village That Died for England: The Strange Story of Tyneham* (London: Jonathan Cape, 1995).

195 See Robert Murphy, "Swinging London Films," presentation at seminar "The Sixties," Department of History, Open University, 5 December 1997. Murphy observes that filmmakers were, like Archigram, slow to respond to the change in mood.

196 Peter Hodgkinson, "Drug-In City," *Architectural Design*, November 1969, p. 586, quoted in Whiteley, *Reyner Banham*, p. 262.

197 Mike Catto, "Futures Seen through British Comics," Design History Society Conference "Futures: Visions and Revisions," University of Middlesex, 14 December 1996.

198 Paul Oliver, ed., *Shelter and Society* (London: Barrie and Rockliff/Cresset Press, 1969).

199 See Paul Oliver, "The Houses In Between," in Gowan, ed., *A Continuing Experiment*, p. 79.

200 Oliver, "The Houses In Between," p. 86.

201 Ibid., p. 82. Fuller's geodesic dome was likewise iconic to both zoomists and ecologists.

202 See, for instance, David Greene's use of a land art piece by Sally Hodgson in David Greene, "Imagining the Invisible University," *Architectural Design*, April 1971, reprinted in Cook, ed., *Archigram*, pp. 116–119.

203 David Greene and Mike Barnard, "Video Notebook," 1972, reprinted in Cook, ed., *Archigram*, p. 119.

204 David Greene, "Imagining the Invisible University," *Architectural Design*, April 1971, reprinted in Cook, ed., *Archigram*, pp. 116–119.

205 David Greene and Mike Barnard, "The Electric Aborigine," 1971, reprinted in Cook, ed., *Archigram*, p. 117. For further discussion of this and other Archigram projects, see also Peggy Deamer, "The Everyday and the Utopian," in Steven Harris and Deborah Berke, eds., *Architecture of the Every-*

day (New York: Princeton Architectural Press, 1997), pp. 194–195.

206 David Greene, "Collage," 1972, reprinted in Cook, ed., *Archigram*, p. 118.

207 Peter Cook, *Experimental Architecture* (London: Studio Vista, 1970), p. 114.

208 Ibid., p. 115.

209 See E. F. Schumacher, *Small Is Beautiful: Economics as if People Mattered* (New York: Harper and Row, 1973).

210 The first Earth Day took place on April 22, 1970.

211 Warren Chalk, "Touch Not," Summer Session '70 presentation, AA, 1970, published in *Architectural Design*, April 1971, reprinted in Archigram, ed., *A Guide to Archigram*, pp. 358–359.

212 Banham, *Megastructure*, p. 101. Men's magazines had been defended by Banham in "I'd Crawl a Mile for . . . *Playboy*," *Architects' Journal*, 7 April 1960, reprinted in Banham, *Design by Choice*, p. 130. As early as January 1966, a hostile reviewer in the *Architectural Association Journal* had realized it was possible to deride *Archigram* for its "playboy text" (quoted in Banham, "Zoom Wave Hits Architecture"). The weakness of Banham's defense of Archigram's collages is taken up in Whiteley, *Reyner Banham*, pp. 177–178.

213 Pawley, "We Shall Not Bulldoze Westminster Abbey," p. 427.

214 "BASA Conference," *Architectural Design*, January 1966, p. 4.

215 Stewart Brand, "Archigram," in Brand, ed., *The Last Whole Earth Catalog*, p. 89.

216 "Emancipation," *Archigram*, no. 8 (1968), n.p.

217 The Hornsey sit-in effectively ended the Light/Sound Workshop where Rickaby, Crompton, and Cook had worked (Tony Rickaby, telephone interview, 27 August 2003).

218 Quoted in Andrea Branzi, *The Hot House: Italian New Wave Design* (London: Thames and Hudson, 1984), p. 54. For discussion on Superstudio, see Peter Lang and William Menking, *Superstudio: Life without Objects* (Milan: Skira, 2003).

219 The prominent Italian conceptual designer Ettore Sottsass depicted Herron's Walking City as a wreck washed up with the architectural icons of New York City in his "Design of a Roof to Discuss Under," part of the 1972–1973 *The Planet as Festival* series of drawings. See Terence Riley, ed., *The Changing of the Avant-Garde: Visionary Architectural Drawings from the Howard Gilman Collection* (New York: Museum of Modern Art, 2002), p. 87.

220 Branzi, *The Hot House,* pp. 54–55.

221 See Arato Isozaki, foreword to Branzi, *The Hot House,* p. 5.

222 The Suit was made by Pat Haines. The Smithsons, with equal and opposite English disengagement, exhibited their "Florence as an ideogram for paradise on earth."

223 Variously known as Architects' Revolutionary Socialist Enclave.

224 Peter Cook, "Letter to ARse," *Archigram,* no. 9 (1970), n.p.

225 Tony Rickaby suggests that *ARse* was primarily edited by AA students (telephone interview, 27 August 2003).

226 Cook, "Letter to ARse."

227 Archigram, "1970: Good Luck from Archigram," 1970 (archive of Jean-Paul Jungmann), reprinted in Marc Dessauce, ed., *The Inflatable Moment: Pneumatics and Protest in '68* (New York: Princeton Architectural Press, 1999), cat. 127, p. 41. The card is also printed in *Archigram* no. 9.

228 Tony Rickaby particularly recalls this change of mood (telephone interview, 27 August 2003).

229 Paul Shepheard, "That Was Then, This Is Now," *AA News,* July 1997, p. 10, reporting on the AA150 "Seventies" seminar. Note however that "that's what David says about everything."

230 Cook, "Letter to ARse."

231 This list was illustrated in David Mellor's lecture for "The Sixties," Sussex Arts Club, Brighton, 5 June 1997.

232 Jeff Nuttall, *Bomb Culture* (London: MacGibbon and Kee, 1968, rpt. London: Paladin, 1970), p. 244. See also the reference to Archigram on p. 204 which claims that Archigram at the time, like "the Fugs and the Beatles," was "caught in a temporary hiatus."

233 The change in mood was acknowledged in the preface, written in the summer of 1968.

234 Oliver, "The Houses In Between," p. 84.

235 "In This Archigram," *Archigram,* no. 9 (1970), n.p. (original ellipses).

236 Antoine Stinco, "Boredom, School, Utopie," in Dessauce, ed., *The Inflatable Moment,* p. 69.

237 See Jean-Louis Violeau, "Utopie: In Acts," in ibid., pp. 37–59.

238 Jean Aubert, in conversation with Tim Benton, Paris, 1998.

239 Herbert Tonka interviewed January 1997, quoted in Violeau, "Utopie," p. 49. Peter Cook confirms his irritation with the lock-in (correspondence, 29 July 2003).

240 See, for example, Utopie's March 1968 "Structures Gonflables" show at the Musée d'Art Moderne, Paris, or the Italian "Urboeffimero 6," Piazza del Duomo, Florence, of May 1968, a traffic-blocking inflatable parade by the UFO Group (formed 1967).

241 Banham, too, tended to dismiss younger radicals as a form of defense. See Whiteley, *Reyner Banham,* chapter 5.

242 Cook, "Archizone 2: Europe," n.p.

243 "In This Archigram," *Archigram,* no. 9.

244 Ibid. (original ellipses).

245 Scott, "Myths, Misses, and Mr. Architecture," p. 168.

246 See particularly the S.F.1 and S.F.2, two blocks of flats on the Greater London Council's Elgin estate, 1968, where glass-reinforced plastic panels were dropped into place by crane, six round-cornered at a time, to create a twenty-two-story block in ten months. See Dennis Sharp, *20th Century Architecture: A Visual History* (London: Lund Humphries, 1991), pp. 292–293, and J. W. Davidson, "S.F.1," *Architectural Design,* March 1967, p. 138.

247 Banham, "Monaco Underground," p. 272.

248 See Martin Pawley and Bernard Tschumi, "The Beaux-Arts since '68," *Architectural Design,* September 1971, p. 553; and George Baird, "1968 and Its Aftermath: The Loss of Moral Confidence in Architectural Practice and Education," in William S. Sanders, ed., *Reflections on Architectural Practices in the Nineties* (New York: Princeton Architectural Press, 1996), p. 64.

249 "Archizone 9: North America," *Archigram,* no. 9 (1970), n.p.

250 Scott Brown, "Little Magazines in Architecture and Urbanism," pp. 223–232.

251 Robert Venturi, Denise Scott Brown, and Steven Izenour, *Learning from Las Vegas,* rev. ed. (Cambridge: Mass.: MIT Press, 1977), p. 100.

252 Scott Brown, "Little Magazines in Architecture and Urbanism," p. 231.

253 Venturi, Scott Brown, and Izenour, *Learning from Las Vegas,* pp. 99–100.

254 Scott Brown, "Little Magazines in Architecture and Urbanism," p. 232.

255 See Hays, ed., *Oppositions Reader,* p. viii. See also Joan Ockman, "Resurrecting the Avant-Garde: The History and Program of *Oppositions,*" in Beatriz Colomina and Joan Ockman, eds., *Architectureproduction,* Revisions, no. 2 (New York: Princeton Architectural Press, 1988), pp. 180–199. The Institute for Architecture and Urban Studies was founded in 1967.

256 Archigram, *Archigram Opera,* 1975 (?) (rescreened at Cornerhouse, Manchester, February 1998).

257 For example, Utopie's Jean Baudrillard attended the 1970 Aspen Design Conference only to round upon experimentalist tendencies of the late sixties as utopian academicism. He had, ironically, been invited by Banham. See Dessauce, ed., *The Inflatable Moment,* p. 8.

258 Peter Eisenman, "Editors' Foreword" to Pawley, "We Shall Not Bulldoze Westminster Abbey," in *Oppositions,* no. 7 (Winter 1975), reprinted in Hays, ed., *Oppositions Reader,* p. 425.

259 See *Oppositions,* no. 6 (Fall 1976), reprinted in Hays, ed., *Oppositions Reader,* pp. 234–239.

260 Colin Rowe, introduction to *Five Architects* (New York: Wittenborn, 1972), reprinted in K. Michael Hays, ed., *Architecture Theory since 1968* (Cambridge, Mass.: MIT Press, 1998), p. 75.

261 See Peter Cook, ed., "The New York Five at Art Net," *Art Net* (London, September-October 1975).

CONCLUSIONS

1 Robert Venturi, Denise Scott Brown, and Steven Izenour, *Learning from Las Vegas,* rev. ed. (Cambridge, Mass.: MIT Press, 1977), p. 102.

2 Martin Pawley, "We Shall Not Bulldoze Westminster Abbey: Archigram and the Retreat from Technology," *Oppositions,* no. 7 (Winter 1975), reprinted in K. Michael Hays, ed., *Oppositions Reader* (New York: Princeton Architectural Press, 1998), p. 428. Pawley admitted, though, that at the time of Archigram's zenith he himself had been "merely picayune, jeering at the interstices in Peter Cook's net of words whilst mighty fish slipped away to Germany, to Italy, to Japan."

3 Dennis Crompton recalls visits to Monte Carlo with Colin Fournier "about once a month for nearly three years." Correspondence, 14 July 2004.

4 For the call to a "Moratorium on Buildings," see David Greene and Mike Myers, dirs., *Warren, I Remember Architecture Too,* Archigram, 1974. For evidence of Peter Cook's determination to build, see Martin Pawley, "Peter Cook—Archiman or Anarchist?," *Building Design,* 15 May 1970, pp. 6–7.

5 Dennis Crompton explains that "there was never enough work or income to support more than three partners and none of us could be full time anyway so we were teaching part-time." Correspondence, 14 July 2004.

6 "Archigram," *Megascope,* no. 3 (November 1966), n.p.

7 Manfredo Tafuri, "L'Architecture dans le Boudoir: The Language of Criticism and the Criticism of Language," *Oppositions,* no. 3 (1974), reprinted in Hays, ed., *Oppositions Reader,* pp. 163–164. For more on the debate between Archigram, Eisenman, and Tafuri, see Felicity Scott, "Architecture or Techno-Utopia," *Grey Room,* no. 3 (Spring 2001), pp. 112–116.

8 "A Comment from Peter Reyner Banham," in Peter Cook, ed., *Archigram* (London: Studio Vista, 1972), p. 5.

9 For further discussion of the SI's politics, see especially Anselm Jappe, *Guy Debord,* trans. Donald Nicholson-Smith (Berkeley: University of California Press, 1999); for more on the SI's architecture, see Simon Sadler, *The Situationist City* (Cambridge, Mass.: MIT Press, 1998).

10 David Greene, "Popular Pak," *Archigram,* no. 8 (1968), n.p.

11 Peter Cook, "The Pluralistic Situation," *Arena,* September 1967.

12 Rem Koolhaas, "Introduction to Report on the City 1 and 2," quoted in David Rock, "Citation for Royal Gold Medal 2002," Royal Institute of British Architects, London, 20 November 2002, <http://www.architecture.com/go/Architecture/Also/Awards_311.html>. Koolhaas studied at the AA from 1968 to 1972.

13 See Sutherland Lyall, *Imagination Headquarters, London: Herron Associates* (London: Phaidon, 1993).

14 Warren Chalk, "Owing to Lack of Interest, Tomorrow Has Been Cancelled," *Architectural Design,* September 1969, reprinted in Archigram, ed., *A Guide to Archigram 1961–74* (London: Academy, 1994), pp. 392–397. The title was taken from a popular song, and was also used by a television documentary on population growth.

15 Warren Chalk, "An Unaccustomed Dream," 1972 (?), in Cook, ed., *Archigram,* p. 32.

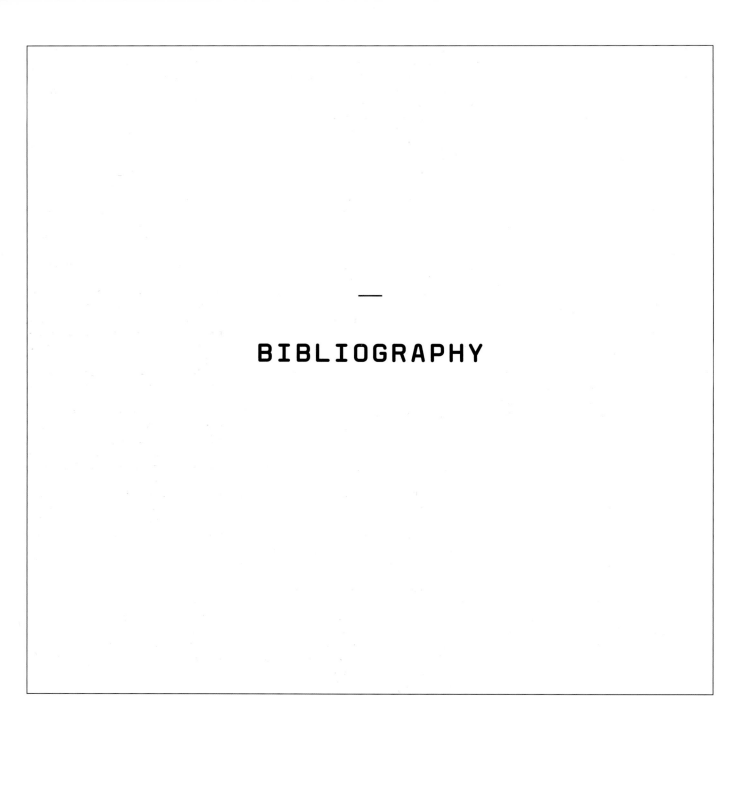

—

BIBLIOGRAPHY

Owing to their proximity to the events recounted, some works published prior to 1975 are listed as primary sources, though their importance varies. Many primary documents are reprinted in anthologies published after 1975 and will be found in the volumes listed in the anthologies section. The following concentrates on documents directly cited in the book text; it does not purport to be a definitive bibliography on Archigram.

PRIMARY SOURCES

WORKS BY MEMBERS OF ARCHIGRAM

Archigram. "The All-In Holiday." *Daily Express Colour Supplement,* 27 July 1970, pp. I–IV.

Archigram. "Amazing Archigram: A Supplement." *Perspecta* 11 (1967), pp. 131–154.

Archigram, ed. *Archigram,* nos. 1–9 1/2. London, 1961–1974.

Archigram. "Archigram Group, London: A Chronological Survey." *Architectural Design,* November 1965, pp. 559–572.

Archigram. "La città al campo." *Domus,* no. 477 (August 1969), pp. 10–13.

Archigram, ed. *Hogar y Arquitectura,* no. 72 (September/October 1967), whole issue.

Archigram Architects. *Monte Carlo Entertainments Centre,* internal report. London: Archigram Architects, 1971.

Chalk, Warren. "Hardware of a New World." *Architectural Forum* 125, no. 3 (October 1966), pp. 46–51.

Chalk, Warren. "The Tiger in the Tank." *Architectural Design,* September 1965.

Cook, Peter, ed. *Archigram.* London: Studio Vista, 1972.

Cook, Peter. *Architecture: Action and Plan.* London: Studio Vista; New York: Reinhold, 1967.

Cook, Peter. *Experimental Architecture.* London: Studio Vista, 1970.

Cook, Peter, ed. *Net,* no. 1. London: Art Net, 1975.

Taylor Woodrow Group. *Urban Renewal: Fulham Study. A Pilot Study of an Area in the Metropolitan Borough of Fulham in the County of London Carried Out by the Taylor Woodrow Group at the Invitation of the Minister of Housing and Local Government.* London: Taylor Woodrow Group, 1963.

ARTICLES, MAGAZINES, AND DOCUMENTS

Advanced Studies Group. *K4: Kinetic Audio Visual Environments, West Pier, Brighton.* London: Hornsey College of Art, 1967.

Alloway, Lawrence. "City Notes." *Architectural Design,* January 1959, excerpted in David Robbins, ed., *The Independent Group: Postwar Britain and the Aesthetics of Plenty.* Cambridge, Mass.: MIT Press, 1990.

Architects' Revolutionary Socialist Enclave. *ARse,* 1968–1970 [?].

Architectural Association. *Ron Herron: Twenty Years of Drawings.* London: Architectural Association, 1980.

Aubert, Jean, et al., eds. *Utopie,* no. 1. Paris: Anthropos, May 1967.

Banham, Reyner. "City as Scrambled Egg." *Cambridge Opinion,* "Living with the 60s" edition, no. 17 (1959), pp. 18–23.

Banham, Reyner. "A Clip-On Architecture." *Design Quarterly,* 1965, whole issue, reprinted *Architectural Design* 35 (November 1965), pp. 534–535.

Banham, Reyner. "Revenge of the Picturesque: English Architectural Polemics, 1945–1965." In John Summerson, ed., *Concerning Architecture.* London: Allen Lane/Penguin Press, 1968, pp. 265–273.

Banham, Reyner, Paul Barker, Peter Hall, and Cedric Price. "Non-Plan: An Experiment in Freedom." *New Society,* 20 March 1969, pp. 435–443.

"BASA Conference." *Architectural Design,* January 1966, p. 4.

Beyfus, Drusilla. "Flexible Space." *Weekend Telegraph Magazine,* no. 126 (3 March 1967), pp. 22–27.

Broadbent, Geoffrey. "Archijam Tomorrow: What Has Archigram Achieved?" *Architectural Association Quarterly* 5, no. 3 (Autumn 1973), pp. 57–59.

Cassidy, Michael. "Space Odyssey on the Rocks: Archigram—Pioneers or Exhibitionists?" *Building* 224, no. 1 (5 January 1973), pp. 43–46.

Chrysalis. "Chrysalis." *Architectural Design* 43, no. 42 (March 1972), pp. 172–174.

Clip-Kit. London: Architectural Association, 1966.

Collins, Peter. "Plug'n Clip." *Sunday Times Colour Magazine,* September 1965.

Colquhoun, Alan. "Symbolic and Literal Aspects of Technology." *Architectural Design,* November 1962, pp. 508–509.

Conway, Dolan, ed. "Three London Schools of Architecture within Ten Minutes Walking Distance of Each Other." *Architectural Design,* March 1969, pp. 129–164.

Crosby, Theo, ed. *This Is Tomorrow.* London: Whitechapel Gallery, 1956.

Crosby, Theo, and John Bodley, eds. *Living Arts,* nos. 1–3. London: Institute of Contemporary Arts and Tillotsons, 1963–1964.

Duffy, Francis, ed. "Some Notes on Archigram." *Arena,* June 1966, pp. 171–172.

"The Euston Story." *Architectural Design,* June 1966, p. 267.

Freeman, Robert, ed. *Cambridge Opinion,* no. 17. Cambridge, 1959.

"IDEA—International Dialogue of Architecture." *Architectural Design,* June 1966, p. 312.

Kassaboff, George, John Outram, Paul Power, and Ian McKechnie. "Student Section—BASA." *Architects' Journal* 129, no. 3342 (19 March 1959), pp. 450–459.

Llewelyn Davies, Richard [and John Weeks]. "Endless Architecture." *Architectural Association Journal,* July 1951, pp. 106–112.

Megascope, no. 3. Bristol, November 1966.

Middleton, Robin. "Folkestone IDEA." *Architectural Design,* July 1966, p. 322.

New Metropole Arts Centre. *International Dialogue of Experimental Architecture.* Folkestone: New Metropole Arts Centre, 1966.

Pawley, Martin. "Peter Cook—Archiman or Anarchist?" *Building Design,* 15 May 1970, pp. 6–7.

Pawley, Martin, and Bernard Tchumi [sic]. "The Beaux-Arts since '68." *Architectural Design,* September 1971, pp. 533–566.

Potlatch, no. 23. Paris, October 1955. Reprinted in *Potlatch 1954–57.* Paris: Editions Gérard Lebovici, 1985.

Price, Cedric. "Reflections on the Team 10 Primer." *Architectural Design,* May 1963, p. 208.

Scott Brown, Denise. "Little Magazines in Architecture and Urbanism." *Journal of the American Institute of Town Planners* 34, no. 4 (July 1968), pp. 223–232.

Sharp, Dennis. "Forecasting Tomorrow's World." *Royal Institute of British Architects Journal* 74 (December 1967), pp. 537–541.

Smithson, Alison, and Peter Smithson. "The Function of Architecture in Cultures-in-Change." *Architectural Design,* May 1960, pp. 149–150.

Smithson, Alison, and Peter Smithson. "The Heroic Period of Modern Architecture." *Architectural Design,* November 1965, pp. 587ff.

Weeks, John. "Indeterminate Architecture." *Transactions of the Bartlett Society,* no. 2 (1963–1964), pp. 83–106.

BOOKS

Alexander, Christopher, and Serge Chermeyeff. *Community and Privacy: Toward a New Architecture of Humanism.* New York: Doubleday, 1963. Reprint, Harmondsworth: Penguin, 1966.

Anderson, Stanford, ed. *Planning for Diversity and Choice: Possible Futures and Their Relations to the Man-Controlled Environment.* Cambridge, Mass.: MIT Press, 1968.

Ant Farm. *Inflatocookbook.* Sausalito: Rip Off Press, 1970.

Banham, Reyner. *The Architecture of the Well-Tempered Environment.* London: Architectural Press, 1969.

Banham, Reyner, ed. *The Aspen Papers: Twenty Years of Design Theory from the International Design Conference in Aspen.* London: Pall Mall Press, 1974.

Banham, Reyner. *The New Brutalism.* London: Architectural Press, 1966.

Banham, Reyner. *Theory and Design in the First Machine Age.* London: Architectural Press, 1960.

Bell, Daniel. *The End of Ideology: On the Exhaustion of Political Ideas in the Fifties.* Glencoe, Ill.: Free Press, 1959.

Benevolo, Leonardo. *History of Modern Architecture,* vol. 2. London: Routledge and Kegan Paul, 1971.

Benthall, Jonathan. *Science and Technology in Art Today.* London: Thames and Hudson, 1972.

Boguslaw, Robert. *The New Utopians: A Study of System Design and Social Change.* Englewood Cliffs, N.J.: Prentice-Hall, 1965.

Booker, Christopher. *The Neophiliacs: A Study of the Revolution in English Life in the Fifties and Sixties.* London: Collins, 1969.

Brand, Stewart, ed. *The Last Whole Earth Catalog.* Santa Cruz: Portola Institute, 1971.

Buchanan, Colin, et al. *Traffic in Towns: A Study of the Long Term Problems of Traffic in Urban Areas.* London: HMSO, 1963.

Burns, Jim. *Arthropods: New Design Futures.* New York: Praeger, 1972.

Colomina, Beatriz. *Privacy and Publicity: Modern Architecture as Mass Media.* Cambridge, Mass.: MIT Press, 1996.

Conrads, Ulrich, and Hans Günther Sperlich. *Fantastic Architecture.* Trans. Christiane Crasemann Collins and George R. Collins. Architectural Press, 1963.

Critchlow, Keith. *Order in Space: A Design Source Book.* London: Thames and Hudson, 1969.

Crosby, Theo. *Architecture: City Sense.* London: Studio Vista, 1965.

Crosby, Theo. *How to Play the Environment Game.* Harmondsworth: Penguin Books and Arts Council of Great Britain, 1973.

Crosby, Theo. *The Necessary Monument.* London: Studio Vista, 1970.

Crosby, Theo, and John Bodley, eds. *Living Arts* nos. 1–3. London: Institute of Contemporary Arts and Tillotsons, 1963–1964.

Drew, Philip. *Third Generation: The Changing Meaning of Modern Architecture.* New York: Praeger, 1972.

Friedman, Yona. *Vers une architecture scientifique.* Paris: Editions Pierre Belfond, n.d. Trans. *Toward a Scientific Architecture.* Cambridge, Mass.: MIT Press, 1975.

Gans, Herbert. *The Levittowners: Ways of Life and Politics in a New Suburban Community.* London: Allen Lane, 1967.

Giedion, Sigfried. *Architecture, You and Me.* Cambridge, Mass.: Harvard University Press, 1958.

Giedion, Sigfried. *Mechanization Takes Command: A Contribution to Anonymous History.* Oxford: Oxford University Press, 1948. Reprint, New York: Norton, 1969.

Goodman, Robert. *After the Planners.* Harmondsworth: Penguin, 1972.

Gowan, James, ed. *A Continuing Experiment: Learning and Teaching at the Architectural Association.* London: Architectural Press, 1975.

Gowan, James, ed. *Projects: Architectural Association 1946–71.* AA Cahiers Series No. 1. London: Architectural Association, 1974.

Habraken, N. J. *Supports: An Alternative to Mass Housing.* London: Architectural Press, 1972.

Hall, Peter. *London 2000.* London: Faber and Faber, 1963.

Jacobs, Jane. *The Death and Life of Great American Cities.* New York: Vintage, 1961.

Jencks, Charles, and George Baird. *Meaning in Architecture.* London: Barrie and Rockliff/Cresset Press, 1969.

Jencks, Charles, and Nathan Silver. *Adhocism: The Case for Improvisation.* London: Secker and Warburg, 1972.

Kidder-Smith, G. E. *The New Architecture of Europe.* Harmondsworth: Penguin, 1962.

Landau, Royston. *New Directions in British Architecture.* London: Studio Vista, 1968.

Le Corbusier. *Towards a New Architecture.* London: Butterworth, 1987 (first published as *Vers une architecture,* Paris, 1923).

Lippard, Lucy R. *Six Years: The Dematerialization of the Art Object from 1966 to 1972.* New York: Praeger; London: Studio Vista, 1973.

McLuhan, Marshall. *Understanding Media: The Extensions of Man.* New York: McGraw-Hill, 1964.

Ministry of Housing and Local Government. *Homes for Today and Tomorrow.* London: HMSO, 1961.

Moholy-Nagy, László. *Vision in Motion.* Chicago: Paul Theobald, 1947.

Nairn, Ian. *Modern Buildings in London.* London: London Transport, 1964.

Negroponte, Nicholas. *The Architecture Machine: Toward a More Human Environment.* Cambridge, Mass.: MIT Press, 1970.

Newman, Oscar. *Defensible Space: People and Design in the Violent City.* London: Architectural Press, 1973.

Nuttall, Jeff. *Bomb Culture.* London: MacGibbon and Kee, 1968. Reprint, London: Paladin, 1970.

Oliver, Paul, ed. *Shelter and Society.* London: Barrie and Rockliff/Cresset Press, 1969.

Pawley, Martin. *The Private Future: Causes and Consequences of Community Collapse in the West*. London: Thames and Hudson, 1973.

Popper, Karl. *The Open Society and Its Enemies*. 2 vols. London: Routledge and Kegan Paul, 1945, 1966.

Popper, Karl. *The Poverty of Historicism*. London: Routledge and Kegan Paul, 1957.

Price, Cedric, Frank Newby, Robert H. Suan, and Felix J. Samuely and Partners. *Air Structures: A Survey*. London: Department of the Environment/HMSO, 1971.

Richards, Brian. *New Movement in Cities*. London: Studio Vista, 1966, 2d ed. 1969.

Rudofsky, Bernard. *Architecture without Architects: A Short Introduction to Nonpedigreed Architecture*. New York: Museum of Modern Art, 1964.

Smithson, Alison, ed. *Team 10 Meetings*. New York: Rizzoli, 1991.

Smithson, Alison, ed. *Team 10 Primer*. London: Studio Vista, 1968.

Smithson, Alison, and Peter Smithson. *Ordinariness and Light*. London: Faber and Faber, 1970.

Summerson, John. *Ten Years of British Architecture 1945–55*. London: Arts Council of Great Britain, 1956.

Tyrwhitt, J., J. L. Sert, and E. N. Rogers, eds. *The Heart of the City: Towards the Humanisation of Urban Life*. London: Lund Humphries, 1952.

Venturi, Robert, Denise Scott Brown, and Steven Izenour. *Learning from Las Vegas*. Cambridge: Mass.: MIT Press, 1972, rev. ed. 1977.

Williams, Raymond. *The Long Revolution*. London: Chatto and Windus, 1961.

Wolfe, Tom. *The Electric Kool-Aid Acid Test*. London: Bantam, 1971 (first published 1968). Reprint, London: Black Swan, 1989.

Wright, Frank Lloyd. *The Living City*. New York: Horizon Press, 1958. Reprint, New York: New American Library, 1970.

Young, Michael. *The Rise of the Meritocracy*. London: Thames and Hudson, 1958.

Young, Michael, and Peter Willmott. *Family and Kinship in East London*. London: Routledge and Kegan Paul, 1957.

Zuk, William, and Roger Clark. *Kinetic Architecture*. New York: Van Nostrand Reinhold, 1970.

ANTHOLOGIES

Archigram, ed. *A Guide to Archigram 1961–74*. London: Academy, 1994.

Banham, Reyner. *Design by Choice*. Ed. Penny Sparke. London: Academy, 1981.

Conrads, Ulrich. *Programs and Manifestoes on 20th-Century Architecture*. Cambridge, Mass.: MIT Press, 1970.

Crompton, Dennis, ed. *Concerning Archigram*. London: Archigram Archives, 1998.

Guiheux, Alain, ed. *Archigram*. Paris: Centre Georges Pompidou, Collection Monographie, 1994.

Harrison, Charles, and Paul Wood, eds. *Art in Theory 1900–1990: An Anthology of Changing Ideas*. Oxford: Blackwell, 1992.

Hays, K. Michael, ed. *Architecture Theory since 1968*. Cambridge, Mass.: MIT Press, 1998.

Hays, K. Michael, ed. *Oppositions Reader*. New York: Princeton Architectural Press, 1998.

Knabb, Ken, ed. and trans. *Situationist International Anthology*. Berkeley: Bureau of Public Secrets, 1981.

LeGates, Richard T., and Frederic Stout, eds. *The City Reader*. London: Routledge, 1996.

Ockman, Joan, with Edward Eigen, ed. *Architecture Culture 1943–1968: A Documentary Anthology*. New York: Rizzoli, 1993.

Riley, Terence, ed. *The Changing of the Avant-Garde: Visionary Architectural Drawings from the Howard Gilman Collection*. New York: Museum of Modern Art, 2002.

Robbins, David, ed. *The Independent Group: Postwar Britain and the Aesthetics of Plenty*. Cambridge, Mass.: MIT Press, 1990.

Whyte, Iain Boyd, ed. and trans. *The Crystal Chain Letters*. Cambridge, Mass.: MIT Press, 1985.

AUDIOVISUAL MATERIALS

Archigram, dir. *Archigram*. BBC Productions, 1966.

Archigram. *Archigram Opera*, 1975 (?) (rescreened at Cornerhouse, Manchester, February 1998).

Greene, David, and Mike Myers, dirs. *Warren, I Remember Architecture Too*. Archigram, 1974.

Postle, Denis, dir. *Beaubourg: Four Films by Denis Postle*. Tattooist International for the Arts Council, 1980.

SECONDARY SOURCES

Amery, Colin. *Architecture, Industry and Innovation: The Early Work of Nicholas Grimshaw & Partners*. London: Phaidon, 1995.

Appleyard, Brian. *Richard Rogers: A Biography*. London: Faber, 1986.

Banham, Reyner. *Megastructure: Urban Futures of the Recent Past*. London: Thames and Hudson, 1976.

Benton, Tim. "The Housing Question: The Exemplary Case of Roehampton." *Rassegna*, issue "The Reconstruction of Europe after World War II" (1993).

Berman, Marshall. *All That Is Solid Melts into Air: The Experience of Modernity*. London: Verso, 1983.

Branzi, Andrea. *The Hot House: Italian New Wave Design*. London: Thames and Hudson, 1984.

Bürger, Peter. *Theory of the Avant-Garde*. Trans. Michael Shaw. Minneapolis: University of Minnesota Press, 1984.

Choay, Françoise. *The Modern City: Planning in the Nineteenth Century*. London: Studio Vista, 1969.

Cole, Barbie, and Ruth Rogers, eds. *Richard Rogers + Partners*. London: Academy, 1985.

Colomina, Beatriz. *Privacy and Publicity: Modern Architecture as Mass Media*. Cambridge, Mass.: MIT Press, 1996.

Cook, Peter. "In Memoriam Archigram." *Daidalos*, no. 4 (15 June 1982), pp. 54–58.

Cook, Peter. *Six Conversations*. London: Academy, 1993.

Coop Himmelblau. *Die Faszination der Stadt / The Power of the City*. Darmstadt: Georg Büchner Buchhandlung, 1988.

Crinson, Mark, and Jules Lubbock. *Architecture, Art or Profession? Three Hundred Years of Architectural Education in Britain*. Manchester: Manchester University Press, 1994.

Crow, Thomas. *The Rise of the Sixties*. London: Weidenfeld and Nicolson, 1996.

Curtis, William. *Modern Architecture since 1900*. 3d ed. London: Phaidon, 1996.

Dessauce, Marc, ed. *The Inflatable Moment: Pneumatics and Protest in '68*. New York: Princeton Architectural Press, 1999.

Esher, Lionel. *A Broken Wave: The Rebuilding of England 1940–1980*. London: Allen Lane, 1981.

Gold, John R. *The Experience of Modernism: Modern Architects and the Future City, 1928–53*. London: E & FN Spon, 1997.

Goldhagen, Sarah Williams, and Réjean Legault, eds. *Anxious Modernisms: Experimentation in Postwar Architectural Culture*. Cambridge, Mass.: MIT Press, 2000.

Guiheux, Alain. *Kisho Kurokawa: Le métabolisme 1960–1975*. Paris: Centre Georges Pompidou, 1997.

Hammond, David. "Is This What the Future Might Hold?" *Huddersfield Daily Examiner*, 31 January 1997.

Handlin, David P. *Amercian Architecture*. London: Thames and Hudson, 1985.

Hanson, Brian. "Polygon." *Rassegna* 4, no. 12, "Architecture in the Little Magazines" (December 1982), p. 72.

Harris, Steven, and Deborah Berke, eds. *Architecture of the Everyday*. New York: Princeton Architectural Press, 1997.

Harwood, Elain, and Alan Powers, ed. "The Sixties." *Twentieth Century Architecture*, no. 6 (2002).

Higgott, Andrew. "Form and Technology: The Idea of a New Architecture." In Iain Borden and David Dunster, eds., *Architecture and the Sites of History*. Oxford: Butterworth, 1995.

Hughes, Jonathan. "1961." In Louise Campbell, ed., *Twentieth-Century Architecture and Its Histories*. London: Society of Architectural Historians of Great Britain, 2001.

Hughes, Jonathan, and Simon Sadler, eds. *Non-Plan: Essays on Freedom, Participation and Change in Modern Architecture and Urbanism*. Oxford: Architectural Press, 2000.

Huyssen, Andreas. *After the Great Divide: Modernism, Mass Culture, Postmodernism*. Basingstoke: Macmillan, 1986.

Jackson, Anthony. *The Politics of Architecture: A History of Modern Architecture in Britain*. London: Architectural Press, 1970.

Jacob, Sam. "Der Futurismus von Archigram." *Arch +*, no. 164–165 (April 2003), pp. 96–101.

Jappe, Anselm. *Guy Debord*. Trans. Donald Nicholson-Smith. Berkeley: University of California Press, 1999.

Jeffrey, Ian. "Young British Architects." In David Alan Mellor and Laurent Gervereau, eds., *The Sixties: Britain and France, 1962–1973*. London: Philip Wilson, 1997, pp. 124–131.

Jencks, Charles. *Architecture 2000*. London: Academy, 1969, 2d ed. 2000.

Jencks, Charles. *Le Corbusier and the Tragic View of Architecture*. London: Allen Lane, 1973; Harmondsworth: Penguin, 1987.

Jencks, Charles. *Modern Movements in Architecture*. Harmondsworth: Penguin, 1973, 2d ed. 1985.

Jones, Edward, and Christopher Woodward. *A Guide to the Architecture of London*, Rev. ed. London: Weidenfield and Nicolson, 1992.

Kirkham, Pat. *Charles and Ray Eames: Designers of the Twentieth Century*. Cambridge, Mass.: MIT Press, 1995.

Krausee, Joachim, and Claude Lichtenstein, eds. *Your Private Sky: R. Buckminster Fuller, the Art of Design Science*. Baden: Lars Müller, 1999.

Kurokawa, Kisho. *Metabolism in Architecture*. London: Studio Vista, 1977.

Lampugnani, Vittorio Magnago. "The Permanent Side: Wishful Thinking about the City of the Telematic Age." In Steven Spier, ed., *Urban Visions: Experiencing and Envisioning the City*. Liverpool: Liverpool University Press and Tate Liverpool, 2002.

Lampugnani, Vittorio Magnago, ed. *The Thames and Hudson Encyclopaedia of 20th Century Architecture*. London: Thames and Hudson, 1986.

Lang, Peter, and William Menking. *Superstudio: Life without Objects*. Milan: Skira, 2003.

Lebesque, Sabine, and Helene Fentener van Vlissingen, eds. *Yona Friedman: Structures Servicing the Unpredictable*. Rotterdam: Netherlands Architecture Institute, 1999.

Leslie, Thomas. "Capsule/Gantry: Two Domestic Archetypes in the Architecture of the 1960s." In *Universal versus Individual: The Architecture of the 1960s, Conference Proceedings 2002*. Jyväskylä: Alvar Aalto Academy, 2002.

Louis, Eleonora, et al., eds. *Archigram: Symposium zur Ausstellung*. Vienna: Kunsthalle Wien/Ritter Verlag, 1997.

Lyall, Sutherland. "Archigram Remembered." *DesignWeek*, 4 February 1994, p. 8.

Lyall, Sutherland. *Imagination Headquarters, London: Herron Associates*. London: Phaidon, 1993.

MacEwan, Malcolm. *Crisis in Architecture*. London: RIBA, 1974.

Marriott, Oliver. *The Property Boom*. London: Hamish Hamilton, 1967.

Marwick, Arthur. *British Society since 1945*. Harmondsworth: Penguin, 1996.

Marwick, Arthur. *The Sixties: Cultural Revolution in Britain, France, Italy, and the United States, c. 1958–c. 1974*. Oxford: Oxford University Press, 1998.

Matthews, J. Stanley. "An Architecture for the New Britain: The Social Vision of Cedric Price's Fun Palace and Potteries Thinkbelt." Ph.D. dissertation, Columbia University, 2002.

McCoy, Esther. *Modern California Houses: Case Study Houses, 1945–1962*. New York: Reinhold, 1962.

Mellor, David, ed. *Fifty Years of the Future: A Chronicle of the Institute of Contemporary Arts*. London: Institute of Contemporary Arts, 1998.

Mellor, David. *The Sixties Art Scene in London*. London: Phaidon, 1993.

Mumford, Eric. *The CIAM Discourse on Urbanism, 1928–1960*. Cambridge, Mass.: MIT Press, 2000.

Ockman, Joan. "Resurrecting the Avant-Garde: the History and Program of *Oppositions*." In *Architectureproduction*, ed. Beatriz Colomina and Joan Ockman. Revisions, no. 2. New York: Princeton Architectural Press, 1988, pp. 180–199.

Pawley, Martin. "Death by Architecture." *Blueprint*, January 1998, pp. 22–24.

Pawley, Martin. *Theory and Design in the Second Machine Age*. Oxford: Basil Blackwell, 1990.

Pelkonen, Eeva-Liisa. *Achtung Architektur! Image and Phantasm in Contemporary Austrian Architecture*. Cambridge, Mass.: MIT Press, 1996.

Phillips, Lisa. *Frederick Kiesler*. New York: Whitney Museum of American Art and Norton, 1989.

Price, Cedric. *Cedric Price: Works.* London: Architectural Association, 1984.

Ross, Kristin. *Fast Cars, Clean Bodies: Decolonization and the Reordering of French Culture.* Cambridge, Mass.: MIT Press, 1995.

Sadler, Simon. "Amazing Archigram." Ph.D. dissertation, Open University, 2001.

Sadler, Simon. "Archigram and Technocracy." In *Universal versus Individual: The Architecture of the 1960s, Conference Proceedings 2002.* Jyväskylä: Alvar Aalto Academy, 2002.

Sadler, Simon. "The Brutal Birth of Archigram." *Twentieth Century Architecture,* no. 6, "The Sixties" (2002).

Sadler, Simon. "The Invisible University." *arq (Architectural Research Quarterly)* 6, no. 2 (2002).

Sadler, Simon. "New Babylon versus Plug-In City." In Martin van Schaik and Otakar Máčel, eds., *Exit Utopia—Architectural Provocations 1956–76.* Munich: Prestel, 2004.

Sadler, Simon. "Portrait of the Architect as a Young Man." *Art History* 26, no. 3 (2003).

Sadler, Simon. *The Situationist City.* Cambridge, Mass.: MIT Press, 1998.

Saint, Andrew. *The Image of the Architect.* New Haven: Yale University Press, 1983.

Saint, Andrew. *Towards a Social Architecture: The Role of School-Building in Postwar England.* New Haven: Yale University Press, 1987.

Sanders, Joel, ed. *Stud: Architectures of Masculinity.* New York: Princeton Architectural Press, 1996.

Scott, Felicity. "Architecture or Techno-Utopia." *Grey Room,* no. 3 (Spring 2001), pp. 112–116.

Scott, Felicity. "Involuntary Prisoners of Architecture." *October,* no. 106 (Fall 2003), pp. 75–101.

Sharp, Dennis. *20th Century Architecture: A Visual History.* London: Lund Humphries, 1991.

Silver, Nathan. *The Making of Beaubourg: A Building Biography of the Centre Pompidou, Paris.* Cambridge, Mass.: MIT Press, 1994.

Smith, C. Ray. *Supermannerism: New Attitudes in Post-Modern Architecture.* New York: E. P. Dutton, 1977.

Sorkin, Michael. "Canticles for Mike." In *Exquisite Corpse: Writing on Buildings.* New York: Verso, 1991.

Steiner, Hadas. "Off the Map." In Jonathan Hughes and Simon Sadler, eds., *Non-Plan: Essays on Freedom, Participation and Change in Modern Architecture and Urbanism.* Oxford: Architectural Press, 2000.

Steiner, Hadas. "The Permanence of Impermanence: From the Futuristic Bathroom to Archigram's Cybernetic Forest." In Patrizia Bonifazio et al., eds., *Tra guerra e pace: società, cultura e architettura nel secondo dopoguerra.* Milan: Franco Angeli, 1998.

Walker, John A. *Glossary of Art, Architecture and Design since 1945.* London: Clive Bingley, 1973.

Walters, David. "The Architect as Superhero: Archigram and the Text of Serious Comics." *Architronic* 3, no. 2 (1994) <http://architronic.saed.kent.edu/>.

Whiteley, Nigel. *Reyner Banham: Historian of the Immediate Future.* Cambridge, Mass.: MIT Press, 2002.

Wigley, Mark. *Constant's New Babylon: The Hyper-Architecture of Desire.* Rotterdam: 010 Publishers, 1998.

Wigley, Mark. "Network Fever." *Grey Room* no. 4 (Summer 2001), pp. 83–122.

Wright, Patrick. "They Came In through the Bathroom Window: Refounding British Architecture in the Tyneham Gap." In *The Village That Died for England: The Strange Story of Tyneham.* London: Jonathan Cape, 1995.

ILLUSTRATION CREDITS

The author particularly thanks those contributors who provided illustration permissions free of charge.

Archigram Archives: **frontispiece, 1.1, 1.3, 1.4, 1.6, 1.7, 1.8, 1.9, 1.10, 1.11, 1.12, 1.14, 1.15, 1.17, 1.18, 1.19, 1.20, 1.24, 1.27, 1.29, 1.31, 1.33, 1.34, 1.35, 1.36, 1.37, 2.1, 2.2, 2.4, 2.5, 2.6, 2.7, 2.8, 2.9, 2.10, 2.11, 2.12, 2.13, 2.14, 2.15, 2.16, 2.17, 2.18, 2.19, 2.21, 2.23, 2.24, 2.25, 2.26, 2.27, 2.28, 2.29, 2.30, 3.1, 3.2, 3.4, 3.5, 3.6, 3.7, 3.10, 3.12, 3.15, 3.17, 3.18, 3.19, 3.20, 3.22, 3.23, 3.24, 3.25, 3.26, 3.27, 3.28, 3.29, 3.30, 3.31, 3.32, 4.1, 4.2, 4.3, 4.4, 4.5, 4.6, 4.11, 4.12, 4.14, 4.15, 4.17, 4.22, 4.23, 4.24, 4.25, 4.26, 4.27, 4.28, 4.29, 4.30, 4.31, 4.32, 4.33, 4.34, 4.35, 4.36, 4.37, 4.38, 4.39, 4.40, 4.41, 4.42, 4.43, 4.45**

Courtesy © 2003 Artists Rights Society (ARS) New York / VEGAP, Madrid (Robert Freeman) / © 2003 Artists Rights Society (ARS) New York / DACS, London (Richard Hamilton): **2.20**
Courtesy of Andrea Branzi: **3.34**
Courtesy Coop Himmelb(l)au: **4.10**
Courtesy of Terry Farrell & Partners: **3.14**
Courtesy of The Estate of R. Buckminster Fuller: **3.8, 3.11**
Courtesy of Elain Harwood: **1.13**
Ron Herron and Ron Herron Archives: **1.32, 3.9, 3.16, 3.33, 4.20, 4.21**
Courtesy of Craig Hodgetts: **4.8**
Balthazar Korab Ltd.: **4.7**
Courtesy of Martin Pawley: **4.16**
Courtesy of Cedric Price: **1.30**
Courtesy of Tony Rickaby: **3.25, 4.29, 4.32**
Courtesy of Richard Rogers Partnership: **4.19**
Courtesy of Simon Smithson: **1.16, 1.28, 2.3**
Courtesy of Barry Snowden: **3.24**
Courtesy of Alan Stanton: **4.9**
Kenzo Tange Associates: **1.5, 3.22**
Courtesy of Peter Taylor: **1.29, 2.1**
Courtesy of Taylor Woodrow Construction: **1.2, 1.6, 1.34, 1.35, 2.24, 2.25, 2.26, 2.27, 2.28, 2.29**

INDEX